Reformed Historical Theology

Edited by
Herman J. Selderhuis

in Co-operation with
Emidio Campi, Irene Dingel, Elsie Anne McKee,
Richard Muller, Risto Saarinen, and Carl Trueman

Volume 52

Kyle J. Dieleman

The Battle for the Sabbath in the Dutch Reformation

Devotion or Desecration?

With 4 figures

Vandenhoeck & Ruprecht

This dissertation has been revised for publication.

Bibliographic information published by the Deutsche Nationalbibliothek
The Deutsche Nationalbibliothek lists this publication in the Deutsche Nationalbibliografie;
detailed bibliographic data available online: http://dnb.d-nb.de.
You can find alternative editions of this book and additional material on our website:
www.vandenhoeck-ruprecht-verlage.com

Typesetting: 3w+p, Rimpar
Printed and bound: Hubert & Co. BuchPartner, Göttingen
Printed in the EU

Vandenhoeck & Ruprecht Verlage | www.vandenhoeck-ruprecht-verlage.com

ISSN 2198-8226
ISBN 978-3-525-57060-9

To Andrea and Emden

Contents

Acknowledgements 11

List of Figures 13

Introduction 15
  Topic 15
  Literature Review 16
  Theological Issues 21
  Argument 22
    Sabbatarianism and the Dutch Reformed Tradition 22
    Sabbath, Pluralism, Confessionalization, and Order in the Dutch
    Reformed Church 26
  Method and Theory 30
  Terminology and Structure 33

Chapter 1: Early Reformed Theology of the Sabbath: Calvin and the
Sabbath 37
  Calvin and Sabbatarianism 41
  Calvin's Works 42
    Institutio Christianae religionis (Institutes of the Christian Religion) . 43
    Genevan Catechism 48
    Biblical Commentaries 50
    Sermons on Deuteronomy 55
  Theological Issues 58
    Ceremonial and Moral 58
    The Jewish Sabbath 60
    Sabbath Rest 61
    Sabbath Worship 63
    Sabbath Work 64
    Eschatological Expectations 64

Genevan Practices 65
Conclusions 70
   Sabbatarianism 70
   Calvin's Conclusions 72

Chapter 2: Sabbath Developments in the Dutch Reformed Tradition:
Johannes A Lasco and Zacharias Ursinus 75
   Emden, Johannes a Lasco, and the Dutch Reformed Church 77
      Large Emden Catechism of the Strangers' Church, London (1551) . . 81
      Emden Catechism (1554) 85
   Zacharias Ursinus 89
      Heidelberg Catechism 89
      Smaller Catechism 93
      Larger Catechism 95
      Commentary on the Heidelberg Catechism 97
      Conclusions: Ursinus and the Sabbath 103
   Conclusions 104

Chapter 3: Wilhelmus à Brakel and the Nadere Reformatie: A
Commandment "Assaulted with highly elevated Shields" 107
   The Nadere Reformatie 107
   Wilhelmus à Brakel 112
      The Christian's Reasonable Service 113
   Conclusions 128

Chapter 4: "Concerning the Profanation of the Sabbath": Dutch
Provinicial Synods and the Sabbath 131
   Introduction 131
   Frequency of Sabbath Complaints 140
   Types of Sabbath Complaints 145
   Interpreting Sabbath Complaints 151
   Theological Impact of Sunday Observance 157

Chapter 5: "Whoredom, Drunkenness, Dice, Dancing, and other
Rashness": Sabbath Ideals, Dutch Classes and Sabbath Complaints . . . 163
   Introduction 163
   Introduction to Dutch Classes 169
   Frequency of Sabbath Complaints 174
   Types of Sabbath Complaints 178
      Worship and Church Attendance 178

Immoral Behavior   180
Improper Activities   182
Working on the Sabbath   185
Results of Sabbath Complaints   185
Interpreting Sabbath Complaints   190
Conclusions   193

Chapter 6: Sabbath Observance in Kampen Consistory Records   197
Introduction to Kampen   197
Kampen Consistory Records   201
Sabbath Concerns and Sunday Observance   205
Remedying Sabbath Desecration   213
Sabbath and Establishing a Reformed Identity   214
Sunday Observance, Order, and Scandal   218
Conclusions   220

Conclusion   223
Dutch Reformed Theological Understanding of the Sabbath   223
Sabbath Practices in Dutch Reformed Church Records   225
Sabbath Theology and Practice   227
Order, Pluralism, and Confessionalization   228
Implications for Understanding the Reformation   229
Opportunities for Further Research   231

Bibliography   233
Primary Sources   233
Manuscript Sources   233
Printed Sources   233
Secondary Sources   236

Index of Names   249

Index of Subjects   251

Acknowledgements

The publication of a book is more of a journey than a document, and completely documenting a journey is a nearly impossible task. My own academic journey, culminating in this book, has been influenced and supported by so many different people it is difficult to know where to begin. Perhaps the best place to begin is actually at the end. Before acknowledging those who made this book stronger, I should note that all lingering errors or weaknesses are only my own responsibility. Unlike so many horror stories I have heard, researching, writing, and editing my dissertation and subsequent book was deeply enjoyable, and I can only hope others find as much satisfaction in reading it as I have had in writing it.

Academically, a number of people, institutions, fellowships, and grants have supported my research and writing. The University of Iowa Graduate College provided me with a Graduate College Post-Comprehensive Research Award, Graduate College Summer Fellowship, and Ballard and Seashore Dissertation Fellowship, each of which allowed for a summer or semester completely dedicated to dissertation research and writing. The University of Iowa College of Liberal Arts and Sciences awarded me a Marcus Bach Graduate Fellowship which allowed for another invaluable semester solely dedicated to research and writing.

I am indebted to several research institutions that provided support and help along the way. In the summer of 2013 the Johannes a Lasco Bibliotheek in Emden, Germany, awarded me its Hardenburg Fellowship which allowed me to study for six wonderful weeks in Emden and prompted the beginnings of my interest in the Sabbath in Dutch Reformed churches. Receiving a Stanley Graduate Award for International Research from the University of Iowa International Programs also made my research in Emden possible. A fellowship from the Leibniz-Institut für Europäische Geschichte, in Mainz, Germany, allowed me to live in Europe, conduct the necessary archival work, and interact with a number of helpful scholars. Finally, the H. Henry Meeter Center for Calvin Studies provided me with a Student Research Fellowship which allowed me to study and write at their fine research center for a month in August of 2016.

I have unrepayable debts to a number of helpful colleagues. Dr. Raymond Mentzer, my adviser, has been everything a doctoral student and early career scholar could ask from the earliest days of my doctoral program. His careful insights, editing, and suggestions have helped make my dissertation stronger and clearer in any number of ways. The entire Religious Studies Department at the University of Iowa has been incredibly encouraging and supportive throughout my program, particularly Dr. Diana Fritz Cates, Dr. Paul Dilley, and Dr. Kristy Nahban-Warren, who all kindly served on my dissertation committee. Maureen Walterhouse and Robins Burns, the two women who actually enable the Religious Studies Department to function, have been so readily available to help with any number of issues and deserve endless thanks. Dr. Julie Hochstrasser also graciously agreed to serve on my dissertation committee and provided insights into the Dutch Reformation I would have missed. Outside of the University of Iowa, Dr. Erik de Boer, of the Theologische Universiteit van Kampen, proved an excellent host during my archival work in Kampen and whose knowledge of Dutch Reformed church history I have only begun to approach. Other professors who deserve special thanks include Dr. Charles Parker, Dr. Christine Kooi, and Dr. Lyle Bierma.

Behind every good scholar is a good librarian. Rachel Garza Carreón, librarian for the Religious Studies Department at the University of Iowa, was always so willing to secure whatever resources were needed. Similarly, Karin Maag and Paul Fields at the Meeter Center provided help with resources on more than one occasion.

Personally, the collegiality of fellow students in the Religious Studies Department has greatly enriched my time at the University of Iowa. My parents have long supported my academic interests, and their continued support has been deeply encouraging. My own family, namely my wife Andrea, has been more patient, understanding, and supportive than I could have imagined. The addition of our daughter Emden during my dissertation research and writing has brought immense amounts of joy to us both. I thank Andrea and Emden, with all my love, for making this work possible.

List of Figures

Figure 1: Emmanuel de Witte, Interior of the Oude Kerk at Delft during a Sermon   165
Figure 2: Emmanuel de Witte, The Interior of the Oude Kerk, Amsterdam, during a   166
           Sermon
Figure 3: Emmanuel de Witte, A Sermon in the Oude Kerk, Delft   167
Figure 4: Gijsbert Janszoon Sibilla, Dutch Reformed Service in the Grote Kerk in   169
           Weesp

Introduction

Topic

Sunday observance has a long history in the Christian tradition. Often referred to as the Lord's Day or the Sabbath, Christians have observed Sunday as a holy day of rest and worship throughout their history. The basis for the Christian Sabbath comes from the Ten Commandments given to the Jewish people, either the third or fourth commandment depending on how the commandments are numbered. The Jewish Sabbath was observed on the seventh day of the week, but early on Christians altered their Sabbath to be held on the first day of the week. Thus, Christians observe their Sabbath on Sunday, and observance has primarily meant gathering for corporate worship and resting from one's work. However, Sunday observance has not been uniform throughout the Christian tradition, and the theological issues related to the Sabbath are surprisingly complex.

While Sabbath observance was important in the medieval Catholic setting, the Protestant Reformation brought significant changes to how Sundays were to be observed. Sunday was still a day of worship, but Protestant worship services were significantly different than Catholic worship. Furthermore, the Reformation also brought different expectations for Sabbath observance, including careful attention at sermon services, catechism services, and ecclesiastical discipline for failing to properly observe the day. As is the case with many aspects of Christian piety, the Protestant Reformation brought about important changes in how pious Christians were to observe the Sabbath.

My project seeks to better understand how the Protestant Reformation understood the theology behind Sabbath observance and how the Sabbath was practiced in Protestant churches. More specifically, my research focuses on the Reformed tradition, also known as "Calvinist," in the Low Countries during the sixteenth and seventeenth centuries. To properly understand the vision the Reformed church authorities had for the Sabbath it is important to begin with the theological understanding of the Sabbath found in the Dutch Reformed tradition. However, it is equally important to at least attempt to ascertain what actual

Dutch Reformed church members were doing on Sundays. Were they willing to attend worship and rest from their work? Were there other activities to which they were drawn?

Attending to the Sabbath in the Dutch Reformation is necessary for understanding more completely how the Protestant Reformation impacted the lived religious experience of Christians. Such an examination also provides fascinating insights into the relationship between theology and religious practice and how that relationship was navigated. As will be described below, assumptions about the importance of the Sabbath in the Dutch Reformation have often led to incomplete and unhelpful understandings of how the Sabbath functioned, both theologically and practically, in the Dutch Reformed tradition. My research will demonstrate that the Sabbath was an important way in which church authorities regulated order within their churches and a helpful way for the Reformed confessional group to establish their identity within the broader Dutch religious setting. As a result, it will become clear that previous attention to the Sabbath in the Dutch Reformation has been lacking and when such research has been undertaken it has underestimated or even misunderstood the importance of the Sabbath in the early years of the Dutch Reformed tradition.

Literature Review

Scholarly attention to Sabbath observance in the Protestant Reformation has been surprisingly sparse. This scholarly vacuum is all the more surprising given that Sabbath observance was of extreme importance in Reformed communities throughout the European Reformations.[1] It has been well established that a strict Sabbatarianism came to occupy a central place in the Puritan reform movement.[2] Unfortunately, scholars have frequently been too quick to dismiss the importance of the Sabbath in the Reformed traditions in the rest of Europe, including the Low Countries.

While studies of the Sabbath in Puritan regions have been numerous, less scholarly attention has been given to the Sabbath in the Continental Reformations. Given the close connection with the Reformed communities in England, the Dutch Reformed Church and its relationship to the Sabbath are of particular interest. By examining both the theological background of the Sabbath and the relationship between discipline and the Sabbath in the Dutch Reformed Church,

---

1 Kenneth A. Strand, "Sabbath and Sunday in the Reformation era," in *Sabbath in Scripture and History*, eds. Kenneth A. Strand and Daniel A. Augsburger, Washington, DC: Review and Herald Publishing Association, 1982, 215–228.
2 Kenneth Parker, *The English Reformation: A Study of Doctrine and Discipline From the Reformation to the Civil War*, Cambridge: Cambridge University Press, 1988.

the importance of the Sabbath observance and what that meant for the Dutch Reformed Church becomes clear, drawing into question the conclusions of previous scholars.[3]

Scholars have done a fair amount of research on the Protestant Reformers' theological understanding of the Sabbath. Not surprisingly, scholars have given Calvin's view of the Sabbath the most attention. However, surprisingly little exists in terms of an in-depth examination of Calvin's understanding of the Sabbath. Recently, Elsie McKee has done a fine job in examining Calvin's theology of the Sabbath but focuses largely only on his *Institutes*.[4] Long ago Robert Cox assembled Calvin's various writings on the Sabbath in his audaciously titled *The Whole Doctrine of Calvin About the Sabbath and the Lord's Day*, though Cox provided no commentary on Calvin's works.[5] Richard Gaffin's short book and Kwok Ting Cheung's doctoral dissertation on Calvin's understanding of the Sabbath are undoubtedly the two most significant treatments of the topic, though not without their issues. Gaffin's book is very helpful but does need to be used with caution given its clear confessional bent.[6] Cheung's dissertation tends to interpret Calvin's understanding of the Sabbath in theological terms Calvin never articulated.[7] Lyle Bierma has dedicated a well-done section of a chapter to Calvin and the Sabbath, but such an examination is hardly in depth.[8] Similarly, Richard Bauckham spends a few pages on Calvin's understanding of the Sabbath in his chapter on the "Sabbath and Sunday in the Protestant Tradition."[9] Others, such

---

3 The notion of a "Dutch Reformed" group of Christians is somewhat problematic for several reasons. First, the Dutch Republic was nonexistent when the Reformed faith began its inroads into the region. Even by the middle of the seventeenth century the Dutch Republic was only beginning to really come into its own. Second, the term "Reformed" is a designation the religious practitioners themselves would not have used. Other scholars have deemed these believers "Calvinists" or "the church under the cross." But, the former is itself quite problematic and the latter quite cumbersome. Thus, the term "Dutch Reformed" is serviceable in conveying the identity of the group in question and, therefore, will be used here.

4 Elsie Anne McKee, *The Pastoral Ministry and Worship in Calvin's Geneva*, Genève: Librairie Droz S.A., 2016, 177–187.

5 Robert Cox, ed., *The Whole Doctrine of Calvin About the Sabbath and the Lord's Day: Extracted from His Commentaries, Catechism, and Institutes of the Christian Religion*, Edinburgh: Maclachlan and Stewart, 1860.

6 Richard B. Gaffin, *Calvin and the Sabbath*, Fearn, Ross-shire: Mentor, 1998.

7 Kwok Ting Cheung, "The Sabbath in Calvin's Theology," Ph.D. Dissertation: University of Aberdeen, 1990, v–vi.

8 Lyle Bierma, "Remembering the Sabbath Day: Ursinus's Exposition of Exodus 20:8–11," in *Biblical Interpretation in the Era of the Reformation: Essays Presented to David C. Steinmetz in Honor of His Sixtieth Birthday*, eds. Richard A. Muller and John Lee Thompson, Grand Rapids, MI: W.B. Eerdmans, 1996, 272–291.

9 Richard J. Bauckham, "Sabbath and Sunday in the Protestant Tradition," in *From Sabbath to Lord's Day: A Biblical, Historical, and Theological Investigation*, ed. D.A. Carson, Grand Rapids, MI: Zondervan, 1982, 311–341.

as Coldwell, Gilpin, Lauer, and Primus, have all written briefly, with varying degrees of thoroughness and success, on Calvin and the Sabbath.[10]

The theological understanding of the Sabbath in the Dutch Reformed tradition has also received significant attention. Most of the theological research has focused on the seventeenth century, particularly after the Synod of Dort (also refered to in English as Dordt) in 1618-1619. It was in the subsequent decades that the Dutch pietist movement, the Nadere Reformatie, became increasingly important. Since the Nadere Reformatie placed a great emphasis on the Sabbath, historical theologians have been drawn to studying these discussions and debates regarding the Sabbath during the middle of the seventeenth century. Undoubtedly, the most comprehensive examination remains Hans Visser's excellent, though slightly dated, work, *De geschiedenis van den sabbatsstrijd onder de gereformeerden in de zeventiende eeuw*.[11]

However, almost no attention has been given to the Sabbath understandings that individual theologians such as Johannes a Lasco, Zacharias Ursinus, and Wilhelmus à Brakel articulated. Bierma's chapter, mentioned above, addresses Ursinus' Sabbath views, but no other scholar has paid any in depth attention to his understanding of the Sabbath. At best, the Sabbath as explained briefly in the Heidelberg Catechism has been occasionally studied, though frequently from a confessional viewpoint.[12] Regarding a Lasco and à Brakel, no significant study, to my knowledge, has been carried out which addresses their theological or even practical understandings of the Sabbath.[13]

While attention to the Sabbath in the Dutch Reformation has been somewhat limited, discipline in the Low Countries has received a great deal of scholarly investigation in the last few decades. Arie van Deursen pioneered the study of discipline in Dutch consistory records, examining some of the records of the Amsterdam church.[14] While van Deursen's work remains a standard, additional

---

10 Christopher Coldwell, "Calvin in the Hands of the Philistines, Or, Did Calvin Bowl on the Sabbath?", *The Confessional Presbyterian* 6, (January 1, 2010): 31–49; Lawrence A. Gilpin, "An Analysis of Calvin's Sermons on the Fourth Commandment," *Presbyterian* 30, no. 2 (September 1, 2004): 90–105; Stewart E. Lauer, "John Calvin, the Nascent Sabbatarian: A Reconsideration of Calvin's View of Two Key Sabbath-Issues," *The Confessional Presbyterian* 3, (January 1, 2007): 3–14; John H. Primus, "Calvin and the Puritan Sabbath: A Comparative Study," in *Exploring the Heritage of John Calvin*, ed. David E. Holwerda, Grand Rapids, MI: Baker Book House, 1976, 40–75.

11 Hans Visser, *De geschiedenis van den sabbatsstrijd onder de gereformeerden in de zeventiende eeuw*, Utrecht: Kemink en Zoon, N.V., 1939.

12 Diedrich H. Kromminga, "The Heidelberg View of the Fourth Commandment: Is it Scriptural?," *The Calvin Forum* 6, no. 9 (April, 1941): 187–190.

13 Michael Stephen Springer, *Restoring Christ's Church John a Lasco and the Forma Ac Ratio*, Aldershot, Hants, England: Ashgate, 2007. Springer addresses some of a Lasco's instructions for proper Sabbath observance, though he does not delve into the theological background.

14 Arie Th. van Deursen, *Bavianen en slijkgeuzen: kerk en kerkvolk ten tijde van Maurits en*

studies have been done that have now moved the scholarly conversation forward even more. Herman Roodenburg has done a careful examination of the process of church discipline and how the Amsterdam consistory dealt with a wide variety of sins.[15] Church discipline, which was separate from social discipline, was focused on peace and reconciliation with an emphasis on honor and respectability.

A number of other scholars have undertaken studies of Dutch consistory records. Charles Parker has used consistory records to examine poor relief.[16] Judith Pollmann and Joke Spaans have examined consistory records with an eye towards relationships among different confessional groups.[17] Christine Kooi has used Leiden's consistory records to examine the relationship between the Reformed church and the political authorities in the city.[18] Heinz Schilling has examined the consistory records in Emden and Groningen from a wide variety of perspectives, though typically with the issue of confessionalization in mind.[19] In the last few decades these scholars have demonstrated, each in his or her own way, that studying Dutch consistory records can bring new, more complete ways of understanding the Dutch Reformation. Yet, no scholars have examined Dutch consistory records with a particular eye on Sabbath observance; my project will use the consistory records of the Reformed congregation in Kampen to do exactly that.

Similarly, a great deal of scholarly work has used church records from other, larger Dutch Reformed Church ecclesiastical bodies, namely the provincial synods and the regional classes. Many of these records have been transcribed and published and, as such, are readily available to scholars. At the level of provincial synods, the works include W. P. C. Knuttel's six volumes on the synod of South Holland, Johannes Reitsma and S. D. van Veen's eight volumes on the provincial synods of the northern Netherlands, and F. L. Rutgers' work on Dutch synods in the sixteenth century. At the level of regional classes, the most expansive records

---

    Oldebarnevelt, 4th ed., Assen: Van Gorcum, 1974, 1991, Franeker: Uitgeverij Van Wijnen, 2010. Citations refer to the 2010 edition.

15 Herman Roodenburg, *Onder censuur: de kerkelijke tucht in de gereformeerde gemeente van Amsterdam, 1578–1700*, Hilversum: Verloren, 1990.

16 Charles Parker, *The Reformation of Community: Social Welfare and Calvinist Charity in Holland, 1572–1620*, Cambridge: Cambridge University Press, 1998.

17 Judith Pollmann, *Religious Choice in the Dutch Republic: The Reformation of Arnoldus Buchelius, 1565–1641*, Manchester: Manchester University Press, 1999; Joke Spaans, *Haarlem na de Reformatie: Stedelijke cultuur en kerkelijk leven, 1577–1620*, 's-Gravenhage: Stichting Hollandse Historische Reeks, 1989.

18 Christine Kooi, *Liberty and Religion: Church and State in Leiden's Reformation, 1572–1620*, Leiden: Brill, 2000.

19 Heinz Schilling, *Civic Calvinism in Northwestern Germany and the Netherlands: Sixteenth to Nineteenth Centuries*, Kirksville, MO: Sixteenth Century Journal Publishers, 1991; Heinz Schilling, *Religion, Political Culture, and the Emergence of Early Modern Society: Essays in German and Dutch History*, Leiden: Brill, 1992.

are found in the nine volumes in Series 49 of the Rijks Geschiedkundige Publicatien.[20]

A substantial number of scholars have used these church records to help arrive at a better understanding of the Protestant Reformation in the Low Countries. For instance, A. Ph. F. Wouters and P. H. A. M. Abels have thoroughly studied Delft and Delfland using, in large part, classis records.[21] Similarly, John Paul Elliot's doctoral dissertation uses the records of Classis Dordrecht to examine religious and social life in Dordrecht.[22] Donald Sinnema has used synod and classis records to examine catechism preaching on Sunday afternoons in Dutch Reformed churches.[23] However, outside of his work nothing has been done using these records with an attention to the Sabbath. So, my project will for the first time explore the records of the provincial synods and regional classes with a direct eye towards Sabbath observance as a whole.

This book will fill a gap in the existing scholarship on the Dutch Reformation. First, I will develop a richer portrait of how Reformed theologians, particularly in relation to the Dutch Reformed tradition, understood the theology of the Sabbath. This will include arriving at a fuller understanding of Calvin's view of the Sabbath than has previously been achieved. Even more significantly, my project will for the first time study in depth the role of the Sabbath in the thought of a Lasco, Ursinus, and à Brakel. The theologians addressed, except à Brakel, were primary authors of catechisms which were used widely in Dutch Reformed congregations. As such, average church members were frequently exposed to their theology. À Brakel, while not the author of a catechism, also wrote his major work with the average Christian in mind, and church members widely read his work. As such, the theologians I address expressed a theology of the Sabbath that would have been familiar to lay Dutch Christians.

Secondly, my research will lead to a better understanding of the role of church discipline the provincial synods, regional classes, and local consistories carried out in the Low Countries. In particular, my attention to the way the Sabbath was policed is something that has not previously been the focus of any in depth research. Finally, my work will seek to bridge the gap between social and intellectual history.[24] In this way, I will expand my focus beyond simply a theo-

---

20 For a complete bibliography, refer to Chapter 5, Note 2.

21 A. Ph. F. Wouters and P. H. A. M. Abels, *Nieuw en ongezien: kerk en samenleving in de classis Delft en Delfland 1572–1621*, Delft: Eburen, 1994. In the Dutch Reformed Church the classis refers to a regional group of churches.

22 John Paul Elliott, "Protestantization in the Northern Netherlands: A Case Study: the Classis of Dordrecht, 1572–1640," Ph. D. Dissertation: Columbia University, 1990.

23 Donald Sinnema, "The Second Sunday Service in the Early Dutch Reformed Tradition," *Calvin Theological Journal* 32, no. 2 (November 1997): 298–333.

24 Karen Spierling, *Infant Baptism in Reformation Geneva: The Shaping of a Community, 1536–*

logical examination or a historical reconstruction. Instead, I will examine how theological ideas impacted historical practices and discipline and how the Sunday practices of Dutch congregants influenced theology. In this way, the research here will provide a more complete picture of the theology and practice of the Sabbath in the Dutch Reformation, a topic to which scholars have previously not given much attention.

Theological Issues

Despite what one might presuppose, the theology of the Sabbath was not a straightforward issue. The Sabbath raised a number of theological issues that divided theologians. Hans Visser has expertly traced the theological debates about the Sabbath throughout the seventeenth century.[25] As Visser demonstrates, the theological debates in the Dutch Reformed tradition regarding the Sabbath involved a number of major figures, and the Sabbath was a major theological topic throughout the seventeenth century.[26] But, these debates dealt with theological issues that were being addressed already in the sixteenth century. It is worth mentioning a few of the important theological issues at stake when theologians were discussing the theology of the Sabbath, issues on which Reformed theologians came to vastly different conclusions.

Perhaps the most important issue relates to the distinction between the moral and ceremonial laws. Christian theology has long made a fairly standard threefold categorization of Jewish laws. In order to understand which Jewish laws still apply to Christians, theologians have noted the differences between moral laws, ceremonial laws, and civil laws.[27] Regarding the Sabbath, the issue is whether the Sabbath is best understood as a moral or ceremonial law. Moral laws are laws binding for all eternity; ceremonial laws were meant only for the Jewish people.

1564, Burlington, VT: Ashgate, 2005. In Reformation studies Spierling's work is one of only a few examples that undertake such a synthesis.

25 Visser, *De geschiedenis van den sabbatsstrijd*, 35–274.

26 Visser, *De geschiedenis van den sabbatsstrijd*, Chapters 2–6. The debates included the provinces of South Holland and Walcheren and the universities in Leiden, Utrecht, and Groningen. Some of the major theologians involved in the debates included Voetius, Cocceius, Koelman, and Vlak.

27 The distinction can be found in any number of major theologians throughout Christian history. Aquinas is typically credited with the origination of the threefold distinction, which Calvin adopts. See John Calvin, *Institutes*, IV.xx.14; Thomas Aquinas, *Summa Theologica*, 2a, Question 99, Article 4. However, while not as neatly systematized as in Aquinas, previous theologians also noted the differences in types of Jewish laws. See Augustine, *Reply to Faustus the Manichæan*, Chapter 6; Tertullian, *An Answer to the Jews*, Chapter 2. For an introduction to the threefold division of the Jewish law, see Jonathan F. Bayes, *The Threefold Division of the Law*, Newcastle upon Tyne: The Christian Institute, 2012.

As such, if the Sabbath is best understood as a Jewish ceremony, then the Sabbath commandment need not apply to Christians. However, if the Sabbath is a moral law, then all Christians must still observe the Sabbath commandment. As will be demonstrated in the following chapters, Reformed theologians debated the question, sometimes fiercely.

In addition, Reformed theologians had differing opinions on what exactly was referred to when the Lord commanded his people to rest on the Sabbath day. Determing what "rest" meant was both an exegetical and theological topic. The options for what "rest" indicated included a physical rest from work, spiritual rest from sin, or rest from all activity. Furthermore, as will be shown below, theologians had to determine whether or not rest was the primary purpose of the commandment. Was the commandment meant to address rest or was it meant to address worship? Reformed theologians would nuance their answers to this question quite differently.

Yet another theological issue relates to the day the Sabbath was to be celebrated. Obviously, the Christian tradition typically observed the Sabbath on the first day of the week, Sunday. This is a clear deviation from Jewish practice where the Sabbath was the last day of the week, Saturday. Theological reasonings for this change were numerous, though not exactly uniform. In addition, theologians had striking disagreements over whether or not Christians could observe the Sabbath on any day of the week. Did the Sabbath have to be Sunday, or could Christians observe the Sabbath on any day throughout the week? Opinions varied widely and so did the theological explanations given to support one's position.

Related to the issue of what day the Sabbath should be celebrated is how often the Sabbath should be observed. In this instance the question revolves around whether the Sabbath must be observed once every seven days or if the Sabbath could be observed more or less often. The answer given was related to one's understanding of the previous theological questions. As we will see, the theology behind these questions led to vastly different answers which, in turn, led to vastly different understandings of how the Sabbath should practically be observed.

Argument

Sabbatarianism and the Dutch Reformed Tradition

Sabbatarianism, the term used in various ways to describe a literal and strict Christian appropriation of the Jewish Sabbath, has long been associated with Dutch Reformed communities.[28] Virtually all scholars have supposed that this

---

28 A more thorough definition of the term "Sabbatarian" will occur in the first chapter.

sabbatarian strain within the Dutch Reformed tradition owes its origins to the influence of English Puritanism and, to a lesser extent, German Pietism. Keith Sprunger has argued for this influence of Puritan Sabbatarianism on the Dutch Reformed tradition. He writes, "An English Puritan influence in the camp of the strict Dutch Sabbatarians frequently is discernible. In fact, wherever in the world a strict Sabbath observance movement of any kind emerged, an English or Scottish connection is likely."[29] Other scholars from both English and Dutch perspectives, such as M. M. Knappen and G. D. J. Schotel, have made similar arguments.[30] Parker notes the tendency among scholars, writing, "Two conclusions seem to be common to studies of sabbatarianism written by religious historians. The first is that sabbatarianism was a puritan [sic] innovation which began to surface in the 1570s and 1580s and was crystallized into a formal doctrine by the 1590s."[31] In his impressive tome, Philip Benedict also connects the emphasis on the Sabbath in Dutch circles as a result of influences from English Puritanism.[32] Scholars have gone so far to assert that a strict Sabbatarianism in the seventeenth century was uniquely English and Scottish. For instance, Sprunger explicitly states, "Although English Protestant religion drew heavily from the international Calvinist movement, strict Sabbatarianism in the seventeenth century was unique to the English and Scottish people."[33] Similarly, Winton Solberg has argued that "the Continental Reformation, including Calvin, produced nothing resembling the Puritan doctrine of the Sabbath. But Reformed theology was highly conducive to the development of such a theory."[34] Carl Trueman, too, has taken such a position: "One of the distinctives of British

---

Scholarly grammatical conventions vary, but I have chosen to capitalize the term when used as a noun (e.g. Sabbatarianisms, Sabbatarians) and to not capitalize the term when used as an adjective (e.g. sabbatarian theology, sabbatarian positions).

29 Keith L. Sprunger, "English and Dutch Sabbatarianism and the Development of Puritan Social Theology (1600–1660)," *Church History* 51, no. 1 (1982): 32.

30 From an English historian, see M.M. Knappen, *Tudor Puritanism: A Chapter in the History of Idealism*, Chicago: University of Chicago Press, 1970, 187. From a Dutch historian, see Gilles Dionysius Jacob Schotel, *De openbare eeredienst der Nederl. Hervormde Kerk in de zestiende, zeventiende en achttiende eeuw*, Haarlem: Kruseman, 1870, 211.

31 Parker, *The English Sabbath*, 3.

32 Philip Benedict, *Christ's Churches Purley Reformed: A Social History of Calvinism*, New Haven: Yale University Press, 2002, 324–326 and 518–526.

33 Sprunger, "English and Dutch Sabbatarianism," 24. Sprunger is correct in noting the influence the Netherlands had on Puritanism both in England and in America, though he does not make such a case regarding the Sabbath. See, Keith L. Sprunger, *The Learned Doctor William Ames: Dutch Backgrounds of English and American Puritanism*, Chicago: University of Illinois Press, 1972, 256.

34 Winton U. Solberg, *Redeem the Time: The Puritan Sabbath in Early America*, Cambridge, MA: Harvard University Press, 1977, 26–27.

Puritan Reformed piety over against its continental counterpart was its vigorous Sabbatarianism."[35]

Dutch Sabbatarianism, the typical argument goes, was not a crucial part of the Dutch Reformed identity and did not develop in its churches until relatively late. Sprunger summarizes such a position, arguing that, "The strict Sabbath practice associated with the Dutch Reformed people in America and elsewhere tends to be a later development."[36]

However, in what follows, I will demonstrate that this understanding of Dutch Sabbatarianism is deeply flawed. The strength of the argument is that, indeed, the Dutch Reformed theological tradition was by and large not sabbatarian. As the subsequent chapters will demonstrate, Sabbatarianism was not the theological norm for early Dutch Reformed theology. Rather, the theological origins of such Sabbatarianism can be found in the Dutch Nadere Reformatie, in the first half of the seventeenth century. English Puritanism, with its emphasis on Sabbatarianism, certainly impacted this movement within the Dutch Reformed Church.[37]

Yet, while a sabbatarian theology was lacking in the early days of the Dutch Reformed theology, the Dutch Reformed tradition was sabbatarian in its piety very early on. As the church records will suggest, Dutch Reformed Sabbatarianism practices came not from English Puritanism but, rather, arose from within the Dutch Reformed churches. While the theological backing for such a Sabbatarianism may have come from English Puritanism, Dutch Reformed church authorities emphasized a careful, sabbatarian observance of Sundays for their own reasons particular to their own religious and cultural setting. This must be the case, I will demonstrate, because the Dutch Reformed concern with Sabbath observance is evident before English Puritanism's influence found its way to the Low Countries.[38]

Thus, part of my overall argument is that the Sabbath in the Low Countries was more important, theologically and practically, than previous scholars have acknowledged. It is my contention that in the sixteenth and seventeenth centuries the Sabbath was an integral aspect of Christian piety in the Dutch Reformed tradition. The Sabbath became for Dutch religious authorities a way to ensure order within the church but was also a way to distinguish Reformed Christians

---

35 Carl R. Trueman, "Reformed Orthodoxy in Britain," in *A Companion to Reformed Orthodoxy*, ed. Herman J. Selderhuis, Leiden: Brill, 2013, 274.

36 Sprunger, "English and Dutch Sabbatarianism," 29.

37 Joel R. Beeke, *Assurance of Faith: Calvin, English Puritanism, and the Dutch Second Reformation*, New York: P. Lang, 1991. Much work has been done tracing the influence of English Puritanism on the Nadere Reformatie, Beeke's being among the best.

38 Trueman, "Reformed Orthodoxy in Britain," 274–275. Trueman notes the emphasis on the Sabbath in Britain became "a focal point" towards the end of the sixteenth century and at the beginning of the seventeeth century. I will demonstrate that the strict concern with the Sabbath was present in the Dutch churches prior to that time period.

from Catholics and Anabaptists. I will go on to argue, however, that the church authorities' efforts at enforcing Sunday observance were met with resistance from the laity and were largely unsuccessful. As Philip Benedict has written, assessing the "success" of church discipline is difficult, but church discipline clearly had its limits and was resisted.[39] Such resistance certainly is evident, my research will demonstrate, in the Dutch Reformed situation.

The importance of the Sabbath becomes clear when studying the attention Reformed theologians give to it. Calvin, a Lasco, Ursinus, and à Brakel all devote a considerable amount of attention to the Sabbath. They are concerned with the theological understanding of the Sabbath, particularly regarding the relationship between the Old Testament and the New Testament.[40] However, they also deal explicitly with what sorts of behaviors and practices are required and forbidden on Sundays.[41] Even for these theologians, then, the Sabbath was important theologically but also for the lived experience of Reformed congregants.

Similarly, Sunday observance was a significant issue for consistories, regional classes, and provincial synods. Simply the number of times the governing bodies dealt with Sunday observance indicates that they were concerned with people's practices. As the later chapters will prove, at each level of church government desecration of the Sabbath was, albeit with varying frequencies, a concern of the church authorities.

The Sabbath was, I will argue, a clear way in which Reformed Christians could demonstrate their piety. This demonstration of piety was important within the Reformed Church but also for the general public. As a demonstration of the genuineness of the Reformed faith, Reformed Christians' piety was to be above reproach. Sabbath observance, namely attendance at worship services and ceasing from work, was a demonstration of piety that everyone could see. On the other hand, a desecration of the Sabbath was equally as noticeable and tarnished the reputation of the Reformed faith and the Dutch Reformed Church. Thus, Sabbath observance was a crucial aspect of the piety expected of Dutch Reformed Christians.

If my argument is correct, then scholars need to reevaluate how and why the Sabbath came to occupy the position that it held within the Dutch Reformed Church. By way of explanation, I offer two main theories. First, the emphasis on Sabbath-keeping in the Dutch Reformed churches was a way for Dutch ecclesiastical authorities to maintain order within their churches and, ideally, society

---

39 Benedict, *Christ's Churches Purely Reformed*, 484–489.
40 For example, reference Calvin, *Institutes*, II.ix.1–2; Zacharias Ursinus, *The Commentary on the Heidelberg Catechism*, Lord's Day 34, I–II; Wilhelmus à Brakel, *The Christian's Reasonable Service*, III.44.
41 Calvin, *Institutes*, II.viii, 28–33; Ursinus, *Commentary on the Heidelberg Catechism*, Lord's Day 38, IV; À Brakel, *The Christian's Reasonable Service*, III.49.

more generally. Second, strict Sabbath observance served to establish a Reformed identity in a religiously plural environment where the Dutch Reformed Church was forced to compete with a number of other religious traditions, including Anabaptists, Catholics, Lutherans, and, later, Remonstrants.

Sabbath, Pluralism, Confessionalization, and Order in the Dutch Reformed Church

Having established the importance of the Sabbath in Reformed theology and lived piety, the book will place Sunday observance within a religiously plural situation where the Dutch Reformed Church was seeking to distinguish itself. In recent years a number of prominent scholars have given much attention to the religiously plural situation in the Dutch Republic. Ben Kaplan, Christine Kooi, Charles Parker, and Judith Pollmann all have given close attention to the presence of Catholics in the Dutch Republic and their interactions with the Reformed Church.[42] Similarly, the presence of Anabaptist movements with its long history in the Low Countries has been well documented and studied, most notably in Samme Zijlstra's work.[43] The Lutheran presence, again quite strong in the Low Countries, has certainly not been ignored but has received less scholarly attention.[44] More generally, and with varying degrees of nuance and success, the religious diversity found in the Dutch Republic has been addressed from a variety of angles in a number of edited volumes and published conference proceedings.[45]

---

42 Benjamin Kaplan et al., eds., *Catholic communities in Protestant states: Britain and the Netherlands c.1570–1720*, Manchester, UK: Manchester University Press, 2009; Christine Kooi, *Calvinists and Catholics during Holland's Golden Age: Heretics and Idolaters*, Cambridge: Cambridge University Press, 2012; Christine Kooi, "Popish Impudence: The Perseverance of the Roman Catholic Faithful in Calvinist Holland, 1572–1620," *The Sixteenth Century Journal*, 26, no. 1 (1995): 75–85; Charles Parker, *Faith on the Margins: Catholics and Catholicism in the Dutch Golden Age*, Cambridge: Cambridge University Press, 1998; Judith Pollmann, *Catholic Identity and the Revolt of the Netherlands, 1520–1635*, Oxford: Oxford University Press, 2011.

43 Samme Zijlstra, *Om de ware gemeente en de oude gronden: Geschiedenis van de dopersen in de Nederlanden 1531–1675*, Hilversum: Verloren, 2000; Samme Zijlstra, "Anabaptists, Spiritualists and the Reformed Church in East Frisia," *The Mennonite Quarterly Review* 75, no. 1 (2001): 57–73.

44 The most complete work, though dated, is J.W. Pont, *Geschiedenis van het lutheranisme in de Nederlanden tot 1618*, Haarlem: E.F. Bohn, 1911. Also, see Alastair Duke, *Reformation and Revolt in the Low Countries*, London: The Hambledon Press, 1990, particularly chapters 1, 2, and 11; Johannes Lindeboom, *De confessioneele ontwikkeling der reformatie in de Nederlanden*, 's-Gravenhage: Martinus Nijhoff, 1946, 1–30.

45 C. Scott Dixon, Dagmar Freist, and Mark Greengrass, eds., *Living with Religious Diversity in Early-Modern Europe*, Farnham, England: Ashgate, 2009; Alastair Duke, Judith Pollmann, and Andrew Spicer, *Public Opinion and Changing Identities in the Early Modern Netherlands:*

Recent scholarship has debated the exact nature of religious pluralism in the Low Countries. What is clear is that the Low Countries consistently were home to any number of religious groups, including Catholics, Lutherans, Reformed, Anabaptists, Socinians, Jews, and Muslims.[46] At the same time, recent scholarship has shown that these various religious groups were more interwoven than previously assumed, and boundary lines were often much more blurred than supposed.[47] Yet, religious authorities in some locales were frequently unhappy with the religious plurality they found in their lands and attempted to eradicate any hint of plurality.[48]

Related to the issue of religious plurality are discussions of tolerance and coexistence in the Low Countries. While a complete recounting of such debates here is impossible and unnecessary, it is important to, at the very least, recognize the complicated nature of tolerance and coexistence in the Low Countries. The Reformed Church was the official state church, yet all citizens were guaranteed tolerance regarding private religious conviction. Still, other religious groups were not tolerated in the modern sense; any religious practices not associated with the Reformed Church were cause for arrest or fine. But, to complicate matters even more, those responsible for enforcing the laws regulating unapproved religious groups were often reluctant to do so and were frequently quite lenient in their enforcement.[49] Willem Frijhoff has done much of the best work on the notion of religious toleration and coexistence in Dutch history, noting that "religious controversy is played out in the field of everyday conviviality between the public and private domain."[50] Perhaps Christine has summarized the complexity of the coexistence best when she writes, "No single type of relationship between Reformed Protestants and Catholics in Golden-Age Holland predominated; coexistence was instead a congeries of connections, interactions, affinities, conflicts,

---

Essays in Honour of Alastair Duke, Leiden: Brill, 2007; Arie-Jan Gelderblom, Jan L. de Jong, and Marc van Vaeck, eds., *The Low Countries as a Crossroads of Religious Beliefs*, Leiden: Brill, 2004; R. Po-chia Hsia and Henk F. K. van Nierop, *Calvinism and Religious Toleration in the Dutch Golden Age*, Cambridge, U.K.: Cambridge University Press, 2002; Piet Visser et al., eds., *Religious Minorities and Cultural Diversity in the Dutch Republic: Studies Presented to Piet Visser on the Occasion of His 65th Birthday*, Leiden: Brill, 2014.

46 Henk van Nierop, "Introduction," in *The Low Countries as a Crossroads of Religious Beliefs*, 2–3.

47 Nierop, "Introduction," in *Crossroads of Religious Beliefs*, 7.

48 Joke Spaans, "Religious policies in the seventeenth-century Dutch Republic," in *Calvinism and Religious Toleration in the Dutch Golden Age*, 72–86.

49 Henk van Nierop, "Sewing the bailiff in a blanket: Catholics and the law in Holland" in *Calvinism and Religious Toleration*, 109–111; Christine Kooi, "Paying off the sheriff: strategies of Catholic toleration in Golden Age Holland," in *Calvinism and Religious Toleration*, 87–96.

50 Willem Frijhoff, *Embodied Belief: Ten Essays on Religious Culture in Dutch History*, Hilversum: Uitgeverij Verloren, 2002, 65.

and conjunctions happening at many levels and in many spaces."[51] While her comment focuses on the relationship between Catholics and Reformed Protestants in the province of Holland, the same can be said for Lutherans, Anabaptists, Jews, Muslims, and, later, Remonstrants throughout the Dutch Republic.

The discussions regarding religious plurality, tolerance, and coexistence are relevant for the examination of the understanding of the Sabbath in the Dutch context on several levels. Regarding religious plurality, as I will argue, religious authorities frequently connected the lack of Sabbath observance with religious plurality. Sabbath desecration was seen as an offense similar to that of practicing Catholicism or Anabaptism. As chapters four through six will verify, the complaints about Sunday observance were frequently directly linked with other confessional groups, mostly the Catholics and Mennonites. In addition, a major argument of my work is that one of the primary reasons the Dutch Reformed religious authorities were so concerned with Sunday observance was precisely in order to set themselves apart from other confessional groups and establish their own Reformed identity.

The issue of tolerance also had links with Sabbath observance. Reformed religious authorities were, not surprisingly, quite intolerant of Sabbath desecration involving their own church members but also regarding society more broadly. Civic authorities, I will argue, were similarly intolerant regarding Sabbath observance and desecration, but they were quite hesitant to take any significant action to enforce a stricter Sabbath observance. Much of their hesitance was indubitably linked to the aforementioned religious plurality in their communities. Average citizens were, it seems, much more willing to tolerate variations in Sabbath observance. As the later evidence will suggest, even those affiliated with the Reformed Church were not above desecrating the Sabbath. Attitudes and actions regarding the Sabbath were certainly not uniform and, as the church records demonstrate, the average Dutch citizen took advantage of such varied expectations to practice the Sabbath however he or she saw fit.

Given the varied expectations regarding Sabbath observance, the issue for religious authorities, civic authorities, and average citizens was how to arrive at a state of coexistence. Religious authorities were less likely to be interested in finding a state of equilibrium regarding Sabbath existence. Instead, they wanted a strict Sabbath observance required of all people and were willing to turn to the political authorities to enforce such a requirement. On the other hand, average Dutch citizens were much more likely to favor a state of coexistence regarding Sabbath observance. Naturally, full members of the Dutch Reformed Church must have had different expectations regarding Sabbath observance than their non-religious or even religiously diverse neighbors. Nonetheless, as other

---

51 Kooi, *Calvinists and Catholics*, 15.

scholars, such as Pollmann and Kooi have noted, citizens were generally quite willing and adept at forming and maintaining relationships even despite these varied religious expectations.[52]

The other interpretative lens I will incorporate into my argument is that of order. As Charles Parker has summarized, "A central feature of early modern social history was the drive by political and church authorities to create a well-ordered society."[53] Scholars have widely acknowledged the importance of order to Protestant authorities.[54] Others, such as Benjamin Kaplan and Peter de Jong, have noted this concern with order in the Dutch Reformed churches.[55] I will argue that Sunday observance was part of the religious authorities' desire to maintain religious and moral order within the church. Religious authorities were also concerned with the disorder Sabbath desecration threatened for the whole of society, hence their continual concern with Sunday observance for the whole of a community, not just the church. However, their ability to regulate Sunday behaviors of those outside of the Dutch Reformed Church was extremely limited. Thus, church authorities focused their efforts of maintaining moral order via Sunday observance on their own members. Church authorities did frequently petition the civic authorities to take action, but, as will be demonstrated later, these authorities were reticent to do so in any meaningful manner.

It is my contention that Sunday observance never followed the path religious authorities desired. First, the complaints about the desecration of the Sabbath continued throughout the seventeenth century. In this book I will attempt to trace the frequency of complaints about Sunday observance in order to demonstrate it was still a significant issue that religious authorities were not able to squelch. In addition, the political authorities (*heeren staten*) continued to issue, at the urging of the consistories and synods, decrees against Sabbath desecration. These continuing appearances indicate that Sunday observance was never achieved as the religious authorities had hoped.

As part of my argument that Sunday observance was never followed as the religious authorities desired, I will argue that a large part of the consistories' and synods' ineffectiveness in persuading people to follow their requirements for Sunday observance can be attributed to the hesitancy of the political authorities.

---

52 Pollmann, *Religious Choice in the Dutch Republic*, 194–195; Kooi, *Calvinists and Catholics*, 175–214.

53 Parker, *The Reformation of Community*, 13.

54 Gerald Strauss, *Enacting the Reformation in Germany*, Aldershot: Variorum, 1993, XIV, 1–16; C. Scott Dixon, *Contesting the Reformation*, West Sussex, UK: Wiley-Blackwell, 2012, 172. Strauss has rightly noted the dangers of the term "order," dangers I attempt to avoid through incorporating perspectives of lay Reformed Christians.

55 Benjamin, Kaplan, *Calvinists and Libertines: Confession and Community in Utrecht, 1578–1620*, Clarendon Press, 1995, 43–45; Peter de Jong, "The Conflict Between Calvinism and Anabaptism in the Netherlands," Master's Thesis: University of Washington, 1963, 83–84.

In the records I have examined, the consistories and synods frequently demanded that the political authorities take appropriate measures to promote Sunday observance. However, these measures, such as declaration, laws, and prosecutions, were rarely carried out. I believe their hesitancy can be attributed to a fear of upsetting the delicate pluralistic religious setting in the Netherlands. Disturbing the religious equilibrium in such a setting could have serious economic, political, and social repercussions that the political authorities were simply not willing to risk.

Method and Theory

The following chapters will seek to take seriously how Dutch Reformed Christians experienced their faith, drawing from the lived religion perspective as pioneered by Robert Orsi and David Hall.[56] Within studies of the Dutch Reformed, Willem Frijhoff also advocates for this perspective, even if not explicitly named as such. Frijhoff's observation, and one that I share, is that scholars should "deal with faith as an embodied phenomenon that takes form in people of flesh and blood."[57] Lived religion is concerned with people's religious experience in a very practical, everyday manner. However, lived religion also seeks to incorporate "official" forms of religion, including theological beliefs. As much as the sources allow for it, this book will attempt to illuminate how people incorporated Sunday experiences into their religious lives, taking into account the role theology and religious authority played in such experiences.

In examining Sunday observance from theological and lived angles, my research must take into account the interplay between religious authorities and the laity. In the Dutch Reformation pastors and theologians had certain expectations of how people would behave on Sundays. Certain activities, such as worship and catechism, were demanded; other activities, such as working and frequenting taverns, were strictly forbidden. These expectations and the subsequent discipline for failing to meet such expectations undoubtedly influenced people's religion as they lived and experienced it.

---

56 See the three Introductions in the third edition of Robert A. Orsi, *The Madonna of 115th Street: Faith and Community in Italian Harlem, 1880-1950*, New Haven: Yale University Press, 2002; David D. Hall, *Worlds of Wonder, Days of Judgment Popular Religious Belief in Early New England*, New York: Knopf, 2013; David D. Hall, ed., *Lived Religion in America: Toward a History of Practice*, Princeton: Princeton University Press, 1997; Robert A. Orsi, ed., *The Cambridge Companion to Religious Studies*, Cambridge: Cambridge University Press, 2011.

57 Frijhoff, *Embodied Belief*, 288.

However, the influence of the laity on theology and religious authorities must also be recognized. Theologians, pastors, and secular authorities were not beyond altering their expectations based on responses from the laity. For example, it would not at all be surprising if Dutch laity refused to cooperate fully with pastors' expectations of Sunday observance causing, in turn, the pastors themselves to alter their expectations. In the Dutch context, Charles Parker has paid particular attention to this interplay between clergy and laity.[58] More broadly, Herman Roodenburg has pointed out that social control in early modern Europe was not simply imposed from above but also negotiated "from below."[59]

Getting a truly accurate picture of lay experiences pertaining to Sunday observance is somewhat difficult because of source limitations. The provincial synod and classis records are, of course, biased and written from the perspective of the powerful, male secretary. Similarly, consistory records are by their very nature selective in what gets recorded and omitted. Pollmann has demonstrated this clearly in her work on the diary of Arnold Buchelius.[60] Unfortunately, actually arriving at an unfiltered portrayal of Dutch Reformed lived religious experience is quite difficult, if not impossible. Even if such a view were to exist, say in a diary or autobiography, it would be quite presumptuous to extrapolate from one person's experience or undoubtedly biased point of view. Thus, the church records provide a helpful perspective so long as their bias and selective nature are taken into account.

Much other work has also been done in the theory of religious studies that will be helpful for this project, though the theory will not be overly explicit. Despite some significant difficulties with Durkheim's understanding of religion, his categories of belief and practices within religion can serve a helpful purpose here.[61] Dutch Reformed Christians in the sixteenth and seventeenth centuries certainly had significant religious practices regarding Sabbath observance. To properly interpret the meaning of these religious practices requires understanding, to borrow Durkheim's language, the "states of opinion" these Re-

---

58 Charles Parker, "Confessionalisation: lay-clerical collaboration in the Dutch Catholic communities during the Golden Age," in *Catholic communities in Protestant States*, 18–32; Charles Parker, "Obedience with an Attitude. Laity and Clergy in the Dutch Catholic Church of the Seventeenth Century," in *Crossroads of Religious Beliefs*, 177–195.

59 Herman Roodenburg, "Social Control Viewed from Below," in *Social Control In Europe Volume 1, 1500–1800*, eds. Herman Roodenburg and Pieter Spierenburg, Columbus, OH: The Ohio State University Press, 2004, 145–158. The subsequent chapters in *Social Control in Europe*, Chapters 9–16, all adopt this "bottom up" approach.

60 Judith Pollmann, "Off the Record: Problems in the Quantification of Calvinist Church Discipline," *The Sixteenth Century Journal*, 33, no. 2 (2002): 423–438.

61 Emile Durkheim, *The Elementary Forms of the Religious Life*, New York: The Free Press, 1915. The most glaring problem with Durkheim's definition of religion is his insistence upon a faulty binary division between the sacred and the profane.

formed Christians had regarding the Sabbath. The methodology of my project draws on Durkheim's distinction between religious beliefs and practices, examining how religious beliefs affected religious practices and vice versa. While the lines between these practices and beliefs cannot be drawn too distinctly, the categories are helpful in framing the examination of the Sabbath in the Dutch Reformed tradition. Such an examination requires delving into the theological understanding of the Sabbath typical of the Dutch Reformed tradition in the sixteenth and seventeenth centuries. Having done so, the book will then move to the religious "practices," investigating how the Sabbath was lived out among Dutch Reformed religious practitioners.

As Matthew Engelke has noted, religion is at its core always material.[62] Therefore, to attend only to the Dutch Reformed theological understanding of the Sabbath is to address only one side of the proverbial coin. As is the case with all theology, the theology finds its expression in the daily practices and material experiences of everyday practitioners. Related to Sabbath observance in the Low Countries, to what material practices were Dutch Reformed church members drawn? As the latter three chapters will substantiate, possession of certain material objects and activities such as drinking alcohol, dancing, working, and playing games were common Sabbath activities. One of the goals of this project is, then, to investigate how the theological ideas regarding the Sabbath impacted how Sabbath observance was practiced. To use the language of Geertz, how was it that the system of symbols (i. e. the theological discourse) formulated, or fail to formulate, a general order of existence for people (i. e. Sabbath practices)?[63]

The relationship between "belief" and "practice" is always reciprocal. This means, of course, that the practices of Sabbath observance also impact how the Sabbath is conceptualized theologically. Colleen McDannell notes this interplay when she writes, "Experiencing the physical dimension of religion helps *bring about* religious values, norms, behaviors, and attitudes (original emphasis)."[64] My book operates with a firm belief in McDannell's observation that religious practices are not only *shaped by* religious thought but also *shape* religious thought. While such impacts may be slightly more difficult to apprehend, paying attention to the influence of religious practice on theology is also important for a proper understanding of the religious lives of Dutch Reformed Christians.

62 Matthew Engelke, "Material Religion," in *The Cambridge Companion to Religious Studies*, 209–229.
63 Clifford Geertz, *The Interpretation of Cultures*, New York: Basic Books, 1973.
64 Colleen McDannell, *Material Christianity: Religion and Popular Culture in America*, New Haven: Yale University Press, 1995, 2.

Terminology and Structure

Acknowledging in theory the intertwined relationship between practice and theology, clergy and laity, and religious and political authorities is important, but conducting a study that carries out such theory proves to be much more difficult. Naturally, one needs to make decisions about how to be as all-encompassing as possible while still needing to use meaningful terms, structure material in helpful ways, and draw reasonable conclusions.

As such, I have chosen to use the first three chapters of the present work to address the theology of the Sabbath as understood in the Dutch Reformed tradition. The final three chapters turn the attention to ecclesiastical records and how the Sabbath was disciplined at the various levels. In addition, these chapters draw conclusions about church members' actual Sabbath practices based on the church records' perspectives, taking into account the particular perspectives and biases these records might contain. In structuring the chapters as such the risk of separating out theology and practice is a real concern. However, I have attempted, particularly in the final three chapters, to link the two categories together as much as possible in an effort to present the reality of actual lived religious experience that includes both theology and practice in overlapping and seamless ways.

In addition, the first three chapters largely focus on individual men who were pastors, theologians, and professors. From Calvin to Ursinus to à Brakel, these men were, I will argue, certainly influential for the Dutch Reformed churches. The danger in such an approach is to overestimate the influence of these individuals or the documents they wrote. In addition, equally as important in shaping the theology of the Dutch Reformed Church, as far as such a monolithic thing existed, were the national and even provincial synods. Regretably, limitations of time and space do not allow for research on these bodies and their assumed or articulated theologies of the Sabbath to be included in this project. However, the influence of, for example, the National Synod of Middleburg in 1581 or the National Synod of The Hague in 1586 or, most famously, the National Synod of Dordrecht in 1618–1619 should not be discounted or underestimated. These bodies and their declarations were crucial for the Dutch Reformed Church. Their understanding of the Sabbath has not been the subject of enough academic study and should be explored in greater detail. Unfortunately, that research is simply not able to be undertaken and included here.

Regarding terminology, it will be helpful for the sake of clarity to briefly mention a couple of items at the outset. While I have made conscious decisions regarding terminology, it is my hope that terminology does not interfere with the larger, more important overall argument and narrative. First, the obvious issue is what the day of rest designated in the Jewish Ten Commandments should be called. The Jewish tradition is, of course, to call that day the "Sabbath." The use of the word "Sabbath" continues in the Christian tradition. But, while the Jewish Sabbath referred to the last day of the week, Saturday, the Christian Sabbath, outside of the Seventh Day Adventists tradition, refers to the first day of the week, Sunday. Christian theologians frequently speak of "Sunday" not simply as a day of the week but as the day of rest and worship. In addition, Christians also speak of a day devoted to rest and worship as "the Lord's Day."

In this project I will use the terms "Sabbath," "Sunday," and "the Lord's Day" interchangeably. While such equivocacy seems to border on imprecision, good reasons exist for such an approach. Most notably, the theologians themselves tend to blur the terms and use them interchangeably. On occasion the writers will be quite intentional to use "Sabbath" when referring specifically to the Jewish Sabbath, so I will explicitly note when the Jewish Sabbath is meant rather than the Christian Sabbath. Like the theologians, the church records frequently use the terms indiscriminately. The records speak of problems regarding "Sundays" or, more rarely, "the Lord's Day," but the records also have complaints using the language of the "Sabbath." As such, it is in keeping with historical realities to use the terms somewhat interchangeably, though when speaking of the theological issues I tend towards the "Sabbath" designation and when speaking of actual practices more towards "Sunday."

Second, scholars have differed in their opinions on what term should be used to refer to what today is called the Netherlands and Belgium. The issue is deeply complicated since the realities of history contain all sorts of blurred lines. Several of the more popular options are the Low Countries, the Dutch Republic, and, occasionally, simply the Netherlands. Here I will stay away from using "the Netherlands" unless speaking of the modern-day country since the Netherlands was not formed into the modern nation in its current form until the nineteenth century. Throughout this project I will use both the "Low Countries" and the "Dutch Republic."[65] When references are made to the time prior to the beginning of the Dutch Revolt in 1568 I will use the "Low Countries" since there was no real republic of which to speak. For the time period after 1568 I will often use the "Dutch Republic," even if the completion of such a republic did not fully occur until somewhat later. In a similar vein, I will refer to the ethnic people group simply as "Dutch" even though French, German, English, and Scottish people could all be found residing in the Low Countries and even attending Dutch Reformed churches.

The final issue of terminology relates to the designation of religious identity. The identification of the Dutch Reformed Church becomes clear later in the sixteenth century after church polity became more firmly established. But, earlier

---

65 Jasper van der Steen, "A Note on Terminology," in *Memory Wars in the Low Countries, 1566–1700*, Leiden: Brill, 2015. Here I am largely following his distinctions which I find to be helpful.

manifestations of Protestantism were frequently called "Lutheran," particularly by their enemies. As the Lutheran presence dwindled, the Reformed presence gained strength. Scholars have frequently denoted this group, especially its stricter adherents, as "Calvinists." However, as mentioned above and validated in what follows, that designation is not particularly accurate.[66] As such, I will refer to the Protestant presence in the second half of the sixteenth century and into the seventeenth century as Reformed or, more specifically, Dutch Reformed. This group includes full members of the church, meaning those who submitted to church discipline, but, also, the partial members, known as *liefhebbers*, who attended church services but did not submit to discipline and were, therefore, not permitted to partake of the Lord's Supper.

With the above introduction, caveats, and theoretical understandings firmly in place, it is time to dive into the Sabbath in the sixteenth and seventeenth centuries. Chapter one begins with an analysis of John Calvin's understanding of the Sabbath. While not Dutch or the originator of Protestantism in the Low Countries, Calvin's influence on the religious life of the Low Countries was significant and, as such, provides an important starting point. Chapter two addresses Dutch Reformed theology more properly, analyzing the theological views of Johannes a Lasco and Zacharias Ursinus on the Sabbath. Chapter three moves into the seventeenth century and examines the theology of the strand of pietism in the Dutch Reformed tradition known as the Nadere Reformatie. Even though his work takes place later in the seventeenth century well after the origins of the Nadere Reformatie, Wilhelmus à Brakel and his carefully nuanced understanding of the Sabbath will be the primary theologian investigated. Chapter four explores the Dutch Reformed church records and focuses on the records of the provincial synods. Chapter five narrows the focus somewhat, turning to the records of the more regional church meetings, known as meetings of the classis. Finally, chapter six examines the Dutch city of Kampen and its local church governing body, the consistory. In examining both the theology of the Sabbath and actual Sabbath practices, the importance of the Sabbath for Dutch Reformed piety, confessional identity, and order will become increasingly clear.

---

66 Several scholars have noted the discontinuity between Calvin's theology and what has traditionally been called "Calvinism." Most notably, Richard Muller has argued against such a confusion: Richard A. Muller, "Calvin and the 'Calvinists': Assessing Continuities and Discontinuities between the Reformation and Orthodoxy, Part Two," *Calvin Theological Journal* 31, no. 1 (April 1996): 134–138; Richard Muller, "Was Calvin a Calvnist?", lecture, Westminster Seminary California, Escondido, CA, February 28, 2012. Similarly, see the discussion in Leo Koffeman, ed., "Hoe Calvijns is het Nederlands Calvinisme?", Special Issue, *Kosmos en oecumene: maandblad gewijd aan het samen-leven in kerk en wereld* 24, no. 9 (1990). The issue is not only theological but also cultural: Willem Nijenhuis, *Hoe Calvinistisch Zijn Wij Nederlanders?*, Amsterdam: Historischx Documentatiecentrum voor het Nederlands Protestantisme, 2009.

Chapter 1:
Early Reformed Theology of the Sabbath:
Calvin and the Sabbath

It would not be difficult to make the argument that Christian life in John Calvin's Geneva was centered on Sundays. Scholars have noted the importance of the sermon service in Calvin's Reformation.[1] While sermon services were offered throughout the week, the Sunday sermon service was of particular importance. Additionally, Christians periodically celebrated the sacraments, the Lord's Supper and baptism, during Sunday services. Catechism services, designed to educate Christians in their faith, were also held on Sundays. In Calvin's Geneva, what occurred on Sundays was one of the primary ways, if not the primary way, a Christian's piety and faith were formed and shaped.

While Sundays were of great practical importance for Calvin and Geneva, scholars have had little success in reaching a consensus on what exactly Calvin believed about the Sabbath. This disagreement is sharpest over whether or not Calvin held to a sabbatarian position. Most of the scholarly attention has focused on Calvin's writings in the *Institutes* on the Sabbath commandment, numbered by Calvin and the Reformed tradition more generally as the fourth commandment, and his two sermons on Deuteronomy 5:12–15, the fourth commandment. Yet, scholars examining Calvin's writings have come to quite different conclusions.

Such disagreements have not resulted from lack of examination. A number of studies have undertaken the task of examining and explaining Calvin's theology of the Sabbath. In his published, revised master's thesis Richard Gaffin, emeritus Professor of Biblical and Systematic Theology at Westminster Theological Seminary, provides the most complete examination of Calvin's theological un-

---

1 Robert Kingdon, *Reforming Geneva: Discipline, Faith and Anger in Calvin's Geneva*, Gene`ve: Librairie Droz S.A., 2012, 24–25; Thomas A. Lambert, "Preaching, Praying and Policing the Reform in Sixteenth Century Geneva," Ph.D. Dissertation: The University of Wisconsin-Madison, 1998; Hughes Oliphant Old, *The Reading and Preaching of the Scriptures in the Worship of the Christian Church: Vol. 4, The Age of the Reformation,* Grand Rapids, MI: Eerdmans, 2002, 90–134; T.H.L. Parker, *Calvin's Preaching,* Louisville, KY: Westminster/J. Knox Press, 1992.

derstanding of the Sabbath.[2] John Primus has also touched on Calvin's understanding of the Sabbath, comparing Calvin with later Puritan theologians.[3] More
recently, Stewart Lauer, missionary in Japan for the Orthodox Presbyterian
Church, has entered the scholarly discussion, challenging the work of previous
researchers.[4] Other scholars have also addressed Calvin's understanding of the
Sabbath, though typically more briefly and with other issues in view.[5] Clearly,
scholarship on Calvin's understanding of the Sabbath is not lacking.

Some scholars clearly believe Calvin to hold to a sabbatarian position. In his
article, Lauer argues that Calvin is indeed a sabbatarian. He writes, bluntly, "This
essay argues that parts of Calvin's Sabbath theology has been seriously misunderstood and that he was sabbatarian in both practice and theology."[6] Lauer's
position echoes that of Calvin Pater, who argued that Calvin was a sabbatarian
and even viewed the Sabbath as a Christian sacrament.[7] On the other hand, John
Primus takes a much different view of Calvin's understanding of the Sabbath,
arguing, "In short, Calvin in his theology is not Sabbatarian."[8] Likewise, Georgia
Harkness denies any Puritan strand of sabbatrianism in Calvin's thought, writing
that, "In the matter of sabbath observance, there is a marked difference between
Calvin's doctrine and that of the New England Puritans."[9] Gaffin's position,
somewhat less starkly stated, is that Calvin's theology was not necessarily sabbatarian, though Calvin does tend toward a "practical sabbatarianism."[10]

At least one of the problems within the scholarly debate has been its largely
confessional nature.[11] Any number of Christians identify with the tradition that
has been associated with John Calvin, including most notably any number of
Reformed and Presbyterian denominations. Rightly or wrongly, many theologians and historians within these traditions view Calvin's theology as author-

---

2 Richard B. Gaffin, *Calvin and the Sabbath*, Fearn, Ross-shire: Mentor, 1998.
3 John H. Primus, *Holy Time: Moderate Puritanism and the Sabbath*, Macon, GA: Mercer
   University Press, 1989; Primus, "Calvin and the Puritan Sabbath," 40–75.
4 Stewart E. Lauer, "John Calvin, the Nascent Sabbatarian: A Reconsideration of Calvin's View
   of Two Key Sabbath-issues," *The Confessional Presbyterian* 3, (January 1, 2007): 3–14.
5 Bierma, "Remembering the Sabbath Day," 277–280; Raymond A. Blacketer, *The School of God
   Pedagogy and Rhetoric in Calvin's Interpretation of Deuteronomy*, Dordrecht: Springer, 2006,
   particularly Chapter 5.
6 Lauer, "John Calvin, the Nascent Sabbatarian," 5.
7 Calvin A. Pater, "Calvin, the Jews, and the Judaic Legacy," in *In Honour of John Calvin, 1509–
   1564: Papers from the 1986 International Calvin Symposium*, ed. E.J. Furcha, Montreal: McGill
   University Press, 1987, 256–295.
8 Primus, *Holy Time*, 120.
9 Georgia Harkness, *John Calvin: The Man and His Ethics*, New York: Henry Holt and Company, 1931, 118.
10 Gaffin, *Calvin and the Sabbath*, 109, 141–143.
11 Gaffin, *Calvin and the Sabbath*, 23–26. Gaffin notes the phenomena of the confessional arguments
   and its problematic results.

itative, and the temptation is to bend Calvin's writings to fit one's own positions. This is particularly true of Calvin's theology of the Sabbath.

The confessional debate over Calvin's view of the Sabbath only gets magnified because of the differences in how the Heidelberg Catechism, published in 1563, and the Westminster Catechism, published in 1647, understand the Sabbath.[12] The Heidelberg Catechism, which will be explored more thoroughly in the next chapter, places the emphasis of the fourth commandment on participating in public worship and on resting from sin throughout one's life. On the other hand, the Westminster Catechism speaks of the Sabbath being on the first day of the week for all of time because God has appointed the Sabbath to be perpetual. In addition, the Sabbath must be observed "one whole day in seven." In sum, the Westminster Catechism takes a much stricter, more sabbatarian attitude than the Heidelberg Catechism.

Those who subscribe to either the Westminster Catechism, primarily Presbyterians, or the Heidelberg Catechism, primarily Reformed churches, have tried to support their position using Calvin's theology.[13] Even scholars who attempt to take an objective examination of Calvin's views of the Sabbath have had a difficult time overcoming their assumptions and biases. What is required, then, is a reexamination of Calvin's understanding of the Sabbath. This is not to make the audacious claim that this examination is without its own biases, though every effort will be made to undertake an objective study. Taking special care not to read later documents or theologies into Calvin is particularly important when examining sabbatarian issues.

Despite the large amount of scholarly work on Calvin and the Sabbath, further scholarly attention is certainly needed on the subject. The lack of scholarly consensus on Calvin's view of the Sabbath demonstrates the issue is obviously not clear or resolved. In addition, much of the previous scholarship focuses only on one or two of Calvin's works, typically his *Institutes* and sermons. Finally, a proper portrayal of Calvin's understanding of the Sabbath is needed in order to fully comprehend the role of the Sabbath in sixteenth and seventeenth century Dutch Reformed theology and practice.

Calvin's theology more generally, not to mention regarding the Sabbath, is important in and of itself. But, Calvin is important for the current project because of his influence on the Dutch Reformed tradition.[14] As will be explained in more

---

12 John Stek, "The Fourth Commandment: A New Look," *Reformed Journal* 22, no. 6 (July 1, 1972): 26–29.

13 Diedrich H. Kromminga, "The Heidelberg View of the Fourth Commandment: Does It Conflict with Calvin's," *The Calvin Forum* 6, no. 8 (March, 1941): 161. Kromminga explicitly states: "In this defense of the Heidelberg view of the Fourth Commandment a comparison with the view of John Calvin turns out to be a first requisite."

14 Herman Selderhuis, ed., *Handbook of Dutch Church History*, Göttingen: Vandenhoeck &

depth in the next chapter, Calvin had an impact on the Dutch Reformation in a number of ways, both theologically and practically. Calvin's final edition of the *Institutes* was published in 1559 and translated into Dutch already in 1560. A number of major pastors and theologians in the Dutch Reformed tradition, such as Jean Taffin and Guido de Bres, were educated at the Genevan Academy.[15] Only when Calvin's theology is taken into account can the Dutch Reformation truly be understood.

Before beginning a more in-depth analysis of Calvin's thought, one quick word regarding notation is in order. When speaking about the fourth commandment, Calvin continues to use the word "Sabbath," *sabbathum*. He does, however, frequently use the phrase "the Lord's Day," *diem dominicum*. The reasoning for Calvin's choice of one over the other is not always clear. The contexts within which Calvin uses one term or the other does not provide any significant conclusions, though at times Calvin does associate the "Sabbath" with Judaism and the "Lord's Day" with Christianity. Nonetheless, overall, Calvin uses the terms quite interchangeably and, for the most part, indiscriminately. So, in this chapter the term "Sabbath" will be used throughout. At several points throughout the chapter when Calvin is particularly addressing the establishment of the first day of the week the term "Lord's Day" is most appropriate and will be used. But, overall, here the term "Sabbath" will be used to denote the principle the fourth commandment sets forth both in the Old Testament for the Jews and for Christians.

This chapter, then, will attend to Calvin's understanding of the Sabbath. To arrive at a proper understanding of Calvin's position this examination will include not only the *Institutes* and sermons on Deuteronomy but also the Genevan Catechism and Calvin's biblical commentaries. Such a comprehensive investigation will shed further light on Calvin's understanding of the Sabbath and, in the process, contribute to the ongoing scholarly discussion. In addition, and most importantly for this project, examining Calvin's theology of the Sabbath is the first crucial step in understanding how Dutch Reformed theologians understood the Sabbath and how Dutch Reformed congregants practiced the Sabbath.

Ruprecht, 2015, 203; Guido Marnef, *Antwerp in the Age of Reformation: Underground Protestantism in a Commercial Metropolis, 1550–1577*, Baltimore: Johns Hopkins University Press, 1996, 61–71; Karin Maag, *Seminary or University?: The Genevan Academy and Reformed Higher Education, 1560–1620*, Aldershot, England: Scolar Press, 1995, 30, 33, 56–57, 83–86. Maag has compiled meticulous charts of students at the Geneva Academy who were from the Netherlands and who went on to serve as ministers in the Netherlands.

15 Selderhuis, *Handbok of Dutch Church History*, 203.

Calvin and Sabbatarianism

Within the scholarly debate about whether or not Calvin should be considered a sabbatarian, scholars largely assume that Calvin must fall rather neatly into either the sabbatarian or non-sabbatarian position. Yet, the idea that Calvin did or did not consider himself a sabbatarian is clearly anachronistic. As Richard Muller has demonstrated, theologians and historians have a tendency to assign theological perspectives to Calvin that he himself did not hold and, furthermore, was not even concerned with.[16]

Determining whether or not Calvin qualifies as a sabbatarian requires, of course, a clear definition of what Sabbatarianism is. Such clarity of a definition is often lacking and is certainly not without debate.[17] Primus holds that a sabbatarian position consists of two major premises. First, "the first premise of Sabbatarian theology is that the fourth commandment is rooted in creation." Second, sabbatarian theology holds that "the substitution of Sunday for the Sabbath is based not simply on an early, somewhat arbitrary, ecclesiastical decision, but is based on divine authority which came ultimately from Christ Himself and was transmitted through His apostles."[18]

Yet, the implications of Primus's definition of Sabbatarianism, particularly the second qualification, are much broader. If the Sabbath is divinely instituted on Sunday, then Christians are obviously required to celebrate the Lord's Day on Sunday and are not free to celebrate the Lord's Day on any other day of the week. Celebrating the Sabbath on Wednesday, for example, would go against Christ's ordaining of the day on Sunday. Moreover, the sabbatarian position maintains that the Sabbath commandment still requires Christians to observe one day out of seven. If God has ordained Sunday as the Sabbath, then Christians are not free to choose to observe the Sabbath any less frequently, requiring Christians to observe the Sabbath at least one day out of seven.

Other scholars have offered slightly different definitions of Sabbatarianism. Gaffin believes the distinctive element of the sabbatarian position is that the "fourth commandment is not merely a piece of Mosaic legislation but rather, along with the other elements of the Decalogue, is an expression of a creation ordinance."[19] Gaffin also notes in the sabbatarian view the Sabbath has been changed from the seventh to the first, but he does not tie Sabbatarianism to the belief that such a change was divinely ordained.

---

16 Richard A. Muller, *The Unaccommodated Calvin: Studies in the Foundation of a Theological Tradition,* Oxford: Oxford University Press, 2001, 3–11.

17 For example, Kenneth Parker's book, *The English Sabbath*, is very good but uses sabbatarian language without ever offering a clear definition.

18 Primus, "Calvin and the Puritan Sabbath," 44–50.

19 Gaffin, *Calvin and the Sabbath*, 13.

While a completely uniform definition of what constitutes a sabbatarian position is lacking, Primus's understanding is quite clear and highlights well the relevant issues. So, in determining whether or not Calvin qualifies as a sabbatarian it must first be determined to what extent Calvin understood the Sabbath as rooted in the creation order. It also must be determined whether or not Jesus instituted Sunday as the day that would act as a substitute to the Sabbath. Related to the second point are issues of whether or not the fourth commandment demands a perpetual observance of one out of seven days. Similarly, a discussion on Sabbatarianism must also determine if Calvin believed Christians were free to observe the Sabbath on any day other than Sunday.

However, Calvin's position on the Sabbath should not be limited to that of sabbatarian issues. Other important aspects of Calvin's theology of the Sabbath include what Christians are required to do on Sundays and what should be avoided on Sundays. While prohibitions and requirements for Sunday observance may seem quite clear, Calvin's perspectives on such issues are more complex than might be expected. In addition, expectations for Sunday observance are critical for understanding Reformed Christians' lived religious experience.

Calvin's Works

A proper methodology is crucial for a proper understanding of Calvin's position regarding the Sabbath. The fairest method to Calvin's own beliefs is to first examine each of the textual locations at which Calvin addresses the Sabbath. As other scholars have noted, two of the most important pieces of Calvin's Sabbath theology are his discussions in the *Institutes* and his sermons on the fourth commandment. As Lauer notes, scholars have often seen a tension between Calvin's thinking as expressed in the *Institutes* and his sermons.[20] In this caricature, the *Institutes* are seen to be non-sabbatarian, and the sermons are believed to advocate for a sort of sabbatarian position.[21]

Calvin's biblical commentaries have not been examined as closely regarding Calvin's understanding of the Sabbath, but the commentaries too are an important aspect of Calvin's overall thought. Unfortunately, limitations of space prevent all the locations in which Calvin addresses the Sabbath within his

---

20 Lauer, "John Calvin, the Nascent Sabbatarian," 3.
21 Lauer, "John Calvin, the Nascent Sabbatarian," 3. While I disagree with his overall argument, Lauer summarizes the positions quite clearly. For the argument regarding the sabbatarian nature of the sermons, see Gaffin, *Calvin and the Sabbath*, 109. For the argument regarding the non-sabbatarian nature of the *Institutes*, see Primus, *Holy Time*, 134.

commentaries from being addressed here.[22] I have chosen the passages from Calvin's commentaries where Calvin deals with the topic extensively and that, in my judgment, clearly elucidate Calvin's understanding of the Sabbath. Similarly, the Genevan Catechism, composed by Calvin, has also not been studied adequately in its explanation of the Sabbath. Given its brevity, the Sabbath as explained in the Genevan Catechism can be examined in its entirety. These works have not been given as much attention as the *Institutes* and Calvin's sermons; as such, dealing with them at length here is important.

Only after having examined each of the above works can a more comprehensive view be undertaken. To attempt to synthesize Calvin's various works from the outset risks misreading Calvin's statements in order to make them fit with one another. An additional danger is to prioritize one particular work over another.[23] The best way forward is instead to take each work individually and then draw conclusions and, if necessary, attempt to explain any contradictions.

Institutio Christianae religionis (Institutes of the Christian Religion)

Undoubtedly, Calvin's most famous work is his *Institutio Christianae religionis*, typically translated into English as the *Institutes of the Christian Religion* and referred to simply as the *Institutes*. Calvin's *Institutes* are so famous that much introduction to the work is not needed here. Mainly meant to prepare and train students of theology, the *Institutes* are not a systematic theology but a handbook for clergy to help them understand the whole of Scripture. Naturally, this includes understanding God's law, the Ten Commandments, and the Sabbath. Not surprisingly, Calvin's understanding of the Sabbath, as explained in the *Institutes*, comes most clearly in his section on the Ten Commandments.[24] As

---

22 Cox, *The Whole Doctrine of Calvin*, 1–72. Cox includes Calvin's commentary on a number of biblical passages that I have not included. Some of these deal directly with the Sabbath, such as Isaiah 56, Ezekiel 20, and Amos 8. Other passages Cox includes, such as 2 Corinthians 3, Galatians 3, and Hebrews 8, deal less directly with the Sabbath and more with the relationship between the law, Jews, and Christians.

23 Gaffin, *Calvin and the Sabbath*, 26. Gaffin makes the mistake of prioritizing Calvin's *Institutes* when he describes his method as follows: "A full and careful statement of the teaching of the *Institutes* will be our point of departure, with the remaining materials considered in that light."

24 Calvin, *Institutes*, II.viii.1–59. Of course, Calvin's *Institutio Chrstianae religionis* went through several editions. The Latin editions were published in 1536, 1539, 1543, 1550, and 1559. The final 1559 edition will be the one referenced here since it was that version that was used in the Dutch Reformed tradition; the 1559 version was translated into Dutch in 1560. The Latin 1559 edition can be found in Ioannis Calvini, *Opera quae supersunt omnia*, eds. Guilielmus Baum, Eduaruds Cunnitz, and Eduardus Reuss, Brunsvigae: C.A. Schwetschke, 1863, Tomes II–IV. The whole *Opera quae supersunt omnia* is available online via the Université de

Primus notes, most of the sections on the Sabbath derive from Calvin's 1536 edition of the *Institutes*, though McKee rightly observes there was some development from the 1536 edition to the 1539 edition with little change thereafter.[25] Calvin begins with a general interpretation of the fourth commandment. He summarizes its overall meaning: "The purpose of this commandment is that, being dead to our own inclinations and works, we should meditate on the Kingdom of God, and that we should practice that meditation in the ways established by him."[26] He goes on to list three conditions for this purpose. First, the seventh day was meant to represent spiritual rest for the people of Israel. Spiritual rest entails turning away from one's own works to allow God to work in oneself. Second, God meant for the Israelites to assemble to hear the law and perform religious rites. Finally, the day was to serve as a day of rest from work for servants and those under the authority of others.

Calvin does give significant attention to the importance of the seventh day and its relationship to the fourth commandment. The seventh day mimics God's resting from creation on the seventh day. However, Calvin offers other explanations as to why the seventh day is significant. One option, for which Calvin appeals to Moses, is that the number seven is in Scripture the number of perfection and denotes perpetuity. Or, the number seven could indicate that the Sabbath will never be perfected until Christ's return on the Last Day. In that sense, Calvin argues, the Sabbath command to rest from sin is a continual process but one that will never be complete in this life.

Yet, Calvin does not feel strongly about interpreting the number seven in either of these ways. Calvin has "no objection" to interpreting the number more

---

Genève; see http://archive-ouverte.unige.ch/vital/access/manager/Repository/unige:650? query=calvin&f0=creator%3 A%22Calvin%2C+Jean%22. Any number of English translations and editions of Calvin's *Institutes* exist. The two most well known translations are Henry Beveridge's translation done in 1845 and the edition edited by John T. McNeill and translated by Ford Lewis Battles in 1960. See Jean Calvin, *Institutes of the Christian Religion*, trans. Henry Beveridge, Grand Rapids, MI: Eerdmans, 1989; Jean Calvin, *Institutes of the Christian Religion*, trans. Ford Lewis Battles, ed. John T. McNeill, Philadelphia: Westminster Press, 1960, Reissued by Westminster John Knox Press, Louisville, KY, 2006. Beveridge's edition is available online at http://www.ccel.org/ccel/calvin/institutes/. In what follows all references to Calvin's *Institutes* will refer to the 1559 edition unless otherwise stated and will adhere to the following format: Calvin, *Institutes*, Book Number [Uppercase Roman Numeral].Chapter Number [Lowercase Roman Numeral].Section Number [Arabic Numeral]. I have consulted the Latin as well as Beveridge's and McNeill's translations.

25 Primus, "Calvin and the Puritan Sabbath," 59; McKee, *Pastoral Ministry and Worship*, 182. Primus is incorrect in his assertion that there are "no substantial additions to his Sabbath theology to be found in the numerous references to the Sabbath that are sprinkled throughout the rest of Calvin's works." As will be demonstrated, Calvin's catechisms, sermons, and commentaries certainly add to the complexity of Calvin's understanding of the Sabbath.

26 Calvin, *Institutes*, II.viii.28.

simply.[27] In this view, God assigned the seventh day "either because he [God] foresaw that it would be sufficient; or that, by providing a model in his own example, he might better arouse the people."[28] Which interpretation one adopts "makes little difference" for Calvin. The importance, according to Calvin, is that the focus of the commandment is the perpetual repose from our own labors in order to let God work in us.

Calvin moves on to argue that the fourth commandment is in fact ceremonial in nature.[29] In regard to the Sabbath commandment, the medieval tradition, most famously articulated by Thomas Aquinas, distinguished between the Old Testament ceremonial nature of the commandment, which was only for the Jews, and the moral aspect of the law that Christians were to continue to follow.[30] The ceremonial nature of the fourth commandment, and all ceremonial laws in the Old Testament, were abolished with Jesus' incarnation. Though occasionally speaking harshly about such a distinction, Calvin largely adopts it.[31] Calvin believes the fourth commandment is at least partly ceremonial and, therefore, has aspects that applied only to Jews and not to Christians. "Still there can be no doubt," he writes, "that on the advent of our Lord Jesus Christ the ceremonial aspect of the commandment was abolished."[32] Nonetheless, the command is still applicable to Christians. Christians are not to follow the "shadows" of the commandment but, rather, are to turn their attention to what Jesus Christ has shown to be the truth of the commandment. This involves "being completely dead to ourselves [themselves]" and being "filled with the life of God." The process is not to be left to only one day out of seven. Instead, it is a process that requires the whole of one's life. Two other aspects of the commandment still resonate, Calvin observes.[33] Christians still should assemble for worship. This worship includes hearing the Word preached, celebrating the sacraments, and holding public prayers. Also, Christians should allow servants and laborers to cease from their work. These aspects of the commandment continue to be

---

27 Blacketer, *The School of God*, 172. Unfortunately, in his chapter on the Sabbath Blacketer does not pay attention to these other possible explanations of why the seventh day was chosen.

28 Calvin, *Institutes*, II.viii.30.

29 For Calvin's thoughts more broadly on the ceremonial laws in the Old Testament see his *Institutes*, II.vii. Mark W. Elliott, "Calvin and the Ceremonial Law of Moses," *Reformation & Renaissance Review* 11, no. 3 (December 2009): 275–293.

30 For Thomas Aquinas on the various types of laws, see his "Treatise on Law" in his *Summa Theologica*, "First Part of the Second Part," QQ 90–108. Aquinas' work can be accessed online: St. Thomas Aquinas, *Summa Theologica*, Benziger Brothers edition of 1947, trans. Fathers of the English Dominican Province, http://www.ccel.org/ccel/aquinas/summa.i.html.

31 Bierma, "Ursinus's Exposition of Exodus 20:8–11," 276–278.

32 Calvin, *Institutes*, II.viii.31.

33 Calvin, *Institutes*, II.viii.32.

binding for Christians and, as such, are not part of the ceremonial aspect of the fourth commandment.[34]

A question that naturally arises is whether or not worship and rest from work for servants are necessitated by the fourth commandment every seventh day or even one out of seven days. Calvin anticipates the question and addresses it directly. As already mentioned, with Christ's coming the ceremonial part of the commandment was abolished. Included in the ceremonial aspect of the commandment was the command to observe one specific day a week. He writes, "We do not celebrate it [the Lord's Day] with most minute formality, as a ceremony by which we imagine that a spiritual mystery is typified, but we adopt it as a necessary remedy for preserving order in the Church."[35] While the original command included the celebration on one specific day of the week, Jesus Christ has repealed that aspect of the command. As a result, "Christians ought therefore to shun completely the superstitious observance of days."[36] Calvin attacks those who argue that the only ceremonial aspect of the Jewish law was the adherence to the seventh day of the week. These false prophets allege that the observance of one day in seven remains part of the moral command. But, Calvin believes this has the effect of "retaining the same typical distinction of days as had place among the Jews."[37] Those who cling to such an idea go farther than the Jews in their "gross and carnal superstition of sabbatism."[38] Christians do not have to observe the Sabbath on any particular day of the week, and they do not have to maintain the pattern of observing the Sabbath one out of seven days.[39]

Why, then, do Christians insist on keeping the Sabbath on Sundays? Is this not clinging to the Jewish, ceremonial aspect of the law? The objection that singling out Sunday maintains the observance of days as in Judaism is one Calvin takes seriously. Calvin observes a fundamental difference between the way the Jews

---

34 Albertus Pieters is certainly mistaken, then, when he summarizes what he believes to be Calvin's position, writing, "Whatever grounds may be adduced for the obligation to observe the Lord's Day, in imitation of God's rest, for the sake of the benefit of such observance for the church or for the individual, or out of a desire to commemorate the resurrection of our Lord, no obligation to such observance arises for the Christian from the fourth commandment." Albertus Pieters, "Three View of the Fourth Commandment," *The Calvin Forum* 6, no. 6 (January, 1941): 120.

35 Calvin, *Institutes*, II.viii.33.

36 Calvin, *Institutes*, II.viii.31.

37 Calvin, *Institutes*, II.viii.34. The Latin text reads, "crassa carnalique sabbatismi suersitione Iudaes ter superant."

38 Calvin, *Institutes*, II.viii.34.

39 Kromminga's assertion that "As far as the Institutes [sic] are concerned, Calvin never suggested the transfer of worship from Sunday to some other day of the week," is technically correct though Calvin did suggest such a change was not theologically objectionable. Dietrich H. Kromminga, "How Did John Calvin Regard the First Day of the Week?," *The Banner* (May 8, 1936): 437.

observed the Sabbath and the ways Christians observe Sundays. Jews celebrated the Sabbath as a "ceremony with the most rigid scrupulousness." Christians, on the other hand, use Sunday "as a remedy needed to keep order in the church." The Jewish Sabbath needed to be cast aside because in Christ it was done away with and was no longer sacred. However, another day, Sunday, was appointed for the purpose of maintaining decorum, order, and peace within the church. Calvin rejects the idea that what Christians have done is simply changed the day of Jewish Sabbath from Saturday to Sunday. Rather, the ancients, specifically the Apostle Paul, carefully chose the first day of the week to observe as the Lord's Day because true rest, which is the purpose of the Sabbath, lies in the Lord's resurrection. Thus, while Christians still observe the Lord's Day they do so not in order to cling to the "shadow rite" but to experience the rest provided by Jesus' resurrection.[40]

Nonetheless, Calvin does strongly believe Christians should continue to observe Sunday. Meetings of the church are required by God's Word, and practically these meetings cannot be held unless their time and day have been established. In addition, Calvin notes that things in the church must be done decently and in good order, alluding to 1 Corinthians 14:40. It would be impossible, Calvin argues, "to preserve decency and order without this political arrangement." Having one day set aside for worship is so necessary for maintaining order that getting rid of such a day "would instantly lead to the disturbance and ruin of the Church."[41]

A few conclusions can be made from Calvin's writing in his *Institutes*. Notably, Calvin rejects the notion that Christians must observe the Sabbath on any certain day of the week.[42] Tying the Sabbath to a certain day of the week was part of the ceremonial aspect of the Jewish law and, as a result, no longer applies. Furthermore, he also rejects the notion that the Sabbath must be observed one time a week. Calvin could not be clearer when he declares, "Nor do I cling to the number 'seven' so as to bind the church in subjection to it."[43]

Calvin is very concerned with distinguishing the Christian Lord's Day from the Jewish Sabbath. Despite their similarities, namely the observance of one day a week, the two practices are very different. Christians "differ widely" from the Jews in how they regard the Sabbath. Christians realize the shadow of the law has been done away with due to the coming of Jesus Christ, whereas Jews still follow a "shadowy ceremony." The truth of the commandment was delivered as a type to

---

40 Calvin, *Institutes*, II.viii.33.
41 Calvin, *Institutes*, II.viii.32.
42 Cheung, "The Sabbath in Calvin's Theology," 295–296.
43 Calvin, *Institutes*, II.viii.34.

the Jews, but now it has been imparted to Christians "without figure."[44] In other words, the Jews had in the Sabbath commandment a shadowy pre-figure of the actual purpose and meaning, the antitype, of the Sabbath that Christians now experience. Thus, while the Jews put an emphasis upon resting from work and observing the seventh day of the week, Christians should recognize the essence of the commandment is about continually dying to the works of one's old self and letting God's work rise within oneself.

Finally, the fundamental thrust of the commandment requires resting from one's own self and letting God work in oneself. This is done mainly through worship and attending the corporate worship services. Resting from work is also necessary, hence the reason servants and laborers need to be freed from their work, but rest from work is not the primary goal of the commandment. Calvin describes this spiritual rest in slightly different terms. But, the essential aspect of the fourth commandment for Calvin is that Christians throughout their lives rest from their sin and own works so that God can work in them. Calvin sums up his position nicely and is worth quoting at length:

> The whole [of the commandment] may be thus summed up: As the truth was delivered under a figure to the Jews, so it is imparted to us without figure; first, that during our whole lives we may aim at a constant rest from our own works, in order that the Lord may work in us by his Spirit; secondly that every individual, as he has opportunity, may diligently exercise himself in private, in pious meditation on the works of God, and, at the same time, that all may observe the legitimate order appointed by the Church, for the hearing of the word, the administration of the sacraments, and public prayer; and, thirdly, that we may avoid oppressing those who are subject to us.[45]

Genevan Catechism

Calvin makes his instructions for the Sabbath clear in the Genevan Catechism, which he authored. The focus here will be on Calvin's Latin edition published in 1545 because it is this final Latin edition with which Dutch Reformed Christians would have been most familiar.[46] Calvin deals with the fourth commandment at

---

44 Gordon Bates, "Typology of Adam and Christ in John Calvin," *Hartford Quarterly* 5, no. 2 (1965): 45–47. Bates addresses well Calvin's use of typology regarding Adam and Christ, but he does not address Calvin's use of typology more generally.

45 Calvin, *Institutes*, II.viii.34.

46 This edition was published in 1541 in French but not released in Latin until 1545. The Latin text can be found in the following two works: H.A. Niemeyer, *Collectio confessionum in ecclesiis reformatis publicatarum*, Lipsiae, 1840, 123–138; E.F. Karl Müller, *Die Bekenntnis-schriften der reformierten Kirche*, Waltrop: Hartmut Spenner, 1999 [1903], 117–153. A number of English translations also exist. I have followed most closely J.K.S. Reid's version: *The Catechism of the Church of Geneva that is a Plan for Instructing Children in the Doctrine*

length. With nineteen Question-and-Answers devoted to the Sabbath commandment, the fourth commandment receives the most Question-and-Answers of any of the Ten Commandments. The only other two commandments to receive more than nine Question-and-Answers are the second commandment, with sixteen, and the fifth commandment, with eleven. The sheer amount of time Calvin spends on the fourth commandment demonstrates its importance to him.

Strikingly, in Question-and-Answer 168 Calvin notes that the demand for rest from work was also part of the ceremonial aspect of the command, meaning that the rest from work was not a binding aspect of the commandment. However, Calvin says the commandment was given for three reasons, almost exactly the same as what is listed in his *Institutes*: to prefigure spiritual rest, to preserve the polity of the church, and for the relief of servants.[47] The "spiritual rest" refers to resting "from our own works, that God may perform his works in us."[48] This requires crucifying one's flesh and renouncing one's own understanding, a task that should be done continually.[49]

Calvin goes on in the Genevan Catechism to explain what should be observed regarding the fourth commandment. He writes that following the fourth commandment means that church members "are to meet for the hearing of Christian doctrine, for the offering of public prayers, and for the profession of their faith."[50] In a later question Calvin gives similar activities that are to be observed, though he does alter his list somewhat. There he writes the purpose of the command is that "we attend the sacred assemblies for the hearing of God's word, for celebrating the sacraments, and the regular prayers as they will be ordained."[51]

The Genevan Catechism also briefly addresses the issue of the seventh day. The Catechism reiterates what Calvin writes elsewhere. The 174th Question asks if it is sufficient to crucify our flesh on the seventh day alone, and the answer replies that it certainly is not but that it needs to be done "during the whole course

---

of Christ, in *Calvin: Theological Treatises*, ed. and trans. J.K.S. Reid, Louisville and London: Westminster John Knox Press, 1954. Hereafter the Genevan Catechism will be cited as follows: Calvin, "Catechism of Geneva," in *Theological Treatises*, QA #, page number." Calvin did produce an earlier catechism, published in French in 1537 and Latin in 1538. The originals of the first edition can be found in *Ioannis Calvini Scripta Ecclesiastica. Volumen II: Instruction et Confession de Foy Dont on Use en L'Eglise de Geneve*; *Catechismus seu Christianae Religionis Institutio Ecclesiae Genevensis*, eds. Anette Zillenbiller and Marc Vial, 2002, 2–113. An English translation of the 1541 French edition was provided by Paul Fuhrmann in 1949: Paul Fuhrmann, *Instruction in the Faith (1537)*, Philadelphia: John Knox Westminster Press, 1949. Ford Lewis Battles translated the 1538 Latin edition in 1997 in *Calvin's First Catechism: A Commentary*, ed. I. John Hesselink, Louisville, KY: Westminster John Knox Press, 1997, 1–38.

47 Calvin, "Catechism of Geneva," in *Theological Treatises*, QA 171, 112.
48 Calvin, "Catechism of Geneva," in *Theological Treatises*, QA 172, 112.
49 Calvin, "Catechism of Geneva," in *Theological Treatises*, QA 173–174, 112.
50 Calvin, "Catechism of Geneva," in *Theological Treatises*, QA 179, 112.
51 Calvin, "Catechism of Geneva," in *Theological Treatises*, QA 183, 113.

of life."[52] Question-and-Answer 176 follows up by asking why the seventh day is prescribed to the commandment rather than any other day. The answer given is that the number seven implies perfection, denotes perpetuity, and indicates the spiritual rest will not be complete until Christians depart this world.

Question 178 asks again whether the meditation of God's works is sufficient to be done one day out of seven. Here Calvin comes very close to indicating that the Sabbath must be celebrated one day out of seven. The Catechism says in response to the 178th Question, "It becomes us to be daily exercised in it, but because of our weakness one day is specially appointed. And this is the polity I mentioned."[53] Here Calvin specifically notes that one day, presumably out of seven, has been appointed, which seems to be a sabbatarian declaration. What is left unanswered, however, is who has appointed the day. Has God appointed one day out of seven or has it been instituted by the church? The reference to polity seems to suggest that Calvin sees the one day out of seven structure as being the church's decision. As such, the one out of seven observance is not a divine ordinance but a matter of practicality and usefulness that the church has established.

Overall, the Genevan Catechism does not deviate a great deal from Calvin's work in the *Institutes*. The Catechism stresses the spiritual rest the commandment points towards and highlights the three purposes of the command that go beyond its ceremonial application. The most striking point Calvin makes in the Catechism is that regarding work and rest on the Sabbath. The statement, responding to the question about whether the commandment "interdicts us from all labor," bears quoting: "As the observance of rest is part of the old ceremonies, it was abolished by the advent of Christ."[54] For Calvin, resting from work is not the purpose of the fourth commandment and, therefore, is not the command's moral imperative. What the commandment is concerned with is that Christians spiritually rest which means resting from their own works so that God can work in them, a task that should extend beyond the Sabbath to the whole of their lives.

Biblical Commentaries

Calvin's understanding of the Sabbath does come up in his biblical commentaries. Given the methodology of his commentaries, Calvin's comments on the Sabbath tend to be more succinct and less explanatory. The main location the Sabbath arises is in Calvin's commentary on the last four books of Moses.[55]

---

52 Calvin, "Catechism of Geneva," in *Theological Treatises*, QA 174, 112.
53 Calvin, "Catechism of Geneva, " in *Theological Treaties*, QA 178, 112.
54 Calvin, "Catechism of Geneva," in *Theological Treatises*, QA 168, 111.
55 The Latin edition can be found in Ioannis Calvini, *Opera quae supersunt omnia*, Tomes XXIV

However, Sabbath discussions do occur in Calvin's commentaries on Genesis, the synoptic gospels, and Hebrews.[56] The method here will be to briefly address each relevant passage; more general theological themes will be examined below.

The Sabbath does come up in Calvin's commentaries prior to the Ten Commandment passages in his commentary on Genesis 2:3. Here Calvin insists that the day was not just designed to be a day of rest but one of worship and meditating on God's works. He is quite explicit: "God did not command men simply to keep holiday every seventh day, as if he delighted in their indolence; but rather that they, being released from all other business, might the more readily apply their minds to the Creator of the world." This worship is part of what endures with the fourth commandment. Christians are meant to "employ themselves in the worship of God" and it is "right that it should continue to the end of the world." One day a week is not, however, sufficient for worship. People should "daily exercise themselves" to contemplate "the infinite goodness, justice, power, and wisdom of God" which is the "proper business of the whole life."[57]

In his comments on Genesis 2, Calvin does broach the issue of what aspects of the Sabbath have been abrogated and what remains. Calvin clearly identifies the Sabbath as preceding the Jewish people and the commandment given at Mount Sinai. But, the Sabbath does change. "Afterwards, in the Law, a new precept concerning the Sabbath was given, which should be peculiar to the Jews and but for a season...." Calvin does not address in any sort of detail the peculiarities of the Jewish Sabbath. But, he does note that the ceremony given to the Jews was "a legal ceremony shadowing forth a spiritual rest, the truth of which was man-

---

and XXV, 1882. Charles William Bingham has also provided an English translation based on the Latin text and compared with the French edition. See John Calvin, *Commentaries on the Four Last Books of Moses Arranged in the Form of a Harmony*, trans. Charles William Bingham, 4 Volumes, Edinburgh: Calvin Translation Society, 1852–55. The English translations of Calvin's biblical commentaries are available online at http://www.calvin.edu/meeter/calvin-works-in-english/ or at http://www.ccel.org/ccel/calvin/commentaries.i.html. I have consulted the Latin texts as found in the *Opera quae supersunt omnia* but have largely followed the English translations. All subsequent references to Calvin's biblical commentaries will follow the following format: Calvin, *Commentaries*, Bible Passage.

56 The Latin edition of Calvin's Genesis commentary is found in the *Opera quae supersunt omnia*, Tome XXIII, 1882. For the English translation see John Calvin, *Commentary on the First Book of Moses Called Genesis*, trans. John King, 2 Volumes, Edinbourgh: Calvin Translation Society, 1847–1850. The Latin edition of Calvin's harmony of the synoptic gospels is found in the *Opera quae supersunt omnia*, Tome XLV, 1891. For the English translation see John Calvin, *Commentary on a Harmony of the Evangelists Matthew, Mark, and Luke*, trans. William Pringle, 3 Volumes, Edinbourgh: Calvin Translation Society, 1845–1846. The Latin edition of Calvin's commentary on Hebrews is found in the *Opera quae supersunt omnia*, Tome LV, 1896. For the English translation see John Calvin, *Commentary on the Epistle of Paul the Apostle to the Hebrews*, trans. John Owen, Edinbourgh: Calvin Translation Society, 1853.

57 Calvin, *Commentaries*, Genesis 2:3.

ifested in Christ." That Christ has abrogated the Sabbath law does not mean the Sabbath no longer applies. Rather, the task is to determine what belongs to the "ancient figures" and what belongs to the "perpetual government of human life." In response, Calvin argues that the perpetual nature of the Sabbath is that Christians should devote themselves to the worship of God and the mortification of the flesh so that "sons of God should no longer live unto themselves." Again, Calvin never clarifies, in this part of his writing, what the actual "ancient figures" that were "abolished when the truth was fulfilled" are.[58]

Calvin begins his discussion of the fourth commandment in his *Mosaic Commentary* as he did for Genesis–with worship. "The object of this Commandment is that believers should exercise themselves in the worship of God," Calvin begins. Calvin notes that all people are prone "to fall into indifference," and the Sabbath helps them in "maintaining their care and zeal for religion." The commandment's purpose was, at its essence, "that the Jews might know that their lives could not be approved by God unless, by ceasing from their own works, they should divest themselves of their reason, counsels, and all the feelings and affections of the flesh." This sanctification continues for Christians and is the essence of the commandment. Thus, worship proves essential for individuals to be "ruled and guided by the Spirit of God."[59]

Calvin spends the majority of his time on the fourth commandment explaining the commandment's spiritual substance. What God was doing for the people of Israel in the commandment was placing "before their eyes as the perfection of sanctity that they should all cease from their works."[60] Referencing Colossians 2, Calvin argues the outward rest was "nothing but a ceremony" and the true substance of the commandment must be seen in Christ. The spiritual substance Christ demonstrates is that the old person is to be crucified with Christ so that the new person can be resurrected to the newness of life. The purpose of the Sabbath, Calvin again highlights, is that Christians should rest from their own works and sin, and let God work in them.

The commandment does, however, have other purposes, Calvin further explains. Calvin again stresses the importance of worship, though now he describes worship in somewhat different terms. Calvin writes that God hallowed the seventh day so that "He might keep His servants altogether free from every care, for the consideration of the beauty, excellence, and fitness of His works." Making the same point, Calvin turns his attention again to corporate worship. In order to prompt people to consider God's works, God established a day for the Jewish people so that they "should meet in the sanctuary, there to engage themselves in

---

58 Calvin, *Commentaries*, Genesis 2:3.
59 Calvin, *Commentaries*, Exodus 20:8.
60 Calvin, *Commentaries*, Exodus 20:8.

prayer and sacrifices, and to make progress in religious knowledge through the interpretation of the Law." This same intent remains for Christians. Christians are to gather for worship in order to be "better prepared to learn and to testify our faith."[61]

The final purpose, as Calvin explains elsewhere, is to provide relaxation for servants. The purpose of even this aspect is still the honoring of God. Calvin expounds little on this part of the commandment. He does not believe this part of the commandment to be primary. If care for those under one's authority was the primary purpose of the commandment it would be grouped with the second half of the Ten Commandments, the section dealing with love of neighbor. Instead, the commandment belongs to the first half, those commandments relating to love and worship of God. Calvin also notes that the reason non-Israelites were included in the Sabbath rest was so that the Israelites themselves would not be tempted but would be incited to observe the Sabbath.

Calvin does address the ceremonial aspects of the law. Most notably, Calvin calls outward rest "nothing but a ceremony." Calvin goes on to quote from Isaiah 58 where Isaiah "reproves the hypocrites for insisting only on the external ceremony of rest." The rest Calvin speaks of is a physical sort of rest that was meant to point to a "spiritual and far higher mystery."[62] What this means, of course, is that physically resting on the Sabbath is not part of the fourth commandment that Christians need to follow.

The Sabbath also comes up in several of Calvin's New Testament commentaries. Several of Jesus' miracles, as recorded in the gospels, occur on the Sabbath. In Luke 14 Jesus heals a man of abnormal swelling on the Sabbath. When the Pharisees and the teachers of the law have no response to Jesus' question about whether his healing on the Sabbath broke the law, Jesus points out that all of them would pull their child or an ox out of a well on the Sabbath. Calvin interprets this story as demonstrating what forms of work are allowed on the Sabbath. The Sabbath goes no further than rest from one's own works. Works of God and works of charity do not violate the holy rest the Sabbath commands.[63] Similarly, Calvin points to Jesus' act of healing a man with a shriveled hand on the Sabbath (Matthew 12, Mark 3, Luke 6) to demonstrate that one who helps his or her brethren on the Sabbath has not violated the Sabbath commandment.[64]

In other instances the gospels narrate stories about Jesus being questioned about the Sabbath. In one story Jesus is questioned by the Pharisees because his disciples have been picking heads of grain on the Sabbath. Rather than condemn

---

61 Calvin, *Commentaries*, Exodus 20:8.
62 Calvin, *Commentaries*, Exodus 20:8.
63 Calvin, *Commentaries*, Luke 14:1–6.
64 Calvin, *Commentaries*, Matthew 12:11.

his disciples, Jesus chastises the Pharisees and claims that he is Lord of the Sabbath. Calvin takes the main point regarding the Sabbath to be that the Sabbath was given that people might be "employed in true and spiritual worship" and be freed from worldly occupations so that they could attend the holy assemblies.[65] In Calvin's view, Jesus does not abolish the Sabbath. Instead, he merely gives the Sabbath its proper use, which is for the spiritual health of humanity.[66]

Outside of the gospels the Sabbath comes up in Calvin's New Testament commentaries in at least two locations. In Colossians 2 the apostle Paul warns against letting people judge others based on a variety of external means, including Sabbath days. Here Calvin points out that feast days are a shadow of the revelation that comes in Christ. Against the accusation that Christians still keep observances of special days, Calvin responds as he did in the *Institutes*–that respect is paid to government and order and not days.[67]

Hebrews 4 is another significant location where Calvin addresses the Sabbath. Here the author of Hebrews speaks of the Sabbath rest that still exists for the people of God. Calvin notes that humans follow God's rest on the seventh day of creation when they rest as he did. This rest consists of being united to God and referring all thoughts and actions to him. In order to gain this union with God Christians must cease from their works in order to mortify their own flesh and live to God. Calvin is clear; this ultimate rest will never be achieved in this life but should continually be sought nonetheless.[68]

The author of Hebrews, Calvin thinks, also brings up the Sabbath in order to draw attention from the external observance of the Sabbath. Here Calvin is particularly vitriolic against the Jewish people. Calvin writes that the apostle shows the true purpose of the Sabbath "in order to reclaim the Jews from its [the Sabbath's] external observances lest the Jews should be foolishly attached to the outward rite." He goes on: "Of the Sabbath's abrogation indeed the apostle does expressly speak, for this is not his subject, but by teaching them that the rite had a reference to something else, he gradually withdraws them from their superstitious notions."[69] Whether external rest or earthly worship, Calvin reiterates, they were part of the external rite Christ abolished with his coming.

---

65 Calvin, *Commentaries*, Mark 2:24, Matthew 12:8.
66 Calvin, *Commentaries*, Matthew 12:8.
67 Calvin, *Commentaries*, Colossians 2:3. The Latin edition of Calvin's Colossians commentary
    is found in the *Opera quae supersunt omnia*, Tome LII, 1895. For the English translation see
    John Calvin, *Commentaries on the Epistles of Paul the Apostle to the Philippians, Colossians,
    and Thessalonians*, trans. John Pringle, Edinburgh: Calvin Translation Society, 1851.
68 Calvin, *Commentaries*, Hebrews 4:10.
69 Calvin, *Commentaries*, Hebrews 4:10.

Sermons on Deuteronomy

The final aspect of Calvin's works that needs to be addressed is his sermons on the books of Deuteronomy. Calvin preached two sermons on the fourth commandment, the first on Thursday June 21, 1555, and the second the very next day on June 22.[70] In fact, the fourth commandment is the only commandment on which Calvin preached two sermons. In his book on Calvin's Deuteronomy sermons, Dr. Raymond Blacketer hypothesizes that Calvin gives more attention to the fourth commandment because the "Decalogue elaborates more on this precept than it does on the others."[71] While Blacketer's explanation is plausible, a better explanation is that Calvin recognized the uniqueness of the fourth commandment. The fourth commandment, Calvin noted, "stands in peculiar circumstances apart from the others."[72] Whatever the reason, Calvin's two sermons on the fourth commandment provide valuable insights into his theology of the Sabbath.[73]

In his first sermon on the fourth commandment Calvin focuses largely on the command to "observe the Sabbath day and keep it holy," verse twelve of Deuteronomy chapter five. Calvin's main objective is to demonstrate to his listeners what import the fourth commandment has for their lives. In order to do that, Calvin explains what are the ceremonial aspects of the command that no longer apply and what are the enduring aspects of the command that are still binding. Calvin tells his listeners that the Sabbath was a "figure" or a "shadow" to the Jews. The shadow of the Sabbath command "was a figure to represent the thing that was fulfilled indeed at the coming of our Lord Jesus Christ." With the coming of Jesus, Christians are no longer held to the figure of the Sabbath. Calvin could not be clearer when he says, "As now we be no more tied to the old bondage of keeping the Sabbath day."[74]

If the shadow of the fourth commandment has been abrogated by Jesus Christ, then what of the commandment remains? Having laid aside the "ceremony

---

70 Blacketer, *The School of God*, 173–174. Blacketer provides important and helpful insights into Calvin's use of the exegetical tradition, including Augustine, Chrysostom, and Bonaventure, and the standard fourfold method of exegesis.

71 Blacketer, *The School of God*, 171.

72 Calvin, *Institutes*, II. viii.28.

73 For Calvin's sermons on Deuteronomy I have relied most heavily on the translation done by Arthur Golding in 1583. Iohn Calvin, *The Sermons of M. Iohn Calvin vpon the fifth booke of Moses called Deuteronomie…*, trans. Arthur Golding, London: Henry Middleton, 1583. The Latin versions can be found in *Opera quae supersunt omnia*, Tomes XXV–XXIX, 1882–1885. Hereafter, the sermons will be cited from Golding's edition as "Calvin, *Sermons on Deuteronomy*, page number." Benjamin Wirt Farley, *John Calvin's Sermons on the Ten Commandments*, Pelham, AL: Solid Ground Christian Books, 2011. Farley's adapted dissertation is the best English translation of Calvin's sermons on the entire Ten Commandments.

74 Calvin, *Sermons on Deuteronomy*, 201.

itself...we must learn to forebear our own wills and all our own thoughts and affections" so that "God only may work in us and guide and govern us by his Holy Spirit."[75]

In his first sermon Calvin also broaches the issue of the Sabbath occurring every seventh day. While the Jews kept the Sabbath on Saturday, the seventh day, Christians are not bound to that day. Christians are no longer required to observe the seventh day because it "was changed because Jesus Christ in his resurrection did set us free from the bondage of the law and cancelled the obligation thereof."[76]

In his discussion of resting one day out of seven Calvin is not clear exactly what the requirements are for Christians regarding what day should be set aside. Are Christians required to still observe one day a week? Or, are Christians free to observe the Sabbath whenever they deem fit? Primus notes the tension in Calvin's thinking: "It is, once again, clear from this passage that while Calvin was not absolutely committed to the one in seven rhythm, he does take it very seriously and assumes it as a normal and typical routine for the Christian community."[77] While Calvin is less than clear, he does hint at his position. He says, "It is convenient to have some one day certain" for the purpose of assembling to "have the sacraments ministered, and to make common prayer unto God, and to show one agreement and union of faith."[78]

The day of rest is meant to be spent in worship, but corporate worship is not the only activity that should be done on the Lord's Day.[79] The day is also meant for rest, but rest does not mean simply a lack of activity. Calvin calls such a use of the Sabbath day "idleness," and he rails against it throughout his sermons. His imagery is quite explicit: "If we spend the Lord's Day in making good cheer and in playing and gaming is that a good honoring of God? No, is it not a mockery and a very unhallowing of his name? Yes." Attending the worship services is not enough: "It is not enough for us to go to some sermon upon the Lord's Day to receive some good instruction and to call upon the name of God; but we must also digest the same things." Rather than profaning the day with questionable activities or simply laziness, Calvin says the rest of the Lord's Day should be spent meditation on the goodness and works of God. In particular, the day should be spent praying to God.[80] Spending the rest of the Lord's Day in such a manner is not only fitting in order to keep the commandment, but it will also prepare Christians for the rest of the week.

---

75 Calvin, *Sermons on Deuteronomy*, 201.
76 Calvin, *Sermons on Deuteronomy*, 205.
77 Primus, "Calvin and the Puritan Sabbath," 70.
78 Calvin, *Sermons on Deuteronomy*, 205.
79 Primus, "Calvin and the Puritan Sabbath," 69.
80 Calvin, *Sermons on Deuteronomy*, 204.

Calvin's second sermon on the fourth commandment has a significant shift in focus. This second sermon focuses on verses 13–15 of Deuteronomy 5, verses that highlight the prohibition on work. Resting from work on the Sabbath is Calvin's primary focus in his second sermon.[81] Calvin begins by noting that the fourth commandment is not a command to work; it is a command to rest. God has been gracious in only demanding one day of the week for Christians to focus on God. Calvin writes, "Our Lord shows us that we have no cause to grudge of the giving and bestowing of one day upon him, seeing he leaves us six for one."[82] Christians should focus on God every day and even "assemble every day to call upon the name of God." Nonetheless, God, in his kindness, only demands one day a week and is "contented if we allow him one day: or rather if that day serve us for all the rest of the week, God is contented with it."[83]

Calvin goes on to explain that another reason God ordained the Sabbath was for the sake of charity. God offers the Sabbath as a day for all people to rest from their work. The day, Calvin says, should be a benefit to Christians and their households. Also included in the command to rest are animals, servants, and foreigners. Animals and foreigners are included in the command not for their own sake.[84] Rather, they are included, Calvin says, so that Christians are not tempted to break the Sabbath but, instead, are affirmed in their keeping of the Sabbath.[85]

Yet, Calvin is repeatedly clear that ceasing from work and reaping any benefit that results are completely secondary to the command. His representative quote is worth quoting at length:

> His chief intent was not that there should be a day in the week wherein men should cease from labor, that they might take breath and not be continually overhauled, so as they should be tired; that was not the cause which moved God to appoint the Sabbath day. But his ordaining of it was so that the faithful might know that they ought to live after such a holy manner, as to rest from all their own lusts and desires that God might work wholly in them.[86]

---

81 Blacketer, *The School of God*, 190–195. Blacketer refers to the "ethical implications" as the emphasis of Calvin's second sermon. Primus, "Calvin and the Puritan Sabbath," 66. Similarly, while perhaps overstating the case, Primus notes the "best source for Calvin's Sabbath ethics are the two Deuteronomy sermons."

82 Calvin, *Sermons on Deuteronomy*, 206.

83 Calvin, *Sermons on Deuteronomy*, 207.

84 Primus, "Calvin and the Puritan Sabbath," 71.

85 On the inclusion of animals, see Calvin, *Sermons on Deuteronomy*, 207–208. On the inclusion of foreigners, see Calvin, *Sermons on Deuteronomy*, 211.

86 Calvin, *Sermons on Deuteronomy*, 208. Golding's 1583 translation has been altered slightly for the sake of accuracy and modern readability. Golding translates Calvin's phrase, "ç'a esté afin que les fideles cogneussent" as "was to do the faithful to understand."

Nonetheless, while the spiritual purpose remains primary, those who follow the Sabbath and are not "too eager in seeking their earthly commodities" will "not fail to find the same profitable to them" if only they look to God.[87]

Theological Issues

Ceremonial and Moral

In Christian history, the fourth commandment was often seen as a unique commandment within the Ten Commandments. Initially, most Christian theologians spiritualized the Sabbath and saw it as an eschatological expectation, something that was not done to the other nine of the Ten Commandments.[88] Most significantly, late medieval theology began to employ the distinction between moral and ceremonial aspects of the Sabbath commandment. As described above, ceremonial commands no longer applied to Christians. Thus, theologians were forced to address how the Sabbath commandment could be ceremonial while still being applicable to Christians. In addition, the Sabbath commandment was the only one of the Ten Commandments that was viewed as at all ceremonial; the other commandments were clearly moral. Calvin also saw the fourth commandment as unique and explicitly stated such a position at the beginning of his discussion in the *Institutes:* "But as this commandment stands in peculiar circumstances apart from the others, the mode of exposition must be somewhat different."[89]

Calvin's understanding of the moral and ceremonial distinction of the fourth commandment is somewhat complicated. Calvin rejects the distinction medieval theologians made between the ceremonial and moral aspects of the commandment, regarding the distinction as at least incomplete for the fourth commandment.[90] At the same time, he frequently uses the language of "ceremonial" and also talks of the enduring aspects of the command. For example, in

---

87 Calvin, *Sermons on Deuteronomy*, 209.
88 Bauckham, "Sabbath and Sunday in the Post-Apostolic Church" in *From Sabbath to Lord's Day*, 252–298; Paul King Jewett, *The Lord's Day: A theological Guide to the Christian Day of Worship*, Grand Rapids, MI: W.B. Eerdmans Publishing Company, 1971, 88–100; Bauckham, "Sabbath and Sunday in the Medieval Church in the West," in *From Sabbath to Lord's Day*, 300–309. For a couple examples of the spiritual, eschatological understanding of the Sabbath, see Tertullian, *An Answer to the Jews*, in *Ante-Nicene Fathers*, Vol. 3, Ch. 4; Augustine, *City of God*, in *Ante-Nicene Fathers*, Vol. 2, Book XXII, Ch. 30.
89 Calvin, *Institutes*, II.viii.28.
90 Calvin, *Institutes*, II.viii.32. Bierma, "Urinsus's Exposition of Exodus 20:8–11," 277. Bierma also rightly points out that Calvin actually misunderstands the medieval position and comes to make essentially the same distinction using only different terms.

Question-and-Answer 169 of the Genevan Catechism, Calvin poses the question "Do you mean that this commandment properly refers to the Jews and was therefore merely temporary?" The answer is as follows: "I do, in as far as it is *ceremonial.*"[91] Yet, the next question asks whether there is "anything under it [the command] beyond ceremony." The answer states that the command was given for three reasons.[92] It is difficult to see how the aspects of the command beyond the "ceremony" are anything other than the moral aspect of the command.

Calvin makes a similar point in his commentaries. Calvin writes that Paul clearly teaches the fourth commandment contained a "ceremonial precept... calling it a shadow of these things, the body of which is only Christ." What is left if "the outward rest was nothing but a ceremony," then, is to determine "the substance of which must be sought in Christ." Elsewhere in his commentary Calvin uses language such as "the spiritual substance of the type" and "the thing the commandment signifies."[93]

What this means for Calvin is the Sabbath commandment is not entirely applicable to Christians. In his sermon on Deuteronomy Calvin tells his listeners, "As now we be no more tied to the old bondage of keeping the Sabbath day."[94] If Calvin does essentially make a distinction between the ceremonial and moral aspects of the fourth commandment, then which aspects are ceremonial and which are moral? How is it that the commandment can be ceremonial and still have application to the Christian life?

The moral aspect of the fourth commandment centers on the command for spiritual rest. Spiritual rest simply means resting "from our own works, that God may perform his own works in us."[95] Calvin makes the same point in his Mosaic commentary, noting again that the "genuine reason" for the commandment is that Christians should rest from their works just like God rested on the seventh day.[96] Two other requirements of the commandment persist, as well. First, the commandment requires Christians to worship. A major aspect of this worship includes communal, organized worship. About this worship Calvin writes, "The Sabbath being abrogated, there is still room among us, first, to assemble on stated days for the hearing of the Word, the breaking of the mystical bread, and public prayer."[97] Second, as one of its objects the Sabbath is to be a "day of relaxation for servants."[98] Servants and all those who live under the authority of others are to

---

91 Calvin, "The Genevan Catechism," in *Theological Treatises,* QA 169, 111–112. Emphasis added.

92 Calvin, "The Genevan Catechism," in *Theological Treatises,* QA 170, 112.

93 Calvin, *Commentaries,* Exodus 20:8.

94 Calvin, *Sermons on Deuteronomy,* 201.

95 Calvin, "The Genevan Catechism," in *Theological Treatises,* QA 172, 112.

96 Calvin, *Commentaries,* Exodus 20:8.

97 Calvin, *Institutes,* II.viii.32.

98 Calvin, *Commentaries,* Exodus 20:8; Calvin, *Institutes,* II.viii.32.

have a day of rest and an intermission from their labors. This aspect of the commandment is meant to cause people to be "disposed to act humanely," but it is not the primary goal of the commandment. The "direct object" of the commandment is focused on honoring God. That is why the commandment is found in the first table of the law, dealing with honoring God, and not the second table, dealing with the honoring of others, what Calvin calls an "extrinsic advantage."[99]

In sum, Calvin believes the fourth commandment is still applicable for Christians. The commandment has other objects even though it is ceremonial in nature.[100] These "moral" aspects of the commandment continue to be relevant for Christians. As mentioned above, Calvin believes the pertinent aspects of the commandment to be threefold. Christians are to practice a spiritual rest in which they rest from their own sin and works and let God work in them. Christians are to worship God and meditate on his works, mainly through public worship but also by contemplating his works in the world. And, Christians are to provide rest for those slaves or other people under their care. So, while the ceremonial signs of the commandment have been abrogated with the coming of Jesus Christ, the moral aspects of the commandment continue to be binding for the Christian.

The Jewish Sabbath

In Calvin's view, the Jewish Sabbath is vastly different than the Christian observance of a Sabbath. The Jewish Sabbath had as its purpose several particulars. First, God meant to "furnish the people of Israel with a type of spiritual rest by which believers were to cease from their own works and allow God to work in them." Second, the Israelites were to have a "stated day on which they should assemble to hear the Law and perform religious rites" and, by meditating on his [God's] works, be trained in piety. Third, God wanted servants and those under the authority of others to have a day of rest and have reprieve from their labors.[101]

Within God's commands to the Jews, the Sabbath commandment was of central importance, Calvin argues. Calvin references Ezekiel 20, where the Jews are chastised for not keeping the Sabbath. Their failure to keep the Sabbath amounted to a rejection of the entire law and "thrust the whole service of God underfoot."[102] The Jewish recounting of the Sabbath law demonstrates the seriousness with which the Sabbath law was considered. In the *Institutes*, Calvin alludes to "many passages" where the Sabbath commandment is strictly enforced

---

99 Calvin, *Institutes*, II.viii.28.

100 Calvin, *Commentaries*, Exodus 20:8.

101 Calvin, *Institutes*, II.viii.28.

102 Calvin, *Sermons on Deuteronomy*, 201.

by God. Calvin writes, "When he [God] would intimate by the Prophets that religion was entirely subverted, he complains that his Sabbaths were polluted, violated, not kept, not hallowed; as if, after it was neglected, there remained nothing in which he could be honored."[103]

As explained above, as with much of Jewish law, Calvin believes the coming of Jesus Christ has abrogated much of the fourth commandment. The ceremonial aspects of the fourth commandment no longer apply precisely because of the coming of Jesus. Calvin says that the "Sabbath day was a figure to represent the thing that was fulfilled indeed at the coming of our Lord Jesus Christ."[104] Christians no longer have "the figure or shadow anymore" but are free to "apply ourselves the better to the serving of God."[105]

To put it lightly, Calvin does not think particularly highly of the Jewish understanding of the Sabbath. In nearly all of his works Calvin makes reference to the misunderstanding the Jews have of the Sabbath command.[106] For example, Calvin argues that Jewish practice of the Sabbath is misguided due to their misunderstanding of what the commandment is really about. But, even more problematic for the Jewish people is their refusal to recognize Jesus as the one who fulfills the law. The Jews have not realized that the sign of the commandment has been fulfilled in the person of Jesus Christ. As a result, they continue to follow the shadows of the law rather than having their eyes opened to the substance of the commandment. Jews keep the superstitious following of certain days, as if the purpose of the commandment was met in keeping certain days. Calvin writes, "To the contemplation of this [the perpetual resting from our works], the Jews were every now and then called by the prophets, lest they should think a carnal cessation from labor sufficient."[107] In Calvin's view, the Jews are unable to arrive at the spiritual substance of the law because they do not look to Jesus for such a reality.

Sabbath Rest

Calvin makes a particular point that the Lord's Day not be wasted. The purpose of the commandment is rest, but it is a very particular sort of rest. Rest does not simply mean that Christians are to do nothing on the Sabbath. Calvin is very clearly and vehemently against this sort of rest, which he characterizes as idle-

---

103 Calvin, *Institutes*, II.viii.29.
104 Calvin, *Sermons on Deuteronomy*, 201.
105 Calvin, *Sermons on Deuteronomy*, 204.
106 The Genevan Catechism is the one place where Calvin does not make explicit mention of the Jewish practice or misunderstanding of the Sabbath.
107 Calvin, *Institutes*, II.viii.31.

ness. In his first sermon Calvin associates idleness on the Sabbath with super-stitious popery. He writes, "For we see how it is an opinion in popery that God is served with idleness. It is not after that sort that we must keep holy the Sabbath day."[108] In short, anything that draws away from the principle of the com-mandment should not be engaged in on the Sabbath. In his commentary, Calvin pointedly declares that "the Sabbath is violated even by good works, so long as we regard them as our own." God takes "no delight in idleness and sloth," so the rest the Sabbath demands cannot be a simple "cessation of labors of their hands and feet."[109]

Similarly, Calvin is surprisingly unconcerned with rest from physical work. While Calvin does recommend such rest from work and includes it as part of the purpose of the commandment, it is not the primary purpose. In fact, the com-mand to cease from all labors "as the observance of rest is part of the old ceremonies" and, as such, "was abolished by the advent of Christ."[110] Clearly, Calvin does believe the primary purpose of the fourth commandment is to command Christians to physically rest on the Sabbath. Thus, the rest the com-mandment speaks of must be different than simply ceasing from work.

The Sabbath rest Calvin speaks of is largely a spiritual rest. This comes through explicitly in numerous locations. In his Genesis commentary Calvin writes about the legal ceremony that shadows the "spiritual rest" that is the essence of the command.[111] The same point is made in his Hebrews commentary: "There is a sabbathizing reserved for God's people, that is, a spiritual rest."[112] Spiritual rest also is mentioned in the Genevan Catechism, *Institutes*, and Calvin's com-mentary on the fourth commandment.[113]

What does Calvin mean, exactly, when he speaks of this "spiritual rest"? The main aspect of spiritual rest consists of resting from sin so that God can do his good work in Christians.[114] In other words, the Sabbath and the theological doctrine of God's work of sanctification in Christians are intimately bound. Spiritual rest is the means by which Christians meditate on God's works, rest from their own works and sin, and allow God to work within them.

---

108 Calvin, *Sermons on Deuteronomy*, 205.
109 Calvin, *Commentaries*, Exodus 20:8.
110 Calvin, "The Genevan Catechism," in *Theological Treatises*, QA 168, 111.
111 Calvin, *Commentaries*, Genesis 2:3
112 Calvin, *Commentaries*, Hebrews 4:8
113 Calvin, "The Genevan Catechism," in *Theological Treatises*, QA 171, 112; Calvin, *Institutes*, II.viii.28–29; Calvin, *Commentaries*, Exodus 20:8.
114 Gaffin, *Calvin and the Sabbath*, 62.

Sabbath Worship

Calvin also emphasizes the importance of worship on the Lord's Day. In his commentary Calvin goes so far as to say, "The object of this commandment is that believers should exercise themselves in the worship of God." Within the Jewish context the requirement for worship was so that people could "engage themselves in prayer and sacrifices and make progress in religious knowledge through the interpretation of the Law." God did not "merely wish that people should rest at home but that they should meet in the sanctuary, there to engage themselves in prayer and sacrifices, and to make progress in religious knowledge through the interpretation of the Law."[115]

Calvin clearly identifies that this requirement of worship carries over to Christian practice. The Sabbath commandment does not require the holding of worship services on one particular day of the week. As such, worship services are not the main objective of the fourth commandment. The command to worship God is, however, part of the commandment. Because of human weakness, Calvin believes the church has established one day, Sunday, for corporate worship, and that day should be observed to ensure Christian piety and order within the church.

However, worship on the Sabbath is not limited to corporate sermon services. Worship also included contemplating God's works in creation. Randall Zachman rightly notes this emphasis in Calvin's works.[116] Christians should also spend time being "attentive to the consideration of the wisdom, power, goodness, and justice of God in his admirable creation and government of the world."[117] Worshipping God on the Sabbath includes spending time reflecting on God's goodness as evidenced through his general revelation, particularly creation.

Like the whole of the commandment, Sabbath worship is not to be limited only to one day a week. The worship that is carried out on the Sabbath should extend to the whole of one's life. Calvin writes that "by the continual meditation on the Sabbath, they [Christians] might throughout their lives aspire to this perfection."[118] Christians should cease sinning on the Sabbath and allow such avoidance of sin to extend to the whole of their lives; likewise, the worship that Christians engage in on the Sabbath should be reflected and imitated every other day of the week.

---

115 Calvin, *Commentaries*, Exodus 20:8.
116 Randall C. Zachman, *John Calvin As Teacher, Pastor, and Theologian: The Shape of His Writings and Thought*, Grand Rapids, MI: Baker Academic, 2006, 176, 197, 231, 239.
117 Calvin, *Commentaries*, Exodus 20:8.
118 Calvin, *Institutes*, II.viii.30.

Sabbath Work

Finally, Calvin asserts that no work is to be done on the Lord's Day. This aspect of the commandment is especially pertinent for those who are "slaves and laborers." It is the third purpose of the commandment that Calvin highlights.[119] The command to cease from work receives the most attention in Calvin's sermons on Deuteronomy.

Yet, outside of Calvin's sermons, the command to rest from work is not emphasized in Calvin's works. Even in his sermons, as quoted above, Calvin says,

> His [God's] chief intent was not that there should be a day in the week wherein men should cease from labor, that they might take breath and not be continually overhauled, so as they should be tired; that was not the cause which moved God to appoint the Sabbath day.[120]

Calvin frequently talks about rest but almost always turns to the idea of "spiritual rest."

Physical rest is a necessary part of the commandment, but it is not the core of the commandment. Physical rest is necessary, in the first place, as an act of charity to one's neighbor.[121] The second reason for physical rest is that it allows time and space for people to attend worship services and occupy themselves considering "the good things that he [God] has done for us."[122] In his Genesis commentary, Calvin writes,

> God did not command men simply to keep holiday every seventh day, as if he delighted in their indolence; but rather that they being released from all other business, might the more readily apply their minds to the Creator of the world.[123]

Thus, Calvin does believe physical rest should be observed on the Sabbath, but that physical rest is always in service of the larger purposes of the commandment, namely spiritual rest and worship.

Eschatological Expectations

Calvin's view of the Sabbath is focused on the Sabbath's eschatological fulfillment.[124] The Sabbath commandment will find its end when Christ comes again and Christians find their ultimate rest in him. All of the Sabbath activities

---

119 Calvin, *Institutes*, II.viii.32; Calvin, *Commentaries*, Exodus 20:8.
120 Calvin, *Sermons on Deuteronomy*, 208.
121 Calvin, *Commentaries*, Exodus 20:8.
122 Calvin, *Sermons on Deuteronomy*, 205; McKee, *Pastoral Ministry and Worship*, 179.
123 Calvin, *Commentaries*, Genesis 2:3.
124 Cheung, "The Sabbath in Calvin's Theology," 316–326.

that are to be carried out here on earth are only a foretaste of what Christians will experience with Christ's second coming.

The problem with the current practice of the Sabbath is humanity's sinfulness. In his *Institutes* Calvin writes, "But because we must still wage an incessant warfare with the flesh, it [the Sabbath] shall not be consummated until the fulfillment of the prophecy of Isaiah: 'From one new moon to another and from one sabbath to another shall all flesh come to worship before me, says the Lord.'"[125] It is precisely this sinful nature of humanity that requires such careful guarding of the Sabbath. If the Sabbath is not followed, then Christians are less able to allow God to work in them and more likely to give themselves over to sin.

Thus, despite humanity's sinfulness, Christians must continue to strive towards a true Sabbath. Even though the true Sabbath will never be fulfilled in this life and "the completion of this rest cannot be attained in this life, yet we ought to strive for it."[126] The spiritual rest, which is the primary goal of the Sabbath, is "only begun in this life and will not be perfect until we depart from this world."[127] Nonetheless, the Christian is to keep the Sabbath and so begin in this life the spiritual rest that will one day be complete in eternal life upon Jesus' return.

Genevan Practices

Having examined closely Calvin's theology of the Sabbath, it is worth addressing how Sundays were observed in Geneva. In turning to the practices in Geneva, it must be recognized that the focus is no longer strictly on Calvin and his vision of the Sabbath. For, while Calvin's influence in Geneva was immense, Calvin was not the sole organizer of Geneva's religious practices.[128] Calvin was forced, no matter how much he resisted, to work with other religious authorities in Geneva as well as the political authorities in the Small Council. Thus, while looking at how Geneva enforced the Sabbath is helpful for seeing how Calvin's theology was worked out in practice, Calvin was not the sole religious authority in Geneva.

One of the best, if not the best, ways to get a true picture of Sunday practices in Calvin's Geneva is via the Genevan consistory records. Famously first studied by Robert Kingdon, the Genevan consistory records have been the subject of further study by Thomas Lambert, Jeffrey Watt, Karen Spierling, and several others. The

---

125 Calvin, *Institutes*, II.viii.30.
126 Calvin, *Commentaries*, Hebrews 4:10.
127 Calvin, "The Genevan Catechism," in *Theological Treatises*, QA 176, 112.
128 Karen Spierling, *Infant Baptism in Reformation Geneva: The Shaping of a Community, 1536–1564*, Burlington, VT: Ashgate, 2005, Chapters 3–4. As just one example of Calvin's lack of absolute power in religious practices, Karen Spierling addresses his inability to completely transform baptismal and godparent practices.

consistory records provide a vast source of information on religious practices in Geneva. Naturally, the focus here will be on what the consistory records can disclose about Sunday practices and, even more particularly, about the importance of worship on Sundays.

Kingdon has shown how worship in Geneva shifted with the Reformation from a Mass-centered worship service to a sermon-centered worship service.[129] Genevans on any given Sunday had the opportunity to attend one of three churches. Recently, Elsie McKee has meticulously described what Sundays in Geneva during Calvin's time were like.[130] On the average Sunday, Genevans had their choice of roughly eight sermon services. An early service was held for servants; a main service was held at around 8:00 AM; and a final service was held in the mid-to-late afternoon. Morning services included the singing of psalms, prayer, a sermon based on a Bible text, the occasional celebration of the Lord's Supper, offerings for the poor, and community announcements. Less is known about the afternoon services, though they included prayer, psalm-singing, Scripture reading, preaching, and reciting the Apostles' Creed. Attendance at each service was not, of course, required, but it was expected that Genevans would attend a worship service on Sunday. For their part, the Genevan municipal ordinances explicitly required holding a number of services. On Sundays the Ordinances required the following: "Each Sunday, there is to be sermon at St. Peter and St. Gervais at break of day, and at the usual hour at the said St. Peter and St. Gervais. At midday, there is to be catechism, that is, instruction of little children in all the three churches, the Magdalene, St. Peter and St. Gervais. At three o'clock second sermon in St. Peter and St. Gervais."[131]

On Sundays at noon catechism services were also held.[132] The catechism services were intended for children learning the faith and were clergy-led. Any adults who wished were allowed to sit in on the sessions, but the consistory also commanded numerous adults to attend in order to remedy their ignorance of the faith.[133] The basic information covered in the catechism services followed the structure of the Genevan Catechism. The catechism, and therefore the services, required catechumens to learn the Apostles' Creed, the Ten Commandments, and the Lord's Prayer. Thomas Lambert has rightly argued that the education efforts of the consistory via catechism services were quite effective, though many Gen-

---

129 Kingdon, *Reforming Geneva*, 27.
130 McKee, *Pastoral Ministry and Worship*, 232–244.
131 Calvin, "Draft Ecclesiastical Ordinances (1541)," in *Theological Treatises*, 62.
132 McKee, *Pastoral Ministry and Worship*, 222–232.
133 Kingdon et al., *Registers of the Consistory of Geneva in the Time of Calvin: Volume 1, 1542–1544*, Grand Rapids, MI: Wm. B. Eerdmanns, 2000, 50, 92, 129, 318. These are just a few of many examples of the Consistory ordering people to attend catechism.

evans remained unwilling or unable to learn the Reformed faith as the consistory desired.[134]

Geneva was quite unique in that Sundays were not the only day sermon services were held.[135] Early on in the Genevan Reformation sermon services were also held on Wednesdays, but eventually sermon services were held virtually every day of the week. The Ordinances required services to be held on these other days as well. "Besides the two preachings which take place, on working days there will be a sermon at St. Peter three times a week, on Monday, Tuesday and Friday one hour before beginning is made at the other places."[136] Calvin himself preached an astonishing amount—typically, twice on Sundays and several times each week at these weekday services.[137] While a thorough examination of these weekday services is not necessary here, such services typically included prayer, Bible reading, a sermon, and the recitation of the Lord's Prayer and the Apostles' Creed. In addition, Calvin established in Geneva a weekly day of prayer, typically held on Wednesdays, with a liturgy based on the Sunday services.[138]

The establishment of church services on days other than Sunday clearly flows naturally out of Calvin's conception of the fourth commandment. As mentioned above, Calvin believed the Sabbath commandment demands that worship should occur as frequently as possible. Having worship services every day of the week is a natural, practical extension of Calvin's theological principle.

The religious authorities in Geneva attempted to regulate Sabbath practices closely. The Genevan consistory frequently inquired as to whether or not people had been attending church services. The concern of the consistory regarding Sunday worship is clearly attendance at these sermon services. People were frequently called before the consistory for not attending services. Similarly, when the consistory found people lacking in any number of ways their recommendation almost always included attending more sermons.

The examples of Genevans being called before the consistory for failing to attend Sunday services are much too voluminous to catalogue here, but a few examples will be helpful and can serve as representative. Pernete, a widow of Pierre Puvel, was called before the consistory on March 23, 1542, and asked about her "frequenting of sermons."[139] Pernete said she had attended church services

---

134 Lambert, "Preaching, Praying and Policing," 520–526.

135 McKee, *Pastoral Ministry and Worship*, 269–270.

136 Calvin, "Draft Ecclesiastical Ordinances (1541)," in *Theological Treatises*, 63.

137 James Thomas Ford, "Preaching in the Reformed Tradition," in *Preachers and People in the Reformations and Early Modern Period*, ed. Larissa Taylor, Leiden: Brill, 2001, 67–68. Ford notes that many Protestant Reformers preached frequently. For instance, Heinrich Bullinger preached between 7,000–7,500 sermons throughout his forty-four-year ministry.

138 McKee, *Pastoral Ministry and Worship*, 327, 344.

139 Kingdon et al., *Registers*, 23–24.

the previous Sunday–one in the morning and one in the afternoon at St. Peter's. However, Pernete failed to recall what was spoken about in the sermons, and she could not even remember who the pastor was in the afternoon service!

On April 4, 1542, Pierre, his last name unidentified, was questioned about his attendance at the church services. He too said he attended on Sunday morning and heard Calvin preach from the gospel of St. John. Pierre was unable, however, to recite the Lord's Prayer, the Apostles' Creed, or the Ten Commandments when he was questioned. The consistory seemed pleased with his church attendance but admonished him to "frequent the sermons and instruct his family in the Word of God."[140]

The consistory also inquired about attendance at the church services throughout the week. Pierre Guilliermet was questioned about his attendance at sermons. Guilliermet reported that he attended services twice on Sundays but did not go throughout the week because he was unable to go. The consistory exhorted Guilliermet to learn the faith better and frequent the sermons, particularly because "he is very avaricious."[141] Ayma Du Chabloz was also questioned about church attendance. Ayma declared that she must not have been at the sermons because she was treating one of her syphilis patients. The consistory reminded her to attend sermons, though Ayma found herself in much more trouble because of her involvement in Catholic masses and novenas to St. Felix.[142] For those more serious offenses Ayma was sent before the more powerful secular authority, the Small Council.

Surprisingly, the consistory placed emphasis on education, not worship, during Sunday services, though the two were hardly contradictory in the consistory's eyes. When people were brought before the consistory they were questioned about what they had learned at the services. It is when people brought before the consistory were unable to validate their knowledge of the faith that they received the ire of the consistory. The clear assumption the consistory had was that worship imparts a certain amount of knowledge. At the same time, the consistory also believed knowledge was needed to worship properly. Ignorance was not an acceptable religious posture; proper worship required knowing what was happening. In the Genevan consistory's view, educating people in this way was a sort of prerequisite needed for people to be able to keep the fourth commandment properly through worship.

On the other hand, the consistory records give less attention to working on the Sabbath. Complaints about work on Sunday rarely come up in the records. While one might assume that work on the Sabbath was absolutely prohibited in Geneva,

---

140 Kingdon et al., *Registers,* 33.
141 Kingdon et al., *Registers,* 235.
142 Kingdon et al., *Registers,* 231.

the consistory records do not support such a conclusion. For instance, when Mamad Buctin was brought before the consistory and questioned about his church attendance he replied that he could not come because he had to work. The consistory seemed remarkably understanding, advising him to "go to catechism on Sundays and frequent the sermons when he can," making no mention of his working on Sundays.[143]

Yet, true to Calvin's theology, when people were castigated for working on the Sabbath it was nearly always connected with their attendance at worship services. The consistory's primary concern did not seem to be working on the Sabbath. Rather, the concern was primarily with work that prevented people from attending sermons. When Franceyse Bellet was brought before the consistory and questioned about her sermon attendance on Sundays she said that she went when she could but could not always go because she had to earn a living. The consistory did nothing about her working on Sunday but did admonish her to frequent the sermons.[144] Similarly, Berthe, the wife of Pierre de Joex, reported to the consistory that she could not go to sermons as often as she should because she had no servant and, therefore, was required to do more of the work herself. The consistory, again, was unconcerned with the work she did but did admonish her to "follow the sermons."[145]

What the consistory records portray is that Sabbath in Geneva was to be dedicated to attending church services. If a person in Geneva consistently chose not to attend services, then he or she was likely to find himself or herself in front of the consistory. In Geneva worship services were a primary method, if not *the* primary method, of practicing one's Christianity. The importance of the fourth commandment in Geneva should not be understated. Calvin's theological understanding of the Sabbath issues found its way into the practices of Geneva and its citizens, but it did not find its limits there. Calvin's theology of the Sabbath was to have a large impact on Reformed Christians throughout Europe, including, of course, Dutch theologians and Reformed churches in the Dutch Republic.

---

143 Kingdon et al., *Registers*, 111.
144 Kingdon et al., *Registers*, 36.
145 Kingdon et al., *Registers*, 306.

Conclusions

Sabbatarianism

Having examined Calvin's various works, a few conclusions are in order. The first issue is to determine to what extent, if any, Calvin can correctly be called a sabbatarian. Using Primus' twofold definition of what constitutes Sabbatarianism, two issues need to be decided. First, does Calvin believe the Sabbath command is rooted in the created order? Second, is it Calvin's contention that the day of the Jewish Sabbath has been changed to Sunday by command of Christ himself?

In short, the answer to the first question is "yes."[146] At several different locations throughout his work Calvin is quite clear that the Sabbath does not find its origins at Mount Sinai and the Ten Commandments. In his commentary on the Mosaic books he writes that, "It may be probably conjectured that the hallowing of the Sabbath was prior to the Law."[147] Here the anachronism of thrusting sabbatarian debates on Calvin comes through quite clearly. Even though he uses very tentative language of "probably conjecture," Calvin does not feel the need to bolster his argument or argue more thoroughly for the point.

The second question is more difficult to answer. Indeed, scholars have given extremely varied, even contradictory answers. Yet, looking at Calvin's overall work leads to the conclusion that Calvin does not believe Sunday is the Sabbath day that Jesus has ordained. Calvin clearly rejects some of the implications of Sunday being the divinely ordained day to observe the Sabbath. Most notably, Calvin rejects the notion that the Sabbath must be observed on Sunday. The day to observe the Sabbath is no longer Saturday. He writes, "It is true that we are not bound to the seventh day; neither do we keep the same day that was appointed to the Jew: for that was Saturday."[148]

Additionally, Calvin does not argue for the necessity of reserving one day of seven as the Lord's Day. In fact, he explicitly states that he does not hold the church to observing one day out of seven. He writes, "I do not cling so to the number seven as to bring the Church under bondage to it, nor do I condemn churches for holding their meetings on other solemn days, provided they guard against superstition."[149] Calvin makes the same point in his first sermon on Deuteronomy, noting that Christians are "set free from the bondage of the law" because Jesus has "cancelled the obligation thereof." Even though Christians

---

146 Bierma, "Ursinsus's Exposition of Exodus 20:8–11," 278–279. Bierma's point that Calvin grounds the fourth commandment in natural law is exactly correct.
147 Calvin, *Commentaries*, Exodus 20:11.
148 Calvin, *Sermons on Deuteronomy*, 205.
149 Calvin, *Institutes*, II.viii.34.

should still observe a time for the Sabbath, they have great freedom in deciding the specifics. Calvin writes, "[Christians] must observe the same order of having some day of the week, be it one or be it two, for that is left to the free choice of the Christians."[150] Here Calvin clarifies that the commandment is not specific about one day a week—it can be more often because there is nothing necessary about one day out of seven.

Despite his arguments that Christians are free in carrying out the particulars of the Sabbath commandment, Calvin argues strongly for the designation of one particular day to set aside, whatever day that may be. It is important to note that his argument is not based in the fourth commandment; in other words, Calvin does not believe the fourth commandment requires the Sabbath must be on one particular day. His argument for Christians still observing a specific day of the week is two-fold. First, people are weak and sinful and, therefore, are prone to neglecting the worship of God. In a discussion in the *Institutes* about why Christians do not assemble for worship every day, Calvin writes, "But if the weakness of many made it impossible for daily meetings to be held, and the rule of love does not allow more to be required of them, why should we not obey the order we see laid upon us by God's will?"[151] If no particular day and time is set aside to worship God, then Calvin is quite sure people will neglect worship altogether. Neglecting to spend time in worship of God would certainly be a breaking of the fourth commandment.

In fact, Calvin believes corporate worship should occur more frequently. However, people's stubbornness and weakness prevent that from happening. In his *Institutes* Calvin poses the hypothetical question: "Why do we not assemble daily?" Calvin answers: "If only this had been given us!"[152] In Question-and-Answer 178 of the Genevan Catechism, Calvin asks whether it is sufficient to devote one out of seven days to meditating on the works of God. He answered as follows: "It becomes us to be daily exercised in it [meditation on God's works], but because of our weakness, one day is specially appointed. And this is the polity which I mentioned."[153] Yet, God, in his mercy, realizes humanity is too weak to set aside more than one day a week. In his sermon Calvin elaborates: "God therefore beholding such rawness and weakness in us, and ruing our inability to discharge ourselves fully of our duty releases us and utters not his uttermost rigor, but says he is contented if we allow him one day."[154]

---

150 Calvin, *Sermons on Deuteronomy*, 205.
151 Calvin, *Institutes*, II.viii.32.
152 Calvin, *Institutes*, II.viii.32.
153 Calvin, "Catechism of Geneva," in *Theological Treatises*, QA 178, 112.
154 Calvin, *Sermons on Deuteronomy*, 207.

Calvin is also deeply concerned with order.[155] As has been well documented, Calvin desired order in virtually every aspect of church life. The guiding biblical text for Calvin which he references in the *Institutes*, is undoubtedly 1 Corinthians 14:40, Paul's guides for worship: "But everything should be done in a fitting and orderly way." Calvin worries that if the church does not set a particular day for worship the church will fall into disorder. He minces no words when he writes, "So impossible, however, would it be to preserve decency and order without this public arrangement that the dissolution of it would instantly lead to the disturbance and ruin of the Church."[156]

Yet, because the appointment of Sunday as the Sabbath is not divinely instituted or required by the Sabbath commandment, Calvin should not be considered a sabbatarian. Calvin's sabbatarian position is not explicit because it was not a theological issue he was addressing directly. However, if a sabbatarian position includes one day in seven, namely Sunday, as being divinely appointed, then Calvin's theology must not be considered sabbatarian because of his clear position that the Sabbath was not changed to Sunday by Jesus Christ.

Calvin's Conclusions

Having concluded that Calvin is not formally a sabbatarian, it is now time to briefly draw some conclusions regarding Calvin's view of the Sabbath. How did Calvin think Christians should practice the Sabbath? What was the import of the Sabbath commandment for Christians? Drawing a few conclusions will highlight Calvin's fundamental understanding of the Sabbath and, going forward, the theological ideas of the Sabbath that eventually influence the Sabbath practices in the Dutch Reformation.

First, the essence of the commandment for Calvin consists of letting God work in oneself and resting from one's own works. This rest is not, it has been demonstrated, a mere physical rest. The spiritual rest Calvin speaks of is one in which a person dies to his or her old self so that God can work in him or her. In theological terms, the Sabbath is meant for sanctification. This sanctification should extend to the whole of the Christian's life.[157] Thus, the Sabbath is not just about a spiritual rest one day a week; it allows God to work every day of one's life.

Second, Calvin emphasizes the importance of worship on the Sabbath. Worship is so vital to the fourth commandment because it is the best way to allow God

---

155 Willem Balke, "Calvijn en de Zondagsheiliging," *Theologica Reforma* 37, no. 3 (September 1994): 181. Balke rightly hightlights that holding worship services on Sunday was, for Calvin, "een zaak van ordre."

156 Calvin, *Institutes*, II.viii.32.

157 Calvin, *Institutes*, II.viii.29.

to work. As such, Sabbath worship is important not only one day of the week but should define the Christian's lifestyle. Christians are, of course, free to worship as much as they please and, furthermore, are not tied to worship on one particular day. Nonetheless, the Sabbath commandment is God's way of ensuring that Christians do not neglect worship, a temptation Christians are likely to give in to given their weakness and sinfulness. As such, the fourth commandment requires that Christians spend time worshipping together, meditating on God's works, and allowing God to work in them.

Finally, Calvin's concern for work on the Sabbath is relatively, if not surprisingly, relaxed. Calvin is concerned about work on the Sabbath but mainly because it threatens Christians' ability to focus on God and God's work in them. Additionally, Calvin believes slaves and workers under the authority of others need to be given time off work. However, Calvin repeatedly refers to physical rest on the Sabbath as a ceremonial aspect of the fourth commandment. As such, the rest from work is important as an act of charity important for slaves and others working under authorities. But, in his works Calvin is clear that the emphasis of the commandment is not resting from work. What remains to be seen, and the subject of the following two chapters, is how theologians within the Dutch Reformation adopted, altered, or rejected Calvin's understanding of the Sabbath.

Chapter 2:
Sabbath Developments in the Dutch Reformed Tradition: Johannes A Lasco and Zacharias Ursinus

The Protestant Reformation set down roots in the Low Countries early in the sixteenth century. Martin Luther's writings were quickly translated into Dutch, published, and distributed throughout the Dutch provinces. As a result, Luther's ideas spread rapidly and became quite popular. The reasons for Luther's popularity are numerous and interconnected, but at least part of Luther's popularity was due to the religious discontent among Catholics, the centrality of Antwerp as a Protestant publishing center, the close relationship between German and Dutch Augustinian monks, and the large number of Dutch students studying with Luther and Philip Melanchthon at the University of Wittenberg.[1] All lay Catholics did not, of course, make the move to Luther's Protestant thinking. Furthermore, as J.J. Woltjer and Guido Marnef have pointed out, a broad middle group of Christians also existed who found common ground with both Protestantism and Catholicism, aligned themselves with Protestantism but did not break from the Catholic Church, or were simply indifferent to the religious issues.[2]

Protestantism became increasingly varied as it continued to spread in the Low Countries. Besides adherents to Luther's thought, the Low Countries became a hotbed for Anabaptists, known as "radical reformers," in the years following 1530. Additionally, spiritualists, such as David Joris, and sacramentarians, such as Hendrik Niclaes and Dirk Volkertsz Coornhert, also found a home in the Low Countries. Religious affiliations in the Netherlands took a wide variety of forms with nuances particular to each community and individual. Many Christians who thought positively of religious reform or who had radical Protestant beliefs defy any accurate categorization to one particular group. What is clear is that Protestantism, in all its variations, was a significant presence in the Low Countries relatively early in the sixteenth century.

---

1 Selderhuis, *Handbook of Dutch Church History*, 173.
2 Marnef, *Antwerp in the Age of the Reformation*, 57–58; J.J. Woltjer, *Friesland in hervorming-stijd*, Leiden: Universitaire Pers, 1962, 90–104.

The influence of Calvin and Reformed Christianity did not find its way into the Low Countries until the second half of the sixteenth century. Calvin's influence did not enter the Low Countries directly. Instead, the Reformed movement and Calvin's theology found their way into the Dutch provinces through foreign influences. Calvin's model of church polity first appeared in the Dutch refugee communities, particularly those of Emden and London. The turn towards "Calvinism" in these exiled Protestant communities was largely a move towards a Reformed church polity rather than a wholesale turn in theology, though theological issues should not be minimized. Calvin's theological influence came to the Low Countries from abroad via several other means. First, Calvin's writings often came to the Low Countries via French-speaking areas.[3] For instance, the Gallican Confession of Faith, largely based on a Genevan model, in France had a significant exposure in the Dutch provinces and was deeply influential in the forming of the Belgic Confession, which quickly became a confessional standard in the Reformed churches in the Low Countries.[4] Secondly, Calvin himself had personal contact with several Dutch Protestants, including Dutch students who were studying or had studied at the Genevan Academy.[5] Finally, numerous Protestant pastors were trained in Geneva and, upon their return to the Low Countries, brought back with them a new adherence to the Reformed faith.[6] While lay preachers did much of the preaching throughout the sixteenth century and educated ministers had been and would continue to be educated in a variety of places, including Heidelberg, Cologne, Louvain, Lausanne, and later Leiden, the Genevan Academy had a significant impact on Dutch Reformed ministers and, by extension, on Dutch Reformed religious life.[7]

The Reformed church, the "church under the cross," was first formally established in the Low Countries at Antwerp in 1555, though the Reformed pres-

---

3 Andrew Pettegree, "The spread of Calvin's thought" in *The Cambridge Companion to John Calvin*, ed. Donald K. McKim, Cambridge: Cambridge University Press, 2004, 211.

4 Nicholaas H. Gootjes, *The Belgic Confession: Its History and Sources*, Grand Rapids, MI: Baker Academic, 2007, 65.

5 Selderhuis, *Handbook of Dutch Church History*, 203.

6 Maag, *Seminary or University?*, 30, 33, 57, 83, 85. Maag notes that from 1559–1564 eleven students from the Low Countries studied in Geneva. From 1565–1572 that number increased to twenty-nine; from 1573–1586 the number increased again to eighty-three. From 1587–1599 a total of forty-six students came from the Low Countries, and from 1600–1620 the number of students from the Low Countries was eighty-eight. Not all of these students necessarily studied theology or went on to become pastors, but the influence of Geneva and, thus, Calvin is undeniable.

7 Phyllis Mack Crew, *Calvinist Preaching and Iconoclasm in the Netherlands, 1544–1569*, Cambridge: Cambridge University Press, 1978, 84–87; Richard Fitzsimmons, "Building a Reformed ministry in Holland, 1572–1585," in *The Reformation of the Parishes: The ministry and the Reformation in town and country*, ed. Andrew Pettegree, Manchester: Manchester University Press, 181–183.

ence had been operating in Antwerp and elsewhere even earlier.[8] Evidence survives of other underground congregations from around 1560 in the provinces of Flanders and Brabant. Reformed communities in the northern Low Countries were certainly present several years later. The iconoclastic activities of 1566, the *Wonderjaar*, and the Spanish Catholic authorities' subsequent repressive response set off a chain of political events but also actually cemented the existence of the Reformed presence in the Low Countries.

As the Reformed movement in the Low Countries developed, the Dutch Reformed movement needed to adopt and develop its own theological positions for its own unique context and issues. Included in these decisions were issues dealing with Sunday observance and the Sabbath. This chapter will address how Dutch Reformed theologians conceived of the Sabbath in the second half of the sixteenth century and into the seventeenth century. Such an examination will demonstrate that the Sabbath was of considerable importance to Dutch Reformed theology and Dutch Reformed polity and piety. The Sabbath was not, as scholars have often presumed, an issue that arose only in Dutch pietistic movements of the seventeenth century or relegated solely to Puritan movements in England.[9] Instead, through examining the theology of Johannes a Lasco and Zacharius Ursinus, this chapter will argue that theologians early in the history of the Dutch Reformed church emphasized strict observance of the Sabbath, particularly the role of corporate worship on the Sabbath, and assigned significant importance to the Sabbath as a matter of piety for Dutch Reformed congregants. More specifically, the following discussion will demonstrate that with Ursinus's theology a shift takes places from an emphasis on the spiritual Sabbath, as seen in Calvin and then a Lasco, to a greater emphasis on participating in the ministry of the Church.

Emden, Johannes a Lasco, and the Dutch Reformed Church

The importance of Johannes a Lasco to the Dutch Reformation should not be underestimated.[10] A Lasco, born into a powerful Polish family, arrived in East Friesland in 1540. A Lasco was well educated and was both an Erasmian and a

---

8 Marnef, *Antwerp in the Age of Reformation*, 61–64; Duke, *Reformation and Revolt*, 77–100.

9 See above: "Introduction," 22–24.

10 Henning P. Jürgens, *Johannes a Lasco, 1499-1560: ein Europäer des Reformationszeitalters*, Wuppertal: Foedus-Verl, 1999; Henning P. Jürgens, *Johannes a Lasco in Ostfriesland: der Werdegang eines europäischen Reformators*, Tübingen: Mohr Siebeck, 2002; Hermann Dalton, *Johannes a Lasco. Beitrag zur Reformationsgeschichte Polens, Deutschlands und Englands.* 1970; Christoph Strohm, ed., *Johannes a Lasco, 1499–1560: Polnischer Baron, Humanist, und*

humanist.[11] A position as a Catholic bishop appears to have been a Lasco's initial career goal, but such a position never materialized. A Lasco's conversion to the Reformed faith came late in life after he was forty years old, following the death of his brother, Hieronymus. Wim Janse notes that Albert Hardenberg and his colleagues in Frankfurt were very influential in a Lasco's conversion to the Reformed tradition.[12] Eventually, after his time in East Frisia, a Lasco was appointed head of the London Strangers' Church in 1550. A Lasco's time in England was quite successful and productive, but when Edward VI died and the Catholic Mary succeeded him, a Lasco and members of the foreign Protestant churches were forced to flee. The London exiles traveled for a while around northern Germany, but the majority of the exiles eventually found their way to the East Frisian city of Emden in 1554.[13]

East Friesland was in a tumultuous situation both politically and religiously during the middle of the sixteenth century. The Reformation in East Friesland began largely as a Lutheran movement, particularly with the accession of Count Enno in 1528. However, as Andrew Pettegree describes, the efforts to make East Friesland a Lutheran territory were not overly successful.[14] Protestant dissenters, particularly Dutch ones, were prominent in East Friesland. These dissenters included leading Anabaptist figures such as Melchior Hoffman, Menno Simons, and David Joris. Protestant thought in East Friesland was hardly uniform, and by 1530 Count Enno was writing to Philip of Hesse for advice on how best to deal with the, at least, five different conceptions of the Lord's Supper present in his lands.[15] However, what is most pertinent about East Friesland for the Dutch Reformed tradition is its early adherence to Protestantism, whatever its flavor.

europäischer Reformator: Beiträge zum internationalen Symposium vom 14.–17. Oktober 1999 in der Johannes a Lasco Bibliothek Emden, Tübingen: Mohr Siebeck, 2000.

11 Nicollete Mout, "Erasmianischer Humanismus und reformierter Protestantismus zur Zeit a Lascos," in *Johannes a Lasco, 1499–1560: Polnischer Baron, Humanist, und europäischer Reformator*, 21–34; Cornel Zwierlein, "Der reformierte Erasmianer a Lasco und die Herausbildung seiner Abendmahlslehre 1544–1552," in *Johannes a Lasco, 1499–1560: Polnischer Baron, Humanist, und europäischer Reformator*, 35–100; Jürgens, *Johannes a Lasco, 1499–1560*, 46–91.

12 Wim Janse, "A Lasco und Albert Hardenberg. Einigkeit im Dissens," in *Johannes a Lasco, 1499–1560: Polnischer Baron, Humanist, und europäischer Reformator*, 261–282; Wim Janse, *Albert Hardenberg als Theologe: Profil eines Bucer-Schülers*, Leiden: E. J. Brill, 1994, 13–14.

13 Harold Ogden Joseph Brown, *John Laski: A Theological Biography, A Polish Contribution to the Protestant Reformation*, Ph. D. Dissertation: Harvard University, 1967, 139–165. At least part of the issue appears to have been their Reformed leanings, which were not welcome in the Lutheran lands. See, Diedrich H. Kromminga, "John A Lasco: Polish Calvinist Reformer," *The Calvin Forum* 5, no. 5 (December 1939): 88.

14 Andrew Pettegree, *Emden and the Dutch Revolt: Exile and the Development of Reformed Protestantism*, Oxford: Clarendon Press, 1992, 29–31.

15 Nicole Grochowina, "Confessional Indifference in East Frisia," *Reformation & Renaissance Review* 7, no. 1 (April 2005): 116.

When Count Enno died, his widow, Countess Anna, took over the government of East Friesland. Countess Anna, along with a majority of East Frisians, was decidedly more Reformed than her husband. In 1542, a Lasco was appointed superintendent of the church in Emden.[16] A Lasco's appointment in Emden had wide reaching effects. Catholicism, which had experienced a resurgence after the death of Count Enno, was curtailed again. A Lasco challenged Anabaptists in public debates, first with David Joris's followers and then with Menno Simons.[17] As a result of the latter debate, Simons and his followers were expelled from East Friesland. While other Protestant traditions, principally Lutheranism, were able to survive in East Friesland, the Reformed tradition became the primary Protestant tradition, and Emden became the center of the Reformed church in East Friesland.

Much like Calvin, a Lasco's church order put a heavy emphasis on church discipline and ecclesiastical structures. Upon his arrival in Emden a Lasco established the *coetus*, which involved public weekly meetings of East Frisian ministers to discuss doctrine. Similarly, in 1544 the *Kirchenrat*, the consistory, was established to regulate morality within the Christian community. The *Polizeiordnung* was enacted the following year; it instituted ministers and elders to regulate the morals of church members. In short, a Lasco's work in Emden led to the consolidation of the Reformed movement there and throughout East Friesland.

However, Charles V's enforcement of the Augsburg Interim in East Friesland in 1548 led to a Lasco's exit from Emden. In 1550, a Lasco was appointed superintendent of the Strangers' Church in London, a church for the many French and Dutch refugees in London.[18] A Lasco returned to Emden in 1554 along with a number of the London refugees. His return cemented Emden's move towards a Reformed church polity. Upon a Lasco's return, church discipline was taken up again, and a new institution, the *Fremdendiaconie*, was established to care for poor immigrants.[19]

While serving as administrator and pastor of the refugee churches in London a Lasco composed detailed instructions regarding worship services. In his *Forma ac ratio tota ecclesiastici ministerii in peregrinorum*, a Lasco describes when worship services were to be held, what they were to include, and even how long they were to last.[20] According to the *Forma ac ratio*, worship services were to be

---

16 Brown, *John Laski*, 89–138.
17 Pettegree, *Emden and the Dutch Revolt*, 32.
18 Springer, *Restoring Christ's Church*, 5.
19 Pettegree, *Emden and the Dutch Revolt*, 36.
20 Johannes a Lasco, *Forma ac ratio tot Ecclessiastici Ministerij, in pereginorum, potissimum vero Germanorum Ecclesia: instituta Londini in Anglica, per Pientissimum Principem Anglicae etc. Regem Eduardum, eius nominis Sextum: Anno post Christum natum 1550. Addito*

held four times a week. Sunday services were held in the morning and afternoon; these services were also held on specific holy days, such as Christmas and Good Friday. The French refugee churches held additional sermon services on Tuesdays and Thursdays, and the Dutch refugee churches held lectures on Scripture on Tuesdays and sermon services on Thursdays. The various services had slightly different orders and elements. Sunday morning services included singing psalms, public prayer and the Lord's Prayer, reading the Ten Commandments, confession of sin, recitation of the Apostles' Creed, collections for the poor, and a sixty-minute sermon. On occasion the Sunday morning services also included the celebration of the Lord's Supper six times per year, baptisms, and marriages. Sunday afternoon services were largely the same, except they included an abbreviated sermon in the form of a thirty-minute explanation of a Lasco's *Larger Catechism*, and the Ten Commandments and Apostles' Creed were omitted. The weekday services were a great deal simpler. These services included singing psalms, confession of sin, prayers and the Lord's Prayer, collections for the poor, and a sixty-minute sermon. Prophecy was a unique item in one of the weekday services. The prophecy, based on the Zurich model and very similar to Geneva's *congre ́gations*, was a discussion of sermons and doctrine where preachers and laity were able to ask questions about sermons given the previous week.[21] The French churches held their prophecies on Tuesdays, and the Dutch churches held theirs on Thursdays.[22]

It is somewhat difficult to know how exactly the schedule and structure of the worship services as practiced in the London churches were carried over to a Lasco's time in Emden. However, as Springer has argued, the influence of the *Forma ac ratio* in Emden should not be underestimated. Schilling also has noted the importance of a Lasco's influence on the Emden community, particularly in terms of discipline.[23] Springer outlines a host of ways in which a Lasco's work was influential in Emden as well as other Dutch refugee churches, including the important Dutch refugee church in Frankfurt. In 1554, a Lasco had the *Forma ac ratio* printed in Emden as well as Marten Micron's German summary of the *Forma ac ratio*, the *Christlicke Ordinancien*.[24] In addition, the *Forma ac ratio* was

ad calcem libelli Privilegio suae majestatis. Autore Joanne a Lasco Polinae Barone, Frankfurt, 1555. The text of the *Forma ac Ratio* can be found in Johannes a Lasco, *Joannis a Lasco Opera tam edita quam inedita*, ed. Abraham Kuyper, Amstelodam: Müller, 1866, Volume 2, 1–283.

21 Erik A. de Boer, *The Genevan School of the Prophets: The Congre ́gations of the Company of Pastors and Their Influence in 16th Century Europe*, Gene ̀ve: Librairie Droz, 2012.

22 Springer, *Restoring Christ's Church*, 77–93.

23 Schilling, *Civic Calvinism*, 21–39.

24 Springer, *Restoring Christ's Church*, 113. For Micron's work see *De Christlicke Ordinancien der nederlantscher Ghemeinten te Londen (1554)*, ed. Willem Frederik Dankbaar, 's-Gravenhage: M. Nijhoff, 1956.

translated into the vernacular for the French congregations in Emden in 1556.[25] While local variety most likely prevented churches from following a Lasco's prescriptions exactly, what is clear is that a Lasco's practical emphasis on worship services found its way to Emden and other Dutch refugee congregations.[26]

In his book *Emden and the Dutch Revolt*, Andrew Pettegree has convincingly demonstrated the importance of Emden in the Dutch Reformation and during the Dutch Revolt.[27] As a result of Pettegree's work, a wide scale analysis of Emden's relationship with and impact on the Dutch Reformed Church is not necessary. Rather, a brief, overarching description will suffice. While religious persecution was present in the Low Countries throughout the 1540s and 1550s, Emden became clearly involved in the religious situation of the Low Countries when Antwerp asked for help from Emden in supporting their fledgling evangelical congregation.[28] Over time, the Emden consistory became increasingly involved with settling disputes, printing Dutch evangelical texts, and sending pastors to evangelical communities in the Low Countries. With the iconoclastic *Wonderjaar* in 1566 and the anticipated reaction from Spanish authorities, Dutch Reformed exiles flooded into Emden in an attempt to recover and reorganize. It was only years later as the Dutch provinces strengthened during the Dutch Revolt, the Dutch economy grew, and the Dutch Reformed Church solidified in the Dutch Republic that the role of Emden in the affairs of the Dutch Reformed movement began to wane.

Large Emden Catechism of the Strangers' Church, London (1551)

Johannes a Lasco wrote his first catechism, in Latin, already in 1546 for the churches in East Friesland. He used the same catechism in London in 1550. Jan Utenhove then translated the catechism into Dutch so that the Dutch refugee children in London could be instructed in the Reformed faith. The original Latin translation of the catechism does not survive, so the Dutch version of 1551 is the earliest extant version.[29] A Lasco's first catechism, often known as the Large

---

25 Johannes a Lasco, *Toute la forme & maniere du Minstere Ecclesiastique...*, Emden, 1556, in *Marian Protestantism: Six Studies*, ed. Andrew Pettegree, Brookfield, VT: Ashgate, 1996, 64.

26 Springer, *Restoring Christ's Church*, 111–132.

27 Pettegree, *Emden and the Dutch Revolt*, 57–86.

28 Pettegree, *Emden and the Dutch Revolt*, 59.

29 The original Dutch version, and Kuyper's Latin translation from the Dutch, can be found in the second volume of *Joannis A'Lasco Opera*, Volume 1, 340–475. I have consulted Kuyper's editions and also relied on James Frantz Smith's translation, which I found to be accurate and reliable. His translation of the Catechism of the Strangers' Church can be found in his dissertation: James Frantz Smith, "John A'Lasco and the Strangers' Churches," Ph.D. Dissertation: Vanderbilt University, 1964, 132–220. His translation has been reprinted in James T.

Emden Catechism of the Strangers' Church, was later shortened and authorized for use in the church of Emden. This revised catechism, the Emden Catechism or the *Catechismus Emdanus Minor*, will be examined more closely below.

The Large Emden Catechism, like most early modern catechisms, addresses each of the Ten Commandments. The Large Emden Catechism devotes around sixty-three questions-and-answers to the Ten Commandments, depending slightly on how exactly one groups the questions-and-answers. Fifty-six of those questions-and-answers deal directly with the commandments. The Sabbath commandment, which a Lasco numbers in typical Reformed fashion as the fourth, is given eleven questions-and-answers (36–46).[30]

The first question simply asks what the fourth commandment is. The second question asks how the command is to be observed. In the answer, a Lasco makes a distinction that is quite unique among Protestant theologians of all sorts. The command "is observed and violated in a double way, just as there is a double kind of Sabbath, or day of rest; namely, the internal and external."[31] The internal and external duality of the Sabbath commandment is different from the ceremonial-moral distinction seen earlier in Calvin, though even that distinction was not particularly unique to Calvin. The main difference lies in what aspects remain relevant for Christians. In Calvin's view, the ceremonial nature of the Sabbath commandment was fulfilled in Jesus and no longer binds Christians. However, for a Lasco's distinction between the internal and external parts of the commandment, both aspects still apply to Christians. Christians are to observe the internal Sabbath and the external Sabbath. Which part is more important is not addressed. Though the internal Sabbath is explained first, the more likely reality is that a Lasco considered the internal and external observance of the Sabbath to be equally important. Violating either meant violating the whole of the command.

The internal Sabbath is observed when "we refrain from our carnal works, dying daily to them, thinking always of the kingdom of God, allowing God to work in us, honoring him and giving thanks with a peaceful conscience in all things, whether favorable or adverse."[32] The language a Lasco uses here comes very close to what Calvin describes as "spiritual rest." A Lasco highlights several major theological themes: mortification of the sinful self (dying daily to carnal works), vivification (allowing God to work in us), and sanctification (refraining

---

Dennison, *Reformed Confessions of the 16th and 17th Centuries in English Translation,* Volume 2, Grand Rapids, MI: Reformation Heritage Books, 2008, 584–642. In what follows I will cite a Lasco's Dutch edition as found in Kuyper's edited work as follows: A Lasco, *Opera,* Vol. number, page number. I will also cite Smith's English translation.

30 A Lasco, *Opera,* Vol. 2, 371–377; Smith, "John A'Lasco and the Strangers' Church," 153–156.
31 A Lasco, *Opera,* Vol. 2, 373; Smith, "John A'Lasco and the Strangers' Church," 153–154.
32 A Lasco, *Opera,* Vol. 2, 373; Smith, "John A'Lasco and the Strangers' Church," 154.

from our carnal works/honoring God). A Lasco does mention something quite unique when he includes "giving thanks with a peaceful conscience in all things, whether favorable or adverse."[33] Such phrasing no doubt comes from a Lasco's historical context where exile communities experienced all sorts of situations, both favorable and adverse. Interestingly, a Lasco uses the Sabbath as an occasion for Christians to exercise thanksgiving and a peaceful conscience regarding the blessings or, more likely, the difficulties of their present situations.

Exactly the opposite of what a Lasco had just described violates the internal Sabbath. The inner Sabbath is violated when carnal works are done and people "are not governed everywhere by the Word of God." Notably, violating the Sabbath is not just about tending to God's Word on Sunday or even any other one day of the week. Instead, a Lasco connects the Sabbath with the Word of God governing Christians "everywhere." Additionally, a Lasco's pastoral concern for persecuted refugee Christians again comes through. His conclusion to the answer states that the inner Sabbath is violated when Christians "impatiently bear all torment and adversity."[34]

Question-and-answer 40 highlights the eschatological nature of the inner Sabbath. The question asks when the observance of the inner Sabbath will be completed. The answer says such observance will be complete "in the resurrection of the dead, when Christ the Lord, appearing in his glory, will create a new heaven and a new earth according to the promise of Scripture, when there will be an eternal, happy Sabbath from all deadly works, and when God will be all in all." Obviously, a Lasco has no inclinations that the inner Sabbath is completed in the present eschaton. A Lasco's conception of the eschatological Sabbath is highly Christocentric and centers on God's fullness. In fact, the answer he gives does not mention humanity at all outside of the "resurrection of the dead."[35]

The external Sabbath is observed and violated in a much different manner. The external Sabbath is observed "when the Church of God is honored in its office and ministry (which was established and appointed at the command of Christ)."[36] Question-and-answer 42 expands on the office and ministry of the Church. It explains that the commandment requires Christians to be diligent in "hearing and learning with longing hearts the Word of God in the company of the faithful." Also, the sacraments are to be rightly administered and received so that "the knowledge of God is increased, his benefits pondered, the name of God honored, and a definite trust in the Church evoked."[37] Finally, the Sabbath is to be

---

33 A Lasco, *Opera*, Vol. 2, 373; Smith, "John A'Lasco and the Strangers' Church," 154.
34 A Lasco, *Opera*, Vol. 2, 373; Smith, "John A'Lasco and the Strangers' Church," 154.
35 A Lasco, *Opera*, Vol. 2, 373; Smith, "John A'Lasco and the Strangers' Church," 154.
36 A Lasco, *Opera*, Vol. 2, 373; Smith, "John A'Lasco and the Strangers' Church," 154.
37 A Lasco, *Opera*, Vol. 2, 373, 375; Smith, "John A'Lasco and the Strangers' Church," 155.

a day devoted to serving one's neighbor and other sacred works, as well as supporting the officers of the Church.

Yet, even those activities are not enough. In response to the follow-up question "Is this enough?" the answer is definite: "Not at all." The answer goes on to describe that every household is to be urged to participate itself in the activities described in the previous answer. It is certainly necessary to participate in the church functions at the "time and place" indicated. But these household practices are also to be used in conjunction with the Church so that the "entire body of Jesus Christ may be edified." A Lasco's argument is that the Sabbath requires more than church rites and even more than participation in those rites. Rather, every household needs to practice the Sabbath, using the practices of the Church, so that all people will be edified.[38]

The violation of the external Sabbath is addressed in the following two questions-and-answers, 44 and 45. Interestingly, the answer regarding the violation of the external Sabbath begins with the ministers. The Sabbath is violated "when the ministers of doctrine, of the Sacraments, and of the remaining Christian practices enjoined by God desert their office, commit adultery, or for some other reason falsely conduct themselves contrary to the command of God." The answer goes on to implicate anyone who "spurns the assemblage, doctrine, Sacraments, and remaining practices of the Christian Church" or who holds the Church and its practices in contempt. In addition, the answer to question 45 states that the Sabbath can be violated in other ways. Violating the Sabbath can also occur when people use the day inappropriately. Activities specifically mentioned include labor, indolence, heedlessness, drunkenness, throwing dice, sports, and other fleshly works.[39]

The final question-and-answer devoted to the fourth commandment addresses what sorts of labors Christians are to carry out on the other six days of the week.[40] This question-and-answer is a unique aspect of a Lasco's catechism, with no question-and-answer like it in Calvin's catechism or the Heidelberg Catechism. The answer given is that each person is to attend to his or her vocation and undertake such work as if in the presence of God. The goal of one's work should be for the glory of God and the support and service of one's neighbor. A Lasco's answer is not necessarily surprising or innovative, but he again draws attention to the Sabbath commandment as dealing with the whole of the Christian's life.

Several important observations are worth noting in regards to a Lasco's view of the Sabbath as evidenced in the Large Emden Catechism. Most notable is a Lasco's unique distinction between the external and internal Sabbath. A Lasco's

---

38 A Lasco, *Opera*, Vol. 2, 375; Smith, "John A'Lasco and the Strangers' Church," 155.
39 A Lasco, *Opera*, Vol. 2, 375; Smith, "John A'Lasco and the Strangers' Church," 155–156.
40 A Lasco, *Opera*, Vol. 2, 375, 377; Smith, "John A'Lasco and the Strangers' Church," 156.

use of the two different categories implies that Christians are required to observe the Sabbath in two distinct manners, and the distinction drives how a Lasco approaches the Sabbath. As described above, Christians are to observe the Sabbath inwardly and outwardly, and these two different aspects of Sabbath observance are quite distinct. Also important for a Lasco is his emphasis on the importance of the Sabbath for the entirety of the Christian's life, the universality of the commandment. This is particularly true regarding the internal Sabbath, which requires a dying to the old self *daily* and allowing God's work to govern one's life *everywhere*. In addition, all people are to dedicate themselves to the Sabbath through participating in the Church's activities, resting from work, and allowing God to work in themselves.

Emden Catechism (1554)

As mentioned above, a Lasco's first catechism was altered for use in Emden and was published as the Emden Catechism of 1554, also known as the *Catechismus Emdanus Minor*.[41] The shorter 1554 version of a Lasco's earlier 1551 catechism was intended to give children a more manageable, age-appropriate version with which to work. In the shortened Emden Catechism, a Lasco addresses the Ten Commandments, the Apostles' Creed, and the Lord's Prayer. East Friesland was not unfamiliar with previous Reformed catechisms. Calvin sent his Genevan Catechism to East Friesland in order to educate people in the Reformed faith and maintain unity among the various, international Reformed communities.[42]

In addition to the Emden Catechism of 1554, the Emden Examination of Faith (1553) was written, as Dennison rightly observes, to "provide a summary of Christian truth which was to be appropriated and understood by those applying to the Lord's Table."[43] The origins of the Emden Examination of Faith, published as *Een korte ondersoeckinge des gheloofs...*, are somewhat unclear, but it appears that a Lasco wrote a Latin version which was then translated into Dutch, possibly by Utenhove.[44] Those who wanted to participate in the Lord's Supper were re-

---

41 The text for the *Catechismus Emdanus Minor* can be found in Lasco, *Joannis a Lasco Opera tam edita quam inedita*, Volume 2, 495–543. Bart Elshout's English translation has been included in Dennison's *Reformed Confession*. See, Dennison, *Reformed Confessions*, Vol. 2, 54–75. Elshout's translation is reliable and has largely been followed here. Again, I will cite Kuyper's work and the English translation as found in Dennison's *Reformed Confessions*.
42 Alasdair I.C. Heron, "Calvin and the Confessions of the Reformation: Original Research," *Hervormde Teologiese Studies/Theological Studies* 70, no. 1 (2014): 1–5.
43 Dennison, *Reformed Confessions*, Vol. 2, 41.
44 Christopher Joy, *The Dutch Language in Britain (1550–1702): A Social History of the Use of Dutch in Early Modern Britain*, Leiden: Brill, 2015, 112. The text of the "Emden Examination

quired to learn and recite the answers therein. The Examination of Faith is quite brief with only forty-one Questions-and-Answers, but one of its questions does ask what is to be learned from the four commandments of the first table of the Ten Commandments. The response for the fourth commandment says, "Lastly, that I am duty bound to be trained in all His divine testimonies, following the holy ordinance of His Word."[45] According to the Examination of Faith, the purpose of the fourth commandment was to be trained in the Christian faith, which attending sermon and catechism services accomplished. Clearly, the emphasis on Sabbath observance is attending the church services in order to be instructed in the faith.

It was this instruction in the faith on the Sabbath that prompted the very composition of the Emden Catechism. The catechism was to be taught on Sundays. The preface states, "It was our [the ministers'] desire to pursue this with the highest degree of diligence so that through the hallowing of the Sabbath day the catechism should be taught in our churches during the afternoon." The catechism services were meant to educate people, primarily children but also ignorant adults, in the faith and, therein, keep the Sabbath holy. In addition, the teaching of the catechism was to guard against the abuse of the Sabbath. The catechism services were to be held "in order that by such means the common people would be kept out of the bars and the young people off the streets, and thus be kept from all manner of vanity, immorality, and mischief."[46] In fact, the connection with the Sabbath comes up twice in the short preface. Just a few sentences later the preface again encourages churches to teach the catechism on the Sabbath:

> Beloved, we therefore beseech you…to teach it [the catechism] diligently and persistently in your congregation on the Sabbath day to the benefit of the children and all who are of simple mind, so that our children who have been dedicated to the Lord in baptism, may by way of pure and true doctrine be raised in the fear of the Lord–and that the common man would refrain from desecration of the Sabbath (that is, from drunkenness, games, walking, shopping, laboring, and other servile activities), so that the Sabbath, according to God's command, may be hallowed in your parts.[47]

The theological importance of the Sabbath in the Emden Catechism is obvious from the beginning. For a Lasco the catechism itself is necessary to ensure the proper observance of the Sabbath.

---

of Faith" can be found in *Joannis a Lasco Opera tam edita quam inedita*, 477–492. Dennison's English translation can be found in his *Reformed Confessions*, Vol. 2, 43–52.

45 A Lasco, *Opera*, Vol. 2, 481; Dennison, *Reformed Confessions*, Vol. 2, 45.

46 A Lasco, *Opera*, Vol. 2, 497; Dennison, *Reformed Confessions*, Vol. 2, 55.

47 A Lasco, *Opera*, Vol. 2, 497, 499; Dennison, *Reformed Confessions*, Vol. 2, 55.

The Emden Catechism begins with the Ten Commandments and addresses the Sabbath in the fourth commandment. The fourth commandment, like all the commandments, receives one question and answer. Question 11 asks, "What does the fourth commandment teach you?". The answer is worth quoting in its entirety:

> That on the Sabbath, I and my entire family would rest in the Lord who has ordained that for the well-being of my body and soul I may engage neither in physical labor, useless frivolity, vain activity, nor works of the flesh, but rather, that I would sanctify this day by exercises of faith, holy ceremonies, and good works as commanded by God, doing so to the glory of His name and the well-being of my body and soul.[48]

A Lasco's Catechism contains lists of both what must be avoided on the Sabbath and what must be done on the Sabbath. First comes the list of prohibited activities: "physical labor, useless frivolity, vain activity, [and] works of the flesh." Physical labor is a broad category, likely meant to encompass any normal work activities. In other words, rest from physical labor meant resting from working at one's occupation. The rest from labor does not encompass all physical work. As demonstrated below, labor that qualifies as "good works" is allowed and even commanded.

The prohibition on "useless frivolity" and "vain activity" is particularly interesting and somewhat unique. Calvin touched briefly, mainly in his sermons, on not simply wasting the Sabbath day in idleness. What a Lasco prohibits in his question and answer is, in short, recreation. Again, the terms a Lasco uses, "frivolity" and "vain activity," beg for greater definition that, unfortunately, is not given. But, what the Emden Catechism does is essentially prohibit any activity that does not sanctify the Sabbath day and serve the glory of God's name. Even activities which are not inherently sinful and perhaps potentially beneficial are to be avoided on the Sabbath if they are not useful for the honoring of God and the well-being of one's body and soul. A prohibition as a Lasco describes places significant limits on what is allowed on the Sabbath and increases greatly the list of activities not allowed.

Since morally neutral activities were not always allowed on the Sabbath, it is not at all surprising that sinful activities were also forbidden on the Sabbath. The Emden Catechism refers to these activities as "works of the flesh." A Lasco uses the phrase "works of the flesh" in the Pauline sense, referring to a rest from sinful

---

48 A Lasco, *Opera*, Vol. 2, 506–507; Dennison, James, *Reformed Confessions*, Vol 2, 59. The Latin text is as follows: "Docet, ut cum familia sabbathum, sive quietem Domini, quod nobis ad utriusque tam corporis, quam animae salutem institutum est, neque corporis labore, neque inutili ocio, neque vanis actionibus, aut operibus carnis transigam, sed contra fidei exercitiis, sacris ritibus, bonisque operibus a Deo praescriptis ad ipsius nominis gloriam illud ipsum sanctificem, et ad corporis animaeque incolumitatem consumam."

ways.[49] As demonstrated in the previous chapter, the idea of resting from "sinful works of the flesh" is something that comes up frequently in Calvin's treatment of the Sabbath. The emphasis continues in a Lasco's Emden Catechism. Especially on the Sabbath, Christians are to abstain from those works of the sinful self, "works of the flesh," that linger in the life of the Christian.

In the second place, the Emden Catechism moves on to what should be done on the Sabbath. These works include "exercises of faith, holy ceremonies, and good works." A Lasco is not clear on what exactly exercises of faith includes. The exercises of faith seem to include more private acts of devotion, such as family devotions, individual prayer, and Bible reading. Holy ceremonies certainly refer to public worship services. Finally, good works are to be done on the Sabbath. What this means, of course, is that all sorts of work are not prohibited. On the contrary, God commanded good works, and Christians are to do good works on the Sabbath.

But, in a Lasco's view, the essential purpose of the Sabbath is to rest. This rest is to include a person's entire family. However, the rest a Lasco mentions is a specific type of rest. The Sabbath rest is a "rest in the Lord." The rest that a Lasco speaks of includes physical rest from labor and, more importantly, spiritual rest from sin. Furthermore, it is an active rest in that it requires certain activities, namely the sanctification of the day, participation in holy ceremonies, and good works. Ironically, the rest a Lasco describes includes *doing* a number of Christian activities.

Twice within the short answer a Lasco includes the phrase "the well-being of my body and soul." The purpose of the Sabbath institution was for the Christian's well-being. A Lasco's words echo Jesus' words in Mark 2 when he tells the Pharisees, "The Sabbath was made for man, not man for the Sabbath."[50] For a Lasco, the Sabbath is meant for the well-being of Christians. Both the prohibitions and the commands of the Sabbath commandment are for the well-being of the Christian. Not engaging "in physical labor, useless frivolity, vain activity, nor works of the flesh" is all done for the purpose of the Christian's physical and spiritual well-being. In the same way, the activities recommended, "exercises of faith, holy ceremonies, and good works," are also to be done because they contribute to the Christian's well being.

However, the Sabbath is not solely for Christians. The Sabbath is also for God. The Sabbath is to give glory to God's name. A Lasco associates God's glory with the activities the Sabbath commandment requires. The exercises of faith, holy

---

49 Galatians 5:19: "The acts of the flesh are obvious: sexual immorality, impurity and debauchery, idolatry and witchcraft; hatred, discord, jealousy, fits of rage, selfish ambition, dissensions, factions and envy; drunkenness, orgies, and the like."

50 Mark 2:27.

ceremonies, and good works Christians do on the Sabbath are done to the glory of God's name. God's glory is not mentioned in connection with the prohibitions regarding the Sabbath. The prohibitions are meant for the good of humanity; the proper activities for the Sabbath are meant both for God's glory and human flourishing. The point a Lasco makes in his Emden Catechism is that the Sabbath is both for the good of humanity and for God's glory, the two naturally not being mutually exclusive.

Zacharias Ursinus

Zacharias Ursinus is extremely important for the development of theology and practice within the Dutch Reformed Church in the sixteenth and into the seventeenth century.[51] Relatively little is known about Ursinus's life with many of his letters and papers having gone unpreserved.[52] Ursinus was well-educated, studying at major Reformed centers such as Strasbourg, Basel, Lausanne, Lyon, Orleans, and Geneva. Frederick III of the Palatinate, on the recommendation of Peter Martyr Vermigli, appointed Ursinus professor at the seminary in Heidelberg, the *Collegium Sapientiae*. It was shortly after his appointment in Heidelberg, in 1562 and 1563, that the Heidelberg Catechism was prepared and published. Ursinus was removed from his professorship when Frederick's Lutheran successor came to power. Ursinus spent the rest of his life, until his death in 1578, as professor in Neustadt an der Weinstrasse at the Reformed school of Casmirianum.[53]

Heidelberg Catechism

The Heidelberg Catechism was, arguably, the most important confessional document for the Dutch Reformed Church at least until the Synod of Dort in 1618–1619. Frederick III, the Elector of the Palatinate, ordered the composition of a catechism. A committee prepared the Catechism in 1562 and published it in 1563.[54] Also in 1563 the Catechism was translated into Dutch in Emden, and

---

51 Derk Visser, *Zacharias Ursinus, The Reluctant Reformer: His Life and Times*, New York: United Church Press, 1983. The most thorough biography of Ursinus to date is still Visser's work.

52 Visser, *Ursinus*, xiv–xvii.

53 Theodor Julius Ney, "Zacharius Ursinus," in *Allgemeine Deutsche Biographie: auf Veranlassung und mit Unterstützung seiner majestät des Königs von Bayern Maximilian II*, Vol. 39, Leipzig: Duncker & Humblot, 1895, 369–372.

54 Lyle Bierma, "The Purpose and Authorship of the Heidelberg Catechism," in Bierma et al., *An*

another Dutch edition appeared in Heidelberg that same year.[55] The first Dutch edition was intended to be of use to Reformed Christians persecuted in the Low Countries as well as those who had fled to Germany.[56] Only a few years later, by 1566, the Catechism was used for catechizing.[57] Dutch editions were frequent throughout the sixteenth and seventeenth centuries. As Karin Maag has demonstrated, no fewer than twenty-two Dutch editions were issued prior to 1600.[58]

The Heidelberg Catechism was distributed widely to theologians across Europe. Reactions were somewhat mixed. Not surprisingly, the strongest negative reactions came from Lutheran rulers and theologians, particularly those of a Gnesio-Lutheran bent.[59] Reactions from Reformed theologians were much more positive. As one notable example, Bullinger commented to a friend that he considered it the best catechism ever published.[60] Calvin received a copy of the Heidelberg Catechism from Caspar Olevianus, one of its contributing authors. Olevianus sent a letter on April 3, 1563, to Calvin in which he mentions his sending a Latin edition of the Catechism both to Calvin and Beza.[61] Unfortunately, no record exists of Calvin's response to the Catechism. Scholars have speculated and disagreed over what Calvin's response might have been. Hendrikus Berkhof takes Calvin's silence to be most likely a sign of his indifference to the Catechism or his disapproval of the publication of yet another Reformed Catechism.[62] On the other hand, Fred Klooster uses Calvin's dedication of his commentary on Jeremiah to Frederick III as evidence that Calvin approved of the Reformed movement in the Palatinate and, in particular, the Heidelberg Catechism.[63]

The authorship of the Heidelberg Catechism has been the subject of much scholarly debate. The composition of the Heidelberg Catechism was almost

---

Introduction to the Heidelberg Catechism: Sources, History, and Theology: with a Translation of the Smaller and Larger Catechisms of Zacharias Ursinus, Grand Rapids, MI: Baker Academic, 2005, 49.

55 Karin Maag, "Early Editions and Translations of the Heidelberg Catechism," in *An Introduction to the Heidelberg Catechism*, 107.
56 Karla Apperloo-Boersma and Herman J. Selderhuis, *Power of Faith: 450 Years of the Heidelberg Catechism*, Göttingen: Vandenhoeck & Ruprecht, 2013, 21.
57 Selderhuis, *Handbook of Dutch Church History*, 209.
58 Maag, "Early Editions and Translations of the Heidelberg Catechism," 103–118.
59 Fred Klooster, "Calvin's Attitude to the Heidelberg Catechism," in *Later Calvinism: International Perspectives*, ed. W. Fred Graham, Kirksville, MO: Sixteenth Century Journal Publishers, 1994, 313–315.
60 Carl Pestalozzi, *Heinrich Bullinger. Leben und ausgewählte Schriften*, Elberfeld: K.K. Friderichs, 1858, 415; Klooster, "Calvin Attitudes to the Heidelberg Catechism," 315–316.
61 Klooster, "Calvin's Attitude to the Heidelberg Catechism," 318.
62 Hendrikus Berkhof, "The Catechism in Historical Context," in *Essays on the Heidelberg Catechism*, Bard Thompson et al., Philadelphia: Philadelphia United Church Press, 1963, 84.
63 Klooster, "Calvin's Attitude to the Heidelberg Catechism," 321–331.

certainly a team project. The main issue is how significant the roles of Zacharius Ursinus and Caspar Olevianus were. Many scholars have been wary of giving Olevianus too large of a role in the composition of the Catechism.[64] Yet, Bierma has recently called such claims into question, arguing that Olevianus may have had a larger role than previously supposed.[65] Bierma's demonstraton of the literary parallels between Olevianus's *Firm Foundation*, which is Olevianus's commentary on the Heidelberg Catechism, and the Heidelberg Catechism itself is quite convincing and hints that Olevianus was active in the composition of the Heidelberg Catechism. However, until more evidence is produced, a more certain conclusion on the role of Olevianus in the composition of the Heidelberg Catechism is impossible. The most reasonable conclusion based on the available evidence still positions Ursinus as the lead author in the team of authors.[66]

As Bierma points out, Frederick's purpose in commissioning a catechism for the Palatinate was three-fold. First, the Catechism was to be a teaching tool for children. Second, it was to be a preaching guide for instructing common people within the church. Finally, the Catechism was to serve as a form for confessional unity among Protestants in the Palatinate.[67] Notably, the Catechism was meant to serve the Christian laity. From the beginning, the Catechism was intended to be familiar to children, via catechesis, and the congregation, via preaching. Given its intention, ideally, the Catechism's teaching on the Sabbath would have been familiar and influential for all Reformed Christians.

While the Heidelberg Catechism was intended to have a wide, ecumenical impact, the Catechism became incredibly important for the Reformed movement in the Low Countries. Already in 1568 the Convention of Wesel highly recom-

---

64 Walter Hollweg, *Neue Untersuchungen zur Geschichte des Heidelberger Katechismus*, Neu-kirchen: Neukirchener Verlag, 1961, 127–152; Fred Klooster, "The Priority of Ursinus in the Composition of the Heidelberg Catechism," in *Controversy and Conciliation: The Reforma-tion and the Palatinate, 1559–1583*, ed. Derk Visser, Allison Park, PA: Pickwick Publications, 1986, 73–100; J.F.G. Goeters, "Entstehung und Fruhgeschichte des Katechismus," in *Hand-buch zum Heidelberger Katechismus*, ed. Lothar Coenen, Neukirchen: Neukirchener Verlag, 1963, 15.

65 Lyle Bierma, "General Introduction," in Caspar Olevianus, *A Firm Foundation: An Aid to Interpreting the Heidelberg Catechism*, ed. and trans. Lyle Bierma, Grand Rapids, MI: Baker Books, 1995, xvii–xxviii.

66 Lyle Bierma, "Ursinus and the Theological Landscape of the Heidelberg Catechism," in *The Spirituality of the Heidelberg Catechism: Papers of the International Conference on the Heidelberg Catechism Held in Apeldoorn 2013*, ed. Arnold Huijgen, Göttingen: Vandenhoeck & Ruprecht, 2015, 11. For background and more detail on the debate reference the following works: Lyle Bierma, "Olevianus and the Authorship of the HC: Another Look," *The Sixteenth Century Journal* 13, no. 4 (1982), 17–27; Fred Klooster, *The Heidelberg Catechism: Origin and History*, Grand Rapids, MI: Calvin Theological Seminary, 1987–88, 160–171.

67 Bierma, "The Purpose and Authorship of the Heidelberg Catechism," 51.

mended the use of the Heidelberg Catechism in Dutch-speaking congregations.[68] The first Dutch national synod was held in exile in Emden in October 1571. That Synod of Emden subscribed to the *Belgic Confession* (i.e. 1561 *Confession of Faith*) as well as the French confession of faith. Similarly, the Synod preferred the Heidelberg Catechism for all Dutch-speaking congregations while it recommended the Geneva Catechism in French-speaking congregations.[69]

The Heidelberg Catechism has only one question-and-answer on the fourth commandment. Nonetheless, given the importance of the Catechism for the Dutch Reformed Church, it is necessary to examine in some detail exactly what the Catechism says about the commandment. Question 103 of the Catechism asks what God's will is in the fourth commandment. The answer is twofold and worth quoting completely:

> First, that the gospel ministry and education for it be maintained, and that, especially on the festive day of rest, I regularly attend the assembly of God's people to learn what God's Word teaches, to participate in the sacraments, to pray to God publicly, and to bring Christian offerings for the poor. Second, that every day of my life I rest from my evil works, let the Lord work in me through his Spirit, and so begin in this life the eternal Sabbath.[70]

The emphasis for the Heidelberg Catechism is on corporate worship. The Heidelberg Catechism includes participating in the ministries of the church first in its answer, a notable and intentional reverse from Calvin's Genevan Catechism. Worship attendance is primary and includes hearing God's word, participating in prayers and the sacraments, and giving offerings to the poor. Attendance at these assemblies of God's people must be "diligent." It is through the church services that the Christian ministry and education is carried out. Without attendance at the service, presumably, the ministry of the church would cease and education in the faith would diminish.

The second point the Catechism makes does not actually deal at all with one particular day of the week. Instead, the commandment intends for Christians to rest from sin every day. Additionally, the Christian is to continually allow the Lord to work in him or her through the power of the Holy Spirit. This dying to

---

68 Frederik L. Rutgers, *Acta van de Nederlandsche Synoden der zestiende eeuw*, Dordrecht: Van den Tol, 1980, 20–21.

69 Rutgers, *Acta*, 57–58; Martin van Gelderen, *The Political Thought of the Dutch Revolt, 1555–1590*, Cambridge: Cambridge University Press, 1992, 105.

70 I have followed the English translation in *Ecumenical Creeds and Reformed Confessions*, Grand Rapids, MI: CRC Publications, 1987, 59. The original German edition, the first Dutch edition, and the first Latin edition can all be accessed online: http://www.prdl.org/author_view.php?a_id=54&sort=date_asc. The original German can also be accessed in August Lang, *Der Heidelberger Katechismus und vier verwandte Katechismen*, Leipzig: Deichert, 1907, 42–43.

one's evil ways and opening oneself to the Spirit is something that begins in this life but finds its completion in the "eternal Sabbath."

Notably absent in the Heidelberg Catechism is any mention of work. The Catechism contains no prohibitions on work of any kind. Rest is mentioned twice, but neither time is it connected with a rest from physical labors. One reference mentions the "festive day of rest" and the other reference is to "rest from my evil ways." While Ursinus and the committee may have simply assumed work was not allowed, not including the prohibition on work was certainly a conscious decision, and its absence says a great deal about where the Heidelberg Catechism's emphasis can be found. That emphasis is emphatically not on ceasing from work.

The Catechism echoes Calvin's and a Lasco's theologies of the Sabbath on several points. Most notably, the second point the Catechism makes about resting from "my evil ways" sounds much like what Calvin referred to as "spiritual rest" and what a Lasco called "refraining from carnal works." Like Calvin and a Lasco, this spiritual rest consists both of resting from one's own evil but also of allowing the Holy Spirit to work inside oneself. Similarly, the Catechism picks up the eschatological tones that Calvin and a Lasco struck earlier when it speaks of the "eternal Sabbath." The Catechism follows Calvin's understanding that the Sabbath will never be complete in this life. Like Calvin and a Lasco, the Catechism argues the actual reality to which the Sabbath points, resting from one's own works and allowing God to work in oneself, will only be completed in the "eternal Sabbath." The emphasis on corporate worship is one final commonality the Catechism has with Calvin and a Lasco. In placing participation in worship first in its answer the Catechism puts more emphasis on worship than Calvin did, but connecting worship with the Sabbath commandment is something both Calvin and a Lasco do. The Catechism's emphasis on corporate worship is, however, more pronounced than in either Calvin or a Lasco.

Smaller Catechism

Ursinus's Smaller Catechism, the *Catechesis minor,* was not published until 1612 in Reuter's collection of Ursinus's works.[71] That edited work claimed the Smaller Catechism to have been written in 1562. The Smaller Catechism was supposedly

---

71 Zacharias Ursinus, "Catechesis minor, perspicua brevitate christianum fidem complectens," in *Zacharias Ursini Opera Theologica,* ed. Quirinus Reuter, 3 Volumes, Heidelberg, 1612, 1:34–39. Lyle Bierma has translated the Smaller Catechism into English in *An Introduction to the Heidelberg Catechism,* 141–162. I have largely followed his translations. Citations to the Smaller Catechism, the Larger Catechism, and the Heidelberg Catechism will be as follows: Ursinus, "Smaller/Larger/Heidelberg Catechism," QA #.

composed for the education of the general population and children. Some scholars have questioned Ursinus's authorship of the Smaller Catechism, arguing instead that it was the result of a committee project.[72] August Lang argued, for instance, that the Smaller Catechism was simply an abridged version of the Larger Catechism with some alterations that resulted from the committee's influence.[73] Nonetheless, more recent research has shown quite convincingly that Ursinus was the likely author of the Smaller Catechism in 1561 or 1562.[74] Thus, the Smaller Catechism was actually composed prior to the Heidelberg Catechism and does seem to have been a sort of preliminary draft for the Heidelberg Catechism designed for uneducated adults and children.[75]

The fourth commandment is given only one question and answer in Ursinus's Smaller Catechism. The question is similar to the one asked in the Heidelberg Catechism: "What is required of us by the fourth commandment?" The answer too mimics the Heidelberg Catechism. The fourth commandment requires two things. First, the ministry of the church is to be maintained and cultivated. This includes meeting at the appointed times to hear God's word, administering the sacraments, calling on God in public prayer, and giving offerings of mercy. Secondly, the commandment requires that "throughout our whole life we think on and practice the things we have learned on these days." The way to do this is to rest from all evil works and present "our members to God as instruments of righteousness."[76]

Several items in this brief answer stand out. First, the answer mentions that Christians should meet "at the appointed times." The answer does not state if God ordains those appointed times or if the church is free to choose those times. The answer also does not highlight how often those appointed times should or must be. In other words, the answer does not broach the sabbatarian issue of whether or not the church is required to observe the Sabbath one in seven days. Similarly, the answer also does not address whether the observance of the Sabbath must be on Sunday.

Second, the emphasis in the second half of the answer highlights the importance of carrying over the Sabbath to the whole of one's life. The Small Catechism's answer clearly points out that the Sabbath is not intended to be

---

72 Bierma, *An Introduction to the Heidelberg Catechism*, 137–140. Bierma's introduction to the Smaller Catechism is the best current summary and analysis of the authorship of the Smaller Catechism. Wilhelm Neuser, "Die Erählungslehre im Heidelberger Katechismus," *Zeitschrift für Kirchengeschichte* 75 (1964): 309–326, 311. Neuser was one notable scholar who argued the Smaller Catechism was a committee project.

73 Lang, *Der Heidelberger Katechismus*, LXXVII–LXXVIII.

74 Erdmann Sturm, *Der junge Zacharias Ursinus: Sein Weg vom Philippismus zum Calvinismus*, Neukirchen: Neukirchener Verlag, 1972, 239–246.

75 Bierma, *An Introduction to the Heidelberg Catechism*, 138.

76 Ursinus, "Smaller Catechism," QA 89.

quarantined to one day a week. In fact, just the opposite is true. The Sabbath is a sort of practice for the whole of one's life; the learning of the Sabbath is to be contemplated and practiced every day. Additionally, much like Calvin's spiritual rest, the answer speaks of a rest from evil works that should be carried out daily and continued throughout this life. The answer also offers a positive corollary to resting from evil. Christians should not just rest from evil but also present themselves to God as "instruments of righteousness." The answer requires not only a continual rest from evil but also a positive statement of carrying out righteous works throughout one's life.

As with the Heidelberg Catechism, the answer makes no mention of physical rest from work. In fact, the only mention of rest is "resting from all our evil works" as the way to "think and practice the things we have learned on these days" that should take place "throughout our whole life." But, the Small Catechism says nothing about resting from work. Outside of resting from evil works, the closest the answer gets to advising rest on the Sabbath is the requirement that "all unnecessary hindrances" to the ministry of the church be removed. Presumably, work on the Sabbath could be a hindrance to the ministry of the church, but it would not necessarily be so.

Larger Catechism

The Larger Catechism, *Catechesis maior*, was first printed in a volume of Ursinus's theological treatises in 1584. As Erdmann Sturm has demonstrated, it is quite likely that Ursinus's Larger Catechism was the result of his first course of university lectures at the University of Heidelberg in 1562.[77] The intention of the Larger Catechism, then, was to serve as a summary of doctrine for university students. As such, it was to be more in depth than a rudimentary catechism but more accessible than typical traditional theological texts.[78]

Ursinus's Large Catechism devotes six questions to the fourth commandment, questions 185–190. The six questions spent on the fourth commandment are fewer than that of the first commandment (8) and the second commandment (16), equal to that of the third commandment, and more than that of the following six commandments. The first question on the commandment simply asks

---

77 Erdmann, *Der junge Zacharias Ursinus,* 239–246.
78 Bierma, *An Introduction to the Heidelberg Catechism,* 138. I have used Bierma's translation of the Larger Catechism, found in Bierma, *An Introduction to the Heidelberg Catechism,* 163–223.

what the fourth commandment is, a necessary question given the Reformed tradition's unique way of numbering the commandments.[79]

The second question asks what the commandment requires. The answer given is quite similar to those found in the Heidelberg Catechism and the Small Catechism. The public ministry of the church is to be carried out, which includes teaching the true doctrine of God, the administration of the sacraments, and public prayers and confession. Ursinus does make a unique addition to the 186th question. He adds that the fourth commandment requires that "obedience and honor be given to this ministry, and each individual earnestly desire to maintain it in his own place."[80] Here Ursinus again gives importance to the ministry of the church, noting that the fourth commandment requires obedience and honor to be given. In addition, the ministry of the church is not only a corporate function but an individual one for every person. Christians at an individual level are to maintain the ministry of the church in their own homes and positions within society.

In the next question Ursinus asks what the fourth commandment forbids. The answer again focuses on the ministry of the church: "All contempt, denigration, and willful hindrance of the ministry."[81] What is noticeably absent, again, is any condemnation of work done on the Sabbath. As in the *Smaller Catechism*, work could certainly fall under the category of a "hindrance of the ministry." However, the absence of work in the list of what is forbidden on the Sabbath is notable. While Ursinus does not mention work as forbidden on the Sabbath, Ursinus is certainly concerned that the ministry of the church be upheld and anything from the ministry on the Sabbath is forbidden.

Question-and-answer 188 asks why God wants a "certain time designated for the ministry of the church."[82] The answer is two-fold. First, humans are weak and need a separate time to meditate on divine things. In other words, if God does not establish a particular time for the ministry of the church to be observed, then people, in their weakness, will indubitably neglect that meditation on divine things. Second, this time is given so that rest from labor may be given to those under another's power. While rest from work was absent in the previous answer, now it shows up in connection with the specificity of a set apart time. As such, rest from labor is still an important aspect of what is necessary on the Sabbath. Nonetheless, this rest from labor remains secondary to the major purpose of the

---

79 Ursinus, "Larger Catechism," QA 185. In Luther's "Larger Catechism" and "Smaller Catechism" the Sabbath commandment is listed as the third of the Ten Commandments. Likewise, in Catholicism the Sabbath commandment is considered the third commandment.
80 Ursinus, "Larger Catechism," QA 186.
81 Ursinus, "Larger Catechism," QA 187.
82 Ursinus, "Larger Catechism," QA 188.

time set apart for the Sabbath–meditating on divine works via the ministry of the church.

The final two questions, questions-and-answers 189 and 190, deal with the seventh day included in the fourth commandment. The first of the questions asks why God designated the seventh day for the Israelites. Ursinus answers that the seventh day is tied to God's resting from creation on the seventh day. His doing so made the seventh day holy and the the day on which the Israelites should rest from their works, namely their sins, and devote themselves to God's work.[83] The second question asks whether Christians are also bound to the seventh day. Here Ursinus answers negatively. Christ has abolished the Mosaic ceremonies, so Christians are not bound to a particular day. Nonetheless, Ursinus writes, "But to the best of our ability we must observe the necessary time and order for ministry set by the church without, however, considering them part of the worship of God."[84]

Commentary on the Heidelberg Catechism

Ursinus's writings on the Sabbath go well beyond what is written in the Heidelberg Catechism and Ursinus's other catechisms.[85] His further explanations of the fourth commandment are found mainly in notes taken from his lectures at Heidelberg University on the Heidelberg Catechism and compiled as his commentary on the Catechism, *Corpus doctrinae Christianae ecclesiarum*. After Ursinus's death several of his students published their notes on Ursinus's catechism lectures, but, unsurprisingly, their versions contained notable discrepancies. After Ursinus's death, in 1591, David Pareus, theologian, pastor, and one of Ursinus's favorite students, published a carefully prepared version of Ursi-

---

83 Ursinus, "Larger Catechism," QA 189.
84 Ursinus, "Larger Catechism," QA 190.
85 One work clearly relating to the Sabbath is an English translation titled *A Verie Profitable and Necessarie Discourse Concerning the Observation and Keeping of the Sabboth Day...*of Ursinus's work. John Stockwood translated the work into English already in 1584 (accessed via Early English Books Online [EEBO], copied from Bedleian Library). However, I take this work to be loosely based on Ursinus's lectures on the Heidelberg Catechism. Having compared *A Verie Profitable and Necessarie Discourse* with the *Commentary*, I have concluded the two are too similar to be completely separate works. Furthermore, John Stockwood studied in Heidelberg, receiving his B.A. there in 1567, which means it is entirely possible he heard Ursinus lecture himself or had easy access to notes from Ursinus's lectures. In addition, I have been unable to find the original work mentioned anywhere in early compilations of Ursinus's writings. As such, I do not treat *A Verie Profitable and Necessarie Discourse* here. It should be mentioned that the material and the essence of the work are extremely similar to the *Commentary*; as such, examining *A Verie Profitable and Necessarie Discourse* separately does not lead to any new insights into Ursinus's understanding of the Sabbath.

nus's lectures.[86] The work was extremely popular, with at least thirteen Latin editions between 1591–1663 and twenty-three English editions between 1587–1663.[87] The *Corpus doctrinae* was a much different document than the Catechism itself. Its tone is much more polemical, particularly defending the Catechism against Lutheran attacks. Ursinus's *Commentary on the Heidelberg Catechism* is his most elaborate explanation of the Sabbath commandment and, as a result, is extremely important for understanding Ursinus's theological understanding of the Sabbath.[88]

Ursinus breaks the fourth commandment into two separate parts to begin his discussion. The first part is the commandment itself, and the second part is the reason for the commandment. He then breaks the first part of the commandment, "Remember the Sabbath day to keep it holy; on it you shall do no manner of work, etc.," into two further parts, a moral, perpetual part and a ceremonial, temporary part.

The first part of the commandment is moral and perpetual because of the end and causes of the commandment, which are also perpetual. The aim of the commandment Ursinus states outright: "The end or design of the commandment is the maintenance of the public worship of God in the church, or the perpetual preservation and use of ecclesiastical ministry." For Ursinus, the ministry of the church serves a number of purposes. The public ministry is necessary so that (1) God is publically served in the world, (2) religion and faith are stirred up in the elect, (3) people may edify one another, (4) doctrine and worship of God continue, and (5) the church is discerned in the world. All of these reasons are perpetual, so it follows, Ursinus argues, that the ministry of the church demanded in the commandment is binding for all people from the "beginning to the end of the world."[89]

The second part of the commandment, its reference to the seventh day, is ceremonial because it was given to the Jews as a type or sacrament. The seventh day serves only as a type of Jesus Christ's sanctification of the church and, as

---

86 Maag, "Early Editions and Translations," 111; Apperloo-Boersma and Selderhuis, *Power of Faith*, 21; Eric D. Bristley, "Appendix 3. Biographical Notes," in Zacharias Ursinus, *Commentary of Dr. Zacharius Ursinus on the Heidelberg Catechism*, trans. G.W. Williard, The Synod of the Reformed Church in the U.S., 2004, http://www.rcus.org/wp-content/uploads/2013/09/UrsinusZ_HC-Commentary-17-NEW-HC.pdf, 1273.

87 T.D. Smid, "Bibliographische Opmerkingen over de Explicationes Catecheticae van Zacharias Ursinus," *Gereformeerde Theologisch Tijdschrift*, 41 (1940): 228–243; Bristley, *http://www.rcus.org/wp-content/uploads/2013/09/UrsinusZ_HC-Commentary-17-NEW-HC.pdf*, Appendix 2, 1214–1270.

88 Zacharias Ursinus, *The Commentary of Dr. Zacharius Ursinus on the Heidelberg Catechism*, trans. G.W. Williard, Grand Rapids: Eerdmans, 1956. In what follows I will cite Williard's translation, referencing the page numbers from his 1956 publication.

89 Ursinus, *Commentary*, 557.

such, is ceremonial. Thus, for Ursinus, the Sabbath is not bound to the seventh day anymore because it has been "fulfilled and abolished by the coming of the Messiah," just like the rest of the ceremonies and types found in the Old Testament.[90]

The reason for the commandment is tied to the Lord resting on the seventh day, blessing and hallowing the day. All people are to imitate God's rest, so while the ceremonial aspect of the seventh day was only relevant to the Jews, the command to rest holds for all people. Ursinus gives three reasons this Sabbath rest is so important. First, a violation of the Sabbath rest is essentially a violation of the "whole worship of God." Second, the Sabbath rest indicates the greatness of the thing it signifies, the spiritual Sabbath. Finally, the external Sabbath is to contribute to the "beginning and perfecting in us that rest which is spiritual."[91]

So, what exactly are Christians to do on the Sabbath? The day is not to be spent in "slothfulness and idleness." Instead, the day is to be dedicated to holy works, including divine worship. Worship is, of course, not to be omitted on all other days, but on the Sabbath it should be public and private. On the other hand, work is not to be done on the Sabbath. However, Ursinus notes that it is not a ban on all work but only on servile work that hinders the worship of God. To prove his point, Ursinus goes on to cite a number of Scripture passages, including Jesus' healing on the Sabbath in Luke and Jesus' vindicating his disciples for picking grain on the Sabbath in Matthew.[92] Ursinus also includes an interesting reference to a passage from 2 Maccabees where Maccabeus gave justification for the army to fight on the Sabbath if the enemy attacked on the Sabbath.[93] Ursinus summarizes his position, writing,

> These declarations teach, that such works as do not hinder or interfere with the proper use of the Sabbath, but which, on the other hand, rather carry out its true intention and so establish it, as all those works do which so pertain to the worship of God or religious ceremonies, or to the duty of love towards our neighbor, or to the saving of our own, or the life of another, as that necessity will not allow them to be deferred to another time, do not violate the Sabbath, but are especially required in order that we may properly observe it.[94]

---

90 Ursinus, *Commentary*, 558.
91 Ursinus, *Commentary*, 558.
92 Ursinus, *Commentary*, 559; Luke 14:1–6; Matthew 12:1–14.
93 Ursinus, *Commentary*, 559; 2 Maccabees 2:40–41. The reference is particularly interesting given that 2 Maccabees was not considered part of the canon of Scripture in the Dutch Reformed tradition. Article 6 of the Belgic Confession includes "the two books of Maccabees" in its list of apocryphal works and distinguishes such books from "the canonical books." That article goes on to say that: "The church may certainly read these books and learn from them as far as they agree with the canonical books. But they do not have such power and virtue that one could confirm from their testimony any point of faith or of the Christian religion."
94 Ursinus, *Commentary*, 559.

The rest is to include children and families as well as strangers. Children and families are included because of God's benevolence so they too can have the opportunity to worship. Strangers are to observe the Sabbath not because it was a sacrament to them but so that they do not give offense to the church. In addition, animals were to rest on the Sabbath so that people were not tempted to work and to act as an example to people as to how they should exercise kindness to fellow mankind.[95]

On the one hand, rest on the Sabbath, Ursinus continues, is meant to "excite us to a consideration of these his works, and to praise and glorify his name for his benefits to mankind."[96] At the same time, Sabbath rest is meant to free Christians from work that would prevent them from worshipping and to encourage Christians to cease sinning. In this way, Christians are to abstain from all sin and also from works that would interfere with his or her ability to participate in the ministry of the church. Resting in such ways imitates God, Ursinus argues. Thus, the Sabbath is meant to prompt Christians to praise and worship God but also to become more like him in resting from their sins, a rest that is signified by resting from one's work.

Ursinus moves on to discuss four main questions. First, what and how manifold is the Sabbath? Second, in what respect does it belong to us [Christians]? Third, why was it [the Sabbath] instituted? Lastly, how is it kept holy and how is it profaned? In order to properly understand the whole of Ursinus's thoughts on the Sabbath, his answers to each of the questions he posed will in turn be summarized briefly.

In answering the first question regarding what exactly the Sabbath is Ursinus returns to his distinction between the moral and ceremonial. The moral part of the Sabbath includes "the study of the knowledge of God and of his works, with a careful shunning of sin, and worshipping God by confession and obedience."[97] The Sabbath is begun in this life but will be perfectly enjoyed in perpetually praising and glorifying God in the life to come. The ceremonial aspect refers to the certain time set apart for the church to hold the worship services. In the Old Testament the ceremonial had multiple aspects, including Sabbath days, months, and years. The New Testament church does still adhere to the ceremonial aspect of the law, but it is under different auspices than the Old Testament. Ursinus writes, "The *new* depends upon the decision and appointment of the church, which for certain reasons has made choice of the first day of the week, which is to be observed for the sake of order, and not from any idea of necessity."[98]

---

95 Ursinus, *Commentary*, 560.
96 Ursinus, *Commentary*, 561.
97 Ursinus, *Commentary*, 561–562.
98 Ursinus, *Commentary*, 562–563, original emphasis.

As Ursinus turns his attention to the second question, how far the Sabbath belongs to Christians, he argues that the ceremonial aspect of the commandment has been abrogated with the coming of Jesus Christ. As he has argued earlier, the moral part of the command still applies; the necessity still remains for the Christian church to set apart time for the preaching of God's word and the administration of the sacraments. What the church is not bound to is any particular day, be it Saturday, Wednesday, or any other day. The crux of Ursinus's argument clearly depends on his premise that the fourth commandment has a ceremonial nature. It is to making this argument that he then turns.

Ursinus anticipates a number of objections to the idea that the fourth commandment could be ceremonial. He lists six possible objections. Two of the objections relate to when the Sabbath command originated. The objections Ursinus lists argue the commandment has its origins prior to the fall into sin or, at least, prior to Moses; either way, the command is therefore perpetual. Ursinus responds with an argument that even laws prior to Moses were figures of what is to come, meaning they could be ceremonial. Similarly, the moral aspect of the Sabbath commandment may have been present prior to the fall into sin, but the aspect of the seventh day does not appear until Moses. Other objections include that all of the Ten Commandments are moral; Exodus 31 speaks of the covenant as everlasting; the cause of the command is perpetual; and some (i.e. Anabaptists) disallow any difference in days. While delineating each response is not necessary here, Ursinus answers each objection in turn, demonstrating that the arguments flow out of faulty premises.

The third question Ursinus proposes is why the Sabbath was instituted, and he gives a list of eight chief ends. The list of ends is as follows: 1) the public worship of God in the church, 2) the preservation of the ecclesiastical ministry, 3) a sign of the eternal and spiritual Sabbath, 4) a reminder of God's creation of the world, 5) that works of charity and kindness towards one's neighbors are done, 6) the bodily rest for man and beasts, 7) that others are provoked to piety and worship, and 8) that the church might be visible to the world.[99] Important to note here is that the primary ends of the Sabbath deal with worship. Of the eight chief ends listed, four of them, numbers one, two, seven, and eight, deal with the ministry of the church and corporate worship. Ursinus's emphasis on the ceremonies of the church is clear in his answer as to why the Sabbath was instituted in the first place.

Ursinus's final question deals with how the Sabbath is kept holy and how it is profaned. Ursinus again makes a list of items that should be done in order to keep the Sabbath day holy. First, on the Sabbath the church is to be rightly taught and instructed concerning God and his will. Secondly, the sacraments should be administered according to their divine appointment. Third, Christians should

---

99 Ursinus, *Commentary*, 566.

learn the doctrine of the church. The fourth item is very similar to the second. The sacraments are to be administered but also to be used according to the divine appointment. Fifth, the church should publicly call upon God through prayer. Sixth, the Sabbath is a day for the collecting of alms and performing works of love for the poor in order to demonstrate charity and generosity. Finally, the Sabbath should remind people to honor the ecclesiastical ministry. Honor for the ministry means showing reverence, love, and gratitude to ministers, as well as obeying ministers and allowing for the ministers' imperfections.[100]

Ursinus concludes his comments on the Sabbath with brief remarks concerning the ministry of the church and concerning ceremonies. Comments on the ministry of the church are relevant because the fourth commandment sanctions the public worship of God. For Ursinus, the ecclesiastical ministry "is that office which God has instituted in his church to which he has committed the preaching of his word and the administration of the sacraments according to the divine appointment."[101] God has graciously given the church the ministry in order to glorify his name, convert people to himself, accommodate himself to people's weaknesses, provoke people to godliness, show his mercy, and make the church visible in the world.[102] Ministers receive different sorts of calls. God calls some ministers "immediately," while the church calls others "mediately." God calls prophets and apostles immediately, but the church calls ministers who are to serve as evangelists, bishops or pastors, doctors or teachers, governors or elders, and deacons.[103] Ministers who are called as pastors, Ursinus says, have a variety of tasks they are to carry out faithfully. These tasks include the faithful and correct exposition of the law and gospel, the administration of the sacraments, providing a good example of the Christian life, diligently tending to their flocks, giving respect to the decisions of the church, and giving attention to the poor.[104] As if ministers' responsibilities were not enough, Ursinus has high expectations for who should be called to ministry. Ursinus is explicit; ministers, which includes pastors, elders, and deacons, should be men, not women. Ministers must have a

---

100 Ursinus, *Commentary*, 570–571.
101 Ursinus, *Commentary*, 571.
102 Ursinus, *Commentary*, 571–572.
103 Ursinus, *Commentary*, 572. In the Latin, which was first printed in 1584 in Geneva by E. Vignon, Ursinus lists *evangeliste, episcopi en pastores, doctores, gubernatores*, and *diaconi*. Using the language of bishop, while surprising given Protestant disdain of Catholic hierarchy, is not unique in the Reformed tradition. Calvin himself used the language of bishop, the Latin *episcopi*, in several locations. See, for instance, his *Institutes*, IV.iii.12. Of course, the Protestant Reformers understood the term quite differently from their Catholic counterparts.
104 Ursinus, *Commentary*, 572–573.

good reputation inside and outside the church, and they must be able to understand and teach doctrine.[105]

Ursinus also expands on what exactly he means when he describes something as ceremonial or as a ceremony. Ursinus defines ceremonies as "external and solemn actions ordained in the ministry of the Church for order's sake or signification." Ceremonies are different from moral works in that they are temporary, all alike, signs of things, special rather than general, and in service to moral works. God or the church can ordain ceremonies, Ursinus argues. Interestingly, Ursinus says ceremonies that God ordains cannot be changed. Such a point seems deeply counterproductive for Ursinus to make. If divinely-ordained ceremonies are unchangeable, how is it that the Sabbath ceremony can be changed? Even more confusing is that as an example of a God-ordained, unchangeable ceremony Ursinus mentions "sacrifices, by which we offer and render obedience to God." Yet, of course, Ursinus does not expect Christians to practice the actual ceremony of offering sacrifices. Unfortunately, Ursinus does not elaborate on his point, simply concluding with the point that ceremonies that the church institutes can be changed.[106]

Ceremonies are not unimportant for Ursinus. In fact, he argues that the church can and *should* enact its own ceremonies. Ceremonies are necessary because "the moral worship of God cannot be observed without defining and fixing various circumstances connected with it."[107] Ursinus does give guidelines for these ceremonies, though the guidelines are extremely general. They must 1) not be impious, 2) not be superstitious, 3) not be too many, and 4) not be idle but edifying for all. Naturally, establishing Sunday as the day to observe the Sabbath is a ceremony that fits all four of these listed criteria.

Conclusions: Ursinus and the Sabbath

For Ursinus, rest does play a role in the Sabbath command. Naturally, resting on the Sabbath day includes ceasing from work. However, not all work is forbidden on the Sabbath. In an effort to avoid what Ursinus calls "Jewish superstition" he allows for work that is necessary, work that is done to help others, and work that promotes the ministry of the church and love of neighbor. While he never defines the term explicitly, Ursinus mentions on several occasions that it is "ordinary work" that needs to be rested from. This rest from ordinary work is to include children, strangers, and even non-Christians.

---

105 Ursinus, *Commentary*, 573.
106 Ursinus, *Commentary*, 573.
107 Ursinus, *Commentary*, 574.

Rest on the Sabbath also means resting from sin. In fact, Ursinus says that work is a "figure" and the thing that is signified is sin. In language that sounds much like Calvin's, Ursinus says that rest from sin is the goal of resting on the Sabbath. Sin is, of course, always forbidden, whereas work is only forbidden on the Sabbath. In addition, resting from sin is much more important than simply rest from work. For Ursinus, as with Calvin, resting from work on the Sabbath is not helpful if not accompanied with a rest from one's own spiritual works and from sin.

What the fourth commandment does not require, Ursinus says, is the observance of any specific day. If scholars can debate whether or not Calvin qualifies as a sabbatarian, little debate is to be had regarding Ursinus. He clearly does not believe the Sabbath must be observed on a specific day of the week, arguing that such observance was part of the ceremonial aspect of the fourth commandment. Ursinus pays less attention to whether the Sabbath must be observed one day out of seven. He seems to regard the one out of seven day pattern established in the Jewish Sabbath as a ceremonial aspect of the commandment that has no further bearing on Christians given the coming of Jesus Christ.

While Ursinus is clear the Sabbath should include rest, albeit mainly a spiritual rest, his primary concern regarding the fourth commandment is the ministry of the church. In his writing on the Sabbath, Ursinus emphasizes the importance of the "public ministry of the Church." For Ursinus, the fourth commandment is primarily about dedicating oneself to the ministry of the church. The ministry of the church mainly consists of attending corporate worship services which include the preaching of the Word, participation in the sacraments, communal prayers, and offerings for the poor. For Ursinus, the Sabbath certainly includes a spiritual rest, as Calvin stresses, but the primary purpose of the Sabbath for Christians is to participate in the ministry of the church.

Conclusions

Throughout the end of the sixteenth century and into the seventeenth century the Sabbath continued to be an important point of theological elucidation. While speaking of a uniform Dutch theology of the Sabbath is somewhat simplistic, theologians largely followed the guidance of Ursinus and, particularly, the Heidelberg Catechism. The Synod of Dort, the most important national synod in the history of the Dutch Reformed Church, stated its view on the Sabbath in six main points.[108] The first point is that the fourth commandment is part ceremonial

---

108 Unfortunately, issues of time and space disallow a greater investigation in the Sabbath

and part moral. Second, the Jewish observance of the seventh day was ceremonial. Third, a fixed and enduring day of worship is appointed as the moral aspect of the law as well as much rest as is necessary to maintain such worship. Fourth, the Sabbath of the Jews has been abrogated, but Christians sanctify the Lord's Day. Fifth, the Lord's Day was observed in the ancient church during the time of the apostles. Sixth, the Lord's Day is consecrated for divine worship as well as rest from all servile works, minus works of charity and necessity, and from recreations impeding the worship of God.[109] However, the theological importance of the Sabbath in the Dutch Reformed Church long pre-dated the Synod of Dort.

Johannes a Lasco's Emden Catechism and Zacharias Ursinus's theological works demonstrate the concern the Dutch Reformed Church, at least in its theology, had for Sabbath observance from its inception. While constraints of time and space have limited the examination here to only two theologians important to the Dutch Reformed tradition, the importance of a Lasco and the Emden Catechism and Ursinus and the Heidelberg Catechism to the overall Dutch Reformed tradition ensured, at least, that their theological ideas were not outliers. Rather, their views on the Sabbath were standard theological positions held in the Dutch Reformed Church in the sixteenth and seventeenth centuries. Their positions, clearly not sabbatarian but also not particularly lax regarding the Sabbath, were well disseminated throughout the Dutch Reformed world. In particular, Ursinus's works and the Heidelberg Catechism would have been extremely familiar to Dutch Reformed Christians.

As has been demonstrated in this chapter, a Lasco largely carried on Calvin's theological tradition, putting a heavy emphasis on what he terms the "interior Sabbath." Like Calvin, a Lasco highlighted the dying to one's own carnal works and, instead, allowing God to work in him or her. A Lasco also emphasized the

---

question at the Synod of Dort. However, the issue is significant and worthy of greater study since little work has been done on the importance of the discussion on Sabbath prior to and at the Synod of Dort. For work that has already been done, see Daniel R. Hyde, "Regulae de Observatione Sabbathi: The Synod of Dort's (1618–1619) Deliverance on the Sabbath," *Puritan Reformed Journal* 4 (2012): 161–184. For an excellent introduction into the current scholarship on the Synod of Dort more generally, see Aza Goudriaan and Fred van Lieburg, "Introduction," in *Revisiting the Synd of Dordt (1618–1619)*, eds. Aza Goudriaan and Fred van Lieburg, Leiden: Brill, 2011, IX–XIV. Also, Donald Sinnema, "The Drafting of the Canons of Dordt: A Preliminary Survey of Early Drafts and Related Research," in *Revisiting the Synod of Dordt (1618–1619)*, 291–311.

109 Herman H. Kuyper, *De Post-Acta of Nahandelingen van de Nationale Synode van Dordrecht in 1618 en 1619 Gehouden, Naar den Authentieken Tekst in het Latijn en Nederlandsch Uitgegeven en met Toelichtingen Voorzien, Voorafgegaan door de Geschiedenis van de Acta, de Autographa en de Post-acta dier Synode en Gevoldg door de Geschiedenis van de Revisie der Belijdenisschriften en der Liturgie, Benevens de Volledige Lijst der Gravamina op de Dortsche Synode Ingediend. Een historische Studie.* Amsterdam: Höveker & Wormser, 1899, 184–6.

prohibition from work, vain activities, and sin and, instead, a turn to good works, exercises of faith, and holy ceremonies.

Ursinus highlights many of the same points as both Calvin and a Lasco. In particular, Ursinus is still quick to emphasize the need for rest from work and, more importantly, a spiritual rest from one's sin and own works. However, with Ursinus's theological approach to the Sabbath a clear turn towards the importance of the ministry of the church comes forward. Ursinus's works put a much greater emphasis on participating in the holy ceremonies of the Church than either Calvin or a Lasco did. The practical implications of Ursinus's slight but important change in emphasis are significant. Instead of an emphasis in ceasing from one's own works and sins, which can be done privately and as the corporate Christian body, Ursinus believes the Sabbath to be primarily about participating in the ministries of the church, an activity that requires participation in the public church events. While neither Calvin nor a Lasco would have undermined the importance of the public ministry of the church for the Sabbath, it is Ursinus who takes such an approach and uses it as the emphasis for his theological approach to the Sabbath.

As the Reformed movement became increasingly entrenched in the Low Countries, the theological importance of the Sabbath only increased. After the Synod of Dort, the theological trajectory of the Reformed movement in the Dutch Republic was largely decided. Yet, the importance, both theologically and practically, of the Sabbath was only to receive more attention throughout the seventeenth century. The movement that contributed most significantly to the rise of Sabbath concerns during the seventeenth century was the Nadere Reformatie, the subject of the next chapter.

Chapter 3:
Wilhelmus à Brakel and the Nadere Reformatie:
A Commandment "Assaulted with highly elevated Shields"

The Nadere Reformatie

Any examination of the Sabbath in the Dutch Reformed tradition would be lamentably incomplete without at least some attention to the Nadere Reformatie ("Further Reformation" or "Second Reformation").[1] The Nadere Reformatie, which began at the beginning of the seventeenth century and lasted until the middle of the eighteenth century, refers to a movement within the Dutch Reformed tradition that emphasized, as one scholar puts it, "a broader programme of purification of religious life and society."[2] An in-depth investigation of the Nadere Reformatie is not necessary for the purposes of this chapter, and numerous excellent discussions, particularly those by Willem van 't Spijker, W. J. op 't Hof, and Arie de Reuver, already exist that have thoroughly addressed the movement.[3] What is important for the current project is how the Nadere Re-

---

1 Joel R. Beeke, *Assurance of Faith: Calvin, English Puritanism, and the Dutch Second Reformation*, New York: Peter Lang, 1991, 383–413; Joel R. Beeke, "The Dutch Second Reformation (Nadere Reformatie)," *Calvin Theological Journal* 28, no. 2 (1993): 300–307. The debate about how to translate the Dutch "Nadere Reformatie" has been given a considerable amount of attention. The clearest and most helpful, in my opinion, is Joel Beeke's analysis. It is important to note that the use of the terms "Further Reformation" or "Second Reformation" in this context is not related to Dr. Heinz Schilling's designation of the "Zweiten Reformation" or "Second Reformation" in broader Reformation studies. See, for instance, Heinz Schilling, *Religion, Political Culture and the Emergence of Early Modern Society: Essays in German and Dutch History*, Leiden: Brill, 1992, 247–301. In a different way, Heiko Oberman has also famously spoken of "Zwei Reformationen." See, Heiko A. Oberman, *Zwei Reformationen: Luther and Calvin, Alte und Neue Welt*, Berlin: Siedler Verlag, 2003. To avoid confusion with Schilling's and Oberman's terms and given the translation difficulties with Nadere Reformatie, I will use the Dutch original, Nadere Reformatie, in what follows.

2 Jonathan I. Israel, *The Dutch Republic: Its Rise, Greatness and Fall, 1477–1806*, Oxford: Clarendon Press, 1995, 474; Beeke, "The Dutch Second Reformation," 298–300.

3 Willem van 't Spijker, "De Nadere Reformatie," in *De Nadere Reformatie: Beschrijving van haar voornaamste vertegenwoordigers*, eds. T. Brienen et al., 's-Gravenhage: Boekencentrum, 1986, 5–16; Willem van 't Spijker, "Bronnen van de Nadere Reformatie," in *De Nadere Reformatie en het Gereformeerd piëtisme*, eds. T. Brienen, et al., 's-Gravenhage: Boekencentrum, 1989, 5–51;

formatie impacted Sabbath theology and Sabbath practices in the Dutch Reformed tradition throughout the seventeenth century.

The origins of this piety movement within the Dutch Reformed Church are somewhat difficult to pin down, but the movement was able to flourish following the Counter-Remonstrant victory at the Synod of Dort.[4] Early proponents of the movement in the seventeenth century coined the phrase "Nadere Reformatie," a term that was likely borrowed from the English Puritans.[5] After the victory of the Counter-Remonstrants at the Synod of Dort in 1619, the Nadere Reformatie was in prime position to thrive within the Dutch Republic. Counter-Remonstrants pressured the political authorities to combat immoral behavior of all sorts. The pressure of the stricter Calvinists would not last long; after 1625 the Counter-Remonstrants lost much of their power and with it the Nadere Reformatie lost some influence. However, the Nadere Reformatie was able to survive and even thrive throughout the seventeenth century and well into the eighteenth century.

Included in the policing of morality the proponents of the Nadere Reformatie advocated for were, not surprisingly, concerns about Sabbath observance. Almost every theologian who adhered to the Nadere Reformatie advocated stricter observance of the Sabbath. Dutch Reformed Christians who aligned themselves with the Nadere Reformatie prided themselves on Sunday observance and considered it central to Christian piety. In sum, it is quite accurate to say that strict Sunday observance became one of the hallmarks of the Nadere Reformatie. As such, it is important to understand and examine the Nadere Reformatie in order to understand the Sabbath within the Dutch Reformed Church, both theologically and practically.

The English Puritan movement quite certainly influenced the Nadere Reformatie and may have even prompted its beginning. William Perkins, often seen as the father of English Puritanism, had a significant influence on Willem Teellinck, the originator of the Nadere Reformatie.[6] More famously, William Ames, who studied under Perkins and had clear Puritan leanings, spent a great

---

W. J. op 't Hof, *Engelse piëtistische geschriften in het Nederlands, 1598–1622*, Rotterdam: Lindenberg, 1987; W. J. Op 't Hof, "Studie der Nadere Reformatie: Verleden en Toekomst," *Documentatieblad Nadere Reformatie* 18, no. 1 (1994): 1–50; Arie de Reuver, *Sweet Communion: Trajectories of Spirituality from the Middle Ages Through the Further Reformation*, trans. James de Jong, Grand Rapids, MI: Baker Academic, 2007, 15–26; Arie de Reuver, "Wat is het Eigene van de Nadere Reformatie," *Documentatieblad Nadere Reformatie* 18, no. 2 (1994): 145–154.

4 Hof, *Engelse piëtistische geschriften in het Nederlands*, 617–625. W. J. op 't Hof dates the beginning of the movement already in 1608 with the first of Willem Teellinck's publications.

5 L. F. Groenendijk, "De Oorsprong van de Utitdrukking 'Nadere Reformatie,'" *Documentatieblad Nadere Reformatie* 9, no. 4 (1985): 128–134. Groenendijk meticulously traces the origins of the term "Nadere Reformatie."

6 Beeke, *Assurance of Faith*, 118–120.

deal of time in the Dutch Republic where his theological influence was considerable.[7] Furthermore, English Puritan works found their way into the Dutch Republic.[8] While Beeke rightfully points out the Nadere Reformatie was not simply a reproduction of the English Puritan movement, the Puritan influence was real and certainly contributed to the emphasis on Sabbath observance that became a significant aspect of the Nadere Reformatie.[9]

A real danger does exist in splitting too starkly the Nadere Reformatie and Dutch Reformed orthodoxy.[10] In fact, as Richard Muller has demonstrated, Reformed orthodoxy was certainly concerned with piety and devotion in addition to theology and philosophy.[11] While part of a much broader point in scholarship, mostly regarding the relationship of the Reformed movement and scholasticism, the relevant point here is that the Nadere Reformatie did not disparage orthodox theology.[12] Similarly, while the Nadere Reformatie was concerned with Christian piety, many of its proponents were also extremely able theologians. Thus, moving forward, the divide between the Nadere Reformatie and Dutch Reformed orthodoxy in the seventeenth century should not be made too quickly or starkly.

Willem Teellinck was the Nadere Reformatie's first major proponent. Teellinck is not as widely known as Gisbertus Voetius or even Wilhelmus à Brakel, but he has not inappropriately been considered the father of the Nadere Reformatie.[13] Arie de Reuver, in his study on spirituality from the Middle Ages

---

7 Jan van Vliet, *The Rise of the Reformed System: The Intellectual Heritage of William Ames*, Eugene, OR: Wipf & Stock, 2013, 162–184; Sprunger, *The Learned Doctor William Ames*, 27–95. Ames was exiled to the Netherlands in 1610. So, while his influence in Dutch theology is clear, the timing of his influence cannot account for the strict Sabbath concerns of the Dutch church authorities, which were present long before 1610, that will be addressed in the subsequent chapters.

8 Hof, *Engelse piëtistische geschriften in het Nederlands*, 585–587.

9 For the differences between Puritanism and the Nadere Reformatie, see Beeke, *Assurance of Faith*, 386–387.

10 Gregory D. Schuringa, "Orthodoxy and Piety in the *Nadere Reformatie:* The Theology of Simon Oomius," *Mid-America Journal of Theology*, 20 (2009): 95–103. Schuringa provides a persuasive example of how orthodoxy and piety were never separated.

11 Richard A. Muller, *After Calvin: Studies in the Development of a Theological Tradition*, Oxford: Oxford University Press, 2003, 17–18, 105–121.

12 Heiko A. Oberman, *Spätscholastik und Reformation, Vol. 1: Der Herbst der mittelalterlichen Theologie*, trans. Martin Rumscheid and Henning Kampen, Zürich: EVZ Verlag, 1965; Maarten Wisse, Marcel Sarot, and Willemien Otten, eds., *Scholasticism Reformed: Essays in Honour of Willem J. van Asselt*, Leiden: Brill, 2010; Carl R. Trueman and R. Scott Clark, eds., *Protestant Scholasticism: Essays in Reassessment*, Carlisle: Paternoster, 1999. These works all give attention to the close relationship between scholasticism and the Reformed movement.

13 W.J.M. Engelberts, *Willem Teellinck*, trans. Annemie Godbehere, Amsterdam: Scheffer & Company, 1898; P.J. Meertens, *Letterkundig leven in Zeeland in de zestiende en de eerste helft der zeventiende eeuw*, Amsterdam: Noord-hollandsche Uitgevers Maatschappij, 1943; Reuver, *Sweet Communion*, 105–106; W.J. op 't Hof, *Bibliografische lijst van de geschriften van Willem Teellinck*, Rotterdam: Lindenberg, 1993.

through the Nadere Reformatie, has gone so far as to assert, "Teellinck's importance for this pietistic tradition is hard to overestimate." Teellinck was born in 1579 and went on to study law at Leiden, St. Andrews, and Poitiers in France. Having obtained his doctorate in jurisprudence Teellinck traveled to England where he encountered Puritan pietists. Consequently, in 1604 Teellinck went back to Leiden to study theology. He went on to serve congregations in Haamstede (1606–1612) and Middelburg (1613–1629). Teellinck's pietistic views were spread through his vast array of publications, numbering somewhere around seventy-five.[14] Teellinck was notoriously intolerant of religious minorities in the Netherlands, most notably Arminians, Catholics, Lutherans, Jews, and Anabaptists. What Teellinck desired for the Dutch church was a purity not only in doctrine but also of lifestyle. Not surprisingly, Teellinck wanted the Reformed Church to fight against any number of immoral lifestyles. While a more exhaustive examination of Teellinck's Sabbath views cannot be undertaken here, included in Teellinck's pietistic vision was a strict observance of the Sabbath.[15] From the very beginning, then, the Nadere Reformatie placed a significant emphasis on a strict observance of the Sabbath.

Gisbertus Voetius (or, in Dutch, Gijsbert Voet) was another major player in the early stages of the Nadere Reformatie. After his education at Leiden, Voetius took up the pastorate in 1611 and attended the Synod of Dort as its youngest member. By 1634 Voetius was appointed as a theology professor at the University of Utrecht where he also served as pastor. Though he was a systematic theologian, Voetius was concerned with Reformed Christians' piety. Voetius wrote extensively about the Sabbath in his *De sabbatho et festis*.[16] Eventually, Voetius's views on the Sabbath brought him into stark conflict with Johannes Cocceius and Abraham Heidanus, professors at Leiden, and his colleague in Utrecht, Franciscus Burman. Cocceius was initially professor of Hebrew at the University of Franeker and later was appointed professor of theology at the University of Leiden. Compared to Voetius, Cocceius was a more liberal theologian who believed in the complexity of Scripture and the importance of careful biblical interpretation and theology.[17]

---

14 Reuver, *Sweet Communion*, 106.

15 Willem Teellinck, *Noodtwendigh Vertoogh, aengaende den tegenwoordighen bedroefden staet van Gods volck*, Middelburg, 1627. The subject is also addressed in W. J. op 't Hof, *Willem Teellinck (1579–1629): Leven, Geschriften en Invloed*, Kampen: De Groot Goudriaan, 2008, 358–370.

16 Gisbertus Voetius, *De sabbatho et festis*, in *Sel. Disputationes* III, 1227–1251, 1252–1281. Addressed briefly in F.G.M. Broeyer, "Gisbertus Voetius, God's Gardener. The Pattern of Godliness in the *Selectae Disputationes*," in *Scholasticism Reformed: Essays in Honour of Willem J. van Asselt*, 147–148.

17 Willem J. van Asselt, *Johannes Coccejus: Portret van een zeventiende-eeuws theoloog op oude*

The theological disagreements between Voetius and Cocceius quickly centered on Sabbath observance. The confrontation regarding the Sabbath became heated, and Dutch Reformed Christians began to choose sides, labeling themselves as either "Voetians" or "Cocceians." Following their leader, Voetians, generally speaking, were strict adherents of the Reformed camp who rejected liberal theology and Cartesian philosophy. In addition, they pushed for a strict enforcement of Christian morality in Dutch society, particularly regarding the Sabbath, since they believed the Sabbath commandment required a literal and rigorous observance. Cocceians, on the other hand, held that the Sabbath commandment, when properly interpreted, did not require strict observance. This dispute between the Voetians and Cocceians often found lived expression in varying Sunday practices. The Cocceians, who were much freer in their interpretation of the Sabbath, taught that after morning church services people could engage in recreation and even some work.[18] The Leiden theology faculty experienced significant disagreement over Sabbath observance, and the debate found its way into the public sphere.[19] In fact, as the rift between the two groups intensified, Cocceian women would sit in front of their windows embroidering on Sundays simply to annoy the Voetian women passerbys.[20] Eventually the States of Holland commanded the provincial synods of North Holland and South Holland to cease debating the Sabbath, and the professors at Leiden were not to discuss the Sabbath either in print or in lectures.[21]

Clearly, the Sabbath was at the center of what the Nadere Reformatie represented. At the root of the sharp disagreements about the Sabbath in the Dutch Reformed tradition were significant theological issues. How theologians understood the Old Testament covenant and its relationship to the New Testament would play a heavy influence into how the Sabbath was to be practiced. Similarly, issues regarding the nature of ceremonial laws versus moral laws and how to determine each were of central importance. However, these theological disagreements were not relegated to the halls of the academy. Rather, Sabbath disagreements had significant impacts on how Christians were to live out their faith. As such, in order to understand the lived religious experience of Dutch Reformed Christians regarding Sunday observance, it is important to understand

---

en nieuwe wege, Heerenveen: Groen, 1997, 5–76. A great deal has been published on Cocceius. Willem van Asselt has carried out much of that work, which remains the most thorough.

18 Maurice G. Hansen, *The Reformed Church in the Netherlands Traced from A.D. 1340 to A.D. 1840, in Short Historical Sketches*, New York: Board of Publication of the Reformed Church in America, 1884, 218.

19 Visser, *De Geschiedenis van den Sabbatsstrijd*, 115–137; Israel, *The Dutch Republic*, 662.

20 Hansen, *The Reformed Church in the Netherlands*, 218.

21 Visser, *De Geschiedenis van den Sabbatsstrijd*, 138–149; Israel, *The Dutch Republic*, 663–664.

the theological disagreements proponents of the Nadere Reformatie had with other Dutch Reformed theologians.

Wilhelmus à Brakel

The focus of this section will be on Wilhemus à Brakel (1635–1711), a later proponent of the Nadere Reformatie, and his theological understanding of the Sabbath. As a representative of the Nadere Reformatie, à Brakel's understanding of the Sabbath represents a significant departure from that of Calvin, a Lasco, or Ursinus. As will be demonstrated in what follows, à Brakel's theological views of the Sabbath were radically different from other Dutch Reformed theologians and how those differences impacted how congregants should observe the Sabbath.

À Brakel was a Dutch Reformed minister and a major proponent for the Nadere Reformatie in the latter half of the seventeenth century. À Brakel was born in 1635 in Leeuwarden to a deeply religious family. At the Franeker Academy in 1654 à Brakel began his study of theology. From there à Brakel studied in Utrecht, beginning in 1660, with the renowned Voetius and Andreas Essenius. After finishing his education, à Brakel served as pastor to the Leeuwarden congregation for ten years, a ministry that was beset with several controversies. From Leeuwarden, à Brakel went to Rotterdam where he served as pastor until his death in 1711. À Brakel's ministry in Rotterdam was well-received, and it was here that his congregants came to affectionately know him as "Father à Brakel."[22]

As will become clear in the subsequent analysis of à Brakel's work, à Brakel was steeped in the scholastic method. As Muller has aptly noted, scholasticism properly understood "does not refer to a particular theology or philosophy but to a *method* developed in the medieval schools in order to facilitate academic argument, specifically argument leading to the resolution of objections, the identification and use of distinctions, and the establishment of right conclusions."[23] À Brakel's method clearly fits this definition. À Brakel's work is littered with long, numbered lists of arguments and objections and distinctions, all of which were used to arrive at the establishment of proper conclusions. The scholastic method à Brakel employs included the use of reason but, as was typical in Reformed scholasticism, also included the use of Scripture as a primary, normative source of truth claims.[24] As recent scholarship has demonstrated, à Brakel's use of the

---

22 Reuver, *Sweet Communion*, 231–260.
23 Richard A. Muller, "Calvin and the 'Calvinists,' Assessing Continuities and Discontinuities between the Reformation and Orthodoxy, Part One," *Calvin Theological Journal* 30, no. 2 (November 1995): 367.
24 Muller, "Calvin and the 'Calvinists,' Part One," 368–369.

scholastic method, including its seemingly never-ending numbered lists and distinctions, was not unique among Reformed theologians.[25] À Brakel's arguments regarding the Sabbath contain the marks of a carefully constructed scholastic method.

At least three reasons for focusing on à Brakel of all the Nadere Reformatie theologians come to mind. First, à Brakel's career occurs during the middle of the Nadere Reformatie movement. As such, his theology and writings provide a sort of middle ground for the Nadere Reformatie, both in terms of chronology and in thought.[26] Secondly, scholars have not given à Brakel's career adequate attention. Other theologians of the Nadere Reformatie, such as Willem Teellinck and Gisbertus Voetius, have been studied in far greater depth. À Brakel, on the other hand, has gone relatively unnoticed. Finally, à Brakel's magnum opus is *The Christian's Reasonable Service*. This work is not primarily a systematic theology but, rather, a guide for everyday piety. *The Christian's Reasonable Service* was extremely popular with lay people in the Netherlands and led to his overall popularity among Reformed Christians in the Dutch Republic. Thus, à Brakel's work connects with the lived religion of everyday Dutch Reformed Christians in a way that other Nadere Reformatie theologians do not.

The Christian's Reasonable Service[27]

Before undertaking his examination of the fourth commandment, it will be helpful to briefly examine à Brakel's understanding of the Ten Commandments as a whole. À Brakel is clear that the laws of the Ten Commandments are of

---

25 Trueman and Clark, *Protestant Scholasticism*, xiv–xv; Muller, "Calvin and the 'Calvinists,' Part One," 367–368.

26 Bartel Elshout, "The Theology of Wilhelmus à Brakel (1)," lecture, Puritan Reformed Seminary, Grand Rapids, MI, August 29, 2014, https://www.youtube.com/watch?v=wnOkw CiPxGY&list=PLHKxt9HSA8B72xMBzMHU8kIUT9aUu5rUw&index=1.

27 Wilhelmus à Brakel, *De Redelijke Godsdienst: In welke de Goddelijke waarheden van het genadeverbond worden verklaard, tegen partijen beschermd en tot beoefening aangedrongen, alsmede de bedeling des verbonds in het Oude en Nieuwe Testament en de ontmoeting der kerk in het Nieuwe Testament, vertoond in een verklaring van de Openbaring van Johannes*, Leiden: D. Donner, 1893. The Dutch version can be accessed online at http://www.theologienet.nl/ theologieindex.html#BRAKELW. À Brakel's work was originally published in Dutch as *De Redelijke Godsdienst* in 1700. I have primarily followed Bartel Elshout's reliable yet readable English translation: Wilhelmus à Brakel, *The Christian's Reasonable Service*, trans. Bartel Elshout, 4 Volumes, Grand Rapids, MI: Reformation Heritage Books, 2012. The English version is also now available online at http://www.abrakel.com/p/christians-reasonable-service.html. Throughout the rest of the chapter, references will cite the online versions of both À Brakel's Dutch edition and Elshout's English translation and be formatted, respectively, as follows: À Brakel, *De Redelijke Godsdienst*, Deel number, Hoofdstuk number, page number; Elshout, *The Christian's Reasonable Service*, Volume number, page number.

eternal duration, a point that will be very significant for his interpretation of the fourth commandment.[28] À Brakel argues that the Ten Commandments are identical to the law of nature; therefore, the laws remain in force and obligate everyone to follow them. The laws were given to Israel, which à Brakel considers the church, with no limitation in time, so the Ten Commandments still apply to Christians.[29] While Jesus has fulfilled the law, Jesus still says the law is binding at all times and commands the performance of the good of the law.[30] Indeed, à Brakel argues, the keeping of the moral law is urged throughout the New Testament.

In beginning his discussion on the Sabbath commandment, à Brakel addresses the basic contents of the fourth commandment. The commandment contains, à Brakel argues, three separate elements: a short exhortation, a declaration, and incentives for observance. À Brakel takes each of these elements in order. The short exhortation, according to à Brakel, is the phrase, "Remember the Sabbath day, to keep it holy." The word "remember" is "a word of great emphasis" in à Brakel's view. The commandment is to be remembered in the sense that one must take care "not to contradict, reject, or forget this commandment."[31] In fact, Christians should prepare themselves for the Sabbath the day prior so that nothing will hinder them on the Sabbath.

The commandment includes the exhortation to "remember," but à Brakel also gives attention to the idea of "the Sabbath day" and the command to "keep it holy." À Brakel says the Sabbath means "to rest" which, in turn, means "the cessation of something."[32] The commandment, à Brakel argues, is to rest from labor and thereby be refreshed. The command to keep the Sabbath holy means sanctifying the day for sacred use. The Sabbath, à Brakel says, is to be set apart for a "holy and lawful use" that makes the day sacred.[33] Exactly what the uses of the day are is something à Brakel will go on to explain later and will be addressed below.

À Brakel then moves on to an explanation of the "declaration" of the commandment. It is in his explanation of the declaration that one can immediately

---

28 À Brakel, *De Redelijke Godsdienst*, Deel 2, Hoofdstuk 6, 41–43; Elshout, *The Christian's Reasonable Service*, Vol. 3, 55–58.
29 À Brakel, *De Redelijke Godsdienst*, Deel 2, Hoofdstuk 6, 40–41; Elshout, *The Christian's Reasonable Service*, Vol. 3, 54.
30 À Brakel, *De Redelijke Godsdienst*, Deel 2, Hoofdstuk 6, 48–49; Elshout, *The Christian's Reasonable Service*, Vol. 3, 64–66.
31 À Brakel, *De Redelijke Godsdienst*, Deel 2, Hoofdstuk 6, 103; Elshout, *The Christian's Reasonable Service*, Vol. 3, 139.
32 À Brakel, *De Redelijke Godsdienst*, Deel 2, Hoofdstuk 6, 103; Elshout, *The Christian's Reasonable Service*, Vol. 3, 139.
33 À Brakel, *De Redelijke Godsdienst*, Deel 2, Hoofdstuk 6, 140; Elshout, *The Christian's Reasonable Service*, Vol. 3, 140.

begin to see how drastically à Brakel departs from Calvin, a Lasco, or Ursinus. In his initial exposition à Brakel notes the commandment has three separate elements–the time of observance, the manner of observance, and the persons called to its observance.[34] À Brakel argues outright that the Sabbath must be observed every one day out of seven. À Brakel holds to this position very strongly, stating that Christians are not to repeat the Sabbath more often even if they are so inclined. He writes, "It [the Sabbath] must be one of the seven days, and it ought not be repeated any earlier or later."[35]

À Brakel also places a heavy emphasis on the "manner of observance." The fourth commandment requires service to God and, particularly, the service the Sabbath requires is a cessation of labor. À Brakel goes on to make several distinctions related to ceasing from labor. Ceasing from labor can mean being idle and not doing anything, but this cannot be what God intends on the Sabbath because God hates idleness. Rest could also be complete non-activity that God commands so that such non-activity is an injunction from God, but à Brakel rejects this as well because God has not commanded that anywhere. Or, not to work can mean not doing something so as to be able to focus on something else or at least do something else conjoined with resting. These options too à Brakel rejects because the cessation of labor is not due to labor being a hindrance to spiritual service. Similarly, the rest and serving God cannot be conjoined because then one could partially observe the commandment by resting but still working or by working but not resting.[36] What the ceasing from labor must mean, à Brakel argues, is that Christians are to be engaged in a "holy rest." Doing no work and religious worship are combined into what it means to cease from labor. This combination is what à Brakel calls "holy rest" and is the primary goal of the fourth commandment.[37]

The third element of à Brakel's exposition concerns those who are under the obligation of the Sabbath commandment. À Brakel's view is that all people are forbidden to work on the Sabbath day. All people, even those who are not Christians, must follow the fourth commandment. À Brakel's position on the universality of the fourth commandment is similar to Calvin's and Ursinus's views that all people should follow the Sabbath, but à Brakel's reasoning is quite distinct from that of Calvin and Ursinus. Calvin and Ursinus believed all people

---

34 À Brakel, *De Redelijke Godsdienst*, Deel 2, Hoofdstuk 6, 104; Elshout, *The Christian's Reasonable Service*, Vol. 3, 140.

35 À Brakel, *De Redelijke Godsdienst*, Deel 2, Hoofdstuk 6, 104; Elshout, *The Christian's Reasonable Service*, Vol. 3, 141.

36 À Brakel, *De Redelijke Godsdienst*, Deel 2, Hoofdstuk 6, 104–105; Elshout, *The Christian's Reasonable Service*, Vol. 3, 141–142.

37 À Brakel, *De Redelijke Godsdienst*, Deel 2, Hoofdstuk 6, 105; Elshout, *The Christian's Reasonable Service*, Vol. 3, 142.

should observe a day of rest so as not to distract Christians. That is to say, the commandment itself did not necessarily require such observance. However, à Brakel believes the commandment itself requires all people to observe the Sabbath. It is not just for the benefit of Christians; rather, it is God's will in the commandment that all people observe the Sabbath, whether they are Christians or not.

Observing the Sabbath and practicing a "holy rest" requires that a number of activities are abstained from on the Sabbath. Obviously, sin is universally forbidden in Christianity. Yet, à Brakel lists seven particular sins which are specific to observing the Sabbath day. Most of the list consists of standard sins, such as making a workday out of the Sabbath (2), making it a day of sin (5), and transforming the day into a market day (3). Additional sins include not setting the Sabbath apart from other days (1) and rejecting or speaking against the Sabbath (7). Also included in à Brakel's list of prohibited activities are turning the day into one of idleness and sleep (6) as well as enjoying worldly pleasures on the Sabbath (4).[38]

À Brakel is not just interested in speculative or vague prohibitions, however. He is pointedly specific with the sins that Christians should avoid. Included in the list of worldly pleasures to be avoided are activities such as sailing, horse-riding, fishing, bird-hunting, playing tennis, playing ball, games of chance, playing cards, or playing with dice. Strolling in the fields or gardens is permitted so long as they are undertaken to observe the works of God and thereby allow one to "be refreshed according to soul and body."[39]

Other activities that make the Sabbath a day of sin include going to church in worldly attire and drinking in bars and inns where one can "hear the violin, the vain chatter and jeering of drunkards, and the playing of drums." Sins that corrupt the Sabbath also included having elaborate meals at home or a buffet in one's yard and courting between young men and women. Sins are, of course, heinous enough on their own, but they are particularly offensive when carried out on the Sabbath. À Brakel writes, "Such sins are double in measure—yes, they provoke God in an extraordinary manner."[40]

À Brakel is similarly specific about the types of work that one must avoid. Christians should not occupy themselves with the work of their profession. Brewers, bakers, laundry men, cooks, tailors, and shoemakers, all included in à Brakel's list, are to avoid practicing their trade on the Sabbath. But, Christians

---

38 À Brakel, *De Redelijke Godsdienst*, Deel 2, Hoofdstuk 6, 106–107; Elshout, *The Christian's Reasonable Service*, Vol. 3, 143–145.
39 À Brakel, *De Redelijke Godsdienst*, Deel 2, Hoofdstuk 6, 107; Elshout, *The Christian's Reasonable Service*, Vol. 3, 144.
40 À Brakel, *De Redelijke Godsdienst*, Deel 2, Hoofdstuk 6, 107; Elshout, *The Christian's Reasonable Service*, Vol. 3, 144.

also break the Sabbath if they bring their work home with them. À Brakel writes, "This [bringing work home] also applies to barbers, those who load and unload ships, those who labor on ferries, luggage porters, and garbage men; it pertains to all the labor whereby one earns a living."[41] Finally, work should not be postponed to the Sabbath, and work in preparation for the next day also should not be done. Such activities include mending, washing children, anything pertaining to laundry, paying bills, and going shopping. À Brakel summarizes the prohibition on work with a blanket condemnation: "On this day God wants universal cessation of activity on the entire face of the earth. This is evident from the commandment."[42]

Paradoxically, à Brakel also says a few types of work are allowed. Religious labors, "such as when ministers preach in the sweat of their brow," are permitted on the Sabbath. Additionally, works of absolute necessity are also allowed. Here à Brakel follows the traditional theological stance that works that are "engendered by unexpected events on the Sabbath–be it that a fire breaks out, a person falls in the water, etc." may be done. Lastly, works of mercy are allowed. À Brakel mentions caring for the sick, the labors of pharmacists, doctors, surgeons, and midwives, feeding cattle in the winter, and providing protection against enemies.[43]

As mentioned above, ceasing from work is something that all beings must do. À Brakel frames this in terms of "the persons who are sanctified by the Sabbath." Christians themselves are to rest, obviously, but they are also obligated to let those rest who are under their care. All men are forbidden to work and this includes members of the church, native residents, and even strangers. Even the animals must rest on the Sabbath. The commandment requires all beings to rest from work. À Brakel states it starkly: "God thus wishes to have complete silence upon the entire face of the earth."[44]

As mentioned above, à Brakel makes a special point of prohibiting going to the market on the Sabbath. His prohibition is brief, but he writes, "This pertains to buying and selling by merchants, store owners, sellers of fruit, vendors of all sorts of edible material, sellers of fish, etc."[45] The mention of market days as a separate point may seem strange, but à Brakel references the biblical prohibition in Ne-

---

41 À Brakel, *De Redelijke Godsdienst*, Deel 2, Hoofdstuk 6, 106; Elshout, *The Christian's Reasonable Service*, Vol. 3, 143.

42 À Brakel, *De Redelijke Godsdienst*, Deel 2, Hoofdstuk 6, 106; Elshout, *The Christian's Reasonable Service*, Vol. 3, 144.

43 À Brakel, *De Redelijke Godsdienst*, Deel 2, Hoofdstuk 6, 105; Elshout, *The Christian's Reasonable Service*, Vol. 3, 142.

44 À Brakel, *De Redelijke Godsdienst*, Deel 2, Hoofdstuk 6, 105; Elshout, *The Christian's Reasonable Service*, Vol. 3, 142.

45 À Brakel, *De Redelijke Godsdienst*, Deel 2, Hoofdstuk 6, 107; Elshout, *The Christian's Reasonable Service*, Vol. 3, 144.

hemiah 13. In Nehemiah 13, Nehemiah is enacting final reforms among the Israelites who have returned to Jerusalem from exile. À Brakel references verses 15–16 where Nehemiah witnesses people "treading on wine presses on the Sabbath and bringing in grain and loading it on donkeys, together with wine, grapes, figs, and all other kinds of loads," and, as a result, warns them against selling food on the Sabbath.[46] À Brakel also references verses 19–21 of Nehemiah 13. In these verses Nehemiah orders the gates of Jerusalem shut on the Sabbath so that no one could bring in his or her goods to sell. When sellers camped out next to the city walls Nehemiah warns them that he will have them arrested. As a final measure Nehemiah orders the Levites, the priests, to guard the gates in order to keep the Sabbath day holy. Without hesitation à Brakel applies the Sabbath prohibitions in Nehemiah to his Christian audience.

À Brakel points out that on the Sabbath Christians should avoid activities which are normally acceptable and harmless. The Sabbath is abused, he writes, when Christians delight themselves "with such things that are lawful at the appropriate time and place, in the appropriate company, and with the appropriate objective."[47] Even these normally permitted works are not, however, allowed on the Sabbath because the Sabbath is meant to be a "delight in the Lord" and not a delight in worldly pleasures.

Notably, à Brakel begins his list of sins prohibited on Sundays with a warning for those who do not set the Sabbath day apart from other days (1). Similarly, he ends the prohibitions with a warning against rejecting and speaking against the Sabbath (7). Both prohibitions are important because they argue against those who emphasize the ceremonial nature of the Sabbath. On the first prohibition à Brakel writes, "We sin...when we fail to acknowledge that this day has been set apart by God by virtue of his example and command."[48] À Brakel takes a similar tone in the last prohibition:

> "We sin when we...draw others away from hallowing this day and give them the liberty to do so; ridicule those who conscientiously hallow the sabbath [sic] according to God's command, railing at them by calling them ignorant, hair-splitters, and hypocrites (how abominable!); are unwilling to hallow the sabbath [sic] ourselves; draw others away from doing so; and mock with those who sanctify this day."[49]

What à Brakel clearly emphasizes is that those who disagree with him and consider the Sabbath ceremonial are participating in sin.

---

46 Nehemiah 13:15–16.
47 À Brakel, *De Redelijke Godsdienst*, Deel 2, Hoofdstuk 6, 107; Elshout, *The Christian's Reasonable Service*, Vol. 3, 144.
48 À Brakel, *De Redelijke Godsdienst*, Deel 2, Hoofdstuk 6, 107; Elshout, *The Christian's Reasonable Service*, Vol. 3, 143.
49 À Brakel, *De Redelijke Godsdienst*, Deel 2, Hoofdstuk 6, 107; Elshout, *The Christian's Reasonable Service*, Vol. 3, 145.

While some activities are prohibited on the Sabbath, other activities are required. À Brakel uses the language of "virtue," and the three virtues the fourth commandment requires are preparation, observance, and reflection.[50] Preparation actually begins prior to the Sabbath and consists of five items: acknowledging one's obligation to hallow the Sabbath, a spiritual desire for the Sabbath, prayer for strength to hallow the day, timely cessation from one's work, and the provision and preparation of food for one's family for the Sabbath. À Brakel is less clear on when reflection on the Sabbath takes place, though he seems to mean at the end of the Sabbath day. Reflection consists firstly of reflecting on how the day was spent both publically and privately. This includes identifying the sins one has committed throughout the day and confessing them before the Lord. Reflection also includes reflecting on the good that was done and the blessings received from the Lord, acknowledging God's gift to the church via the Sabbath, and longing for the rest that remains for the people of God.

While preparation and reflection are essential in à Brakel's view, he is most concerned with the activities of the Sabbath day itself. Observance of the Sabbath, the final virtue, includes a list of seven things, according to à Brakel. First, one must focus on the commandment and the example of God resting from his creation. Second, one must rest and withdraw from the world. Third, one is to behold God's works in the creation, preservation, and government of the world, with a particular focus on Christ's work of redemption. Fourth, Christians are to attend the public gatherings of God's people. The sixth aspect of Sabbath observance is closely related to the fourth; Christians must exercise the communion of the saints through private gatherings focused on God's Word, singing songs, and exhorting one another. À Brakel's fifth point is that one should visit the sick and destitute. Finally, Christians should contribute to the poor.[51]

In à Brakel's view, three primary incentives exist for keeping the Sabbath.[52] First, humanity has motivation to follow God's example of resting on the seventh day because humanity is created in God's image. Second, followers of the command are promised comfort, joy, and holiness of soul. In fact, those who keep the Sabbath commandment will experience greater prosperity during the other six days of labor. Finally, God himself hallowed the seventh day which means he set it apart and made it holy. A number of secondary incentives also exist.[53] Reflecting

---

50 À Brakel, *De Redelijke Godsdienst*, Deel 2, Hoofdstuk 6, 107; Elshout, *The Christian's Reasonable Service*, Vol. 3, 145.

51 À Brakel, *De Redelijke Godsdienst*, Deel 2, Hoofdstuk 6, 108–109; Elshout, *The Christian's Reasonable Service*, Vol. 3, 145–146.

52 À Brakel, *De Redelijke Godsdienst*, Deel 2, Hoofdstuk 6, 106; Elshout, *The Christian's Reasonable Service*, Vol. 3, 142–143.

53 À Brakel, *De Redelijke Godsdienst*, Deel 2, Hoofdstuk 6, 109–111; Elshout, *The Christian's Reasonable Service*, Vol. 3, 147–149.

on the harm that comes on desecrators of the Sabbath should prompt careful observance of the Sabbath. The desecration of the Sabbath, à Brakel says, is a dreadful sin and, therefore, God pronounces judgments on those who desecrate his day. On the other hand, meditating on the benefits promised those who observe the Sabbath should also lead to its hallowing. In a point somewhat repetitious to his second incentive above, à Brakel summarizes another incentive when he writes, "He who therefore desires all these benefits ought to hallow the sabbath [sic]—the promise being that they will be given on this day."[54]

Having dealt with the substance of the fourth commandment, à Brakel moves on to deal with whether or not the fourth commandment is moral or ceremonial in nature; what he calls the "great point of contention."[55] À Brakel minces no words about those who misunderstand the nature of the Sabbath. In only three sentences à Brakel accuses Jews, Socinians, Anabaptists, and Antinomians. About those who oppose the Sabbath, à Brakel writes,

> First, the Jews – to whom must be added some heretics in the early church – admit that the Sabbath is of eternal duration. They insist, however, that the seventh day after creation (or the day which has always been observed by the Jews) is to be observed. Secondly, the Socinians, Anabaptists, and Antinomians (opponents of the law) reject the entire law – and thus also this commandment.[56]

However, other opponents, who à Brakel does not identify by name, also exist. Some argue there are only nine commandments and eliminate the fourth commandment, à Brakel accuses, though only "ignorant people" hold to such a view. The next group à Brakel mentions poses the greatest challenge since it comes extremely close to the position of many Reformed theologians, the group à Brakel surely had in mind. Here à Brakel accuses those who "are less offensive in their words, but in very deed reject the entire commandment."[57] This group believes the fourth commandment has both ceremonial and moral aspects. The moral aspect refers to the "requirement of public worship without any reference to day or time," but the seventh day represents the rest of Christ in the grave and, as such, is ceremonial and has been abolished with the resurrection of Christ. Lastly, à Brakel addresses those who have a more nuanced view of how Christ has impacted the fourth commandment. These advocates believe those outside of the church are to labor everyday as a punishment for sin. Prior to Christ's coming

---

54 À Brakel, *De Redelijke Godsdienst*, Deel 2, Hoofdstuk 6, 111; Elshout, *The Christian's Reasonable Service*, Vol. 3, 149.
55 À Brakel, *De Redelijke Godsdienst*, Deel 2, Hoofdstuk 6, 111; Elshout, *The Christian's Reasonable Service*, Vol. 3, 149.
56 À Brakel, *De Redelijke Godsdienst*, Deel 2, Hoofdstuk 6, 111; Elshout, *The Christian's Reasonable Service*, Vol. 3, 150.
57 À Brakel, *De Redelijke Godsdienst*, Deel 2, Hoofdstuk 6, 111; Elshout, *The Christian's Reasonable Service*, Vol. 3, 150.

those who were part of God's covenant of grace were given the seventh day to rest. Those after Christ's resurrection still mark a seventh day of rest as a memorial of the resurrection. All the while those outside of Christ's covenant continue to labor everyday as punishment for sin. In this view, both dispensations, prior to Christ's coming and after, signified the benefits of Christ's resurrection and the eternal life that is to come.

À Brakel rejects all of the positions the various groups, be they real or imagined, put forth and actually argues that "the church of all ages" has also always been opposed to them. In summary, the commandment is of the same moral nature as the other nine of the Ten Commandments and "does not typify Christ in the least." Therefore, à Brakel concludes, the opponents he mentioned have misunderstood the fourth commandment. The commandment really "enjoins public worship" and also the "hallowing of the seventh day following six workdays, and that this day be spent in holy rest."[58]

Before tackling the views he believes to be misguided, à Brakel objects to the use of the word "ceremonial."[59] À Brakel notes that the word is not biblical, but, more significantly, he argues that ceremonies are not only associated with the Old Testament. Rather, the New Testament church also has ceremonies, such as sprinkling once or three times in baptism, sitting or standing during the Lord's Supper, and preaching with a covered or uncovered head. These ceremonies do not, of course, alter the essence of the practices. À Brakel admits that such ceremonies can be found in the Sabbath commandment, namely that the Sabbath was practiced on the last day of the week but is now practiced on the first day of the week. However, since most theologians use the language of ceremonial to describe something that typified Christ's coming, à Brakel rejects the use of the term in association with the fourth commandment. The commandment should not be described as ceremonial because "there is no typification of Christ in the fourth commandment."[60]

À Brakel offers five proofs for why the Sabbath commandment is not ceremonial. After every proof except the final one à Brakel also raises several "evasive arguments" that can be raised in opposition to his proofs.[61] Of course, à Brakel goes on to refute, so he believes, the evasive arguments offered in response to his

---

58 À Brakel, *De Redelijke Godsdienst*, Deel 2, Hoofdstuk 6, 112; Elshout, *The Christian's Reasonable Service*, Vol. 3, 150.

59 À Brakel, *De Redelijke Godsdienst*, Deel 2, Hoofdstuk 6, 112; Elshout, *The Christian's Reasonable Service*, Vol. 3, 151–152.

60 À Brakel, *De Redelijke Godsdienst*, Deel 2, Hoofdstuk 6, 112; Elshout, *The Christian's Reasonable Service*, Vol. 3, 151.

61 À Brakel, *De Redelijke Godsdienst*, Deel 2, Hoofdstuk 6, 113–122; Elshout, *The Christian's Reasonable Service*, Vol. 3, 152–164.

proofs in methodical fashion. These proofs are central to how à Brakel arrives at his understanding of the Sabbath, so it is worth discussing each one individually.

The first proof à Brakel offers is that the commandment was given prior to the fall into sin, so it is unchangeable. À Brakel creates a simple syllogism. "If the commandment pertaining to the sabbath [*sic*] was given to Adam prior to the fall, it then belongs to the unchangeable rule of holiness…."[62] Then, "that the sabbath [*sic*] has been given to Adam prior to the fall is evident from Genesis 2:1–3."[63] Thus, à Brakel concludes that it is "immovably true that the sabbath [*sic*] was given to Adam prior to the fall–and thus to the entire human race. Consequently, it is not a ceremonial command, but of the same nature as all other moral commands which are a perpetual rule of holiness for all men."[64] À Brakel anticipates the objection that the seventh day requirement of this commandment was added later after the fall, but he counters this objection by pointing out that the Lord rested on the seventh day prior to the fall.

The second proof argues that the moral law regulates the observance of the commandment. The reasoning here is quite simple. The Ten Commandments are moral laws; as part of the Ten Commandments, the fourth commandment is necessarily a moral law. À Brakel rejects as an "evasive argument" those who would except the fourth commandment as the lone ceremonial commandment of the Ten Commandments. À Brakel simply sees no evidence for such a position and believes the topic of God-glorifying rest to be moral in nature.

À Brakel's third argument is that the moral law has eternal duration. Here à Brakel's argument is less clear. Essentially, à Brakel argues that Jesus does not abolish the Sabbath commandment because the Sabbath commandment is a moral law. He argues that Jesus did not come to abolish the moral law. Since the fourth commandment is moral (as shown in the second proof), Jesus did not come to abolish it. The simple, logical conclusion à Brakel draws as a result is that the fourth commandment has eternal duration. In his refutation of "evasive arguments" à Brakel again rejects the idea that the Sabbath commandment is not actually a moral law, despite its inclusion in the Ten Commandments. The second "evasive argument" is more substantial: the fourth commandment may be moral and therefore not abolished, but the moral aspect of the commandment only

---

62 À Brakel, *De Redelijke Godsdienst*, Deel 2, Hoofdstuk 6, 113; Elshout, *The Christian's Reasonable Service*, Vol. 3, 152.

63 À Brakel, *De Redelijke Godsdienst*, Deel 2, Hoofdstuk 6, 113; Elshout, *The Christian's Reasonable Service*, Vol. 3, 152. Genesis 2:1–3 reads, "Thus the heavens and the earth were completed in all their vast array. By the seventh day God had finished the work he had been doing; so on the seventh day he rested from all his work. Then God blessed the seventh day and made it holy, because on it he rested from all the work of creating that he had done."

64 À Brakel, *De Redelijke Godsdienst*, Deel 2, Hoofdstuk 6, 117; Elshout, *The Christian's Reasonable Service*, Vol. 3, 157–158.

"pertains to the public worship of God and not to its ceremonial aspect, which is the hallowing of the seventh day."[65] Notably, this argument is exactly the one numerous theologians make, including Calvin, a Lasco, and Ursinus. However, à Brakel calls such a position a "self-fabrication" that has "not one jot or tittle" that can be produced to support it, and he rejects the "twofold" distinction made in such an argument.

The fourth proof à Brakel offers is that observance of the Sabbath command continues after the abrogation of other ceremonial laws. In another complicated argument, à Brakel points specifically to Matthew 24, where he understands the Sabbath to be given an enduring nature even after Jewish ceremonies end. In Matthew 24 Jesus speaks of the end of times and in verse 20 he is speaking of those who are fleeing persecution from the abomination that will accompany the apocalypse. In Matthew 24:20, which à Brakel cites, Jesus says, "Pray that your flight will not take place in winter or on the Sabbath." The passage demonstrates, à Brakel reasons, that the Sabbath will still be relevant at the end of time. Because the Sabbath endures to the end of time it must be part of the moral law and, therefore, not a ceremonial law.

For his final proof à Brakel points to Jesus, the apostles, and the early church all observing the Sabbath. He enlists an impressive array of supporters, citing the likes of Jesus, Paul, John, Irenaeus, Athanasius, Augustine, Justin Martyr, and John Chrysostom. After his resurrection Jesus affirms the observance of the first day of the week, and Paul conducted his ministry on the first day of the week. So, à Brakel concludes, "Take note here that a different day is never mentioned in the New Testament, but that the first day of the week is mentioned repeatedly."[66] À Brakel goes on to conclude that the Sabbath continues to be relevant, based on the New Testament and on quotes from church fathers.[67] What à Brakel does not do is describe how the change from the seventh day to the first day of the week is made. In a curious omission, à Brakel simply avoids the obvious issue of how the church can celebrate the first day of the week when the Old Testament Sabbath is clearly on the seventh day of the week. For reasons unmentioned and difficult to surmise, à Brakel simply skips the topic. His emphasis is on the continued observance of the Sabbath on a specific day, something he believes demonstrates the moral nature of the Sabbath.

---

65 À Brakel, *De Redelijke Godsdienst*, Deel 2, Hoofdstuk 6, 119; Elshout, *The Christian's Reasonable Service*, Vol. 3, 160.

66 À Brakel, *De Redelijke Godsdienst*, Deel 2, Hoofdstuk 6, 120; Elshout, *The Christian's Reasonable Service*, Vol. 3, 162.

67 À Brakel, *De Redelijke Godsdienst*, Deel 2, Hoofdstuk 6, 120–122; Elshout, *The Christian's Reasonable Service*, Vol. 3, 162–164.

After his list of proofs, à Brakel addresses seven general objections.[68] For each, à Brakel raises an objection his opponents put forth, and he then goes on to refute the objections. These objections mostly deal with the moral or ceremonial nature of the Sabbath. Many of the issues à Brakel raises are repetitive of early points, so only a brief summary of each objection and response is needed here. The first objection à Brakel raises is that the Sabbath does not "issue forth from the character of God."[69] The objection, essentially, claims that God could have chosen not to give the Sabbath command and, as such, the command is not an enduring command. À Brakel meticulously rejects the objection on a number of points, rejecting the propositions and arguments.

The second objection is a previous one à Brakel returns to: the Sabbath is part of the ceremonial law.[70] In this instance the objection cites Ezekiel 20:12 which speaks of the Sabbath as a "sign," meaning the Sabbath is only temporary and ceremonial.[71] Again, à Brakel rejects the objection on numerous points, but his main argument is that the Sabbath commandment is no different than the rest of the Ten Commandments and, therefore, is a moral law just as the other nine commandments are.

The third objection à Brakel raises is that Christ abolished the Sabbath.[72] Here à Brakel quotes Jesus words from Matthew 12:8 where Jesus says, "For the Son of man is Lord even of the Sabbath day." However, à Brakel argues, this statement does not abolish the Sabbath. Instead, Jesus was preserving the Sabbath and merely correcting the "superstition of the Jews" who had distorted the meaning of the Sabbath. In the same way, Jesus speaking of the "Son of man" as Lord of the Sabbath only affirms the moral nature of the commandment.

That the Sabbath is actually rejected in the New Testament as detrimental to the gospel is an objection à Brakel gives a great deal of attention to and is the fourth objection à Brakel addresses.[73] Here the relevant biblical texts are Romans 14:5–6, Galatians 4:10–11, and Colossians 2:16–17, all of which seem to remove the distinction of days and, subsequently, the observance of the Sabbath day.[74]

---

68 À Brakel, *De Redelijke Godsdienst*, Deel 2, Hoofdstuk 6, 122–135; Elshout, *The Christian's Reasonable Service*, Vol. 3, 164–183.

69 À Brakel, *De Redelijke Godsdienst*, Deel 2, Hoofdstuk 6, 122; Elshout, *The Christian's Reasonable Service*, Vol. 3, 164–167.

70 À Brakel, *De Redelijke Godsdienst*, Deel 2, Hoofdstuk 6, 123; Elshout, *The Christian's Reasonable Service*, Vol. 3, 167–169.

71 Ezekiel 20:12 reads, "Also I [the Lord] gave them my Sabbaths as a sign between us, so they would know that I the Lord made them holy."

72 À Brakel, *De Redelijke Godsdienst*, Deel 2, Hoofdstuk 6, 125; Elshout, *The Christian's Reasonable Service*, Vol. 3, 169–171.

73 À Brakel, *De Redelijke Godsdienst*, Deel 2, Hoofdstuk 6, 126–130; Elshout, *The Christian's Reasonable Service*, Vol. 3, 171–176.

74 Romans 14:5–6 reads, "One person considers one day more sacred than another; another

But, à Brakel responds, the "distinction of days" has no reference to the Sabbath and the fourth commandment. In addition, other evidence from the New Testament clearly demonstrates that the apostles commanded the early church to continue to celebrate the Lord's Day.

À Brakel plunges more deeply into theological language with the fifth objection, addressing the position that the Sabbath in the New Testament refers to a spiritual rest.[75] The biblical passage in question is Hebrews 4:1-11. The passage seems to suggest that the Sabbath was a sign that pre-figured belief in Jesus Christ and, as such, does not need to be observed as in the Old Testament. In response, à Brakel first argues that those who hold to any measure of a moral commandment, namely other Reformed theologians, also have difficulty with this text. If the passage negates the observance of one particular day a week, then it must also negate the need to gather and worship, something no one would accept. À Brakel then goes on to argue that none of the Old Testament ceremonies are discharged in the passage or anywhere else; rather, the final, spiritual rest that Hebrews 4 speaks of is added in addition to, not in replacement of, the rest of the Sabbath.

The Jewish Sabbath is the subject of the sixth objection.[76] Here à Brakel sets out to refute the objection that the Sabbath is to be observed on the seventh day following six work days. À Brakel argues the commandment deals with "time" and "matter." The "matter" deals with holy rest and is clearly primary; the "time" is the seventh day but is not the primary concern. In addition, in almost comical practicality, à Brakel notes that it would be impossible for everyone around the world to observe the Sabbath on the same day. He writes, "Thus, when one part of the world began and observed the Sabbath, the other part was still permitted to work twelve hours, and whereas the other portion was finished and had begun to work, the other was still observing the Sabbath."[77] More substantially, à Brakel goes on to make a distinction between "the commandments" and "the circumstances surrounding the commandments," a distinction that will be addressed more fully below. Finally, à Brakel argues, the Sabbath day consists of a seventh

---

considers every day alike. Each of them should be fully convinced in their own mind. Whoever regards one day as special does so to the Lord. Whoever eats meat does so to the Lord, for they give thanks to God; and whoever abstains does so to the Lord and gives thanks to God." Galatians 4:10-11 reads, "You are observing special days and months and seasons and years! I fear for you, that somehow I have wasted my efforts on you." Colossians 2:16-17 reads, "Therefore do not let anyone judge you by what you eat or drink, or with regard to a religious festival, a New Moon celebration or a Sabbath day. These are a shadow of the things that were to come; the reality, however, is found in Christ."

75 À Brakel, *De Redelijke Godsdienst*, Deel 2, Hoofdstuk 6, 130–132; Elshout, *The Christian's Reasonable Service*, Vol. 3, 176–178.
76 À Brakel, *De Redelijke Godsdienst*, Deel 2, Hoofdstuk 6, 132–134; Elshout, *The Christian's Reasonable Service*, Vol. 3, 178–182.
77 À Brakel, *De Redelijke Godsdienst*, Deel 2, Hoofdstuk 6, 132; Elshout, *The Christian's Reasonable Service*, Vol. 3, 179.

day of rest following six workdays, but God has simply "advanced the Sabbath by one day." Important to note, à Brakel is clear this change has "not come about by human initiative, but by the initiative of Christ and His apostles."[78] In other words, the change has been divinely instituted!

The final objection is that the Sabbath is a ceremony typifying spiritual worship.[79] Here à Brakel takes direct aim at those who speak of a "spiritual rest," which would have included Calvin and Ursinus. À Brakel rejects again the notion that the fourth commandment can be ceremonial and also rejects the premise that the Old Testament ceremonies exemplify the spiritual worship of the New Testament.

Clearly, à Brakel denies the ceremonial nature of the Sabbath commandment, but he is still forced to acknowledge a difference between the Jewish Sabbath and the Christian Sabbath. After all, à Brakel still advocates for observing the Sabbath on Sunday and not Saturday. À Brakel uses a separate distinction to justify such a switch. The distinction for à Brakel comes between the *commandment* and *circumstantial application*.[80] In other words, most, if not all, moral commandments have an essence to them that defines the commandment; however, each commandment also has elements that apply only to certain circumstances. The commandment aspect of the Sabbath commandment, à Brakel argues, is observing a day of rest and worship and doing so once every seven days. The circumstantial application of the Sabbath law is that the one day of rest out of every seven need be the seventh day of the week, Saturday.

À Brakel mentions the distinction twice in his writing on the fourth commandment. The first occurrence comes in his refutation of the first objection to the Sabbath as a moral command. Within that objection one "evasive argument" offered is that the phrase "because you were slaves in Egypt" in Exodus 20 only applies to Israel and, therefore, the whole command only applies to Israel.[81] However, à Brakel argues, here the distinction between the circumstantial application and the commandment itself are crucial. The reason for the command in this instance ("because you were slaves in Egypt") is clearly circumstantial only to the people of Israel and not to Christians. However, the commandment as such still applies as a moral, eternal command.

---

78 À Brakel, *De Redelijke Godsdienst*, Deel 2, Hoofdstuk 6, 133; Elshout, *The Christian's Reasonable Service*, Vol. 3, 180.
79 À Brakel, *De Redelijke Godsdienst*, Deel 2, Hoofdstuk 6, 134–135; Elshout, *The Christian's Reasonable Service*, Vol. 3, 182–183.
80 À Brakel, *De Redelijke Godsdienst*, Deel 2, Hoofdstuk 6, 124, 132; Elshout, *The Christian's Reasonable Service*, Vol. 3, 167, 179.
81 À Brakel, *De Redelijke Godsdienst*, Deel 2, Hoofdstuk 6, 124; Elshout, *The Christian's Reasonable Service*, Vol. 3, 167.

The second mention of the distinction comes in à Brakel's refutation to the objection that the Sabbath is to be observed on the seventh day of the week after six days of work, not on the first day of the week. Here à Brakel answers in part by saying the seventh day can be changed because it is only part of the circumstantial application of the commandment. To prove his point à Brakel cites two different examples. First, à Brakel points to the second commandment and its regulations for worship. À Brakel draws attention to that fact that not all of the second commandment still applies. He writes, "However, in the Old Testament God wanted to be served by external elements, as being shadows. God abolished this entire method in the New Testament and replaced it by an invisible manner of worship–without this ceremonial framework–although the commandment remained in force."[82] Secondly, à Brakel points to the fifth commandment and its promise of long life in Canaan if fathers and mothers were honored. This promise was only applicable to the Jews, but the commandment still remains in full force. So it is for the fourth commandment, à Brakel argues.

Human initiative cannot simply change the circumstantial aspect of the commandment. Instead, Christ and his apostles bring about the alteration.[83] The change in the circumstantial application is such that the Sabbath is now to be observed on the first day of the week. À Brakel believes the primary evidence for this change lies not necessarily in Jesus' resurrection on the first day of the week but, rather, in Jesus' appearance before the disciples on the first day of the week after his resurrection. The disciples likewise testify to this circumstantial change; à Brakel cites Acts 20:7, 1 Corinthians 16:1–2, and Revelation 1:10.[84] À Brakel has little patience for those who question why no explicit command was given to make the change or those who question the reason for the change in circumstances. In both cases à Brakel replies simply by pointing out that God is superior to humanity and, therefore, no answers can be demanded of God that God does not choose to give.

---

82 À Brakel, *De Redelijke Godsdienst*, Deel 2, Hoofdstuk 6, 132; Elshout, *The Christian's Reasonable Service*, Vol. 3, 179.

83 À Brakel, *De Redelijke Godsdienst*, Deel 2, Hoofdstuk 6, 133; Elshout, *The Christian's Reasonable Service*, Vol. 3, 180.

84 À Brakel, *De Redelijke Godsdienst*, Deel 2, Hoofdstuk 6, 133–134; Elshout, *The Christian's Reasonable Service*, Vol. 3, 180–181. Acts 20:7 reads: "On the first day of the week we came together to break bread. Paul spoke to the people and, because he intended to leave the next day, kept on talking until midnight." 1 Corinthians 16:1–2 reads: "Now about the collection for the Lord's people: Do what I told the Galatian churches to do. On the first day of every week, each one of you should set aside a sum of money in keeping with your income, saving it up, so that when I come no collections will have to be made." Revelation 1:10 reads: "On the Lord's Day I was in the Spirit, and I heard behind me a loud voice like a trumpet...."

Conclusions

At this point it should be quite clear that à Brakel's understanding of the Sabbath represents a definite divergence from that of Calvin, a Lasco, and Ursinus. In fact, à Brakel's position represents a significant departure from much of the earlier Dutch Reformed theological tradition. À Brakel clearly holds a sabbatarian position. As discussed in the first chapter, a sabbatarian position roots the Sabbath commandment in the creation order and believes the change of the Sabbath from Saturday to Sunday to be divinely ordained. Without any equivocation à Brakel asserts that the Sabbath is indeed rooted in the creation order. Similarly, à Brakel is quite clear the change from Saturday to Sunday was divinely instituted and cannot be undone. Therefore, à Brakel's position is certainly sabbatarian, in stark contrast to the previous theologians examined.

In the same way, à Brakel is emphatic in rejecting any ceremonial nature of the fourth commandment. As the above discussiom should make clear, à Brakel is meticulous and forceful in his arguments against the idea that the Sabbath command is in anyway ceremonial. However, his argument is more than mere theological nuance. À Brakel's insistence on the moral nature of the Sabbath commandment leads him to stress the continued requirements of rigid Sabbath observance for Christians. There simply cannot be any spiritualizing of the Sabbath commandment, in à Brakel's view.

The conclusions à Brakel reaches (or, perhaps more accurately, pre-suppositions à Brakel has) regarding the sabbatarian and ceremonial nature of the fourth commandment have drastic impacts on how à Brakel thinks Sunday should be observed. Much of à Brakel's understanding of the Sabbath flows naturally out of his rejection of the distinction between the moral and ceremonial aspects of the fourth commandment. Because the fourth commandment has no ceremonial aspects, the Sabbath command must be moral and, as such, a binding law for Christians.

Interestingly, à Brakel still holds in common with other Dutch Reformed theologians that the commandment requires public worship and a holy resting. À Brakel actually spends remarkably little time on public worship, though it is included in his list of requirements for activities to be engaged on Sundays. While his emphasis on worship certainly does not match that of Ursinus, à Brakel's insistence that the Sabbath commandment requires public, corporate worship falls in line with the likes of Calvin, a Lasco, and Ursinus. In the same way, à Brakel's emphasis on physical rest on Sundays is not especially unique. Though his overall tenor regarding physical rest is more severe than other Reformed theologians, especially than Ursinus, his allowance for necessary work is a theologically standard distinction. In short, it is not as if à Brakel's Sabbath expectations are completely alien to the Reformed tradition.

Yet, in certain respects à Brakel is definitely at odds with other Reformed theologians in regards to what the Sabbath commandment requires. À Brakel rejects Calvin's notion of a "spiritual rest," disqualifying the idea specifically in several locations. Similarly, though he never uses the term explicitly, a Lasco's "interior Sabbath" is a theological interpretation à Brakel did not believe to be part of the fourth commandment. À Brakel does not believe the fourth commandment prefigures Christ in any way, saying it does not "typify Christ in the least." As a result, as demonstrated above, à Brakel rejects completely the idea that the Sabbath for Christians now deals with any sort of spiritual rest. Such a spiritual rest, whether present or eschatological, very well might exist, but, for à Brakel, that rest is not what the fourth commandment is addressing. Such a position clearly puts à Brakel in conflict with earlier theologians, such as Calvin and a Lasco.

À Brakel is also insistent on the Sabbath being tied to only one specific day a week. This conviction impacts à Brakel's expectations regarding the Sabbath. Most obviously, the day to be observed must be Sunday, not any other day of the week. In à Brakel's view, which is different than Calvin's, Christians do not have the option to fulfill their Sabbath duties, namely attend public worship services, on any other day than Sunday. By extension, church authorities were also not allowed to hold their Sabbath activities on any day other than Sunday. This was theoretically possible in the theological positions of Calvin, a Lasco, and Ursinus, even if it was not typical in actuality.

À Brakel's emphasis on the virtues of preparation and reflection makes little sense unless the Sabbath is considered as a separate, particular day. For à Brakel, the fourth commandment does not obligate Christians to worship more than once a week, and Christians should feel no obligation to do so. This is, of course, in direct opposition to Calvin, who emphasizes that the Sabbath should only be the beginning of corporate worship. Because à Brakel sees Sunday as the only day for holy rest and worship, its importance is increased and the preparation and reflection in regards to Sunday are also increasingly important.

In addition, à Brakel is much stricter than Calvin, a Lasco, and Ursinus on what sorts of activities are prohibited on Sundays. Of course, all theologians agreed sinful activities were prohibited on the Sabbath, as they were on every day of the week, and à Brakel is no exception. A Lasco also prohibits "vain activity" and "useless frivolity," and Ursinus prohibits anything that prevents one from attending "the ministries of the church." But, à Brakel spends a significant amount of time and energy with amazing specificity listing the exact sorts of behaviors that are not allowed on the Sabbath. When à Brakel lists activities such as sailing, fishing, hunting, and playing games, he is much more specific and much more expansive in his prohibitions than any of the theologians previously examined.

The conclusion of this chapter is, then, that à Brakel's understanding of the Sabbath, which was typical of the Nadere Reformatie, followed a much different pattern than that of earlier Reformed theologians. Such a position was also quite unique within the earlier Dutch Reformed theological tradition. With his emphasis on the Sabbath being observed on Sunday, his adamant rejection of any ceremonial aspects of the Sabbath commandment, and his strict approach to what was required in observing the Sabbath, à Brakel assigned the Sabbath, which for him equated Sunday observance, a meaning and practical importance much different than that of Calvin, a Lasco, or Ursinus.

The question, now, is what sort of influence the various theological traditions had on the actual practices of Dutch Reformed Christians. Was the sabbatarian position of the Nadere Reformatie and à Brakel how most believers viewed and practiced the Sabbath? Or, did Calvin's emphasis on a spiritual rest from sin gain primary traction? Or, did a Lasco's and Ursinus's emphasis on Sabbath worship find clearest expression in practice? Better understanding the lived religion of Dutch Reformed Christians requires examining not only theological views but also practices and habits. While difficulties with available sources, source biases, and the like complicate determining actual lay practices, turning to church records can provide extremely helpful insights. The methodology followed here will examine such church records, beginning at the national level and moving down to the local level. Doing so will demonstrate how everyday Dutch Reformed Christians adopted, altered, or ignored the theological ideas about the Sabbath examined thus far.

Chapter 4:
"Concerning the Profanation of the Sabbath": Dutch Provinicial Synods and the Sabbath

Introduction

In June of 1604 the provincial synod of Friesland gathered in the modern-day city of Dokkum. The provincial synod, composed of delegates from a number of area classes, addressed several issues. The hosting classis, Classis Dokkum, raised a complaint about "the great disorder and desecration." Their complaints included a number of items including the ringing of the church bells, the drunkenness during the burying of the dead, and the celebration of marriage with maypoles, shooting, and bonfires. However, the majority of Dokkum's complaint dealt with the Sabbath. The classis complained that Sundays were not being kept holy. The specific complaints covered a vast array of offenses. The classis complained of work being done on Sundays, including "plowing, sowing, masonry, carpentry, and other handywork." In addition, the complaint listed all sorts of despicable behaviors during the preaching, behaviors such as "drunkenness, dancing, playing, *kaatsen*, commerce, and shouting in the churchyards." The classis sought a resolution from the political authorities, the *E. heeren Staten*, and demanded that these works be banned and dismissed.[1]

The episode in Dokkum was not unique. As this chapter will prove, Sabbath observance was a frequent topic at provincial synods. In the above instance, proper Sabbath observance focused on issues of work, immoral or improper behaviors, and how to best find a solution to the Sabbath desecration. The complaints at the Friesland provincial synod are certainly not representative of all the issues regarding the Sabbath that provincial synods addressed. Yet, the complaints found in the provincial synod at Dokkum indicate the importance

---

1 Johannes Reitsma and S. D. van Veen, *Acta der provinciale en particuliere synoden gehouden in de noordelijke Nederlanden gedurende de jaren 1572–1620*, 8 Volumes, Groningen: J.B. Wolters, 1892–1899, Vol. 6, 139. References in this chapter will be as follows: Reitsma and Van Veen, *Acta*, Volume Number, Page Number. All translations from the volumes are my own. I have included the original text in the footnotes when I thought it helpful.

church authorities placed on Sabbath observance within their regions and churches.

This chapter will address the provincial synods held in the Low Countries during the sixteenth and seventeenth centuries. These records will reveal that Sunday observance was a significant concern voiced at the provincial synods. As already seen in the above example, issues included working on the Sabbath, disrupting worship, improper recreational activities, and immoral behaviors. Before diving in to the specifics regarding Sabbath complaints in the provincial synods, a brief introduction addressing some methodological issues, the nature of provincial synods, and their role in regulating the Sabbath will help situate the discussion.

Dutch Reformed theologians throughout the sixteenth and seventeenth centuries had very developed and strongly held theological views regarding the Sabbath. From Calvin emphasizing spiritual rest to a Lasco and Ursinus emphasizing public worship to the strict prohibition on work and other activities of the Nadere Reformatie and Wilhelmus à Brakel, the Sabbath had a long theological tradition in the Dutch Reformed tradition. However, thus far relatively little attention has been paid to the actual practices of Dutch Reformed Christians in the early modern period. Did members of the Dutch Reformed Church faithfully and attentively participate in sermon services and catechism services? Did the majority of Dutch Reformed Christians cease from working on the Sabbath? Was the average Dutch Reformed church member willing to go along with À Brakel's more severe observance of the Sabbath, or was he or she willing only to strive for the spiritual rest of which Calvin spoke? In order to understand fully the Sabbath and its relationship with the Dutch Reformation, it is important to now turn to these everyday, lay beliefs and practices regarding the Sabbath.

Several issues arise when attempting to describe the everyday religious practices of the sixteenth and seventeenth century Dutch Reformed Christian, a number of which were raised in the Introduction. First, the relationship between religious beliefs and religious practices must be addressed. The division between the two categories, as described in Durkheim's definition of religion, is not without its difficulties.[2] At the least, practices and beliefs are so closely intertwined in lived religious experience that they could never be fully separated. Nonetheless, in the Dutch Reformation it is helpful and legitimate to think of theology and religious practices in somewhat separate terms, all the while realizing the overlap between the two. This chapter begins to address more directly the relationship between Dutch Reformed theology and the actual religious practices of Dutch Reformed Christians regarding the Sabbath.

---

2 Emile Durkheim, *Elementary Forms of Religious Life*, New York: Free Press, 1915, 51–63.

Second, and more significant here, is the issue of elite religion versus popular religion. Of course, as recent religious studies scholarship has shown, even using the categories of "elite" and "popular" is misleading, reductionist, and overly simplistic.[3] Nonetheless, the fact remains that religious history is frequently told from the perspective of the religiously powerful and influential. To properly understand the lived religious experience of ordinary Dutch Reformed Christians in the sixteenth and seventeenth centuries requires taking into account their actual beliefs and practices as much as possible.

In fact, it was not just the church authorities imposing their expectations for Sunday observance on lay church members. The lived religious experience of these church members certainly affected the way theologians and church authorities enforced Sabbath observances. This "bottom-up" process demonstrates the agency church members had in their religious experience and piety, and it shows that church authorities, the religious "elites," did not have complete control over lived religious experiences. Regarding observing the Sabbath, the provincial synod records show this to be true, though rarely explicitly. For instance, as will be addressed later in this chapter, the church authorities recognized their relative inability to control Sunday observance in rural areas and even resigned themselves to the inevitable Sabbath desecration to which such freedom would lead. Similarly, church authorities recognized they could do little to alter Sunday behaviors without the help of the secular authorities. In this case, the provincial synods recognized they could not always enforce Sunday observance as they would have liked. The agency their church members possessed led the church authorities to seek general enforcement of Sunday observance from the political authorities. Yet, even though church members did experience some freedom in their Sabbath practices, church authorities were resistant to allowing lay ideas regarding the Sabbath to influence their theological understandings. As this chapter will show, even the resistance of church members did not lead to the church authorities complaining about the Sabbath less frequently or altering what was acceptable behavior on the Sabbath.

Of course, several hurdles make accessing these lay voices a rather difficult task. The first issue is the ubiquitous challenge in early modern studies of sources. While the occasional diary or court record is able to shed light on lay religious experience, relatively few existent sources provide any pure and unfiltered perspective of lay Christians.[4] Consistory records, the subject of a later

---

3 See Robert Orsi's critique in *The Madonna of 115th Street Faith and Community in Italian Harlem, 1880–1950*, New Haven: Yale University Press, 1985, 2002, 2010, particularly the "Introduction to the Second Edition" and the "Introduction to the Third Edition" in the 2010 edition.

4 Pollmann, *Religious Choice in the Dutch Republic,* 11–16. Judith Pollmann has powerfully proven how different a lay perspective can be in her work on the diary of Arnold Buchelius.

chapter, begin to provide such a perspective, but even these sources are still told from the dominant perspective of the authority.[5] A second challenge exists in the anecdotal nature of specific accounts of lay religious experience. While an individual diary or biography of an individual Dutch Reformed Christian may provide fascinating insights, it is dangerous, if not disingenuous, to make summary claims about the religious experience of a larger group based on the activities or beliefs of one individual. As a result of these challenges and others, one of the best ways to investigate the Sabbath beliefs and practices of lay Dutch Reformed Christians is to turn to church records.

In seeking to identify the Sabbath practices and beliefs of these lay Christians, it may seem odd to begin with provincial synod records. Church authorities called, held, attended, and recorded the proceedings of these ecclesiastical meetings. Indeed, reading through the provincial synod records does not leave one with many particulars about specific individuals' practices or beliefs. Nonetheless, these records do give instructive insights into how church authorities viewed lay religious experiences of the Sabbath. In a sort of second hand manner, then, the provincial synod records give a picture of the lived religious experience of the Sabbath for ordinary Dutch Reformed Christians. It is not unreasonable to assume that while the pastors and theologians attending the provincial synods indubitably had their own agendas they also were concerned with the actual practices and situations of the congregations with which they were so familiar. The foundation of this chapter subsequently relies on the argument that while the portrayal of Sabbath practices in these records is no doubt biased and must be used carefully, the records do provide indications as to how ordinary Dutch Reformed Christians understood and practiced the Sabbath throughout the sixteenth-and-seventeenth-century Dutch Republic.

While further research into provincial synods is clearly needed, this chapter will reveal that the Sabbath was a major issue discussed at the provincial synods held throughout the Dutch Republic. What the records of the provincial synods suggest is that people's everyday practice of the Sabbath was quite different than the idealized theology of the Dutch pastors and theologians. This chapter argues that Dutch Reformed provincial synods exhibit the struggles that Dutch Reformed churches had in enforcing their theological vision of the Sabbath throughout the sixteenth and seventeenth centuries, and Dutch Reformed Christians actually undertook a wide variety of practices on the Sabbath, many of which the religious authorities disparaged.

Provincial synods were frequent throughout the sixteenth and seventeenth centuries in the Dutch Republic. Nine separate regional groups held provincial synods–Drenthe, Friesland, Gelderland, Groningen, Overijssel, North Holland,

---

5 Pollmann, "Off the Record," 423–438.

South Holland, Utrecht, and Zeeland. A brief word regarding the structure of the Dutch Reformed Church is helpful for understanding the importance of provincial synods. As early as 1571, at the synod at Emden, the ecclesiastical structure was formed.[6] In subsequent years the structure agreed upon in Emden was picked up at synods held in Edam (1572) and Alkmaar (1573), and the structure of the Dutch Reformed churches was firmly established.[7] The Dutch Reformed church consisted of a four-tier structure–consistories, regional classes, provincial synods, and national synods.

The most basic ecclesiastical bodies of the Dutch Reformed Church were the local consistories (*kerkeraad,* plural *kerkeraden*). Local consistories served as the oversight bodies for individual churches and were composed of preachers, elders, and deacons. These consistories met weekly and dealt with a wide variety of matters. The Synod of Emden designated such a structure, requiring, "Each church shall have assemblies or consistories, composed of the ministers of the Word, the elders and deacons. These shall meet at least once a week at a time and place which each congregation finds most convenient and suitable."[8] A more in-depth description of the Dutch consistories will be pertinent later and will be undertaken in subsequent chapters.[9]

In addition to consistories, the Synod of Emden established classes (singular: classis). Act 7 of the Synod of Emden states, "Besides these consistories, classical meetings of neighboring churches shall take place every three or six months, as seems expedient and necessary."[10] Regional classes encompassed small geographical areas and were primarily responsible for keeping village churches connected with the towns. Dutch Reformed regional classes were similar to the French Reformed *colloquy* and the Scottish *presbytery*. These gatherings consisted of preachers and elders, though elder attendance was far from guaranteed and ministers had much greater roles.[11] A major aspect of their function was keeping rural preachers from becoming isolated from the ecclesiastical developments in the urban centers. But, regional classes were also tasked with forming

---

6 Raymond A. Mentzer, "The Synod in the Reformed Tradition," in *Synod and Synodality: Theology, History, Canon Law and Ecumenism in New Contact: International Colloquium Bruges 2003*, eds. Alberto Melloni and Silvia Scatena, Münster: Lit Verlag, 2005, 177–178. As Mentzer rightly notes, the French model largely influenced the Dutch church order.

7 Israel, *The Dutch Republic*, 367.

8 Alastair Duke, Gillian Lewis, and Andrew Pettegree, eds., *Calvinism in Europe, 1540–1610: A Selection of Documents*, Manchester: Manchester University Press, 1992, 158; Rutgers, *Acta*, 58.

9 Van Deursen, *Bavianen en slijkgeuzen*, 101–120.

10 Duke, Lewis, and Pettegree, *Calvinism in Europe*, 158; Rutgers, *Acta*, 58.

11 Cornelis van den Broeke, *Een geschiedenis van de classis: classicale typen tussen idee en werkelijkheid (1571–2004)*, Kampen: Kok, 2005, 533.

new consistories and coordinating education, welfare, and other church affairs.[12] Political provinces within the Dutch Republic were broken up into anywhere from three to eight regional classes. In 1581 South Holland had the most classes with eight; North Holland had six; Zeeland had four; Utrecht had three; Gelderland had four; Friesland had three; Overijssel had five; and Drenthe had three.[13]

Provincial synods were larger ecclesiastical bodies that corresponded to the division of the political provinces of the Dutch Republic. The only exception was the province of Holland which was broken up into two provincial synods–North Holland and South Holland. Each regional classis was to send a certain number of pastors to the provincial synod meetings. These provincial synods were to meet every year to attend to affairs within the province and to work for cooperation among the provinces. Provincial synods were attended by clergy members; the local elders and deacons did not attend. As such, these organizations were composed entirely of religious professionals. National synods were supposed to oversee the provincial synods; however, this oversight body rarely met.

Church discipline was largely to take place at the local level. The Synod of Emden laid out explicit instructions for the process of church discipline. In each congregation the pastor, along with the elders, were to privately exhort and admonish congregants as needed. If such offenses were private, then two or three people were to confront the offender privately, as laid out in Matthew 18. If the sinner repented, then no further action was needed; if no repentance was offered, then the individual should be reported to the consistory. Public sins, on the other hand, were to go immediately before the consistory. Rejecting the admonitions of the consistory led first to suspension from the Lord's Supper and, if persistent, full excommunication. Obstinate sinners were to have their offenses read from the pulpit during Sunday sermon services three times. The first reading was to omit the sinner's name; at the second reading the sinner was to be named. On the third occasion the congregation was to be told that the sinner would be excommunicated unless he or she repented. The length between the three readings was left up to the individual consistories.[14] Importantly, the discipline process differed depending on whether or not the sin was deemed to be public or private in nature. Public sins were clearly seen as more harmful and dealt with more harshly. Although public and private sins were not explicitly delineated, as will

---

12 Gerrit Groenhuis, *De predikanten: de sociale positie van de gereformeerde predikanten in de Republiek der Verenigde Nederlanden voor 1700*, Groningen: Wolters-Noordhoff, 1977, 22–23.

13 Israel, *The Dutch Republic*, 367–368.

14 Rutgers, *Acta*, 68–72.

become evident in the next chapters, Sabbath desecration was typically considered a public sin.[15]

Classis meetings also took up ecclesiastical discipline. The president of classis
was to ask each church in turn what had taken place in their churches, including
any discipline that had been enforced. In addition, any matters the local consistory could not resolve, including matters of discipline, were to be brought
before the classis for a decision.[16] In the same way, provincial synods dealt with
matters of discipline the classes could not resolve.[17] The Synod of Emden charged
the provincial synods to deal with "matters of ecclesiastical discipline" by reading
such items and carefully putting them in writing.[18] Obviously, the matter of
discipline was an important one from the very beginning of the Dutch Reformed
Church, and the churches had a clear process for carrying out discipline in their
churches.

Provincial synods became extremely important in the Dutch Reformed tradition because of the relative lack of national synods. Despite the fact that a
"general assembly of all the Netherlands churches" was to be held every two years,
the actual frequency of these national synod meetings was much less.[19] Although
there is some debate over exactly what constituted a national synod, the 1571
Synod of Emden, the 1578 Synod of Dordrecht, and the 1618–1619 Synod of
Dordrecht were the only strictly national synods held in the Dutch Reformed
Church during the sixteenth and seventeenth centuries. In fact, after the Synod of
Dordrecht ended in 1619 the government of the Dutch Republic forbade any
national synods of the Dutch Reformed Church.[20] Only after the end of the Dutch
Republic in 1795 were national synods again held. The intention was for national
synods to meet every two or three years, but this was anything but the reality of
the situation in the Dutch Republic.

The rarity of national synods added to the importance of the provincial
synods. Practically speaking, in most situations the provincial synods were a sort
of "last resort" for the ecclesiastical authorities. As such, it is safe to presume that
the provincial synods only dealt with matters that were deemed significant
enough to merit attention. Items that could be resolved on the local level would

---

15 Discussion about whether certain sins should be considered private or public did occur at the
   Synod of Emden. These sins included acquiring indulgences, being married or having one's
   children baptized by Catholics, denying Christ in the presence of a magistrate, and swearing
   by saints. An answer was not decided upon because opinions were divided. See Rutgers, *Acta*,
   99.
16 Rutgers, *Acta*, 106–107.
17 Rutgers, *Acta*, 113.
18 Rutgers, *Acta*, 111.
19 Duke, Lewis, and Pettegree, *Calvinism in Europe*, 158.
20 Karel Blei, *The Netherlands Reformed Church, 1571–2005*, trans. Allan J. Janssen, Grand
   Rapids, MI: W.B. Eerdmans, 2006, 37.

not need to be addressed at the level of the provincial synod. In fact, the 1571 Synod of Emden explicitly declared that only matters "which could not be resolved in the consistorial or classical meeting or which concern all the churches of the province" should be raised at the provincial synods.[21] Similarly, any issue that was limited to only a certain locale would also not typically be relevant for provincial synods. Thus, the very presence of complaints about Sabbath observance at the level of the provincial synods suggests the Sabbath issues must have been beyond the control of local consistories or regional classes and deemed serious enough to bring before the provincial synods. Similarly, the Sabbath desecration must also have been widespread enough to warrant discussions and attempted solutions from entire provinces.

Provinical synods dealt with a wide variety of topics, including issues related to the Sabbath. Typically, items the provincial synods addressed came from the "bottom-up." That is to say, concerns of the aforementioned classes that were not resolved or needed further attention were brought before the provincial synods. This was indeed the case for complaints regarding Sunday observance. If an individual classis desired to have the topic of Sunday observance addressed at a provincial synod, the classis would formulate and submit a gravamen to the upcoming provincial synod. The records of the regional classes, the subject of the next chapter, indicate just such a procedure. Classis Dordrecht, for example, requested that the upcoming provincial synod remedy the profanation of the Sabbath in rural areas.[22] Occassionally classes would collaborate and submit a joint gravamen. For instance, in 1590 Classis Delft wanted the upcoming provincial synod that was to be held in Dordrecht to discuss Sunday observance in rural areas and was going to work with Classis Rotterdam on formulating a gravamen.[23] The provincial synod would then discuss and, if necessary, take appropriate action regarding the gravamen. This process can also be seen in the provincial synod records. The North Holland provincial synod of 1606 dealt with a question from Classis Alemair, present-day Almere, about the desecration of the Sabbath. The synod agreed it would be good to talk about the issue and seek a resolution.[24] The records do not always include the particular classis presenting the gravamina. This was the case, for instance, at the 1607 provincial synod held in Groningen. In this case the records include the complaint about the Sabbath

---

21 Rutgers, *Acta*, 109.
22 J. Roelevink, ed., *Particuliere Synode Zuid-Holland: Classis Dordrecht 1601–1620, Classis Breda 1616–1620*, Volume 2, Den Haag: Instituut voor Nederlandse Geschiedenis, 1991, 245. The synod took place from November 7–9, 1606.
23 P. H. A. M. Abels and A. Ph. F. Wouters, eds., *Provinciale synode Zuid-Holland: Classis Delft en Delfland 1572–1620*, Volume 7, Den Haag: Instituut voor Nederlandse Geschiedenis, 2001, 96. The exact date was July 19.
24 Reitsma and Van Veen, *Acta*, Vol. 1, 394. The synod was held on May 30, 1606.

abuses and the resolution of the synod to address the problem.[25] Typically, then, the provincial synods addressed Sabbath desecration at the request of the regional classes. As such, it is appropriate to view the work of the provincial synods regarding the Sabbath not as something church authorities imposed from above but, instead, as the synodical bodies addressing the concerns the more local classes brought to the attention of the provincial synods.

Before diving into the statistics of Sabbath complaints at the provincial synods, a few words regarding methodology are in order. When determining the frequency of Sabbath complaints, I have only counted each provincial synod in which Sabbath complaints occur as one occurrence of Sabbath complaints. Naturally, Sabbath complaints could occur more than once at a particular provincial synod. This did indeed happen quite frequently, particularly when individual churches and classes were giving their own gravamina. So, for instance, at Overijssel's provincial synod in Kampen in 1620 complaints came up regarding the Sabbath three separate times. Similarly, at Utrecht's provincial synod of 1606 Sabbath issues were raised no fewer than four times. However, I have counted all such instances as only one occurrence of a Sabbath complaint. Thus, the frequency of Sabbath complaints that I calculated is only a sort of bare minimum.

In what follows the provincial synod records edited and published by Reitsma and Van Veen as well as by Knuttel have been the focus.[26] In addition to being easily accessed in their published form, the volumes have the added advantage of providing a portrayal of multiple classes throughout the Dutch Republic. Not surprisingly, several limitations do exist. First, the volumes compiled by Reitsma and Van Veen do not extend deep into the seventeenth century; the records end in 1620. Knuttel's volumes overcome this limitation in that they extend all the way until 1700. However, the limitation of Knuttel's volumes is that they focus only on the province of South Holland. Nonetheless, these records are helpful in determining what sorts of items were important to churches throughout the Dutch Republic. More specifically, the records are helpful in deducing what sorts of problematic behaviors persisted in Dutch Reformed churches, including, of course, Sabbath desecration.

---

25 Reitsma and Van Veen, *Acta*, Vol. 7, 133.
26 W.P.C. Knuttel, *Acta der particuliere synoden van Zuid-Holland, 1621–1700*, 6 Volumes, 's-Gravenhage: Nijhoff, 1908–1916. For Reitsma and Van Veen's work, see above, Chapter 4, note 1.

Frequency of Sabbath Complaints

The frequency of Sabbath complaints at the provincial synods varies widely. Yet, all nine of the Dutch provincial synods regularly registered complaints about the Sabbath. As I will argue below, the frequency of complaints was largely due to the strength of the Reformed presence in the province which was also closely tied to geographical location. However, first it will be helpful to establish the frequency of Sabbath complaints in each of the nine provincial synods. For the time period from 1572–1620, the synods fell roughly into three groups–provinces with complaints that occurred in at least two-thirds of the synods; provinces with complaints that occurred roughly half of the time; and provinces with complaints that occurred at around one-third of the provincial synods.

Groningen's provincial synods raised the issue of the Sabbath most frequently. The complaints were found at twenty-one of the twenty-six meetings, meaning complaints were found at 81 % of the provincial synod meetings.[27] In the records of Friesland and South Holland the complaints also arose frequently, with both synods having complaints in 68 % of the meetings. Friesland had complaints in twenty-seven of forty synods, and South Holland had complaints in twenty-one of thirty-one synods.[28]

Several other regions saw complaints about Sabbath desecration at roughly 50 % of their meetings. With a small sample size of only six provincial synods over thirty-five years, Utrecht provincial synods had complaints at three of the six synods.[29] Drenthe had complaints of Sabbath desecration at 47 %, nine out of nineteen, of their synods.[30] Overijssel was slightly lower, with complaints arising at ten out of their twenty-four meetings, or at 42 % of the meetings.[31]

The final three provincial synods saw Sabbath complaints at roughly one-third of their gatherings. Zeeland had only twelve synods during forty-two years, and Sabbath complaints occurred at four of those twelve (33 %) gatherings.[32] Gelderland met more frequently, though still sporadically, meeting twenty-eight times during a forty-two-year period. Their synods contained Sabbath complaints for nine of those meetings for a total of 32 %.[33] North Holland met every year, minus a hiatus from 1609–1617, and had the lowest frequency of Sabbath

---

27 All calculations are my own and are based on my own reading of the published records in combination with the volumes' wonderful indices. For Groningen, see Reitsma and Van Veen, *Acta*, Volume 7.
28 For South Holland, see Reitsma and Van Veen, *Acta*, Volumes 2 and 3. For Friesland, see Reitsma and Van Veen, *Acta*, Volume 6.
29 Reitsma and Van Veen, *Acta*, Volume 6.
30 Reitsma and Van Veen, *Acta*, Volume 8.
31 Reitsma and Van Veen, *Acta*, Volume 5.
32 Reitsma and Van Veen, *Acta*, Volume 5.
33 Reitsma and Van Veen, *Acta*, Volume 4.

complaints of all the provincial synods. Their synods raised the Sabbath complaint at twelve out of forty synods for a total of 30 %.[34]

When comparing and contrasting the various provincial synods, it becomes clear that geographical location played a significant role in the frequency of Sabbath complaints. The northernmost provinces of Groningen and Friesland have the two highest rates of complaints. It is the southernmost provinces, Zeeland and Gelderland, where Sabbath complaints were least likely to occur. Provinces more centrally located, such as Utrecht and Overijssel, were quite average in the frequency of Sabbath complaints.

The geographical distribution of more Sabbath complaints in the northern provinces fits well with the historical development of the Reformed movement in the Dutch Republic. The Dutch Revolt fought with Catholic Spain was waged largely in the southernmost provinces. When fighting erupted in the southern areas, hordes of Reformed adherents fled north. Hans Knippenberg has closely studied the Dutch religious geography. He rightly notes that intitally Protestants fearing Catholic retribution for the iconoclasm of 1566 fled to Germany and England.[35] However, Knippenburg and others have described, as tensions continued the migration of Reformed people was frequently to northern areas.[36] While geographical shifts were not only north-south, the general movement of supporters of the Reformed movement led to a situation where the Reformed presence lessened significantly in the southern provinces but was strengthened substantially in the northern provinces.[37] If Sabbath complaints followed this geographical distribution, as the provincial synods suggest, then one conclusion that can be drawn from the provincial synod records is that Sabbath complaints were more frequent in provinces with a stronger Reformed presence. This suggests that in the Dutch Republic one of the defining aspects of the presence of the Dutch Reformed Church was an emphasis on Sunday observance.

In addition to geography, the Sabbath complaints also appear to be correlated to population density. The provincial synod records suggest that Sabbath complaints were more frequent in rural areas than in urban areas. The intricacies of population distribution do complicate the issue. At least three issues complicate the matter. First, provinces that could be considered rural still might have one or more major cities. For instance, though Groningen was a rural province, the city

---

34 Reitsma and Van Veen, *Acta,* Volumes 1 and 2.
35 Hans Knippenburg, *De religieuze kaart van Nederland: omvang en geografische spreading van de godsdienstige gezindten vanaf de Reformatie tot heden,* Assen: Van Gorcum, 1992, 14.
36 Knippenburg, *De religieuze kaart van Nederland,* 15–17; Willem Frijhoff and Marijke Spies, *Dutch Culture in a European Perspective, 1650: Hard-Won Unity,* trans. Myra Heerspink Scholz, New York: Palgrave Macmillan, 2004, 165.
37 Israel, *The Dutch Republic,* 196–204. Israel aptly describes the political, social, and economic differences between the northern and southern provinces.

of Groningen was significant. Second, populations of cities and provinces fluc-
tuated substantially during the latter half of the seventeenth century, particularly
as Reformed Christians from the south fled to the northern provinces to avoid
persecution.[38] Finally, the Low Countries as a whole was a highly urbanized
society when compared to the rest of Europe. While certain provinces might have
been considered rural in modern times, in the sixteenth and seventeenth centuries the whole of the Low Countries was actually quite urban.[39] Thus, while
complaints about Sabbath desecration appeared more frequently in rural areas,
connecting Sabbath desecration primarily with rural areas rather than urban
areas should not be highlighted too definitively.

Nonetheless, several trends are worth noting. Generally speaking, Sabbath
concerns are found much less frequently in the highly urbanized provinces. The
urbanized areas of North Holland and Gelderland had the lowest frequency of
complaints. On the other hand, rural provinces of the North, notably Groningen
and Friesland, had high rates of complaints. Those provinces which were rural
but had significant urban areas, such as Overijssel and Utrecht, tended to fall in
the middle regarding the frequency of Sabbath complaints. The two exceptions
are Zeeland and Drenthe. Both of these provinces were extremely rural. Yet,
Zeeland had ones of the lowest rates of Sabbath complaints, and Drenthe was
quite average in how often it addressed the Sabbath. So, urban areas tended to
have fewer Sabbath complaints, while rural areas tended towards highers frequencies of complaints, though exceptions certainly did exist.

The question, then, is whether it was geography or population that was the
primary impetus behind Sabbath complaints. Put another way, were Sabbath
concerns more frequent in the North because of its more rural nature or because
the North tended to be more strictly Reformed? Similarly, were Sabbath complaints less frequent in the South because these areas tended to be more urban or
because they were less solidly Reformed? Likely both issues impacted the frequency of Sabbath concerns, but the Sabbath concerns were brought more frequently in provinces where the Reformed presence was stronger. Consequently,
the geographical distribution of Sabbath complaints explains better the frequency of Sabbath complaints than the urban or rural nature of a province.
Generally speaking, the Reformed presence was much stronger and stricter in the
North than in the South, which helps account for the greater frequency of Sab-

---

38 J.G.C. Briels, *Zuid-Nederlanders in de Republiek 1572–1630: een demografische en cultuur-
historische studie*, Sint-Niklaas: Danthe, 1985; Geoffrey Parker, *The Dutch Revolt*, London:
Penguin Books, 1977, Reprinted 2002, 118–119; Israel, *The Dutch Republic*, 307–311; Johannes
M. Müller, *Exile Memories and the Dutch Revolt: The Narrated Diaspora, 1550–1750*, Leiden:
Brill, 2016. Recently, Johannes Müller has examined the memory culture of these mass
migrations.

39 Israel, *The Dutch Republic*, 113–115.

bath complaints in the northern provinces. The provinces of North Holland and South Holland further establish the connection between the relative strength of the Reformed presence in each province and the frequency of Sabbath complaints, with geographical location playing a minimal role.

The two provinces that do not fit nicely into the geographical schema laid out above are North Holland and South Holland. Yet, here too the political circumstances and the strength of the Reformed presence of each particular area are important for understanding the Sabbath complaints. Holland was a single province, but because of its size and population it was split into two provincial synods. North Holland, while remote geographically from the southern provinces under the control of Catholic Spain, had significant remnants of Catholicism. This is especially true of several of the main cities in North Holland. Haarlem held on to Catholicism the longest and most tenaciously of any northern city.[40] Likewise, in the eyes of Reformed authorities Amsterdam was notoriously tolerant of religious minorities and maintained a large number of Catholic residents.[41]

On the other hand, within South Holland were several staunchly Reformed cities. Most significant was Dordrecht. Dordrecht was notorious for its anti-Catholic placards and contained fewer Catholics than many other Dutch cities. Dordrecht was able to secure, as one scholar describes it, "academically-trained, socially-strong and orthodox men," which further cemented the strength of the Reformed movement there.[42] Other major cities in South Holland with strong Reformed presences included Leiden, Delft, and Rotterdam.

Thus, while South Holland was geographically closer than North Holland to the Catholic influences of the Spanish, ideologically North Holland allied with Catholicism more than South Holland. This is particularly true of the major cities within the two regions, shown most clearly in the polar opposites of Haarlem and Dordrecht. So, if Sabbath complaints are connected to a Reformed presence in the Dutch Republic, then it is not surprising that South Holland would have significantly more complaints regarding the Sabbath than North Holland.

While geographical location played a significant role in Sabbath complaints, the types of complaints lodged do not vary widely by geographical location. A few categories of complaints are somewhat peculiar to particular provinces. For example, on several occasions the Zeeland church authorities complained about people marrying on the Sabbath or other prayer days. In Zeeland's provincial

---

40 Israel, *The Dutch Republic*, 363–364.
41 Israel, *The Dutch Republic*, 379–380.
42 Elliott, "Protestantization in the Northern Netherlands," 205. Elliot's discussion of the clergy in Dordrecht comes in the third chapter of his dissertation, especially pages 170–220. Elliott's work remains the best and most complete study of the classis of Dordrecht.

synod of 1602 the synod resolved that people not marry on the prayer days.[43] But, these complaints were found almost exclusively in Zeeland. Nonetheless, the large majority of types of complaints were found with relatively similar frequency throughout the provinces.

What this suggests is that the provinces as a whole shared similar concerns about Sabbath desecration. While certain provinces (e.g. South Holland) were certainly overall more worried than others (e.g. North Holland) about Sabbath desecration, the actual concerns about such desecration were quite uniform. It was not the case, the records indicate, that some provinces were very concerned with worship on Sundays while others were more concerned with work being done. More specifically, it does not appear that particular offenses, such as dancing or drinking, were the focus of any one province over and above any other province.

A somewhat more general conclusion can also be drawn regarding the frequency of Sabbath complaints. In total, Sabbath complaints were raised in 116 of 226 provincial synods through 1620, a total of 51 % of all provincial synods. While how significant that number is lies somewhat in the proverbial eye of the beholder, the fact that at least half of the provincial synods dealt explicitly with the Sabbath is significant. The appearance of Sabbath concerns in these early provincial synods indicates that Sabbath apprehensions in the Dutch Republic were not simply the result of the happenings at the Synod of Dort or connected solely with the rise of the pietistic Nadere Reformatie movement. Rather, Sabbath concerns were important to Dutch Reformed churches early on, with complaints beginning already at the end of the 1570s and continuing throughout the 1580s and 1590s. The prevalence of complaints about desecration of the Sabbath leaves little doubt that the Sabbath was a significant theological and liturgical issue in Dutch Reformed churches from the very beginning of their existences.

However, the Sabbath complaints did not end in 1620. Current source limitations force the focus to be solely on the South Holland synods. Between the years of 1621 and 1700 the South Holland synod met every single year. Sabbath complaints are found in all but fifteen of the eighty provincial synods held from 1621 to 1700. This means that Sabbath complaints can be found in 81 % of the South Holland synods during this time frame. While South Holland as a province was "more Reformed" than the Dutch Republic as a whole, the persistence of Sabbath complaints is striking. As mentioned above, from the years 1571–1620 Sabbath complaints occurred at 68 % of the South Holland synod meetings. Clearly, the frequency of Sabbath complaints in South Holland did not decrease throughout the seventeenth century but, indeed, actually increased.

---

43 Reitsma and Van Veen, *Acta*, Vol. 5, 55.

What the South Holland records suggest is that Sabbath concerns were not solved over time. Evidently the efforts of the provincial synods were not effective in bringing about any real change to people's Sunday behaviors. Despite Sabbath complaints occurring in South Holland already in 1574, the complaints continue in earnest through 1700. The intentions of the South Holland synods to have a holier Sabbath were evidently never met to their satisfaction. The data from other provinces support the same conclusion, though to a much lesser extent given the more limited number of years. While the other provincial synod records examined here end in 1620, in no province did Sabbath issues abate as the years progressed. More research on the provincial synods of other provinces throughout the seventeenth century is needed to definitely establish the persistence of Sabbath concerns throughout the Dutch Republic in the seventeenth century. However, the records support the initial conclusion that the provincial synods were not able to significantly enforce what the authorities regarded as proper Sabbath observance.

Types of Sabbath Complaints

Having examined the frequency of Sabbath complaints, the question now becomes what sorts of complaints were lodged. What were the main issues the provincial synods were concerned with? As was elucidated in the previous chapters, the primary theological concerns were spiritual rest, worshipping on Sundays, and ceasing from work. Did these concerns voiced by the Dutch theologians find expression in the records? Was there a greater emphasis on either worship or refraining from work? In order to properly understand how the religious authorities conceived of the Sabbath and how Reformed Christians observed Sundays, these are the sorts of questions that now need to be answered.

Complaints could come before the provincial synods by several different methods. Presentation of complaints by the regional classes was the most common way complaints appeared before the provincial synods. Sometimes the provincial synod records contain whole lists of complaints individual classes brought or include the minutes from various regional classes. Frequently included in these lists or minutes are complaints regarding Sabbath desecration.[44] Other times the complaints arise in the general synod records with the particular classis lodging the complaint simply identified at the beginning.[45] Most of the

---

44 For examples of this sort, see Reitsma and Van Veen, *Acta*, Vol. 5, 353–354; Vol. 6, 188–191; Vol. 7, 389, 393.
45 For examples of this sort, see Reitsma and Van Veen, *Acta*, Vol. 1, 171, 207; Vol. 6, 220, 276; Vol. 8, 260.

time, however, the complaints simply appear in the records without any mention of who raises them.[46]

Notably, these Sabbath complaints at the provincial synods arise from the local level. Regional classes and their pastors experienced enough problems with Sabbath observance within their own congregations to bring the complaints before the larger provincial synods. This "bottom-up" process suggests at least two further points. One, the problem of Sabbath observance must have been widespread enough that an individual classis thought it worth discussion at the larger provincial synods. When a classis brought Sabbath complaints before the provincial synods it is unlikely these complaints referred to only one person or a small group of people. Such individual cases were more likely to be solved at the level of the consistory or the classis. In fact, nowhere in the provincial synod records, to my knowledge, are any individuals ever named in association with Sabbath desecration. Instead, the Sabbath desecrations likely involved a substantial number of people and were quite widespread, at least from the perspective of the clergy. Second, the process of Sabbath complaints being brought before the provincial synods also suggests that Sabbath desecration must not have been easily solved at the local level. Problems that consistories or regional classes could have resolved would not have needed to be brought before the provincial synods. Only those issues that were unresolved or needed further attention were "worthy" of being raised at the provincial synod. Sabbath observance was not, then, simply a local matter or one that local church authorities could handle on their own. Instead, they sought the advice, help, and authority of the larger ecclesiastical body, indicating the importance pastors placed on Sabbath observance among church members and the pastors' perception of the extent of Sabbath desecration.

Complaints about the Sabbath in the provincial synod records are extremely varied, and even broad categorizations become difficult. Many of the Sabbath complaints themselves are of a very general nature. Nonetheless, Sabbath complaints typically fall into three broad categories. First, general complaints about working on the Sabbath come up frequently. The second group of complaints deals with various forms of recreation on the Sabbath. The final group relates to immoral behavior that took place on the Sabbath.

Complaints about working on the Sabbath frequently mention the markets that are held on Sundays. These markets were, of course, an extremely popular tradition and many people frequented them. Sunday markets were typically held in the open space in the town square, often near the church building. Much to their dismay, the church authorities found it very difficult to put an end to the

---

46 For examples of this sort, see Reitsma and Van Veen, *Acta*, Vol. 3, 217; Vol. 4, 111; Vol. 5, 224; Vol. 6, 76, 113; Vol. 7, 10, 368.

markets. Two things in particular bothered the church authorities about the Sunday markets. First, the markets required people to work. Whoever was selling at the market was, as far as the provincial synods were concerned, working and, thus, violating the Sabbath. The other factor the provincial synods found upsetting was the buying and selling that took place at such markets. As mentioned above, Nehemiah 13 forbid commercial activity on the Sabbath. The provincial synods believed such commercial activity desecrated the Sabbath day and certainly did not meet the requirements of resting on the Sabbath.

Related to Sunday markets were complaints from the provincial synods about businesses remaining open on Sundays. The shops, inns, and bars were evidently all frequently open on Sundays, despite protests from the religious authorities. Again, from the perspective of the church authorities, the danger was multifaceted. The issue of work was again relevant. Having the establishments open meant people had to work and that buying and selling was taking place. The Gelderland province of 1605 complained of the "open stores and the handling of public commerce."[47] The second concern of the provincial synods had to do with the activities that occurred at these establishments. In particular, drinking alcohol, dancing, and sexual misconduct seemed to be the inescapable result of convening at inns and bars on Sundays. Unsurprisingly, the provincial synods could not tolerate these behaviors.

Lay people working on the Sabbath was reprehensible enough to the synods, but even more egregious were the occasions when the magistrates were involved. The synod of North Holland in 1601 wanted the usual abuses of the Sabbath brought to an end, but the synod in particular decried the continuing work of the magistrates on Sundays. The magistrates, the synod reported, were gathering rents, overseeing work on ditches and dikes, and meeting tenants.[48] The complaint of collecting taxes and other monies reappears at the North Holland provincial synod held in 1618.[49] In another instance government militia in the Utrecht province were openly practicing on Sundays, much to the dismay of the provincial synod.[50] All of these offenses were particularly troubling because they were both public and government-sponsored. The very authorities who were supposed to be working to eliminate work on Sundays were themselves authorizing and participating in it.

---

47 Reitsma and Van Veen, *Acta*, Vol. 4, 134.
48 Reitsma and Van Veen, *Acta*, Vol. 1, 306. "ende by name het vergaderen der magistraten op de Sondagen om lant te verpachten, dycken ende slooten te besteden, item het byeencomen der pachteren"
49 Reitsma and Van Veen, *Acta*, Vol. 2, 20.
50 Reitsma and Van Veen, *Acta*, Vol. 6, 355. Unfortunately, the records do not describe what these exercises entailed.

It was not just work on Sundays that the provincial synods sought to overcome. The provincial synods were equally opposed to various types of recreational activities. Rules on recreation were quite strict within the Dutch Reformed churches generally speaking.[51] However, on the Sabbath rules became even stricter. Activities normally permitted were forbidden on Sundays, and the provincial synods complained about these activities again and again. Games of multiple sorts were mentioned on numerous occasions. In particular, the game of *kaatsen* received attention in multiple instances.[52] *Kaatsen* is a traditional Dutch game most commonly associated with the Frisian provinces and is similar to American handball.[53] Other activities included singing, hunting, shooting, and boating/rowing. For instance, the South Holland synod of 1600 sought to prohibit the "riding and sailing of boats or wagons."[54]

Finally, the provincial synods regarded a number of Sunday activities as outrightfully sinful and, as such, clearly problematic. The most frequent complaint the provincial synods lodged regarding illicit behavior on the Sabbath is drinking alcohol. The complaints take numerous forms–"drinking," "drunk-drinking," "keeping taverns." As mentioned above, much of this drinking took place at taverns or inns, which meant the offenses were no longer in the privacy of one's home but now out in public. The provincial synod of Utrecht in 1606 complained about "drunken orgies" and other "wildness" that occured in a number of towns at the inns and bars. The results of these sins were even more disastrous. The drinking that Utrecht complained about in 1606 led to all sorts of other "sad accidents" such as "quarreling, fighting, murders, and deplorable things." Not unexpectedly, the provincial synods did not look favorably on innkeepers or tavern owners. The same 1606 Utrecht synod incredulously mentioned that some innkeepers pretended they did not have clocks, presumably as an excuse for why they were open during worship services.[55]

Other sinful behaviors mentioned frequently are dancing, dating ("courting"), and sexual immorality.[56] The North Holland synod of 1618 had a host of con-

51 For recreation and popular culture in the Dutch Republic more generally, see Arie Th. van Deursen, *Plain lives in a golden age: popular culture, religion, and society in seventeenth-century Holland*, trans. Maarten Ultee. Cambridge, New York: Cambridge University Press, 1991, particularly Chapter 7, "The Natural Life." Van Deursen's work was originally published in Dutch as *Het kopergeld van de Gouden Eeuw*, 4 Volumes, Assen: Van Gorcum, 1978–1981.

52 Reitsma and Van Veen, *Acta*, Vol. 6, 182, 283; Vol. 7, 133.

53 For those unfamiliar with *kaatsen*, Wikipedia provides a fairly clear summary, in English, of the game: https://en.wikipedia.org/wiki/Frisian_handball. Additionally, one can find on YouTube quite a few videos of *kaatsen* being played.

54 Reitsma and Van Veen, *Acta*, Vol. 3, 151.

55 Reitsma and Van Veen, *Acta*, Vol. 6, 321. "...daer d'herbergiers voorwenden, dat dewyle sy geen klock hebben, d'uyre niet en konen weten...."

56 Van Deursen suggests Sundays were a prime day for dating because, first, it was the only day

cerns, including dancing and the brothel houses.[57] Complaints of dancing also came up in the provincial synods of Gelderland, Friesland, South Holland and Groningen.[58] The 1593 provincial synod of Gelderland covered a wide variety of sinful offenses that were desecrating the Sabbath, including cursing and swearing, dancing, fighting, and even visiting whorehouses.[59]

Whether the Sabbath issue was related to work, recreation, or immorality, one of the main sources of irritation for the synods was that these activities distracted from worshipping on the Sabbath. Sometimes the complaint was that these activities kept people away from the church services themselves. In other words, people engaged in such activities rather than attending worship. In 1607 Groningen's provincial synod noted that people on Sundays were engaging in all sorts of labors, such as plowing and harrowing, during the preaching. This meant, of course, that these people were not at the church services.[60] Another synod complained that people were traveling outside the cities on Sundays during the services, again preventing them from attending worship.[61]

The other complaint the synods had was that these activities were an actual distraction during the worship service. In these cases, the activities were occurring during the services and were somehow disruptive, typically because of excessive noise and commotion. Much of the larger commotions likely took place outside of the church buildings. For example, a South Holland provincial synod lamented the drinking that was against God's commandments but especially noted that such drinking bouts took place "during the preaching."[62] However, Dutch Reformed services were typically held in the previously Catholic buildings, and much of the building was no longer needed. As such, the parts of the church building not used for worship became known as the *wandelkerk*, an area the townspeople could use for social and recreational purposes.[63] Undoubtedly, complaints of noise and commotion during worship services must have included activities occurring in the *wandelkerk*, within the actual church building. For instance, in Zeeland the provincial synod resolved to not let anyone be walking or

young people would not have been required to work long hours and, secondly, prospective mates could meet before or after church services. See Van Deursen, *Plain lives in a golden age*, 85.

57 Reitsma and Van Veen, *Acta*, Vol. 2, 20.
58 Reitsma and Van Veen, *Acta*, Vol. 4, 44, 303; Vol. 6, 91; Vol. 7, 16; Knuttel, *Acta*, Vol. 3, 64.
59 Reitsma and Van Veen, *Acta*, Vol. 4, 44.
60 Reitsma and Van Veen, *Acta*, Vol. 7, 133.
61 Reitsma and Van Veen, *Acta*, Vol. 4, 44.
62 Reitsma and Van Veen, *Acta*, Vol. 3, 151.
63 Andrew Spicer, *Calvinist Churches in Early Modern Europe*, Manchester: Manchester University Press, 2007, 125; Herman Roodenburg, "Smelling Rank and Status," in *Class Distinctions: Dutch Painting in the Age of Rembrandt and Vermeer*, ed. Ronni Baer, Boston: Museum of Fine Arts Publications, 2015, 41.

talking in the churchyards during the services since this was causing disruptions.[64]

Also important to note is that the provincial synods consistently portrayed the rural areas (*platten landen*) as very difficult to control. The provincial synods were quite clear that the desecration of the Sabbath was often worse in these rural areas and much harder to regulate. In 1606 the North Holland synod discussed how best to get rid of abuses on the Sabbath, particularly those in the rural districts.[65] The synod of Gelderland in 1620 complained of the "great disorder in the rural areas" that included "running in the church, walking and chatting in the churchyard and church doors during preaching."[66]

Strict Sunday observance faced several obstacles unique to the rural areas. Sunday market days were much more important in the rural areas because people traveled considerable distances to towns in order to attend the markets. Because of the distances, people living in rural areas could not attend the markets as frequently or easily as people living in urban areas. The Friesland provincial synod in 1620 noted that the markets held in rural areas on Sundays could not be abolished because of their importance to the populace, but they did want market dates that fell on Sundays to be postponed to another day.[67] Markets held in town on Sundays were particularly convenient for those who lived in rural areas since they would have already been traveling to town on Sunday for the worship services. Holding the market on Sunday between services was abundantly practical but was not met with approval from the provincial synods. Additionally, farming on the Sabbath was a temptation too great to bear for many rural Reformed Christians. The Friesland provincial synod of 1597 complained about the desecration of the Sabbath which was particularly bad in the rural lands. The synod noted its exasperation with the "plowing, sowing, and threshing" of these rural men and women.[68] Matters of planting and harvesting were often time-sensitive, so it is hardly surprising that farmers were tempted to carry out their work on Sundays. One can imagine the pressure a destitute farmer would feel to plant or harvest his crop on Sunday if the weather cooperated, particularly if severe weather was threatening.

Worship services in the rural areas faced their own challenges. Already in 1593 the South Holland synod demanded efforts be made to remedy the desecration of the Sabbath in the rural areas. Such measures included [Heidelberg] Catechism

---

64 Reitsma and Van Veen, *Acta,* Vol. 5, 297.

65 Reitsma and Van Veen, *Acta,* Vol. 1, 394.

66 Reitsma and Van Veen, *Acta,* Vol. 4, 343.

67 Reitsma and Van Veen, *Acta,* Vol. 6, 231.

68 Reitsma and Van Veen, *Acta,* Vol. 6, 91. "van den ontheiliginge des sabbats insonderheyt ten platten landen, eensdeel duer ergerlijck arbeit van ploegen, saijen, dorschen, ambachten te plegen van vrouwen en mannen."

preaching in the afternoons no matter how few people attended![69] In his article on the Sunday afternoon catechism services, Don Sinnema notes several obstacles rural areas had to overcome regarding afternoon catechism services. Afternoon catechism services were not only for educating children; all church members were expected to attend. Yet, such catechism services were not always held and often not well attended. Often rural churches would share a pastor, making it impossible for each church to hold two services on Sundays.[70] Where afternoon services were held in the rural areas, attendance at such services was so low pastors were frequently tempted to cease holding them.[71] As mentioned above, provincial synods heavily favored holding services regardless of attendance. In regard to those churches sharing a pastor, such churches were to rotate afternoon services among the churches.[72] Quite simply, church authorities were not willing to bend on holding afternoon catechism services.

Interpreting Sabbath Complaints

A final question that must be addressed deals with why the provincial synods viewed Sabbath infractions as such a serious offense. What was it about Sabbath observance that was deemed so essential? Here I offer two arguments, which the records support, in way of explanation. First, the Dutch Reformed churches viewed the Sabbath as a way to distinguish themselves from other religious groups, particularly Catholics and Anabaptists. Second, Sabbath observance was a way for the Dutch Reformed church to ensure a godly and orderly community, both as a church community and society at large.

The relationship between the Dutch Reformed Church and other religious groups in the Dutch Republic was a complicated and varied one. As outlined in the Introduction, much research has been done addressing the tolerance or lack thereof for these groups as well as their interactions with Reformed Christians.[73] Scholars have increasingly noted the coexistence of various religious groups within the Dutch Republic, particularly among laity.[74] Yet, toleration in its purest form remained elusive for any group other than the official Reformed Church.[75]

69 Reitsma and Van Veen, *Acta*, Vol. 3, 7.
70 Donald Sinnema, "The Second Sunday Service in the Early Dutch Reformed Tradition," *Calvin Theological Journal* 32, no. 2 (November 1, 1997): 318.
71 Sinnema, "The Second Sunday Service," 332.
72 Sinnema, "The Second Sunday Service," 318.
73 See above: "Introduction," 26–28.
74 Wayne Te Brake, "Emblems of Coexistence in a Confessional World," in *Living with Religious Diversity in Early-Modern Europe*, 53–79.
75 Willem Frijhoff, "Shifting Identities in Hostile Settings," in *Catholic communities in Protestant states: Britain and the Netherlands: 1570–1720*, 4–5; Willem Frijhoff, "How Plural were

While coexistence at the daily level was evidently quite common, at the clerical level tensions remained high. As Christine Kooi summarizes: "Thus, [Catholic] priests and [Reformed] preachers created rhetorical and institutional cultures that reinforced the confessional divide. Within the most direct, ecclesiastical, and clerical space the relationship between Catholics and Calvinists in Holland was one of hostility."[76] Kooi goes on to explain that these hostilities were largely confined to rhetoric rather than physical violence; nonetheless, in "the confessional arena these two churches and their respective clergies were officially enemies."[77] Sabbath observance, I will argue, functioned as one important way in which Reformed clergy could seek to distinguish themselves from their Roman Catholic counterparts and strengthen confessional boundaries among their Reformed congregants.

Within the provincial synod records Sabbath complaints were frequently found in combination with complaints about Catholics (*papisten*) and Anabaptists (*Wedderdoperen*). Occasionally complaints regarding the Catholics and Anabaptists are actually mentioned in the same gravamen as those about Sabbath desecration.[78] However, complaints about Catholics or Anabaptists which either preceded or followed gravamen about Sabbath desecration were much more common in the records.[79] It is quite unlikely that the grouping of Sabbath complaints with Catholic and Anabaptist complaints was a mere coincidence. Rather, the grouping of these complaints together demonstrates that the delegates to the provincial synods and the individual classes lodging the complaints considered Sabbath offenses and the presence of Catholics and Anabaptists to be similar in nature.

The complaints regarding the two groups differ slightly. Sunday was a prime day for Catholic "superstition." The North Holland synod of 1595 complained that the "Papists" were carrying out much superstition in the churchyards and elsewhere.[80] Because Sunday also was a day of worship for Catholics, complaints often relate to Catholic worship. These complaints take two major forms. The first set of complaints refers to the continued misguided nature of Catholic worship, such as Catholic insistence on fasting and observing feast days. For instance, the provincial synod of Zeeland in 1620 complained about the feast days, evening fasts, presumably intended to purify oneself before Mass the next morning, and superstitions of the Catholics, all which led to the scandalous

---

the Religious Worlds in Early-Modern Europe? Critical Reflections from the Netherlandic Experience," in *Living with Religious Diversity in Early Modern Europe*, 33–42.

76 Kooi, *Calvinists and Catholics*, 88–89.

77 Kooi, *Calvinists and Catholics*, 89.

78 Reitsma and Van Veen, *Acta*, Vol. 7, 149.

79 Reitsma and Van Veen, *Acta*, Vol. 6, 276, 283.

80 Reitsma and Van Veen, *Acta*, Vol. 1, 207.

profanation of the Lord's Day.[81] The second issue the provincial synods had with Catholic worship was the freedom the Catholics had in holding their own worship services. Public Catholic services were banned throughout the Dutch Republic, but Catholics continued to worship privately. However, these services often became more public than Reformed authorities desired. These services, the provincial synods complained, were desecrating the Sabbath. The South Holland synod of 1631 complained about the license Catholics were taking in using the Reformed churches, an offense they connected with the desecration of the Sabbath.[82]

The complaints about Catholic desecration of the Sabbath were most frequent at the South Holland synods. Time and again the Sabbath desecration complaints are connected with the insolence (*insolentie*) of the papists (*papisten*).[83] For example, in 1630 a gravamen spoke of the "profaning of the sabbaths and the insolence of the papacy."[84] The situation was so bad that each classical delegate was to report such insolence to his classis within three weeks so the issues could be discussed in combination with the North Holland synod.

In particular, the South Holland synods were concerned with the activities of the Jesuits. In 1626 the South Holland synod complained of "the profaning of the Sabbaths, together with the running of the papists and the Jesuits."[85] The next year the exact same language was used, again highlighting the Sabbaths, papists, and Jesuits.[86] The Jesuits were connected with Sabbath desecration numerous other times throughout the records, and it is almost always in connection with their "running" around on the Sabbath. The prevalence of the Jesuits is not at all surprising given their efforts toward reconversion via the Holland Mission.[87] What is intriguing is the connection between Jesuit activity and the Sabbath. This is not to say, of course, that complaints about Jesuits and Catholics do not occur apart from the connection with the Sabbath. However, why do the Jesuits get

---

81 Reitsma and Van Veen, *Acta*, Vol. 5, 169. "dat het onderhouden van de affgodische feestdaghen der Papisten, als zijn kermissen, vastelavonden ende diergheljicke, den Papisten in haere superstitien stijven, de ghemeijnte Christi onstichten ende groote aenlijdinghen zijn tot alle ongheregelde wulpsheden…"

82 Knuttel, *Acta*, Vol. 1, 377.

83 Knuttel, *Acta*, Vol. 1, 377, 492; Vol. 2, 15.

84 Knuttel, *Acta*, Vol. 1, 358.

85 Knuttel, *Acta*, Vol. 1, 188.

86 Knuttel, *Acta*, Vol. 1, 216.

87 For insights into the work of the Holland Mission and subsequent responses from Reformed groups, see the following: Christine Kooi, "'A Serpent in the Bosom of Our Dear Fatherland'. Reformed Reaction to the Holland Mission in the Seventeenth Century," in *The Low Countries as a Crossroads of Religious Beliefs*, 165–176; Charles Parker, "Caught Between Reformation: Catholics in the Holland Mission," in *Faith on the Margins*, 24–68; Joke Spaans, "Orphans and students: recruiting boys and girls for the Holland Mission," in *Catholic communities in Protestant states*, 183–199.

associated with Sabbath complaints in particular? Unfortunately, the records do not permit more than speculation. What seems likely is that Jesuits were, naturally, holding their own worship services on Sundays. These worship services were typically secretive, but Jesuits were often responsible for conducting services for multiple "congregations." What the "running" about of Jesuits likely refers to is either these secretive gathering themselves or the Jesuits moving about on Sundays from place to place.

Complaints about the Anabaptists were usually more general in nature. This is not particularly surprising since Anabaptists typically regulated morals very closely.[88] In fact, Christians who left the Reformed Church for Anabaptist groups often did so because they did not think the Reformed Church policed morality, including Sabbath observance, closely enough. Nonetheless, their typically stringent Sunday observance did not keep Reformed authorities from complaining. Already in 1598 the South Holland provincial synod, held in Dordrecht, complained of the Anabaptists, a complaint that included the desecration of the Sabbaths.[89] The Groningen synod of 1608 wanted to be certain that the Anabaptists better observed the Sabbath; the synodical deputies resolved to go to the political authorities, the *"E.E. heren Gedeputeeren,"* to seek an unspecified remedy.[90] More dramatically, in 1611 the Groningen synod again wanted to be sure that the Anabaptists who "spit on the Reformed Sundays are completely gone."[91]

The second interpretive lens through which to examine the provincial synods' concerns with the Sabbath is that of order. For the church authorities order was of utmost importance. In the provincial synod records the notion of disorderly (*onordentlickheden* or *ongeregeltheden*) conduct occurs in a variety of different forms. Many of the general complaints regarding the desecration of the Sabbath note the "disordering of Sundays."[92] Marriage ceremonies, which in some locations were required to take place at the Sunday afternoon services, were often noted as being disorderly.[93] For example, the 1610 synod of Zeeland wanted the placard against "disorderly marriage" on the Sabbaths renewed.[94] When rem-

---

88 Alastair C. Duke, *Dissident Identites in the Early Modern Low Countries*, eds. Judith Pollmann and Andrew Spicer, Burlington, VT: Ashgate, 2009, 95.

89 Reitsma and Van Veen, *Acta*, Vol. 3, 108.

90 Reitsma and Van Veen, *Acta*, Vol. 7, 149.

91 Reitsma and Van Veen, *Acta*, Vol. 7, 193.

92 Reitsma and Van Veen, *Acta*, Vol. 3, 7; Vol. 4, 343; Vol. 5, 103; Vol. 6, 130; Vol. 8, 111.

93 Van Deursen, *Plain lives in a golden age*, 107. Throughout the Dutch Republic civil authorities governed marriage, and the involvement of Reformed clergy was not required. Actual requirements and practices varied widely because each province set its own regulations. See Parker, *Faith on the Margins*, 60–61.

94 Reitsma and Van Veen, *Acta*, Vol. 5, 103.

edies were sought, the synods wanted to ensure that such measures were done in "good order."[95]

In a political and religious situation that was continually on the verge of chaos and even collapse, Reformed church authorities were very keen on keeping their churches in good order. This order stabilized the Reformed Church as a whole but also served to function as a way to establish the legitimacy of the Church. Catholics, Anabaptists, and the religiously indifferent were willing to pounce on any immorality and the subsequent disorder they saw in the Reformed Church. Thus, for many church authorities, moral behavior was the bedrock of an ordered church. Sunday observance was crucial to this order within the church because worship was so fundamental to the church's existence. When activities were undertaken on Sunday besides attending the preaching of the Word, the entire structure of the church was undermined and the very existence of the Reformed Church was threatened. After all, if church members did not need the church for the preaching of God's word, what would they need it for? And, if the Reformed Church could not order its own congregants and bodies, how could it continue to exist in the Dutch Republic?

The provincial synods demonstrated how quickly Sabbath desecration could descend into hostility towards religion in general. Several provincial synods recorded concerns about people, even children, mocking the Sunday services and the preachers.[96] The provincial synod in Utrecht in 1619 associated the desecration of the Sabbath with the "degrading of the religion" that puts the "souls of men in significant peril."[97]

Order was important within the church, but it was also crucial for society as a whole. Maintaining order within society was very difficult for church authorities given their lack of authority. The political situation in the Dutch Republic was certainly complicated and varied quite widely depending on the particular city. Yet, what was consistent throughout were the pleas for the political authorities (*Heeren Staten, E.E. Heeren Staten, E.E. Heeren Gedeputeerde,* or some combination) to better enforce the Sabbath. These *E.E. Heeren Staten* were the nobles who controlled the provincial government. The provincial governments held significant power since the national government, the States General, was comprised of a representative from each provincial state. In other words, political power was in the hands of the provinces and these ruling *E.E. Heeren Staten.* Thus, it is not so surprising that the provincial synods would appeal to these ruling nobles in their efforts to curb Sabbath desecration.

---

95 Reitsma and Van Veen, *Acta*, Vol. 4; 134.
96 Reitsma and Van Veen, *Acta*, Vol. 5, 297; Vol. 6, 321.
97 Reitsma and Van Veen, *Acta*, Vol. 6, 436.

The appeals to the *heeren staten* took several different forms. First, the church authorities frequently asked the *heeren staten* to issue or reissue placards against desecration of the Sabbath. For example, the Friesland provincial synod of 1609 noted the "shameful abuse of Sundays" involving "evening games, bird shooting, *kaatsen* during the preaching, etc."[98] In response the synod demanded that the *E.E. Heeren Staten* uphold the placards that had previously been published and even reissue them. Similarly, Zeeland's synod of 1610 sought that the *hare E.* carry out the publishing of a placard and the renewing of a previous placard in response to the desecration of the Sabbath.[99] As one final example, the provincial synod of Overijssel requested in 1615 that the *E. collegio* renew a wide-reaching placard. This placard demanded that "no one works on Sundays, feast, and prayer days," "during the preaching no one is found in the churchyard walking, talking, or other sins," "no one slander the [church] service and the servants of the church," and "people do not put off the baptism of young children too long."[100]

However, the political authorities were often not willing to comply. The frustration of the provincial synods is almost palpable. Returning to the 1609 synod of Friesland, after calling for the enforcement and reissuing of the placard regarding the Sabbath, the synod noted that if the *heeren staten* are found negligent in this regard the ministers will have to take recourse regarding its complaints.[101] Their very mentioning of that possibility suggests their anticipation of an apathetic response on the part of the officials. The South Holland church authorities had the same worries, though their problem was both with the *Heeren Staten* and the lower deputies who were to enforce the placards. If the placards of the *Heeren Staten* were not properly issued and enforced, the Court of Holland itself "will announce and seek a remedy."[102] In other words, if the national regents of the States General would not take action, the leaders of the province of South Holland would take the matter into their own hands.

The provincial synods believed their requests of the provincial authorities were not the least out of line. In fact, the religious authorities believed their requests had theological backing. The Belgic Confession, written in 1561 by

98 Reitsma and Van Veen, *Acta*, Vol. 6, 182. "Aengaende het tweede gravamen van het schandelicke misbruijck des Sondachs als te weten het awontspeelen, papegaijschieten, caetsen onder predicatie etc."

99 Reitsma and Van Veen, *Acta*, Vol. 5, 103. "Item zal versocht worden aen de voorsz. heeren, dattet hare E. believe het laetste placcaet, tegen de ontheyliginghe des sabbaths ghepubliceert, te doen wtvoeren, mitzgaders te vernieuwen het placcaet

100 Reitsma and Van Veen, *Acta*, Vol. 5, 297.

101 Reitsma and Van Veen, *Acta*, Vol. 6, 182.

102 Reitsma and Van Veen, *Acta*, Vol. 3, 72. "Ende alsoo vele officieren de voorsz. brieven van hare E. niet naer en commen, sal tselve oock den Hove van Hollandt aengediendt ende remedie versocht worden.

Guido de Brès, was one of the early confessions of the Dutch Reformed Church.[103] Article XXXVI of the Belgic Confession is entitled "The Civil Government," and the article includes the instruction that,

> Their [the magistrates'] office is not only to have regard unto and watch for the welfare of the civil state, but also that they protect the sacred ministry, and thus may remove and prevent all idolatry and false worship, that the kingdom of antichrist may be thus destroyed and the kingdom of Christ promoted.[104]

In the view of the Dutch religious authorities, it was not just the right of the political authorities to support the Reformed faith, it was their divinely ordained duty.

That the political authorities were less than willing partners in combating Sabbath desecration is not entirely surprising. The Dutch Reformed Church rarely, if ever, compromised the majority of the population in any of the provinces. In some locations the Reformed population was a considerable minority. For example, in the city of Haarlem only about twenty percent of the total population was Reformed.[105] Similarly, the Reformed Church in Friesland never comprised more than thirty percent of the population and in Delft included only roughly one-fourth of all people.[106] Secular authorities could not let their support of the Reformed Church alienate the other religious groups in their provinces. Rosemary Jones describes the situation aptly when she writes, "Conflicts arose when the provincial states considered that the Reformed church, still comprising only a small minority of the population, was threatening to wreck the Union by demanding extreme measures against other religious groups."[107]

Theological Impact of Sunday Observance

Before leaving the provincial synods to look more closely at classes and consistories it will be helpful to observe briefly the influence, or lack thereof, Dutch Reformed theological traditions had on how provincial synods dealt with the

---

103 Gootjes' *The Belgic Confession: Its History and Sources*, 113–115.

104 Dennison, *Reformed Confessions*, Vol. 2, 447–448.

105 Spaans, *Haarlem na de Reformatie*, 104, 299.

106 Wiebe Bergsma, "The Intellectual and Cultural Context of the Reformation in the Northern Netherlands," in N. Scott Amos, Andrew Pettegree, and Henk F. K. van Nierop, eds., *The Education of a Christian Society: Humanism and the Reformation in Britain and the Netherlands: Papers Delivered to the Thirteenth Anglo-Dutch Historical Conference, 1997*, Aldershot, Hants, England: Ashgate, 1999, 253–255; Wouters and Abels, *Nieuw en ongezien*, I, 229–239.

107 Rosemary L. Jones, "Reformed Church and Civil Authorities in the United Provinces in the Late 16th and Early 17th Centuries, As Reflected in Dutch State and Municipal Archives," *Journal of the Society of Archivists* 4, no. 2 (1970): 109–123.

Sabbath. Did the provincial synods take their cues from Dutch theologians? Do the provincial synods show evidence of attaching importance to the same sorts of things Calvin, a Lasco, Ursinus, and à Brakel did? In other words, does the theological understanding of the Sabbath of the Dutch Reformed tradition find expression in the lived experience of the provincial synods?

The provincial synods clearly took working on the Sabbath very seriously. As proven earlier, this prohibition of work found very early expression in the Dutch Reformed theological tradition. Calvin and Ursinus both contain prohibitions on working in their theologies of the Sabbath, but the provincial synods attempted to impose an even stricter ban on work than the theologians advocated.

The theological emphasis on resting from sin on the Sabbath also clearly comes through in the provincial synod records. In Calvin's theology, resting from sin on the Sabbath is of central importance. The Sabbath is to act as a sort of first fruits in the Christian life; resting from sin on the Sabbath is to carry over into resting from sin throughout one's life. As shown from the records, the provincial synods were clearly concerned with sinful behavior occurring on the Sabbath.

As noted in earlier chapters, much of Dutch theology did not believe the Sabbath must be observed on Sunday. However, the provincial synods indicate less flexibility on the day on which the Sabbath can be kept. Nowhere in the entire volumes of the provincial synods is there any hint that the Sabbath could be celebrated on any other day than Sunday. In this sense, the Dutch provincial synods appear to have been much more sabbatarian in their demands than Calvin, Ursinus, and a Lasco. On this issue, the provincial synods align most closely with the insistence of à Brakel that Sunday must be the day of the Sabbath.

A second area of focus that is found in the provincial synods that is not a major theme in the Dutch Reformed theological tradition is the emphasis on ceasing from recreational activities. Calvin, a Lasco, and Ursinus all prohibit work and sinful activities, but they are largely silent on recreational activities.

Interestingly, of the four theologians examined earlier the provincial synods seem to have the most in common with à Brakel. It is not the case, of course, that à Brakel has heavy influence on the provincial synods since the majority of the provincial synods examined met before à Brakel's career had begun. However, that does not mean the sabbatarian movement of the Nadere Reformatie as a whole was not influential. As explained earlier, the Nadere Reformatie began in earnest with Willem Teellinck who was ordained already in 1606. As numerous scholars have shown, the Nadere Reformatie was influential throughout the seventeenth century.

It is, therefore, not surprising that the Nadere Reformatie's influence would be seen clearly in the provincial synod records. But, what the provincial records demonstrate is that Sabbatarianism had deep roots in the lived experience of Dutch Reformed Christians, deeper than many scholars have previously allowed.[108] The emphasis on the Sabbath was clearly a major tenet of the Nadere Reformatie, as was clearly substantiated in à Brakel's thought above. The provincial synods provide clear support for the conclusion that the theological emphasis on the Sabbath found in the Nadere Reformatie worked its way into the lives of Dutch Reformed Christians.

In order to better understand the provincial synods and their concept of the Sabbath it is helpful to highlight the varied understandings of the clergy and the laity. As discussed at the beginning of this chapter, divisions between elite and lay religion are, of course, fraught with dangers. The divide between clergy and laity is always an artificial one. Nonetheless, the synods certainly have a different perspective than ordinary church members. As mentioned above, the provincial synods were composed solely of clergy; no lay elders or deacons were involved in the synods. As such, the provincial synods represented a definite clerical perspective, whereas the lay congregants they were attempting to bring into line had much different viewpoints.

The provincial synods clearly had strict notions about what Sabbath observance should entail. First and foremost, Sundays were meant for worship. Attending worship services was of absolute importance, including afternoon catechism services. Any activity that kept people from attending the services or that caused disruptions during the services was not allowed. The second major emphasis of the provincial synods was ceasing from work on Sundays. As detailed above, work most often consisted of farming or work associated with the markets. Finally, the provincial synods were quite critical of recreational activities. The recreational activities were a problem in themselves, according to the provincial synods, because the activities could keep people from church services and distract people from worshipping God. At the same time, recreation was also dangerous because it could quickly fall into immoral, sinful behaviors. Indeed, many of the recreational activities were themselves considered sinful and profligate. Yet, even more innocent recreation was viewed suspiciously because of tendencies for recreation to lead to immorality.

The provincial synod records suggest that the laity, on the other hand, had much different ideas about the Sabbath. Again, any consideration of a lay perspective must be approached cautiously. After all, the provincial synods were written entirely from the perspective of the clergy. Yet, what the records suggest is

---

108 Keith Sprunger is incorrect, or at least lacking nuance, when he states, "Although English Protestant religion drew heavily from the international Calvinist movement, strict Sabbatarianism in the seventeenth century was unique to the English and Scottish people." Sprunger, "English and Dutch Sabbatrianism," 24. Winton Solberg makes a similar mistake when he argues that "the Continental Reformation, including Calvin, produced nothing resembling the Puritan doctrine of the Sabbath." Solberg, *Redeem the Time*, 26–27.

that congregants were much less willing to follow the Sabbath in the terms dictated by the religious authorities.

It does appear that the laity were quite willing to attend morning worship services. Very few complaints arise in the provincial synod records regarding attendance at morning sermon services. Complaints do exist about disruptions during the morning services, but there is no assurance the offenders were even full members of the Dutch Reformed Church. Overall, attendance at morning services evidently was to the provincial synods' satisfaction, whose standards can be assumed to be quite high.

However, after the Sunday morning services Reformed Christians were much less giving of their time. According to the provincial synods, afternoon catechism services were not well attended. Rather than returning to their homes to contemplate God's goodness, many people found their way to the marketplaces. In a world where leisure was at a premium, Reformed Christians could not always resist the temptation to engage in a wide variety of recreational activities. The provincial synods paid the most attention to the morally questionable activities, such as drinking, dating, and dancing. It is not necessarily the case that drinking was the most prominent Sunday activity of choice, though the love of alcohol in the early modern Dutch Republic is well documented, but it is the one to which the synods pay most attention.[109] Besides drinking, other more harmless activities also filled up people's Sundays. They could range from boating to playing games to shooting competitions. From the perspective of the laity, Sunday after the morning church service must have been one of the few opportunities for relaxation and recreation. Congregants were quite unwilling, the provincial synods suggest, to cease from their recreation in order to spend time contemplating and worshipping God privately or attend a second service in the afternoon.

In sum, what emerges from the provincial synod records is a picture of religious authorities with quite radically different Sabbath expectations than most lay Dutch Reformed Christians. The Dutch Reformed theological traditions find expression in the expectations of the provincial synods. These expectations included church services twice on Sunday, ceasing from work, and refraining from sinful and recreational activities. However, the laity did not hold these same expectations throughout the Dutch Republic. Lay believers were willing to attend morning church services. Yet, for the most part this attendance is evidently as far as the laity was willing to acquiesce. Lay Christians were much less willing to attend afternoon services and give up drinking and other recreational activities, and they were more than willing to carry out various kinds of work and commerce. The picture the provincial synod records paint is one where the clergy

---

109 Van Deursen, *Plain lives in a golden age*, 100–102.

would continually attempt to thwart Reformed Christians working, playing, and sinning on the Sabbath.

As this chapter has confirmed, the provincial synod records provide evidence that religious authorities were deeply concerned with the practice of the Sabbath. Congregants were not keeping the Sabbath as they should and, instead, were drawn to work, recreation, and immoral and unruly activities. What the provincial synod records provide is an overarching picture of the Sabbath in the sixteenth and seventeenth centuries in the whole of the Dutch Republic. In order to better understand exactly how individual communities and congregants were practicing the Sabbath, it is now appropriate to give attention to the church records of individual classes and consistories. The question is whether the desecration of the Sabbath as described in the provincial synods is reflected in these more local church bodies or whether individual communities were more inclined toward devotion to the Sabbath.

Chapter 5:
"Whoredom, Drunkenness, Dice, Dancing, and other Rashness": Sabbath Ideals, Dutch Classes and Sabbath Complaints[1]

Introduction

The previous chapter made plain that religious authorities had a very specific idea of what the Sabbath should entail. The provincial synods of the sixteenth and seventeenth centuries were quite clear about what sorts of activities needed to be avoided and what was to be done to ensure proper Sunday observance. Primary among the activities that were to be undertaken was attending worship services. Yet, not all people in the Low Countries had the same conceptions of what Sunday observance should entail. The provincial synod records demonstrated a concern that Sunday worship services in the Dutch Reformed churches were not well attended and were often disorderly. Before turning to the Dutch classes' records, it will be helpful to take only a brief look at another perspective of Dutch church services–scenes Dutch painters painted of Dutch Reformed services in the seventeenth century.

Dutch paintings of the early modern period relating to the Reformation are, of course, well studied.[2] While the current work makes no attempt at art history and the author no claim to be an art historian, numerous Dutch painters portray the interiors of any number of churches. Unfortunately, only a few of these paintings

---

1 J.P. van Dooren, ed., *Classicale acta, 1573–1620: particuliere synode Zuid-Holland*, Volume 1, Den Haag: Nijhoff, 1980, 59. The quote in the chapter title comes from the records of Classis Dordrecht in 1578. "Die ahm sohndaghe onder predicatie ende godtzdienst, nicht allein mit wercken ende arbeiden maer ock mit allerlei untucht ende hoerdoem, drunckenschap, dobbelen, dantzen ende andere lichtverdigheidt."

2 Though not an expert in Dutch art history, the following are a few of the works I have found most helpful: Mia M. Mochizuki, *The Netherlandish Image After Iconoclasm, 1566–1672: Material Religion in the Dutch Golden Age*, Aldershot, England: Ashgate, 2008; Angela Vanhaelen, *The Wake of Iconoclasm: Painting the Church in the Dutch Republic*, University Park, PA: The Pennsylvania State University Press, 2012; C.A. van Swigchem, *Een blik in de Nederlandse kerkgebouwen na de ingebruikneming voor de protestantse eredienst*, The Hague: Voorhoeve, 1979; Paul Corby Finney, ed., *Seeing Beyond the Word: Visual Arts and the Calvinist Tradition*, Grand Rapids, MI: Eerdmans, 1999.

display Sunday services in churches.[3] Four such paintings will be briefly examined here only as an introduction into how painters and the religious authorities, as portrayed in the Dutch classes records, described Sundays so very differently. These paintings serve as a gateway into how other members of society viewed Sunday services and the Sabbath ideals the religious authorities associated with Sunday observance.

Emmanuel de Witte's painting *Interior of the Oude Kerk at Delft during a Sermon* from 1651 displays exactly what its title indicates. The painting portrays the majestic Delft church with a preacher speaking from the pulpit in a demonstrative manner. The service itself appears to be quite orderly and well attended. In fact, it appears that the church is filled to capacity with only standing room left. However, not all is well in De Witte's painting. Most notably, dogs, a constant in the paintings depicting Dutch Reformed church services, are present in the sanctuary. Vanhaelen helpfully notes that the presence of dogs in the paintings signals the descralized space of the church, an important point in the context of Catholicism's emphasis on sacred space. She argues, "Dogs are of the world; earthly, immanent creatures fully at home in a desacralized church."[4] Vanhaelen's further argument that dogs act as an ironic device, "deflating the loft aims of art," is especially relevant in the context of worship services.[5] In fact, as Herman Roodenburg has noted, dogs were such a continual problem in Dutch Reformed churches that churches employed *hondenslagers*, dog-chasers, to chase dogs out of the buildings.[6] For the most part, the dogs in this painting appear not to be disrupting the service, save for one dog who is clearly defecating on the church floor. While the image is obviously humorous, it also speaks to the disruptions of church services that were so undesirable yet difficult to control. In addition, a woman to the right of the picture is breast-feeding her child, a potentially distracting activity which is likely why the woman is on the physical fringe of those gathered.

De Witte has a similar painting titled *The Interior of the Oude Kerk, Amsterdam, during a Sermon*. Again, the preacher is in the pulpit speaking to the audience with a dramatic interactive hand gesture. The service here does not appear to be quite as well attended since a bench on the left is obviously not filled. Nonetheless, the women who are visible are clearly engaged in reading their

---

3 None of the paintings listed explicitly mention that they are portrayals of Sunday services rather than services held on other days of the week. However, given the large attendance at all of the services in the paintings, it is quite likely the artists intended for these services to be those of a Sunday morning. Services on another day of the week or even on a Sunday afternoon would not have been as well attended, a point the painters certainly would have taken into account.

4 Vanhaelen, *The Wake of Iconoclasm*, 167.

5 Vanhaelen, *The Wake of Iconoclasm*, 173.

6 Roodenburg, "Smelling Rank and Status," 41.

Figure 1: Emmmanuel de Witte, Interior of the Oude Kerk at Delft during a Sermon, 1651.
© The Wallace Collection, London

books, presumably their Bibles or psalters. As in most Reformed services, men
and women were seated separately, with children being seated with the women. In
this painting a wooden partition separates the sexes and prevents any distractions
or temptations. Again a dog makes an appearance, though this time the dog
appears to be quite well behaved and is causing no disruptions to the service.

De Witte's third painting of a church service is his *A Sermon in the Oude Kerk,
Delft* from 1651–52. This painting is similar to his depiction of the sermon in
Amsterdam. Again, a dog is present, though it appears to be relatively well
behaved. Attendance seems to be quite high, since at least what can be seen in the
painting appears to be full. The preacher appears to be preaching in typical
fashion, wagging a finger demonstratively. Again we find a woman (to the far left)

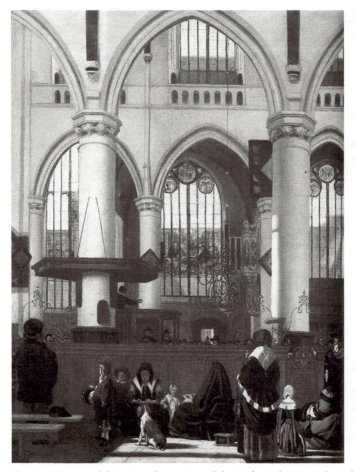

Figure 2: Emmanuel de Witte, The Interior of the Oude Kerk, Amsterdam, during a Sermon, 1658–1659. © The National Gallery, London.

who is breast-feeding her child, something that could potentially distract or disrupt but does not appear to be doing so in the painting.

The last painted church interior examined here is Gijsbert Janszoon Sibilla's painting titled *Dutch Reformed Service in the Grote Kerk of Weesp*. Sibilla's painting is striking because a man in the audience is standing up and reading from a text. The preacher is up in the pulpit, in the left of the painting, but is not speaking at all. Attention is clearly focused on the reader or cantor who is either reading from the Bible or leading the psalm-singing, though the painting gives no explicit evidence that such is the case. *Voorzangers* typically led the psalm-singing in Dutch Reformed services, but *voorlezers* also served as readers of Scripture in

Figure 3: Emmanuel de Witte, A Sermon in the Oude Kerk, Delft, 1650–1651. © National Gallery of Canada, Ottawa.

the services.[7] Since it is not clear whether church members would sit or stand during the psalm-singing, it is difficult to know if Sibilla's painting portrays the singing of a psalm or the reading of Scripture. It appears that no one else is singing along, suggesting the man is a *voorlezer* reading from the Bible. Whatever

7 Bert Polman, "A History of Worship in the Christian Reformed Church," in *Psalter Hymnal Handbook*, eds. Emily R. Brink and Bert Polman, Grand Rapids, MI: CRC Publications, 1998, 111; Bert Polman, "A History of Music in the Christian Reformed Church," in *Proceedings, a Conference on Liturgy and Music in Reformed Worship, July 18–20, 1979, Grand Rapids, Michigan*, ed. A. James Heynen, Grand Rapids, MI: Board of Publications, Christian Reformed Church, 1979, 20–21.

the case, as in De Witte's paintings, the scene is generally one of order and attention.

However, Sibilla's painting also contains elements that portray a service that is not without distractions or disruptions. Again, dogs appear to be the main problem. Seated just behind the reader are two children paying much more attention to the dog at their feet than anything else. The young boy, with a mischievous grin on his face, is yanking the small dog's tail with both of his hands while a young girl, presumably his younger sister, appears to be pulling on her brother's arm in an effort to stop him. A somewhat older girl, likely the older sibling of the other two children, is sitting right behind them but has her head leaned against a short wall and is clearly asleep. The woman to the right of these children, presumably their mother, is not concerned with the distracting children but is, instead, breast-feeding another young child. Many viewers would undoubtedly find the familial nature of the painting endearing, but the religious authorities would have certainly not looked favorably on anything that drew attention away from the religious service taking place.

Other people in Sibilla's painting also appear to be quite distracted during the service and paying little attention to the reading or singing. Towards the left of the painting, in front of the reader, are two standing children who are also concerned with the dog at their feet. One child, a boy, has the dog on a leash while the other child, a girl, is feeding something to the dog. Children are not the only ones distracted. A group of women seated to the right of the reader, just to the left of the reader on the canvas, are in noticeable conversation with one another. One woman is bent over whispering into another woman's ear, while another two women have their faces turned directly towards each other and appear quite unaware of anything other than their own conversation. Similarly, two men just behind these women are standing and also facing each other, likely in conversation themselves.

What Sibilla's painting portrays, then, is a church service that is only somewhat orderly. Notably, the service is well attended and the vast majority of people are paying quite close attention. Nonetheless, Sibilla's painting also displays several instances where people are distracted or disrupting the service. In fact, he deliberately makes these scenes noticeable and prominent in his painting. The overall sense in Sibilla's painting is that the church service was, for the most, part pious and respectable; however, not all people were interested in the service and some, instead, were quite unconcerned with the happenings of the service.

Overall, what these four paintings portray is, with a few notable exceptions, a well ordered and well observed sermon service, along with some very human touches. However, such a reality is not in line with what was previously observed in the provincial synod records. In this chapter attention will be given to an ecclesiastical body directly beneath the provincial synod–the Dutch classis. By

Figure 4: Gijsbert Janszoon Sibilla, *Dutch Reformed Service in the Grote Kerk in Weesp*, 1635. © Museum Catharijnecovnent, Utrecht.

examining these classes' records this chapter will demonstrate that Sunday services were not the ideal picture portrayed in the Dutch paintings but were, instead, filled with disruptions, poorly attended, and often disregarded for other Sunday activities. Indeed, the Sabbath in the sixteenth and seventeenth centuries was far from the harmonious ideal the religious authorities had in mind even as the classes attempted to enforce their strict desires for a holy Sunday observance.

Introduction to Dutch Classes

In the Dutch Reformed Church polity of the sixteenth and seventeenth centuries the local church and its consistory were the most elementary institutional form. As mentioned in the previous chapter, provincial synods, while technically less broad than national synods, often functioned as the highest ecclesiastical meetings in the Dutch Reformed Church. In between these provincial synods and the local consistory, so to speak, were the regional classes meetings. As mentioned in the previous chapter, the Dutch classis had its equivalent in other Reformed traditions and was largely similar to the Scottish presbytery and the French colloquy.

In this chapter the focus will be on the frequency, types, and results of Sabbath complaints in a number of Dutch Reformed classes. The classes' records examined in this chapter are those published in the Rijks Geschiedkundige Publicatien Series, Series 49 of the overall series which contains nine volumes of classes' records.[8] These classes' records cover nineteen different Dutch classes over nearly a half century from 1573 to 1620. The various classes are located in the provinces of Holland, Zeeland, Overijseel, and Gelderland and, therefore, provide a respectable representation of the seven provinces of the Dutch Republic. Unfortunately, the provinces of Friesland, Groningen, and Utrecht are unrepresented. This is even more unfortunate because Friesland and Groningen are the northernmost two provinces in the Dutch Republic. If these classes were included an even fuller picture of how Dutch classes dealt with the Sabbath could be given. However, such undertaking, no matter how worthy, is far beyond the scope of this project. Even so, the wealth of information available in these volumes is immense, yet very few scholars have used them in any depth, part of the problem being their relative lack of availability.

Several works have paid close attention to these classes' records, and the results have been extremely fruitful. Most famously, Wouters and Abels' two volumes on the classis of Delft and Delfland, *Nieuw en ongezien: kerk en samenleving in de classis Delft en Delfland 1572–1621*, draw heavily on the classes' records, and the result is a work that, as one scholar puts it, "will no doubt be the last word on the early history of the Reformed Church in Delft for many years to come."[9] John Paul Elliot's examination of Classis Dordrecht in his doctoral

---

8 The Instituut voor Nederlandse Geschiedenis (ING) originally published this smaller series with the Huygen Instituut voor Nederlandse Geschiedenis publishing the ninth volume following the merging of the ING with the Huygens Instituut. J.P. Van Dooren, ed., *Classicale acta, 1573–1620: particuliere synode Zuid-Holland*, Volume 1, 1980; J. Roelevink, ed., *Particuliere Synode Zuid-Holland: Classis Dordrecht 1601–1620, Classis Breda 1616–1620*, Volume 2, Den Haag: Instituut voor Nederlandse Geschiedenis, 1991; J. Bouterse, ed., *Particuliere Synode Zuid-Holland: Classis Rotterdam en Schieland 1580–1620*, Volume 3, Den Haag: Instituut voor Nederlandse Geschiedenis, 1991; J. Bouterse, ed., *Provinciale synode Zeeland, Classis Walcheren 1601–1620, Classis Zuid-Beveland 1579–1591*, Volume 4, Den Haag: Instituut voor Nederlandse Geschiedenis, 1995; M. Kok, ed., *Provinciale synode Zuid-Holland: Classis Leiden 1585–1620, Classis Woerden 1617–1620*, Volume 5, Den Haag: Instituut voor Nederlandse Geschiedenis, 1996; J. van Gelderen and C. Ravensbergen, eds., *Provinciale synode Overijssel: Classis Deventer 1601–1620, Classis Kampen 1596–1601 en 1618–1620, Classis Steenwijk/Vollenhove 1601–1620*, Volume 6, Den Haag: Instituut voor Nederlandse Geschiedenis, 2000; P. H. A. M. Abels and A. Ph. F. Wouters, eds., *Provinciale synode Zuid-Holland: Classis Delft en Delfland 1572–1620*, Volume 7, Den Haag: Instituut voor Nederlandse Geschiedenis, 2001; A.J. Verschoor, ed., *Classis Gorinchem 1579–1620*, Volume 8, Den Haag: Instituut voor Nederlandse Geschiedenis, 2008; C. Ravensbergen, ed., *Provinciale synode Gelderland. Bd. 1. Classis Nijmegen 1598–1620. Classis Tiel/Bommel 1606–1613. Classis Tiel 1613–1620. Classis Bommel 1614–1620. Bd. 2. Classis Zutphen 1593–1620. Classis Over-Veluwe (Arnhem) 1598–1620. Classis Neder-Veluwe (Harderwijk) 1592–1620*, Volume 9, Den Haag: Huygens ING, 2012. In what follows the works will be cited as follows: Editor, *Classicale Acta*, Vol. [Number], Page [Number].

9 Christine Kooi, Review of *Nieuw en ongezien: kerk en samenleving in de classis Delft en*

dissertation also pays close attention to the classes' records and, as a result, provides fascinating insights into the religious and social life of Dordrecht and the surrounding region.[10] The records of Dutch classes are a wonderful way to gain deeper insights into the religious life of local religious communities while also allowing one to gauge the concerns of local religious authorities.

The classis was an extremely important aspect of Dutch Reformed church polity.[11] Cornelis van den Broeke has carried out the most comprehensive investigation of the classis in the Dutch Reformed tradition. His doctoral dissertation, later published in book form, spans a number of centuries, but the chapters on the early modern period are most helpful. Broeke traces the origins of the Dutch classis model back to the 1568 Convent of Wesel and 1571 Synod of Emden.[12] Subsequent synods affirmed the structure of the Dutch classis, and the classis model found its definitive structure with the approval of the Synod of Dort. As Broeke notes, the Dutch classis was to meet four times per year and was to be composed of ministers and elders. Each consistory was to send one minister and one elder to classis meetings. Consistories were to select their own delegates to each classis meeting. Deacons were not included, and if a consistory had more than one minister all ministers could be sent as voting members. However, elders were clearly of less importance than the ministers and often were not included at all.[13]

At each classis meeting, after opening prayer, a president and a secretary were chosen. The president was required to be a minister, but the clerk could be either a minister or elder, though elders were rarely appointed. After the elections of a president and clerk, the minutes of the previous meeting were read and approved, and the classis followed up with any items from the previous meeting that had required action. Then, the classis, at the president's discretion, examined a variety of topics, including the oversight of consistories, supervision of the Reformed schools, and any help particular congregations needed. After those issues were addressed, a minister gave a sermon followed by discussion of that sermon. Before closing, plans were made for the following classis and a time of self-discipline, *censura morum*, was held.[14]

While national synods and provincial synods made significant decisions regarding the overall direction of the Dutch Reformed Church, the classis was the

---

Delfland 1572–1621, eds. A. Ph. F. Wouters and P. H. A. M. Abels, *The Sixteenth Century Journal* 27, no. 2 (Summer, 1996), 532–533.

10 See above: "Introduction," Note 22.

11 Selderhuis, *Handbook of Dutch Church History*, 240; Van Duersen, *Bavianen en Slijkgeuzen*, 20–24.

12 Van den Broeke, *Een Geschiedenis van de Classis*, 62–66.

13 Van den Broeke, *Een Geschiedenis van de Classis*, 534–535.

14 Rutgers, *Acta*, 105–109; Van den Broeke, *Een Geschiedenis van de Classis*, 535.

ecclesiastical body that was directly responsible for the spiritual health and well-being of a region. The renowned Arie van Deursen was certainly correct in characterizing the Dutch church as a "composition of classical relationships."[15] The classis was in a unique position with advantages neither the national or provincial synods nor the local consistories had. The classis was distanced enough from individual churches to be able to resolve issues consistories could not handle on their own. In this way, the classis had an authority the consistory did not.

On the other hand, while the classes' authority did not match that of the provincial or national synods, the classes dealt with local issues in a way these greater synods typically did not. Local churches, via their consistories, were to send their own concerns or any topics they wanted classis to address at each meeting. Indeed, much of the classes' records are filled with concerns and questions the individual churches had. For instance, in 1589 the church in Vlaardingen sought the help of classis relating to an issue about how a certain member of their church should be disciplined. Should they announce his name from the pulpit, or could they withhold his name in order to keep from publically shaming him?[16] Similarly, in 1595 the church in Schipluiden complained to the classis about a certain woman in its congregation. This woman was questioning why certain people who were sorry for their sins were not allowed to participate in the Lord's Supper. The classis answered that such a person as the woman they described will "not be allowed to stay [in the congregation]," but that they should warn her and pray for her.[17]

Thus, in a manner similar to the provincial synods of the previous chapter, the agendas of the regional classes were also largely determined from lower ecclesiastical bodies, namely the local consistories. The classes' records make clear that this was frequently how Sabbath concerns came before the classis. A few examples will help elucdiate the process. The church in Hillegerberg, called Heijlgersberch in the records, was dealing with "drinking [alcohol] during the preaching" and requested help from their classis, Classis Rotterdam. The classis resolved to send Franciscus Lansbergius and Christophorus Hellerus, along with Hillegerberg's pastor Jacobus Bonteballio, to remedy the situation.[18] Such an instance was not unique. In 1610 the consistories of churches in Walcheren, Schouwen, and South-Beveland all sent gravamina to Classis Walcheren about all sorts of Sabbath desecration.[19] Similarly, churches from the towns of Nootdorp and Wilsveen both petitioned Classis Delft regarding Sunday afternoon cate-

---

15 Van Deursen, *Bavianen en slijkgeuzen*, 20.
16 Abels and Wouters, *Classicale Acta*, Vol. 7, 60.
17 Abels and Wouters, *Classicale Acta*, Vol. 7, 159.
18 Bouterse, *Classicale Acta*, Vol. 3, 392.
19 Bouterse, *Classicale Acta*, Vol. 4, 165–167.

chism services.[20] Typically the requests come from a church consistory as a whole. More rarely, the request comes from a particular pastor frustrated with Sabbath observance in his congregation. Petrus Paludanus was pastor of Giessen-Nieuwkerk and complained about the Sabbath profanation in his congregation and his inability to do anything about it. Classis Dordrecht sent two pastors, Johannes Boccardus and Johannes Celossa, to help remedy the situation.[21] Antipas Levini van den Borre had a similar situation in his congregation in Ottoland; he complained to the classis about his difficulties getting cooperation from the town sheriff.[22] In all these cases, in typical fashion, the complaints about Sabbath observance came from the lived religious experience, albeit of pastors and consistories, of individual Dutch Reformed churches and their members. When the issues could not be adequately resolved at the local consistorial level, appeals were made to the more authoritative regional classes.

The classis, then, was in a unique and important position within the Dutch Reformed Church. The classis held authority that could give help and direction to consistories who needed advice or their problems resolved. At the same time, because the concerns the classis dealt with arose from local consistories, the classes also dealt with issues that were relevant to local situations. Indeed, the consistories themselves were able to raise the issues they were dealing with in their congregations at classis meetings. As such, examining the classes' records can provide insights into the religious life of a given region and is crucial for properly understanding the religious situation in the Dutch Reformed Church as a whole. In fact, the classes' records can portray what the local consistories wanted the regional classes to address. As this chapter will argue, the observance of the Sabbath was a topic that consistories frequently needed addressed at the regional classis meetings.

Yet, the classes' records do, of course, have limitations and weaknesses. As with all church records, the classis notary is the one recording the proceedings and, as such, can edit or filter the issues being discussed or even how the discussion or decision proceeded. In addition, because the classes' records deal with a region of churches the records do not frequently deal with individual cases. There are instances in which individuals or particular situations are addressed directly, but such cases are the exception rather than the rule. Thus, the classes' records still do not portray the lived religious life of individual Dutch Reformed church members the way the modern reader might hope. Nonetheless, if used carefully and with these limitations in view, the classes' records can provide

---

20 Abels and Wouters, *Classicale Acta*, Vol. 7, 54.
21 Roelevink, *Classicale Acta*, Vol. 2, 789.
22 Roelevink, *Classicale Acta*, Vol. 2, 542.

insights into the lives of Dutch Reformed congregants and into the concerns and desires of the religious authorities. Such will be the approach of this chapter.

Frequency of Sabbath Complaints

Dutch classes were extremely varied in how frequently they convened. Ideally, each classis was to meet quarterly. However, many classes averaged far fewer meetings. It was not uncommon for entire years to be skipped, and frequently a classis met only once per year. On the other hand, several classes were prone to meeting more often than four times per year. Some classes consistently met over ten times per year. Not surprisingly, large classes or classes with large cities typically met much more frequently than smaller or more rural classes. Classis Dordrecht, for instance, averaged between six and seven meetings per year. Other classes, such as Classis Rotterdam and Classis Delft, averaged even more meetings per year. These classes also met consistently throughout the years, rarely missing a meeting and virtually never going a year without a meeting.

Other classes met much less frequently. For example, Classis Deventer met only thirty-four times over twenty years (an average of 1.7 meetings per year), and they went five of those twenty years without meeting at all. Similarly, Classis Tiel-Bommel met only twelve times over eight years; Classis Nijmegen met roughly twice a year over twenty-three years; Classis Over-Veluwe met only thirty times over twenty-three years. These smaller classes were also much more likely than the larger classes to go a year, or even a series of years, without meeting at all.

Sabbath complaints at these regional classes meetings were also somewhat varied. A few general observations can be made initially, particularly related to the Sabbath complaints of the provincial synods. First, the regional classes raised the issue of Sabbath observance at a much lower percentage of their gatherings than the provincial synods. The large number of classes meetings compared to relatively few meetings of provincial synod meetings easily explains the discrepancy. Because provincial synods met less frequently, the Sabbath concerns occurred at a high percentage of the meetings. On the other hand, because classis meetings were so numerous, Sabbath complaints were lodged at a lower percentage of those meetings. Second, when the regional classes did raise such concerns, they were often more detailed than the somewhat formulaic complaints of the provincial synods. Again, this is likely due to the nature of the particular governing bodies. Because regional classes were more local bodies, they tended to deal with more specific issues. Provincial synods, on the other hand, were dealing with more generalized problems facing a large number of churches.

Just how frequent were Sabbath complaints at the regional classes? Again, the answer varies widely depending on the individual classis. Calculating the frequency of complaints can be done in two separate ways, either as the percentage of years Sabbath complaints arise out of the total years a classis met or as the percentage of meetings Sabbath complaints occur out of the total meetings a classis had. Because many years had multiple meetings the percentage of meetings that contained Sabbath complaints is quite low.[23]

In several cases, Sabbath complaints were lodged at only a fraction of the total classis meetings. For instance, in Classis Rotterdam Sabbath complaints occurred in only 2.33 % of all the meetings held. Of all classes that have Sabbath complaints, Sabbath complaints were lowest in Classis Leiden with complaints being lodged at only 1.59 % of the total meetings. With similarly low numbers, Classis Zuid-Beveland had Sabbaths complaints at only 2.74 % of their meetings; Classis Delft had complaints at 3.23 % of their meetings; Classis Walcheren recorded complaints in 3.50 % of their meetings; and Classis Gorinchem registered Sabbath complaints at 4.24 % of their meetings. In fact, two classes, Classis Breda and Classis Werden, recorded no complaints about the Sabbath in their meetings, though each classis met for only five and four years, respectively.

On the higher end of the spectrum, several classes had Sabbath complaints at roughly one-third to one-half of all meetings. The highest percentage was in Classis Tiel, where complaints occured 42.86 % of the time. Prior to their classis splitting, the joint Classis Tiel-Bommel had complaints at 33.33 % of their meetings. The sample sizes for these classes are somewhat small as Classis Tiel-Bommel had only twelve total meetings, and Classis Tiel had only fourteen total meetings. Classis Bommel had Sabbath complaints at 29.17 % of their meetings. Classis Bommel had slightly higher numbers with twenty-four meetings, providing for a more indicative percentage. Sabbath complaints also occurred at 36.66 % of Classis Over-Veluwe's thirty total meetings.

The majority of classes had rates of Sabbath complaints at somewhere between 10 % and 25 % of their meetings. Classis Dordrecht fell just under those levels with complaints at 8.31 % of their meetings. Classes with complaint rates between 10 %–20 % include Classis Steenwijk-Vollenhove (14.58 %), Classis Deventer (17.65 %), and Classis Kampen (15.79 %). Finally, classes with complaints at their meetings ranging from 20 %–25 % of the time include Classis Nijmegen (21.74 %), Classis Nede-Veluwe (21.43 %), and Classis Zutphen (20.45 %).

The frequency of Sabbath complaints is very closely related to the number of total meetings a particular classis had. Those classes with higher numbers of meetings typically had Sabbath complaints at a low percentage of their meetings. Classes with few meetings generally had Sabbath complaints at a higher per-

---

23 The following figures are, of course, based on my own calculations.

centage of their meetings, and classes with an average number of meetings had Sabbath complaints that fell somewhere in the middle of the spectrum.

Not surprisingly, the rates of Sabbath complaints based on the percentage of years, not meetings, were significantly higher. Other than the two classes with no complaints, the lowest rate was found in Classis Leiden, where complaints were found in only two of the twenty-seven years, totaling 7.41 %. Classis Zuid-Beveland, where the classis met thirteen years and a Sabbath complaint occurred in only one year, had a similarly low rate, equaling 7.69 %. Classis Rotterdam's yearly percentage was also quite low at 12.20 %. However, several classes had Sabbath complaints in a much higher percentage of the years in which they met. For example, Classis Tiel met eight different years and had complaints in six of those years, totally 62.50 %. A number of classes had Sabbath complaints in roughly 30 %–50 % of the years the classes met. Classis Over-Veluwe had Sabbath complaints in 47.83 % of the total years they met. Also included in this range are Classis Nijmegen (42.86 %), Classis Bommel (42.96 %), Classis Kampen (37.50 %), Classis Zutphen (32 %), and Classis Neder-Veluwe (32.14 %). Other classes had lower rates with Sabbath complaints somewhere between 15 %–30 % of the years the classis met. This category included Classis Dordrecht (29.17 %), Classis Walcheren (21.05 %), Classis Deventer (20 %), Classis Steenwijk/Vollenhove (25 %), and Classis Gorinchem (23.08 %).

As a whole, the rates of Sabbath complaints were much higher in classes that met less frequently. These classes also tended to be smaller classes in more rural areas. These classes, such as Classis Tiel-Bommel, Classis Zutphen, or Classis Over-Veluwe, had fewer administrative sorts of concerns than larger, more urban classes, such as Classis Delft, Classis Rotterdam, or Classis Dordrecht. Perhaps the lack of Sabbath complaints in several of the larger classes can be attributed to an already full plate, so to speak. In other words, larger, urban classes had other issues to deal with, many simply regarding administration, and were not able to address Sabbath concerns overly frequently. Conversely, the smaller classes were able to address Sabbath observance more frequently because they simply had more time and opportunity to do so.

Whether or not Sabbath complaints should be regarded as frequent in the Dutch classes' records depends largely on definitions. What, exactly, constitutes frequent mentioning of the Sabbath? How often do Sabbath complaints need to be lodged to demonstrate a serious concern about Sabbath observance on the part of the classes? The parameters no doubt are a matter of interpretation. Nonetheless, a few observations are in order. First, the frequency of complaints suggests that Dutch classes did have concerns about Sabbath desecration. The fact is that the vast majority of classes raise the Sabbath issue at least occasionally. The very existence of Sabbath complaints at the classes meetings signals that the topic was deemed worthy of attention. In addition, when the classes do mention the Sabbath they are clearly concerned with attempting to remedy whatever the problem is deemed to be.

At the same time, the classes evidently did not see the need to attend to Sabbath complaints at every meeting; far from it, in fact. Sabbath complaints certainly did not dominate the various classes' meetings. As shown above, a number of classes hardly ever mentioned the Sabbath, and two classes made no mention of it at all. Indeed, in those classes where the Sabbath complaints were most frequent, the complaints never were lodged at more than half the meetings and never in more than two-thirds of the years a classis met. Frankly, one must be careful not to overstate the case of how frequent Sabbath concerns arose in the classes' records.

So, what is needed is a balanced view of how to interpret the classes' concerns with the Sabbath in light of the frequency of complaints. It is, of course, overly simplistic to determine the importance of the Sabbath to the classes simply based on rates the issue arises. But, the frequency of complaints is helpful in at least proving that the classes viewed the Sabbath as an important aspect of their churches' piety. Certainly, devotion to the Sabbath was not the classes' only, or even primary, concern, and the low rate at which certain classes raised Sabbath concerns indicates that they often had more pressing issues to address. At the same time, a number of classes spent a significant amount of time addressing Sabbath concerns. Even those classes with fewer mentions of the Sabbath took time at their meetings to raise the issue of Sabbath desecration and seek solutions for such desecration.

Also helpful for interpreting the frequency of Sabbath complaints in the classes' records is understanding how the complaints came before the classis. Often times the classis as a whole addressed the situation of the Sabbath in the churches; in these cases it is not immediately clear how the issue was raised.[24] Other times individual churches raised the issue of Sabbath observance.[25] Here the individual churches were typically dealing with an issue relating to Sabbath observance or simply saw the need for better Sunday practices throughout the Dutch churches. What does not show up in the classes' records are cases where individuals are appealing the ways in which they have been disciplined for Sabbath desecration. The classes were not apt to deal with individual cases of Sabbath desecration, and individuals did not bring their particular concerns regarding Sabbath observance before the classes. As such, the Sabbath concerns raised in the classes appear to be issues the church authorities believed needed to

---

24 Van Dooren, *Classicale Acta*, Vol. 1, 153; Kok, *Classicale Acta*, Vol. 5, 3; Abels and Wouters, *Classicale Acta*, Vol. 7, 61; Verschoor, *Classicale Acta*, Vol. 8, 46.
25 Roelevink, *Classicale Acta*, Vol. 2, 524, 708; Abels and Wouters, *Classicale Acta*, Vol. 7, 54; Ravensbergen, *Classicale Acta*, Vol. 8, 31.

be addressed. It was either the concensus of the whole classis or individual churches within the classis that would typically raise the issue of the Sabbath. The religious authorities, either consistories or classes delegates, were the ones, then, who brought concerns about the Sabbath to the fore at classis meetings.

In sum, in strictly terms of frequency, the Sabbath was not an overwhelming issue for most Dutch classes, but neither was it an unimportant complaint lodged in only a few classes. Rather, concern for the Sabbath was something most classes had, and they were willing to raise the issue of Sabbath desecration at least occasionally in hopes of creating greater devotion to the Sabbath among their congregations.

Types of Sabbath Complaints

Given that Sabbath complaints are found in the classes' records, what were the complaints about, exactly? Complaints about Sabbath desecration took a wide variety of forms.[26] Many of the complaints followed the pattern found in the provincial synod records. As will be shown in what follows, the classes' concerns regarding the Sabbath fall into four main categories: problems regarding worship or church attendance; immoral behaviors on Sunday more generally; improper activities, including recreation and the holding of markets; and working on Sundays, during worship or otherwise.

Worship and Church Attendance

Worship services were of primary importance for Dutch classes. Attendance at Sunday services was expected, and any absence from these services was seen as a problem. From the classes' perspective, far too many people were absent from worship services on Sundays. The classes were very concerned with those who were absent from worship services and engaged in other activities. Notably, it was not just immoral or disruptive activities that were disallowed during the Sunday worship services. For example, Classis Rotterdam-Schieland sought to forbid "riding in carriages and sailing on boats," two recreational activities, during the preaching on Sundays.[27] Absence from the worship services was not acceptable

---

26 The translations of all quotes taken from the classes' records are solely my own. Because the volumes are not readily available, I have included in the footnotes the quotations as found in the cited volumes.

27 Bouterse, *Classicale Acta*, Vol. 3, 215. "Dat ordre mochte ghestelt worden tot verbiedinghe van 't rijden ende varen, met waghenen ende schuijten des sondaegs onder den predicacien ende voornaemlijck op den ghemeijnen vast- ende bidtdaghen."

even if the activities engaged in during the services were otherwise harmless. The classes did not allow recreation during the worship services precisely because it kept people from attending the services.

Of course, engaging in immoral and frivolous behavior rather than attending worship services was a grave concern for the classes. Particularly concerning were the immoral behaviors people participated in while services were being conducted and during the preaching, *onder die predicatie*. Classis Gorinchem complained about the "druncken-drinking" that took place during the preaching.[28] That same complaint goes on to mention the "playing in the churchyards, dancing, dance schools, [and] preparing of food during the preaching."[29] Similarly, Classis Nijmegen lamented the profanation of the Sabbath with "rash things, such as shooting clay pigeons, tapping and drinking in the garden during the preaching."[30] Classis Dordrecht also complained of "the clay pigeon-shooting, *balslaen* [a game similar to *kaatsen*], *kaatsen*, dancing, playing instruments, drunk-drinking, holding auctions, playing court games, et cetera" that took place "during the preaching."[31]

Disruptions during the church services was also a continual problem. Classis Dordrecht complained of the disorder "on Sundays during the preaching and church services."[32] These disruptions were of all different sorts but included walking around, chatting or gossiping, dancing, and playing games. Classis Walcheren covered a number of offenses when they complained about the "riding, going to play, *kaatsen*, bowling, opening taverns, drinking, et cetera."[33] Classis Tiel complained on multiple occasions about activities causing disorder and disruption during the preaching.[34]

---

28 Verschoor, *Classicale Acta,* Vol. 8, 46. "prophanatien des sondachs, mit droncken drencken oeck onder die praedicatie...."

29 Verschoor, *Classicale Acta,* Vol. 8, 46. "mit speelen op den kerckhoofven, danssen, danschoelen, vergaderinge der gerechten onder die praedicatie."

30 Ravensbergen, *Classicale Acta,* Vol. 9, 72. "maer oock met anderen lichtvaerdigen dingen, als clootschieten, tappen ende drincken in de herbergen onder die predicatie wert geprophaneert...."

31 Roelevink, *Classicale Acta,* Vol. 2, 711. "met clootschieten, balslaen, kaetsen, danssen, op instrumenten spelen, droncken drincken, boelhuys houden, gerechtssaecken plegen etcetera."

32 Van Dooren, *Classicale Acta,* Vol. 1, 59. "der unordnung halven, die ahm sohndaghe onder predicatie ende godtzdienst."

33 Bouterse, *Classicale Acta,* Vol. 4, 165–67. "alsoo dezelve byna allomme in steden ende ten plattenlande gemeyn is in ryden, speelegaen, caetsen, bollen, taveernen oopenen, drincken, etcetera."

34 Ravensbergen, *Classicale Acta,* Vol. 9, 312; "Alsoo in veele plaetsen groote abusen voorvallen met tappen, drincken, varen ende klappen onder die predicatie." Ravensbergen, *Classicale Acta,* Vol. 9, 315. "Iss van D. Isaaco dem classi vorgestelt, begerende datt van den broederen der kercken te Tyll aen den Edelen heeren van Zoelen versocht werde om door die bequaemste

Church attendance at afternoon services appeared to be a particularly sensitive topic for several classes. These afternoon services were meant, primarily, for catechism preaching. These services were not well attended, and such was the case even more so in the rural areas where people were not apt to want to travel to church twice on one day. Classis Deventer was having difficulty establishing afternoon preaching services where the "fitting and edifying" catechism would be preached.[35] Classis Dordrecht included the "afternoon preaching" in its complaint about the profanation of the Sabbath.[36] Classis Zutphen complained that a "frivolous woman" was permitted to run her kitchen during the afternoon preaching.[37] For the Dutch classes Sundays were meant for public, communal worship, and this included morning and afternoon services. Any sort of absence from or disruption of these services was a profanation of what the Sabbath was intended to be.

Immoral Behavior

Immoral behavior was a concern of the classes regardless of when it took place, but such events taking place on the Sabbath were especially troublesome. Drinking alcohol was a particularly frequent complaint. As already mentioned above, sometimes the drinking offenses occurred during the preaching. Classis Over-Veluwe complained about the "tapping and drinking of brandy-wine" that occurred "during the preaching."[38] Classis Nijmegen had the same complaint at their 1608 classis meeting when they complained of the "tapping and drinking in the inns during the preaching."[39] Classis Delft's complaint was a little different in that the people were not only drinking during the preaching but were "sitting in the taverns drinking."[40]

---

middelen het tappen, voeren end andersins alle ongeregeltheitt des sonnendags onder praedicatien."
35 Van Gelderen and Ravensbergen, *Classicale Acta,* Vol. 6, 67. "Also die namiddaghspredicatie des categismus ten plattenlande so bequaemlijck ende stichtelijck niet can angevangen worden als 't behoort."
36 Roelevink, *Classicale Acta,* Vol. 2, 764. "De namiddaechsche predicatien ende weeringhe van alle profanatien des sabaths volgens art."
37 Ravensbergen, *Classicale Acta,* Vol. 9, 498. "also dat de koechlers end desgelicken lichtverdige personen vergunt wort haere koechelijn under des namiddags predicatie ock in den rae-thuyseren te drijven."
38 Ravensbergen, *Classicale Acta,* Vol. 9, 659. "groot misbruick gespuert door tappen ende brandewijn drincken onder die predicatie."
39 Ravensbergen, *Classicale Acta,* Vol. 9, 72. "tappen ende drincken in de herbergen onder die predicatie wert geprophaneert."
40 Abels and Wouters, *Classicale Acta,* Vol. 7, 55. "onder de predicatie sitten drincken in de tavaernen."

But, drinking was not simply a problem during the preaching and the church services. The records again and again complain of drinking alcohol and frequenting taverns throughout the day on Sunday. Classis Nijmegen noted in 1598 the "tapping and drinking happening in the taverns."[41] Classis Walcheren mentioned that, among a host of other activities, the "opening of taverns, [and] drinking, et cetera" were desecrating the Sabbath.[42]

Complaints of other immoral behaviors on Sundays could include any number of activities. In 1610, in addition to drinking, Classis Walcheren lamented dancing and fighting taking place on the Sabbaths.[43] Classis Neder-Veluwe also complained of the "carousing and fighting" taking place that desecrated the Sabbaths, preaching, and church services.[44] Dancing, a morally questionable activity, was also a complaint the classes had.[45] For instance, one of the items Classis Gorinchem complained about was "dancing and dance schools" that were profaning the Sundays.[46] While dancing was typically a folk activity, the mention of "dance schools" seems to indicate the participation of the upper class. Similarly, Classis Delft included dancing in their complaints about the disordered nature of Sundays.[47] Sexual offenses were also mentioned occasionally, such as when Classis Dordrecht complained about the "debauchery and whoredom" found on Sundays and during the preaching.[48] This rampant immorality was never acceptable to the classes, but the presence of immorality on a day that was supposed to be dedicated to the Lord was particularly offensive and needed serious attention.

---

41 Ravensbergen, *Classicale Acta,* Vol. 9, 4. "tappen ende drincken in den tavernen geschyet."

42 Bouterse, *Classicale Acta,* Vol. 4, 165. "an de ontheyliginghe des sabbaths, alsoo dezelve byna allomme in steden ende ten plattenlande gemeyn is in ryden, speelegaen, caetsen, bollen, taveernen oopenen, drincken, etcetera."

43 Bouterse, *Classicale Acta,* Vol. 4, 166. "Item alle sabbathsbreucke door drincken, caetsen, danssen, vechten etcetera, daervan onse kercken groote clachten hebben."

44 Ravensbergen, *Classicale Acta,* Vol. 9, 854. "hetwelck daer grote inconvenienten, abusen, lichtveerdigheyt, suyperije ende gevechten, mitssgaders prophanatie ende verstoringe van sabbaten, predicatien ende godessdienst."

45 Van Dooren, *Classicale Acta,* Vol. 1, 711; Bouterse, *Classicale Acta,* Vol. 4, 165-7; Abels and Wouters, *Classicale Acta,* Vol. 7, 55, 120, 153, 179; Ravensbergen, *Classicale Acta,* Vol. 9, 903.

46 Verschoor, *Classicale Acta,* Vol. 8, 46. "prophanatien des sondachs, mit droncken drencken oeck onder die praedicatie, mit speelen op den kerckhoofven, danssen, danschoelen, vergaderinge der gerechten onder die praedicatie."

47 Abels and Wouters, *Classicale Acta,* Vol. 7, 61. "sondach vast in alle plaetsen onser classe ende met namen ten plattenlande noch zeer ontheilicht werdt met drincken, spelen, dansen ende andere ongeregeltheit."

48 Van Dooren, *Classicale Acta,* Vol. 1, 59. "die ahm sohndaghe onder predicatie ende godtzdienst, nicht allein mit wercken ende arbeiden maer ock mit allerlei untucht ende hoerdoem, drunckenschap, dobbelen, dantzen ende andere lichtverdigheidt."

Improper Activities

The classes' records also repeatedly mentioned a number of other activities that people were doing on the Sabbath. Some of these activities were certainly viewed as immoral, but other activities seem much less harmful. Many of these activities were those complained about in the provincial synods and mentioned in the previous chapter. Such activities included the aforementioned *kaatsen* and rhetoric games (*rhetoryckspelen*). These "rhetoric games" quite certainly refer to the popular Chambers of Rhetoric found throughout the Low Countries.[49] These acting groups were extremely popular and would perform a wide variety of stage plays (*Spelen van Sinne*). It was these groups and the plays they performed that the classes complained were desecrating the Sabbath. In addition, activities such as shooting, physical fighting, and all others sorts of "insolence" were also raised.

One of the most frequent specific complaints the classes' records mentioned was the holding of markets on the Sabbath and the accompanying buying and selling. One particular incident involved Classis Over-Veluwe. At its first classis meeting of 1598 the records mentioned that, "One also still finds great profanation of the sabbaths."[50] The records go on to describe that "in particular, in Nijckercken the weekly markets are held during the preaching."[51] Even more discouraging for the classis was that the situation stood no chance of being remedied unless the municipal government decided to hold the markets on another day of the week, a solution the classis was going to seek.

Classis Neder-Veluwe seemed equally as disturbed when it noted the "great profanation of the Sundays" with "buying and selling."[52] In particular, the town of Nieckerck (present-day Nijkerk) was a trouble spot. On Sundays during the preaching Nieckerck held their "great market" and all sorts of people attended. In fact, the records complained, "with all honesty, all the surrounding villages do their best to come to the market."[53] The classis seemed rather pessimistic about

---

49 The Chambers of Rhetoric have been well studied. See, for instace, Elsa Strietman and Peter Happe', eds., *Urban Theatre in the Low Countries, 1400–1625*, Turnhout: Brepols, 2006; Gary Waite, *Reformers On Stage: Popular Drama and Propaganda in the Low Countries of Charles V, 1515–1556*, Toronot: University of Toronto Press, 2000; Joke Spaans, "Public opinion or ritual celebration of concord?: politics, religion and society in the competition between the Chambers of rhetoric at Vlaardingen, 1616," in *Public Opinion and Changing Identities in the Early Modern Netherlands*, 189–209.

50 Ravensbergen, *Classicale Acta*, Vol. 9, 789. "Mann befindt oick noch grote profanatie des sabbaths."

51 Ravensbergen, *Classicale Acta*, Vol. 9, 789. "insonderheit dat tu Nijckercken onder die praedicatie weckenmarckt gehouden werdt...."

52 Ravensbergen, *Classicale Acta*, Vol. 9, 810. "Dewijle grote prophanatie des sonnendages gespuert werdt doer het copen ende vercopen."

53 Ravensbergen, *Classicale Acta*, Vol. 9, 810. "Aldaer op sonnendachs onder de predick een

its ability to put an end to the market, noting only that "the synod therein will remedy as much as possible."

The "buying and selling" on Sundays was a serious problem the classes tried to combat. Complaints about buying and selling, *kopen en verkopen*, on Sundays were very frequent in the classes' records. These complaints were, naturally, often associated with the weekly markets, but the complaints about buying and selling are also often connected with complaints about shops being open on Sundays. Classis Gorinchem noted the violation of the Sabbath days with selling and shops being open.[54] In the classes' views, shops being open on Sunday not only led to people engaging in commerce but also required people to work on the day of rest. As a result, stores and shops were to be closed on Sundays in addition to the prohibition on the weekly markets.

The classes' records demonstrated a particularly serious concern for Sabbath offenses in the rural areas, the *platten lande*. Repeatedly, the classes' records noted complaints about Sabbath desecrations in the rural lands. Complaints about Sabbath keeping in the rural areas were also lodged in the provincial synods, as shown in the previous chapter. It is safe to conclude, then, that Reformed Christians in the rural areas were especially prone to violating the Sabbath.

A number of complaints can be found regarding the rural areas. Some of the complaints were quite general. For instance, in 1589 Classis Gorinchem complained of all sorts of games being played on the Sabbath in addition to the markets that were being held.[55] However, other complaints are much more specific. Classis Nijmegen, in the province of Gelderland, complained that there were many unregulated activities in the "churchyard in the villages of the rural areas, with clay pigeon shooting, *kaatsen*, gossiping, buying from merchants, [and] tapping and drinking happening in the taverns."[56] On two occasions Classis Over-Veluwe also mentioned the rural areas and the "exorbitant" abuse of the Sabbath in those places, including "working, drinking, shooting," and other offenses.[57]

---

groote marckt werdt geholden daer alle omliggende dorpen met alleley waer, beesten ende alles anders toe marckt koemen, dat der synodus daerin wolle sovoel moegelick remedieren."

54 Verschoor, *Classicale Acta*, Vol. 8, 504. "Ende het violeren van de sabbathdagen door vercopen, winckelhouden, optrecken en teeren van schutteryen."

55 Verschoor, *Classicale Acta*, Vol. 8, 46. "Besonder ten plattenlanden merct houden, schermspeelen, guyschelspelen ende dergelycken, van kermissen, vastelavent ende battementspeelen, mommerien, kindermalen [ende] geeltbruyloften."

56 Ravensbergen, *Classicale Acta*, Vol. 9, 4. "Op ende omtrent die kerckhoven in de dorpen ten plattenlande, met clootschieten, catzen, clappen, copmanschappen, tappen ende drincken in den tavernen geschyet."

57 Ravensbergen, *Classicale Acta*, Vol. 9, 739. "Alsmede van die profanatie des sabbaths die daer geschiet doer des sondachs arbeiden, drincken klincken, schieten, schuttebieren, ganse-

Reasons as to why those in rural areas were more prone to Sabbath desecration than urban Christians were proposed in the previous chapter. As the provincial synods suggested, rural Christians were more reliant on market days being held on Sundays given the distance they had to travel. Church members were unlikely to want to travel to the market day in town on another day since they would already be traveling to town on Sunday to attend the church service. Additionally, rural Christians relied heavily on agriculture, an occupation that made it particularly tempting to work on the Sabbath. Even pious church members no doubt found it difficult to refrain from harvesting crops on Sundays when bad weather threatened to destroy their livelihoods.

The classes' records suggest another reason why Sabbath observance was more of a problem in rural areas. The records indicate that it was difficult for authorities to police Sabbath observance in rural areas. This was true for both the ecclesiastical and political authorities. Not surprisingly, rural areas were harder to oversee than urban areas. This was true for a variety of reasons, including travel difficulties, more sparsely populated locales, and time restraints. Without the close supervision of authorities, rural Christians were more able to do as they pleased on Sundays without fear of punishment. The classes' records from Classis Nijmegen, for example, reported that "the visits to the churches in the rural areas is almost impossible."[58] Visits to rural churches from ecclesiastical authorities could be difficult for any number of reasons, including issues such as travel, weather, and time commitments. Reformed Christians in rural areas, it appears, were abler than their urban brothers and sisters to keep the authorities in the dark regarding their Sabbath desecration.

But, it was not just rural areas that were engaged in improper activities on the Sabbaths. Classis Dordrecht noted that the profanation of Sundays was happening "in cities as in rural districts."[59] Classis Delft complained of disorder on the Sabbath in "all places in our classis" that included immoral activities such as drinking and dancing but also simply "playing."[60] Classis Gorinchem likewise complained of "men everywhere" who violated the Sabbath days with all forbidden activities such as shopping, shooting, and the activities of the Chambers

---

trecken ende andre exorbitantien op den plattenlande seer gebruicklick." Also, Vol. 9; 745. "Handelende van de prophanatie des sabbaths, te weeten door het arbeyden, drincken, klyncken, schieten, vaselavontsbieren, gansentrecken, knuppelen, papegaeyschieten, schutebieren, buegelen ende andre exorbitantien op den plattenlande seer gebruyckelijck."

58 Ravensbergen, *Classicale Acta*, Vol. 9, 72. "Is den visitatoribus classis belast: eerstelijck, de visitatie der kercken ten plattenlande soe haest het mogelijck is te verrichten."

59 Van Dooren, *Classicale Acta*, Vol. 1, 245. "De profanatie der zondagen ende bidtdagen in steden als ten platten lande."

60 Abels and Wouters, *Classicale Acta*, Vol. 7, 61. "Dat de sondach vast in alle plaetsen onser classe ende met namen ten plattenlande noch zeer ontheilicht werdt met drincken, spelen, dansen ende andere ongeregeltheit."

of Rhetoric.[61] Evidently, Dutch church members, both urban and rural, were interested in participating in all sorts of activities the Dutch classes deemed inappropriate for the Sabbath.

Working on the Sabbath

Working on the Sabbath was a problem the classes highlighted, but it is not a complaint that was found overly frequently.[62] The complaints were typically quite general in nature. For example, Classis Deventer complained of "working on Sundays, feast-and-prayer days."[63] Classis Nijmegen complained about people working on Sunday but also noted that it was "not only work" that was desecrating the Sabbath but other offenses as well.[64] In the classes' views one of the problems with working on the Sabbath was, not surprisingly, that it kept people from attending worship services. Classis Tiel complained about work being done on Sundays and noted that it needed to be abolished so that people could "go to the godly services."[65] Interestingly, when working on the Sabbath was mentioned it was often the first offense mentioned regarding Sabbath desecration. Too much should not be read into such an ordering, but it does seem working on the Sabbath was an offense the classes took seriously, even if the frequency of such complaints were not as frequent as other complaints.

Results of Sabbath Complaints

Generally, the classes had three different methods of seeking resolutions to the Sabbath desecration. First, the classis could bring their concerns before the larger synodical bodies. Often these were referred to in the classes' records as the national synods but, in reality, such petitions were brought before the provincial

---

61 Verschoor, *Classicale Acta,* Vol. 8, 504. "Dat men noch allenthalven siet in swange gaen de onnutte bachusdagh ende het violeren van de sabbathdagen door vercopen, winckelhouden, optrecken en teeren van schutteryen, teeren van de gilden, verhetoryespelen ende andere kennelyke abusen."

62 The complaint about work comes up, according to my count, ten times in the records. This is not an insignificant number but is many fewer times than complaints such as drinking or playing games.

63 Van Gelderen and Ravensbergen, *Classicale Acta,* Vol. 6, 42. "Dat het arbeyden op sondagen, fest- ende beededaghen."

64 Ravensbergen, *Classicale Acta,* Vol. 9, 72. "Dewijle dat den sondach niet alleen met arbeyden, maer oock met anderen lichtvaerdigen dingen."

65 Ravensbergen, *Classicale Acta,* Vol. 9, 319. "Soo die jegenwoordichlick tot groot achterdeel des godsdiensts in swang gaen, te weeren."

synods, as described in the previous chapter. For instance, in 1591 Classis Delft noted the problem of the profanation of the Sabbath and was going to correspond with the provincial synods of North Holland and South Holland to seek a resolution.[66]

A second option was for the classis to contact the local sheriff (*baljuw, bailliu, balliu*) in hopes that he would more strictly enforce local laws pertaining to the Sabbath. The sheriff was responsible for enforcing any civil laws that related to the Sabbath. Classis Dordrecht was particularly active in pursuing the sheriff's stricter enforcement of Sunday observance. For instance, in 1583 at Classis Dordrecht, Pastor Wilhelmum Lontium noted the unregulated state of Sundays. The classis, upon Lontium's recommendation, sent Lontium and another pastor, Heinricus Corputius, to speak with the sheriff to seek a solution.[67] Classis Dordrecht had a particularly difficult time with the sheriff in Strijen. In 1594 the classis resolved to speak with all the sheriffs of South Holland to more strictly enforce the Sabbath, taking care to emphasize that they would also speak with the sheriff of Strijen.[68] Again in 1595 Classis Dordrecht sought a letter from the *heeren Staten* regarding better Sabbath observance that was to be submitted to all public officials and "in particular, the sheriff of Strijen."[69]

Finally, the classes could send their complaints to the political officials, generally at the local level. While the provincial synods appealed to the lords of the Dutch provinces (the *herren Staten*), the classes' political appeals were directed to local authorities. In 1610 Classis Walcheren desired that the city magistrates would "prevent the desecration of the Sabbath."[70] Similarly, Classis Rotterdam was having difficulty controlling the disorder of the Sabbaths in rural areas, so they called on the "lords of Rotterdam" to take action.[71] Frequently the classes' records began or ended their complaints regarding Sabbath desecration with a

---

66 Abels and Wouters, *Classicale Acta,* Vol. 7, 115. "Men sal oock voorstellen ende braghen welck het middel is, waerdoor de synoden van Suyt- ende Noort-Hollandt goede ende behoorlycke correspondentie metten anderen sullen houden."

67 Van Dooren, *Classicale Acta,* Vol. 1, 153. "Is goedt bevonden, dat Corputius ende Lontius zullen aenspreken den bailliu ende hem de saecke levendich remosntreren, hem biddende datter inne versien mochte worden."

68 Van Dooren, *Classicale Acta,* Vol. 1, 400. "Is tot wechneminge van sulxs geresolvert, dat men wederom den biliou van Suythollandt ende oock van Strijen zall aenspreken, dat zij sulxs willen wereen."

69 Van Dooren, *Classicale Acta,* Vol. 1, 421. "De gedeputeerden wordt opnieuw opgedragen de secretaris C. de Rechtere te verzoeken de missive van de Staten betreffende de zondag-sheiliging aan alle ambtenaren, in het bijzonder aan de baljuw van Strijen te zenden."

70 Bouterse, *Classicale Acta,* Vol. 4, 165. "Het ware te wenschen dat ordre gestelt, ende by alle magistraten aengehouden wierde tot weeringhe van de ontheyliginghe des sabbaths."

71 Bouterse, *Classicale Acta,* Vol. 3, 167. "Belangende de ongeregeltheden ende enorme abuysen welcke ten platte landen getolereert werden, is goetgevonden sulcks myn heeren van Rotterdam te remonstreren."

general note that they would seek remedies from the political authorities. For example, Classis Dordrecht sought remonstrants from the "noble lords, the magistrates of Dordrecht," to help put an end to Sabbath abuses.[72] These requests were often sent via delegates from a classis, but a classis would occasionally send letters to the authorities lodging their complaints.[73]

Issuing placards, government-issued laws or regulations posted in public places in print form, against desecrating the Sabbath was one way the classes sought to prevent Sabbath offenses via political authorities. When classes mentioned reaching out to the magistrates, they frequently also mentioned the placards. Placards were issued in the Dutch Republic to outlaw all sorts of things, particularly heresy, but also included behaviors deemed to desecrate the Sabbath. Typically, placards had already been issued from the authorities regarding keeping the Sabbath, and the classis recommended renewing or reemphasizing the existing placards. However, placards in the Dutch Republic were enforced with a great deal of laxity.[74]

At least in the classes' views, the placards regarding Sabbath observance were not being enforced as they should have been. In one of its complaints regarding Sabbath desecration, Classis Dordrecht concluded its entry with the resolution to "obtain a placard thereof from the E.[dele] heeren Staten."[75] Likewise, Classis Tiel resolved to have deputies from their classis meet with the political authorities in order to seek the "execution of the placards."[76] Occasionally a classis would recommend that placards be issued either for the first time or reissued as a new placard. Classis Over-Veluwe did exactly that when they appealed to the *Edelen heeren* to publicize the placards regarding Sabbath observance and subsequently enforce the placards.[77]

---

72 Van Dooren, *Classicale Acta,* Vol. 2, 769. "Is geleesen een seeckere remonstrantie aen de Edele Heeren de magistraet van Dordrecht noopende de abuysen die op den sabbath vallen."

73 For an example of delegates being sent, see Van Dooren, *Classicale Acta,* Vol. 1, 413. "dat men de gedeputeerden des synodi vermanen sal Conraedt de Rechtere hiervan te spreken ten eynde zijne E. daernae wilde sien ende hem tot exempel voorstellen den bailluw van Strijen, dewelcke seyt geene ontfanghen te hebben, ende dese sake te vorderen." For an example of a letter being written, see Abels and Wouters, *Classicale Acta,* Vol. 7, 120. "Is goetgevonden dat de dienaren van Delf aen hem schryven sullen ende generalick daerinne versoecken dat in zyne jurisdictie alle dansspelen ende andere profanatien der sabbath ende bededaghen moghen afgeschaft werden. Welcken brieff oock eenige dyenaren van 't landt sullen ondertekenen."

74 See Kooi, "Paying off the sheriff," 87–101. Kooi notes how placards outlawing Catholic worship were not strictly enforced.

75 Van Dooren, *Classicale Acta,* Vol. 1, 393. "dat sij dan aenhouden sullen om een placcaet daervan te mogen van de E. heeren Staten te vercrijgen."

76 Ravensbergen, *Classicale Acta,* Vol. 9, 372. "Noopende de verscheiden onordere in de kerck voorkomende ende profanatien des sabbaths, is geadvisert dat D. deputati synodi sulx mede den Edele Hove remonstrerende versoecken executie der placaten daerop gegeven."

77 Ravensbergen, *Classicale Acta,* Vol. 9, 739. "'tsij bij den Edelen heeren drost, den schout ofte

Unfortunately, the classes' records do not give descriptions of whether actions to curb Sabbath desecration were actually taken and, if so, what sorts of effects they had in creating greater Sabbath devotion. The records do not describe whether placards were indeed issued or whether local authorities took any specific actions at the requests of the regional classes. However, more implicitly, the records of the Dutch classes portray a picture in which the church authorities were frequently fighting the indifference of the local sheriffs and political authorities.

Sheriffs were the first group with whom the classes battled. The Classis of Dordrecht appealed frequently to the sheriffs to help curb Sunday abuses, but their pleas were evidently ineffective. In 1597, the records of Classis Dordrecht note that D. Becius and Tavernier sent a request to the sheriff regarding the profanation of the Sabbath, but they received no reply to their inquiry. The records note succinctly, implying annoyance, that, "They will insist on this."[78]

The classes also ran into difficulties with the local magistrates. Mostly, the classes complained of the indifference they encountered when appealing to the magistrates regarding the Sabbath. Classis Walcheren's frustrations were palpable when they "pleaded" with the *heeren de Staten* to pay attention to the placards regarding the Sabbath.[79] Classis Zuid-Beveland sent three delegates from their classis who earnestly exhorted the *stathouder* to avert "insolence and disorder" and "hinder the abuses of Sundays."[80] The magistrates were rarely as responsive as the classes would have liked, so the classes' battle for the Sabbath continued. The classes frequently appealed to the local authorities but frequently received tepid responses.

It is somewhat difficult to know whether the efforts of the Dutch classes to rein in the desecration of the Sabbath were successful or not.[81] However, it does not appear that Sabbath complaints were effective in eradicating Sabbath desecration

---

andere daerto gestelt, aenhoude om daerin te versien dat des Landtscaps placaten, tot weringe van sulcks gepubliciert, geexecutiert werden."

78 Van Dooren, *Classicale Acta,* Vol. 1, 465. "Op het request betreffende de prophanatien des sabbaths ende andere onordeninge, door D. Becius en Tavernier aan de baljuw en de oge vierschaar gezonden, is nog geen antwoord gekomen. Zij zullen hierop aandringen."

79 Bouterse, *Classicale Acta,* Vol. 4, 13. "Datt myn heeren de Staten believe te letten op 't placaet van policye, ende order te stellen dat hetselve onderhouden worde, voornemelick in de pointen van de heyliginge des sabbaths, weiringe aller pauselicker superstitien, als luyden der clocken, bedevaerden, etcetera."

80 Bouterse, *Classicale Acta,* Vol. 4, 441. "Syn by den broederen des classis gecommitteert Andries Canen, Jacop de Volder ende Loys van der Veste, om voer de laetste reyse den stathouder desees eylants ernstelick over syn ampt ende offitie te vermanen, dat hy alle insolentien ende ongeregeltheden weere, waerdoer insonderheyt op sondaghen ende biddaghen den dienst Godts verhindert wordt."

81 Benedict notes the difficulty with assessing the "success" of church discipline in Reformed churches. See, Benedict, *Christ's Churches Purely Reformed,* 484.

over time. In almost every classis the complaints continued with a stable frequency until 1620. Of the seventeen classes registering Sabbath complaints, twelve of those classes had their last complaint in 1615 or later. If anything, the complaints became more frequent as classes became more established, met more frequently, and were more aware of the religious issues they were facing.

Further archival research also hints that Sabbath complaints continued consistently after 1620. In consulting the archival records of Classis Kampen and Classis Vollenhove, complaints about Sabbath desecration continued well past 1620. The archival records from Classis Kampen examined spanned the years from 1618–1651; for Classis Vollenhove the archival records examined were from 1597–1636.[82] An in-depth analysis of the frequency, types, and results of Sabbath complaints is not vital for these years, and indeed not possible for this given project, but the important point is that the years up to 1620 are not exceptional. Rather, in both classes the records continue to portray a concern with Sabbath observance. For example, a relatively quick perusal of the Classis Kampen manuscript records found Sabbath complaints in 1621–23, 1629–30, 1639, 1641, 1643, and 1644.[83] A similar overview of the Classis Vollenhove manuscript records found Sabbath complaints in 1622–23, 1627, 1631–32, and 1636.[84] The complaints are extremely similar to those described above.

For example, Classis Kampen continued to complain about attendance at Sunday afternoon services, particularly in the rural areas. The proposed solution was also strikingly similar to earlier years; a placard would be issued emphasizing attendance at afternoon services and forbidding the similar abuses of the Sabbath.[85] The complaint and solution were again raised in 1644.[86] After complaining generally about the "desecration of Sabbath-days" in 1622, Classis Kampen proposed to again reach out to the *Ed. Gedeputeerden.*[87] Other complaints echoed those of earlier years. In 1639 the Classis again raised the issue of markets being held on Sundays.[88] Drinking and other profanation of the Sabbath were also raised at a classis meeting in 1643.[89]

Similarly, Classis Vollenhove continued to raise Sabbath issues. In 1623 Classis Vollenhove lodged the general complaint regarding the "skandelijke prophana-

---

82 I accessed and examined the classes' records manuscripts at the Archief van Gemeent Kampen in Kampen, NL.

83 Archief van Gemeente Kampen [AGK], "Acta der vergaderingen van de Classis Kampen (1618–1651)," X.I.A.18.

84 AGK, "Acta der vergaderingen van de Classis Vollenhove (1597–1636)," X.I.C.157.

85 AGK, "Acta der vergaderingen van de Classis Kampen," October 9, 1621.

86 AGK, "Acta der vergaderingen van de Classis Kampen," April 30, 1644.

87 AGK, "Acta der vergaderingen van de Classis Kampen," April 29, 1622.

88 AGK, "Acta der vergaderingen van de Classis Kampen," October 14, 1639.

89 AGK, "Acta der vergaderingen van de Classis Kampen," April 17, 1643.

tion" of the Sabbaths.[90] Again a few years later the Classis complained "as previously mentioned that the Sabbath was profaned."[91] Raising previously seen topics, in 1636 Classis Vollenhove complained of the "pigeon-shooting" and "profanation of the Sabbaths" and, similar to earlier years, determined that the deputies of the classis would talk with the local political authorities.[92] Complaints about Catholics also continue. In 1622 Classis Vollenhove complained about the "great abuses," principally the continued existence of Catholic services and the associated "superstitions of the papists."[93]

Naturally, research into Sabbath complaints in the second half of the seventeenth century would be interesting and informative. Such research would only add to a fuller picture of Sabbath discipline and practices in Dutch Reformed churches. However, the demands of such a task require that it must be put off to a later project or for other scholars. Nonetheless, what has been demonstrated above is that a wide variety of Sabbath complaints can be found early on at the level of the Dutch classis. If early research is any indication, these complaints continued well into the seventeenth century, giving the impression that religious authorities continued to battle Sabbath desecration among their congregants in the sixteenth century and throughout the seventeenth century.

Interpreting Sabbath Complaints

As this chapter has made clear, Sabbath observance was not just a matter of importance at the national level. Rather, ecclesiastical authorities at the regional level were also concerned with what they perceived to be the abuses of the Sabbath. The question remains as to why the classes were concerned with Sabbath observance. Of course, the reasons for their concern were likely a confluence of a number of factors. Nonetheless, the classes' records themselves suggest several reasons why the classes were concerned with Sabbath observance.

A concern for order is the most significant concern the classes had regarding the Sabbath. Notably, the complaints about the Sabbath frequently included some form of the Dutch word *ongeregeldheid*, spelled in the records in any number of different ways. The word, difficult to translate exactly, means "unregulated" or "disordered."[94] The classes' records demonstrated a deep fear of

---

90 AGK, "Acta der vergaderingen van de Classis Vollenhove," May 7, 1623.
91 AGK, "Acta der vergaderingen van de Classis Vollenhove," May 21, 1627.
92 AGK, "Acta der vergaderingen van de Classis Vollenhove," June 9, 1636.
93 AGK, "Acta der vergaderingen van de Classis Vollenhove," April 20, 1622.
94 For an excellent examination of the meaning of the word, see the online lexicon, "Historische Woordenboeken op Internet," by the Instituut voor Nederlandse Lexicologie. The general

such disorder in their churches. When their congregations were not properly observing the Sabbath it threatened the orderly worship and piety the church authorities so desired. Reformed Christians were to be moral and pious, and doing so required orderly observance of Christian laws. From the classes' perspectives, failing to keep the Sabbath threw their congregations into chaotic disorder hardly characteristic of faithful Christians.

In addition, the classes' records also portrayed a situation in which the Reformed churches were attempting to establish their own confessional identity within the setting of greater religious plurality. Most notable in the records were the direct mentions of Catholics and Anabaptists. Complaints about Catholics often surrounded Sabbath complaints. But, occasionally the Sabbath complaints themselves contained concerns about Catholic practices. For example, Classis Gorinchem complained of "all the yearly faults" which included the "profanation of the Sabbaths" and the "running around of the Jesuits."[95] Classis Zutphen, in 1598, complained that children were being sent to study with the Jesuits and, even more scandalously, were "enjoying holy benefices," presumably to finance such education.[96] The sentence immediately following that complaint mentioned the "great abuses of Sundays during the preaching."[97]

In particular, the classes were concerned with the threat the Catholics posed to educating Reformed congregants in the Reformed faith. Children were particularly susceptible. The situation Classis Gorinchem described in 1620 was one where people would "openly find the running around, preaching, and misdoings of papists and Jesuits."[98] The classis record continues that parents had their children in "popish and Jesuit schools," that many places had "popish images in their churches," and "crosses in the churchyards remain[ed] allowed."[99] Again,

---

website is <http://gtb.inl.nl/>. The specific webpage for *ongeregeldheid* is <http://gtb.inl.nl/iWDB/search?actie=article&wdb=WNT&id=M044364.re.1&lemma=ongeregeldheid>.

95 Verschoor, *Classicale Acta*, Vol. 8, 137. "In de repetitie de alle jaer valt van profanatie der sabbathdages, dermissen, loppen van jesuiten, weduwen der predicanten onder de particuliere heeren, ordeninge van de schoelen op de dorpen."

96 Ravensbergen, *Classicale Acta*, Vol. 9, 481. "Item dat de derde parth der vicarien, na Landtags recess, bi der kercken und scholen gelecht worden. Item dat de kindren so bi den jesuiten um te studieren gesonden worden, genietende giestlicke beneficien, weder tehuys geforderth end tother der scholen der hoftstadth deser graffschap gesonden."

97 Ravensbergen, *Classicale Acta*, Vol. 9, 481. "Item daer die gruwlicke abusen so des sondages under die predige, hetsi in steden oft in plathenlande, mit bier ofte brandewijn tappen, kopen end verkopen, afgeschaft mochte worden, ende dat doer vernewerunge der placaten daervan voermaels in der Veluwen uthgegangen."

98 Verschoor, *Classicale Acta*, Vol. 8, 51. "Opentlyck verneemt het loopen, prediken ende misdoen van papen ende jesuyten."

99 Verschoor, *Classicale Acta*, Vol. 8, 504. "Datt de ouders haere kinderen in paepsche ende jesuytsche scholen bestellen; dat men in vele plaetsen paepse beelden in de kercken ende cruycen op de kerckhoven laet blyven."

the following sentence complains of further Sabbath desecration.[100] As other scholars have noted, worship services in the Reformed tradition had a distinctly didactic purpose.[101] If congregants were not attending these services, then they were not going to be well-educated in the Reformed faith.

Such a concern also helps shed light on the issue of afternoon catechism services and special weekly church services. The afternoon catechism services were of extreme importance for educating church members in the basics of the Reformed faith. This was particularly the case for adults who would not have had any other significant avenue of education in Reformed theology if they did not attend afternoon catechism services. Uneducated Christians were simply unacceptable to the Reformed religious authorities. In their view, such religious ignorance was characteristic of Catholicism and made church members more susceptible to a host of other theologies, including Catholicism, Lutheranism, and Anabaptist movements.

Catholic Sunday practices also posed a threat to Reformed Christians in other ways. The classes had serious worries that Sunday practices among their congregants were filled with "papal superstition." Unsurprisingly, problems with Catholics came up frequently in the records on a wide array of topics. In 1616 Classis Bommel complained about those marrying Catholics.[102] In addition, Catholic services held on Sundays were a problem. The 1620 meeting of Classis Gorinchem laments the "misdoings and preaching of papists and Jesuits."[103]

Additionally, the classes' records support the argument that Sabbath concerns were present early on in the existence of the Dutch Reformed Church. Out of the seventeen classes that registered Sabbath complaints, eleven of those classes had such complaints within the first five years of the classes' records. Classes included in this category include Classis Dordrecht, Classis Walcheren, Classis Leiden, Classis Steenwijk-Vollenhove, Classis Nijmegen, Classis Tiel-Bommel, Classis Tiel, Classis Bommel, Classis Zutphen, Classis Over-Veluwe, and Classis Nede-Veluwe. One classis, Classis Gorinchem, had its first Sabbath complaint within five to ten years of the origination of the classis. Four classes had their first complaints ten to twenty years after the records begin. These classes were Classis Rotterdam-Schieland, Classis Zuid-Beveland, Classis Deventer, and Classis Delft-Delfland. And, one classis, Classis Kampen, did not have its first complaint until

---

100 Verschoor, *Classicale Acta,* Vol. 8, 504. "Dat men noch allenthalven siet in swange gaen de onnutte bachusdagh ende het violeren van de sabbathdagen door vercopen, winckelhouden, optrecken en teeren van schutteryen, teeren van de gilden, verhetoryespelen ende andere kennelyke abusen."

101 Kingdon, *Reforming Geneva,* 38, 55–63.

102 Ravensbergen, *Classicale Acta,* Vol. 9, 393. "Item het trauwen bij papen."

103 Verschoor, *Classicale Acta,* Vol. 8, 504. "Prediken ende misdoen van papen ende jesuyten."

more than twenty years after the records begin, though the Classis did take a seventeen-year hiatus with no records from 1601 until 1618.

This suggests that for most classes Sabbath concerns were of substantial importance. Sabbath concerns were not something that typically developed only after years of classis meetings. Instead, classis members viewed the Sabbath desecration as an issue that was already present and that needed to be dealt with quickly. Again, this highlights the importance Dutch Reformed classes placed on the Sabbath and, as will be discussed below, should cause scholars to reconsider the role the Sabbath played in the Dutch Reformation from the very beginning.

Geographically, it is rather difficult to draw any conclusions from the classes' records regarding the Sabbath complaints. Overall, those classes in the province of Gelderland had the highest rates of Sabbath complaints. However, Gelderland's classes typically met less frequently and encompassed more rural areas where Sabbath issues were often more problematic. Thus, Gelderland's higher rates of Sabbath complaints likely were due to factors other than geographical location. Classes in Zeeland had the lowest rates of Sabbath complaints. This is somewhat surprising given Zeeland's concern with the Sabbath at the Synod of Dort and its close proximity to the Habsburg provinces and Spanish Catholicism.[104] The province of Holland is more difficult to assess. Several of its classes, such as Classis Dordrecht and Classis Delft, had relatively high numbers of Sabbath complaints. However, Classis Breda and Classis Werden each had no Sabbath complaints and both were found in the province of Holland. In addition, Classis Rotterdam and Classis Leiden were both found in Holland, and each classis had relatively low numbers of Sabbath complaints. Thus, while further research might provide insights into how geographical location impacted the importance given to the Sabbath, the current picture the classes' records provides remains too varied to provide any solid judgments or correlations.

Conclusions

In large part, the classes' records reaffirm what was seen in the provincial synods in the previous chapter. Namely, religious authorities were concerned with Sabbath observance and believed the eradication of Sabbath desecration to be of significant importance. Furthermore, the classes' records demonstrate a concern for the Sabbath very early on. Sabbath concerns were not, then, something that developed only later in the Dutch Reformation. As such, it would be a mistake to downplay the Dutch Reformed emphasis on Sabbath observance or attribute the concerns for strict Sabbath observance only to later Puritan influences, both of

---

104 Visser, *De Geschiedenis van den Sabbatsrijd*, 50–60.

which other scholars have often done.[105] Instead, the Dutch classes' records demonstrate that from the earliest days of their existence the Dutch Reformed churches sought to bring about a strict Sabbath observance, a process that continued well into the seventeenth century.

The classes' theological understanding of the Sabbath is not explicit in the records. That is to say, the classes never attribute their actions or concerns to particular theological concerns or a specific theologian. As a result, one must be careful not to draw links too directly between theologians and the Dutch Reformed classes. However, the issues the classes raised suggest a great deal about their theological stance on the Sabbath and provide at least glimpses into the theological positions the classes had most readily adopted and interiorized.

Theologically, the classes clearly viewed worship as the most important aspect of the Sabbath. The emphasis on church attendance was clear in the complaints regarding congregants absenting themselves from morning or afternoon church services for any number of other activities. In addition, the church services were meant to be honored; the disrupting of the services was something the classes could not tolerate.

Physical rest does also seem to be a concern of the classes. However, the rest was almost always tied to corporate worship. Congregants were to rest from their work, but the purpose of the rest, the records emphasized, was so that they could attend the worship services. Rest alone without attendance at worship was not acceptable. Such rest, perhaps following Calvin's point, would have been mere idleness and in no real way spiritually edifying. Instead, the Sabbath was meant to be a day dedicated to the Lord and to one's own spiritual devotion, and the best way to do that, in the classes' views, was to participate in the corporate worship services.

In the same way, the classes demonstrated a concern for spiritual rest, found so clearly in Calvin, but it was certainly not the main focus of their complaints. The concern for immorality on the Sabbath certainly comes through in the classes' records. The persistent complaints regarding drinking, fighting, dancing, and the like highlight that classes saw immoral behaviors as particularly objectionable on the Sabbath. The Sabbath was meant to be a day of spiritual edification; to Calvin's point, the classes believed using the day to engage in immoral, sinful activities perverted the day to its core.

The complaints regarding recreation on the Sabbath seem to anticipate the sabbatarian theology of Wilhelmus à Brakel. Again, however, the classes' complaints almost always mentioned recreation in connection with worship services. The recreational activities were not necessarily problematic in themselves, even if done on Sundays. Instead, the recreational activities were an issue precisely

---

105 See above: "Introduction," 22–24.

because they distracted people from corporate worship or even caused people to be absent from the worship services.

While it is too dangerous to assign direct theological influences to the Dutch Reformed classes' attitudes to the Sabbath, the classes' records seem to reflect most closely the attitudes found in a Lasco and Ursinus. À Brakel's sabbatarian position did also come through, particularly in the complaints regarding improper activities on the Sabbath, but the emphasis on worship was found most clearly in a Lasco and Ursinus. Of course, Calvin too put a heavy emphasis on worship in conjunction with the fourth commandment, but his emphasis on spiritual rest did not feature prominently in the classes' records. In sum, a Lasco's and Ursinus's theological positions could be seen clearly in the classes' Sabbath complaints, particularly in the classes' emphasis on the Sabbath being primarily for worship. At the same time, à Brakel's later sabbatarian positions were already seen in the classes' strict attitudes toward Sabbath activities. Perhaps Calvin's influence could be seen in the classes' abhorrence for sinful activities on the Sabbath, though, naturally, all theologians agreed sinful activities were forbidden.

An examination of Sabbath practices and discipline has now been undertaken at the levels of both the Dutch Reformed provincial synods and the regional classes. Yet, these levels still had relatively little contact with individual Dutch Reformed church members. Thus, in order to gain a complete picture of how religious authorities sought to regulate the Sabbath and how church members observed the Sabbath, attention will now be given to the local level of Dutch Reformed church polity, the consistory. Turning to consistory records will provide further insights into how church members practiced the Sabbath, how religious authorities wanted the Sabbath observed in their communities, and how local ecclesiastical bodies attempted to bring those two perspectives together.

Chapter 6:
Sabbath Observance in Kampen Consistory Records

Introduction to Kampen

The Dutch city of Kampen is in the province of Overijssel, today an hour and a half train ride northeast of Amsterdam. Kampen has a long history, gaining its city rights in 1236. Because of its position on the Ijssel River, Kampen was a prosperous shipping city, connecting the Rhine River with the Zuiderzee.[1] Kampen reached its peak as a city both in population and in economic success around 1400. Kampen's population in 1400 was somewhere around 12,000, a figure not to be reached again in the early modern period.[2] Trading along the Ijssel slowed considerably in the fifteenth and sixteenth centuries, largely due to the silting of the Ijssel River.[3] The economic decline continued into the sixteenth century, and by the seventeenth century the city of Kampen was struggling to adjust to its new, harsh reality.

Kampen, like so many Dutch cities, was not immune to the struggles of the Dutch Revolt against the Spanish. Rients Reitsma has provided an excellent account of the history of the province of Overijssel, which included Kampen, from 1566–1600.[4] Only a brief overview is needed here. Already in 1572 William van den Bergh, the brother of William of Orange, took the city from the Spanish along with several other local cities.[5] However, the Spanish response was swift and harsh. Only a few months later the Spanish, led by Don Frederick the son of the Duke of Alva, besieged the nearby city of Zutphen. After breaking through the city wall, the Spanish forces captured the city in brutal fashion. Having seen the

---

1 Joop W. Koopmans, *Historical Dictionaries of Europe: Historical Dictionary of the Netherlands*, New York: Rowman & Littlefield, 2016, 173.
2 Israel, *The Dutch Republic*, 114.
3 Israel, *The Dutch Republic*, 119.
4 Rients Reitsma, *Centrifugal and Centripetal Forces in the Early Dutch Republic: The States of Overijssel, 1566–1600*, Amsterdam: Rodopi, 1982.
5 Reitsma, *Centrifugal and Centripetal Forces*, 107–108.

cruelty of the Spanish forces nearby Dutch cities voluntarily surrendered to Don Frederick. Kampen was one such city.

The Spanish rule of Kampen was relatively short-lived, however. In 1578 the Dutch reclaimed the city. The count of Rennenberg, George van Lalaing, led a siege of Kampen, and the Dutch forces were able to defeat the Spanish. Rennenberg served the General Union as the *stadholder* of Friesland, Groningen, Drenthe, Lingen, and Overijssel and was, at the same time, both pro-Dutch and Catholic. The Kampen city regents pushed for continued Catholic practice and demanded the Protestant minister cease preaching, citing the Pacification of Ghent and the religious toleration it provided to Catholics.[6] The Reformed authorities appealed to the Archduke Matthias in Antwerp who asked the Kampen city officials to be tolerant, but the Catholic city officials would not relent. However, the Catholic presence did not have popular support among Kampen's populace, and the Catholic leaders in Kampen were arrested in 1580.[7] From this time forward Kampen remained in the possession of the Dutch, though the danger of the Spanish retaking Kampen and surrounding cities was occasionally present.[8] Most dangerously, in 1580 Rennenberg broke ties with Orange and the cause of the Revolt and declared his loyalty to the Spanish king, calling for the full restoration of the Catholic Church. However, Rennenberg's calls went largely unheeded and the Catholic resurgence Renneberg sought failed, including in Kampen where support for a Catholic insurgency was almost completely lacking.[9] All in all, Kampen's Reformed congregation established a church around 1578 and proceeded with little public opposition.[10]

Relatively little is known about the early Reformed community in Kampen. Prior to the Protestant Reformation, Kampen was a center of Catholicism.[11] Van der Pol describes in detail the vital Catholic religious life in Kampen prior to the Reformation. The Catholic presence in Kampen included three monastaries and five convents.[12] In addition, the Catholic Church was active in caring for the poor and disabled, offering masses, and promoting religious devotion in people's personal lives.[13] The latter can be seen clearly in the popularity of the *Devotio*

---

6 Reitsma, *Centrifugal and Centripetal Forces*, 130–131.

7 Reitsma, *Centrifugal and Centripetal Forces*, 206–215; Israel, *The Dutch Republic*, 204.

8 James Tracy, *The Founding of the Dutch Republic: War, Finance, and Politics in Holland, 1572–1588*, New York: Oxford University Press, 2008, 158–160.

9 Israel, *The Dutch Republic*, 206.

10 Frank van der Pol, *De Reformatie te Kampen in de Zestiende Eeuw*, Kampen: Uitgeversmaatschappij J.H. Kok, 1990, 231–232.

11 Van der Pol, *De Reformatie te Kampen*, 17–87. Van der Pol provides a thorough and excellent, if not lengthy, review of Kampen's religious situation prior to the Reformation in his chapter entitled "De Kerk in de Laat-Middeleeuwse Ijsselstad Kampen."

12 Van der Pol, *De Reformatie te Kampen*, 44.

13 Van der Pol, *De Reformatie te Kampen*, 52–67, 28–41, 73–79.

Moderna movement in Kampen.[14] In Kampen, Catholicism was anything but a dying afterthought in the lives of the citizens and the city as a whole.

Nonetheless, Protestantism in Kampen, as in most of the Low Countries, had a long history and was present from the early 1520s.[15] This included both a substantial Lutheran presence and a more radical and diverse Anabaptist strand.[16] Persecution of Protestants was scant in the Overijssel province more generally, though a few Anabaptists were executed throughout the 1530s. This persecution lasted the longest in Kampen but had ceased by 1543, and Protestants of all sorts were not persecuted until the Duke of Alva arrived.[17] In fact, in 1539 the Catholic authorities in Kampen attempted to remove a secretly Lutheran preacher, but their efforts prompted a riot and were shut down by the city magistrates.[18]

However, even after the official establishment of the Reformed congregation in 1578 membership was still rather low, particularly as a percentage of Kampen's total population. Based on estimates taken from communion lists, membership in the Dutch Reformed Church in the first decade of the seventeenth century appears to have been somewhere from 1,130-1,265.[19] If, as Reitsma has concluded, Kampen's population was around 8,000 people in 1600 and church membership was 1,265, then only around 16% of the population were official church members.[20] Church membership appears to have grown in the next couple decades, the 1620s and 1630s, with an average of fifty to sixty new members per year.[21] But, even if by 1620 membership had gained 1,200 members, as suggested by van der Pol, and the city's population held steady at 9,000, church members still only accounted for about one-third of the total population.[22]

While the Reformed presence in Kampen remained a vast minority of the overall population, not an uncommon occurrence in the Dutch Republic, the Reformed congregation did experience significant growth. Van der Pol has used

---

14 Selderhuis, *Handbook of Dutch Church History*, 124–126; Van der Pol, *De Reformatie te Kampen*, 79–88.

15 Van der Pol, *De Reformatie te Kampen*, 91–92.

16 For the Lutheran presence, see Van der Pol, *De Reformatie te Kampen*, 89–113. For the Anabaptist presence, see Van der Pol, *De Reformatie te Kampen*, 114–126.

17 Israel, *The Dutch Republic*, 94–95.

18 Israel, *The Dutch Republic*, 95.

19 Frank van der Pol, "Religious Diversity and Everyday Ethics in the Seventeeth-Century Dutch City Kampen," *Church History* 71, no. 1 (2002): 27.

20 Reitsma, *Centrifugal and centripetal forces*, 14–15. Reitsma calculates Kampen's population in 1599 to be 8,104.

21 Van der Pol, "Diversity and Ethics in Kampen," 28.

22 Van der Pol, "Diversity and Ethics in Kampen," 27–28. Van der Pol notes that in the first two decades of the seventeenth century church membership grew at a rate of fifty to sixty members per year. Over twenty years, figuring generously, that church membership was up a total of 1,200 members. Added with the earlier number of 1,265, by 1620 church membership was somewhere around 2,465.

Kampen's communion lists to demonstrate this growth since those participating in communion would have needed to be church members. The communion lists from 1579 indicate 180 total participants. For the next ten years the total participants increased from the previous year anywhere from twelve to ninety-one participants. By 1589 the total increase in participation of the Lord's Supper had increased 255 % from the 1579 numbers.[23] The Reformed presence continued to grow in the late sixteenth century. As mentioned above, Van der Pol has demonstrated that participation in the Lord's Supper continued to grow in the first three decades of the seventeenth century.[24] Thus, while the Reformed presence in Kampen was never a vast majority, the Reformed presence experienced considerable growth throughout the late sixteenth and early seventeenth centuries.

The Synod of Dordrecht, held in 1618–1619, had a profound influence on religious life in Kampen. In a city previously split between Remonstrants (i.e. Arminians) and Contra-Remonstrants (i.e. Calvinists), the Remonstrants lost virtually all power after the Synod. In 1620 Prince Maurits dismissed the entire Kampen city council. Thereafter, signing a confession of faith stating one's agreement with the three Dutch confessional standards, the Belgic Confession, the Heidelberg Catechism, and the Canons of Dort, became mandatory for all those holding public office. In addition, city officials were now required to be full members of the Dutch Reformed Church; they could not simply be *liefhebbers*, those who attended services but did not submit to discipline and could not participate in the sacraments. As will be discussed below, many Kampen residents maintained sympathies with the Remonstrants. Despite lay sympathies towards the Remonstrants, local political and ecclesiastical authorities simply did not welcome Remonstrants in Kampen. This was not the case throughout the Dutch Republic. As van der Pol notes, in cities such as Rotterdam, Amsterdam, and Tiel the Remonstrant communities were able to worship together already in the 1630s and 1640s. The Reformed community in Kampen was not particularly large or powerful, but they were intent on maintaining a pure, orthodox church.

Choosing to examine Kampen's consistory records is not entirely arbitrary. Much of the scholarly work on Dutch consistories has focused on the major province of Holland.[25] In addition, the focus of work on the Dutch Reformation more generally has most often been on larger cities.[26] Kampen, on the other hand,

---

23 Van der Pol, *De Reformatie te Kampen*, 428–249.
24 Van der Pol, "Diversity and Ethics in Kampen," 27–28.
25 Kooi, *Liberty and Religion*; Parker, *The Reformation of Community*; Roodenburg, *Onder censuur*; Spaans, *Haarlem na de Reformatie*.
26 This has been the case for the studies of the province of Holland mentioned above. But, it is also the case in the majority of studies outside of the Holland province. See the following excellent studies done on major Dutch cities: Kaplan, *Calvinists and Libertines*; Marnef, Guido, *Antwerp in the Age of Reformation*; Wouters and Abels, *Nieuw en ongezien*.

is located in the much less studied province of Overijssel and, while not an insignificant city, could not be considered a major city in the Dutch Republic.

As a city, Kampen's population in the fifteenth century was steadily declining. By 1572 estimates place Kampen's population around 10,000, and less than twenty years later that number was closer to 7,500. The city made an effort to attract new citizens, offering for eighteen months in 1592 free and immediate citizenship to any new residents from whatever nation without any qualifications for religious adherence.[27] These efforts were mildly successful, but by 1647 Kampen's population had fallen again to around 7,000 people.[28] These population figures are significantly less than any number of other Dutch cities. Of course, a number of major Dutch cities in the powerful provinces of Holland and Zeeland had populations that dwarfed Kampen. Cities such as Amsterdam, Leiden, Haarlem, Middelburg, and Delft had many times the number of people as Kampen. Even somewhat smaller cities, such as Dordrecht, The Hague, and Gouda, had almost twice as many citizens as Kampen. Similarly, cities outside of Holland and Zeeland also had significantly higher populations than Kampen. By 1590, cities such as Utrecht, Groningen, Leeuwarden, and Maastricht were much larger than Kampen, and the disparity only continued in the seventeenth century.[29] Even in the relatively sparsely populated province of Overijssel, Kampen's population always lagged behind nearby Zwolle's and was similar to that of Deventer.[30] In sum, while Kampen was not an unimportant city in the Dutch Republic in the sixteenth and seventeenth centuries, its consistently smaller population and decreasing economic importance put it on a different level of importance than other major Dutch cities and, as such, make it a unique and valuable case study regarding Sabbath observance.

Kampen Consistory Records

Kampen's consistory records, housed in the Stadtsarchief Kampen, survive for the period 1618–1900. The records are found in twelve volumes in the Archief Hervormde Gemeente Kampen collection of the city archives.[31] The consistory

---

27 Israel, *The Dutch Republic*, 331.

28 Reitsma, *Centrifugal and Centripetal Forces*, 15–17.

29 Israel, *The Dutch Republic*, 332. Compared to Kampen's 7,500 people, Israel estimates the populations in 1590 as follows: Utrecht—25,000, Groningen—19,000, Leeuwarden—10,000, Maastricht—10,000.

30 Israel, *The Dutch Republic*, 332.

31 In the Stadtsarchief Kampen the consistory records are catalogued under the Gemeente Archief Kampen (GAK) in the Archief Hervormde Gemeente Kampen (AHGK) collection as II.A.9–20 and labeled "Register van handelingen van de Algemene Kerkeraad van Kampen 1618–1900." The consistory records are found in twelve volumes; the years examined here are

existed before 1618, but when the Remonstrants were separated from the official Reformed church they took the prior consistory records with them. Those records have now been completely lost.

Relatively little scholarly work has been done on Kampen, particularly research utilizing its consistory records. Most notable is the excellent work of Dr. Frank van der Pol, emeritus Professor of Church History at the Theologische Universiteit Kampen. His dissertation, which was then published as a book and is cited above, remains the most comprehensive study of the Reformed community in Kampen in the sixteenth and seventeenth centuries. As already noted, Van der Pol has also written on Simon Oomius in a work that makes excellent use of the Kampen consistory records, albeit largely from the second half of the seventeenth century, to shed light on the lived religious experience of Reformed Christians in Kampen.

The years addressed in this chapter are from 1618–1649. The Kampen consistory records do continue after 1649, all the way to 1900 in twelve volumes. However, time and space demands require an end point, and 1648 is a natural stopping point for several reasons. First, the Dutch Republic's war with Spain ended in 1648, so the years around 1648 were a transitional time for the Dutch in general. More practically, a break in the Kampen consistory records exists from 1650–1654 when no records exist, and the records beginning in 1654 are found in a separate records book. It should be noted, as well, that the consistory records in the last several years, namely from 1646–1649, are increasingly incomplete, and the records themselves are quite out of order.

In very practical terms of methodology, I scanned through all of the consistory records, approximately 650 pages of records, of the aforementioned years completely two different times. While I did not transcribe the entirety of the records, I took special note of entries that mentioned Sundays, the Sabbath, preaching, the Lord's Supper, and the like. The paleography necessary to read the handwriting occasionally proved a difficult task, at times verging on impossible, but overall the records are in good physical shape and the handwriting quite readable. Three different handwritings make up the vast majority of the Kampen consistory records, indicating three different scribes over the years. One hand is wonderfully clear and quite frequent; a second hand is fairly readable and very frequent; a third hand is very difficult to read but, thankfully, quite infrequent. On a few occasions I cite cases Dr. van der Pol noted in his work on the Kampen consistory; in all such cases prior to 1650 I have substantiated his findings with my own reading of the records. All of the references to the consistory records come, naturally, from my own examination of the records.

---

found in the first three volumes. Hereafter the consistory records will be referenced as follows: GAK, AHGK, Date [Month, Day, Year].

The Kampen consistory typically met weekly with exceptional regularity, though it did occasionally meet more frequently as the need arose. The day of the week the consistory met varied. Ironically, much of the time the consistory met on Sundays.[32] Meeting on Sundays was not uncommon for consistories since Sunday worship guaranteed pastors, elders, and deacons would all be present and available to meet. These Sunday meetings took place between the morning and afternoon church services. However, there were periods of times when the consistory met on other days. The most frequent day other than Sunday was Tuesdays,[33] but the consistory also met on Mondays,[34] Wednesdays,[35] Thursdays,[36] Fridays,[37] and Saturdays.[38]

The consistory was composed of pastors, elders, and deacons. The election of elders and deacons took place in November each year. Echoing the 1571 Synod of Emden, the Synod of Dort recommended that elders and deacons serve two year terms with half of the members retiring each year, a process Kampen followed.[39] In this way the institutional memory and experience was preserved with half of the consistory remaining each year.[40] Both synods noted that elders and deacons could be appointed for a longer or shorter period of time at the discretion of the particular consistory. However, the Kampen consistory appears to have followed the recommendation of the synods, annually replacing half of the six elders and half of the eight deacons.[41] Nominations for elders and deacons would be recorded at a consistory meeting, and the names of those selected would be recorded the next time the consistory met. The standard was for six elders to be nominated and three chosen. Eight deacons were normally nominated and four of those eight chosen.[42] At times, there were actually two rounds of narrowing, with a large list of names whittled down to official nominations of six elders and

---

32 GAK, AHGK, June 9, 1630.

33 GAK, AHGK, August 1, 1623.

34 GAK, AHGK, July 4, 1639.

35 GAK, AHGK, September 24, 1642.

36 GAK, AHGK, May 4, 1645.

37 GAK, AHGK, May 30, 1642.

38 GAK, AHGK, July 6 1630.

39 The Kampen consistory records are not explicit about this, but it can be deduced from the names of those nominated. For example, Jan Sabe was elected in as a deacon in 1628, an elder in 1630, and again as an elder in 1632. Obviously, his terms could not have been more than two years.

40 I am currently studying the Kampen consistory records and the process of selecting elders and deacons. Preliminary research indicates that men were frequently nominated repeatedly, and the office of elder was deemed more prestigious than the office of deacon.

41 GAK, AHGK, November 17, 1626; November 23, 1627; November 28, 1628. These are merely a sampling of the typical process found in each year.

42 GAK, AHGK, November 22, 1633; November 4, 1635; November 20, 1645. Again, these examples are representative of the typical method found in any number of years.

eight deacons of whom three and four, respectively, were then chosen.[43] Elders were frequently involved in the city government as either *"burgemeesters"* or *"burgers."* In the latter half of the seventeenth century, van der Pol notes, typically two burgermeesters were members of the consistory. Such a practice was not unique to Kampen but also took place in other towns throughout the provinces of Overijssel and Holland.[44] Appointing civic officials as members of the consistory was typical practice throughout the seventeenth century in Kampen, a point which will prove relevant below in how the consistory related to the city magistrates.

Consistory records, more so than either provincial synod records or classis records, are extremely local documents. Kampen's consistory records are no exception. Reading through the records one finds a great deal of attention to very local, practical matters. Most of the matters are quite routine. For instance, when the Lord's Supper was to be celebrated and preparations for such services are found frequently in the records. Similarly, the consistory undertook the annual event of nominating and choosing elders and deacons to serve on the consistory, as described in the above paragraphs.

Nonetheless, the consistory records also address topics that were much more serious, public matters. Some of the accounts are quite dramatic and poignant. In September of 1634 the consistory dealt with a woman whose husband had abandoned her.[45] The woman reported to the consistory that she had not heard from her husband for seven years! On another occasion the consistory noted the great thanksgiving they owed God for their "great victory over the Sea."[46] What they meant was that the flooding of the Ijssel River did not inundate the city, a fact they credited to God's mercy. Or, in 1642 the consistory dealt with an organist in the main church, the Bovenkerk, who evidently played music other than the psalms during the preaching services.[47] The National Synod of Dordrecht in 1578 had forbidden the use of organs during worship, following the tradition of Calvin in Geneva. In many churches the organs continued to be played before and after the services for entertainment. However, in the 1640s the debate in the Dutch Republic began again about whether or not organs could be used during worship. The relevant complaint in the Kampen consistory records occurs in 1642. Evidently, by that date the use of the organ was allowed in Kampen.[48] However, the

---

43 GAK, AHGK, November 26, 1643.
44 Van der Pol, "Diversity and Ethics in Kampen," 28.
45 GAK, AHGK, September 10, 1634.
46 GAK, AHGK, October 26, 1639.
47 GAK, AHGK, November 11, 1642.
48 Israel, *The Dutch Republic*, 694–695; Randall D. Engle, "A Devil's Siren or an Angel's Throat?: The Pipe Organ Controversy among the Calvinists," in *John Calvin, Myth and Reality: Images*

consistory was clear only the psalms were to be played and sung during the services![49]

Sabbath Concerns and Sunday Observance

Sabbath concerns are frequent in the Kampen consistory records. Kampen's consistory is not the only one to address Sabbath concerns. Unfortunately, most of the consistory records of Dutch Reformed congregations remain housed at various archives in manuscript form. Two notable exceptions exist. First, Schilling and Schreiber have famously transcribed and published the consistory records, *die kirchenratsprotokolle*, from 1557–1620 of the Dutch Reformed congregation in the city of Emden.[50] Second, Jensma has made available the consistory records of Dordrecht.[51] While substantial studies of each set of consistory records is not possible here, it is worth noting the consistory of each congregation addressed Sabbath concerns at least occasionally. The Emden consistory addressed the desecration of the Sabbath at least fifteen times over the sixty-four years. The Dordrecht consistory recorded Sabbath concerns at least five times over seven years.[52] More work on Dutch consistories and their interest in the Sabbath is certainly needed, but initial inquiries into other consistories suggest the Kampen consistory was not unique in its concern for the Sabbath.

As Judith Pollmann has demonstrated so carefully and convincingly, using statistics drawn from consistory records can be a dangerous endeavor. Pollmann has shown that much of the consistory's work was not necessarily recorded, which means any conclusions based on statistics drawn from the records are apt to be, at best, incomplete or, at worst, misleading.[53] Nonetheless, the frequency with which the Sabbath complaints are found in the Kampen consistory records can at least hint at the seriousness the consistory attached to proper Sabbath observance.

---

and Impact of Geneva's Reformer; Papers of the 2009 Calvin Studies Colloquium, ed. Amy Nelson Burnett, Eugene, OR: Wipf and Stock, 2011, 107–125.

49 GAK, AHGK, November 11, 1642.

50 Heinz Schilling and Klaus-Dieter Schreiber, *Die Kirchenratsprotokolle der Reformierten Gemeinde Emden, 1557–1620: Teil I: 1557–1574*, Köln: Böhlau, 1989; Heinz Schilling and Klaus-Dieter Schreiber, *Die Kirchenratsprotokolle der Reformierten Gemeinde Emden, 1557–1620: Teil II: 1575–1620*, Köln: Böhlau, 1992.

51 Theunis W. Jensma, *Uw Rijk Kome: Acta van de Kerkeraad van de Nederduits Gereformeerde Gemeente te Dordrecht, 1573–1579*, Dordrecht: Uitgeverij J. P. van den Tol, 1981, 1–189.

52 For each congregation, I have simply consulted the wonderful indices of the published consistory records to see how many times Sabbath issues were addressed.

53 Pollmann, "Off the Record," 423–438.

In the thirty-two years of records covered in this chapter, Sabbath complaints occur in twenty-six of those years, a percentage of 81.25.[54] Arriving at a total number of Sabbath complaints can vary depending on how one categorizes certain complaints. For instance, does a complaint about the desecration of the Lord's Supper belong to Sunday observance since the Supper was part of Sunday observance? Should complaints about attendance at preaching services on Sunday be categorized with Sunday observance or with complaints about attendance at services held during the middle of the week? Nonetheless, at a sort of estimated minimum, I counted 109 total complaints relating to desecrating the Sabbath and proper Sunday observance. Using this total of 109 over thirty-two years, that means the Kampen consistory averaged nearly three-and-one-half complaints about the Sabbath per year. It should be stressed that such an estimate is likely a bare minimum; it does not include complaints about the desecration of the Lord's Supper, the problem of drinking that was to be addressed in sermons, the "insolence" of young people in the church, and other similar complaints.

The exact numbers are not necessarily important. What is important is noting that Sabbath concerns arise quite frequently in the Kampen consistory records. Given the data, it is safe to conclude that the consistory took Sabbath observance seriously. In addition, the consistory was clearly not satisfied with the state of observance among its congregants, feeling the need to address the issue of proper Sunday observance time and again.

Unfortunately for the interested reader, the complaints rarely have the flair of other transgressions. In fact, the consistory's dealings with the Sabbath are typically phrased in relatively general terms and lack many specifics. Scholars using consistory records are always tempted to draw out detailed cases where a person or group is caught in some scandalous behavior. The temptation also exists when using the Kampen consistory records, but in regards to Sabbath observance those exciting, personal cases are few and far between. While such records are tantalizing for the reader, they are not representative of how the Kampen consistory typically dealt with the Sabbath in the first half of the seventeenth century.

The consistory records regarded Sabbath desecration as a communal offense. In the years under consideration I was able to find only a handful of instances in which a particular individual was mentioned directly in relation to Sabbath desecration. Instead, the complaints were typically general and spoke of such a

---

54 I am quite confident in my readings of the records and, thus, my calculations. However, I am not too arrogant to admit that I may have overlooked a complaint(s), particularly when the handwriting bordered on unreadeable. Good caution warrants the percentage be considered an estimate.

desecration at the group level. This is somewhat surprising given that individuals did frequently come up for various offenses in the Kampen consistory records, as well as early modern consistory records throughout Europe. A few explanations for the anonymity of Sabbath desecration exist. Perhaps the consistory did not view Sabbath desecration as a serious enough offense to warrant addressing a particular individual. Or, perhaps Sabbath desecration was so widespread that it would have simply been impractical and nearly impossible to chastise each individual offender. Another possible explanation is that the consistory viewed Sabbath observance as a communal activity and, therefore, believed the best way to attempt to police the Sabbath was not via individuals but, rather, by bringing the entire community into proper observance.

On the rare occasion when an individual was mentioned, the person's name was usually not mentioned. On May 31, 1639, a certain person from the town of Hessen was disciplined for a number of "public offenses" including drunkenness, fighting, and "disturbances made on Sundays."[55] Even in this instance the man was not disciplined only for Sabbath desecration; his failure to properly observe Sundays was included with a list of other offenses. Singling out one person for his or her Sabbath desecration was certainly not the norm for the Kampen consistory.

For the Kampen consistory, church attendance was of primary importance for properly keeping the Sabbath. While the provincial synods and classes also emphasized church attendance as essential to keeping the Sabbath, the Kampen consistory emphasized such a view to an even greater extent. Church attendance, as the consistory conceived of it, meant being present for two Sunday church services, a morning service and an afternoon service. These church services were, as will be demonstrated, of the utmost importance in the consistory's view. In no uncertain terms, devotion to the Sabbath meant devotion to the church services.

One of the most frequent concerns with Sunday observance was attendance at the afternoon services. The consistory had a particularly difficult time convincing people to attend these Sunday afternoon services. These services were so important because it was at these services where the Heidelberg Catechism was preached. Evidently, these afternoon services were not well attended. The consistory continually pushed for better attendance and more emphasis on the afternoon catechism services.

While the complaints regarding the afternoon services are too numerous to include them all, a few examples will demonstrate the flavor of some of the consistory's concerns. Similar to the concerns of ecclesiastical bodies seen in earlier chapters, the consistory did have to deal with the afternoon attendance of rural congregants who lived just outside of Kampen proper. Already in 1623 the

---

55 GAK, AHGK, May 31, 1639.

consistory noted that those who lived in the rural areas were not attending the afternoon church services. The entry pays particular attention to the children who were not present. The emphasis on children is not surprising since catechism services were especially important for educating children in the Reformed faith.[56] In fact, it appears from the consistory's complaint that the children were traveling to the city for the services but, rather than attending the church services, were instead involved in less desirable activities, such as "copulation."[57] The complaint was raised a few months later that year when the consistory noted the people from the rural areas needed to attend the Sunday afternoon catechism services.[58]

Beyond the rural areas, the consistory had other concerns relating to the afternoon catechism services. The main concern dealt with the preaching at the afternoon services. Here the preaching refers to the explanation of the Heidelberg Catechism, though the consistory often just refers to the *predicatie* at the afternoon services. The consistory was persistent in its attempts to get more people to attend. In 1638 the consistory "declared" that the people needed to attend the "afternoons in the church" so they could hear the preaching.[59] A couple of years later, in 1640, the consistory appealed to the magistrates to get people to "attend the Sunday afternoon catechism preaching held in the church."[60] A year later the consistory held an "extraordinary" meeting, which were actually held relatively frequently and not all that extraordinary, to address the fact that the catechism preaching held in the churches on Sunday afternoons was still not well attended.[61]

Persuading people to attend the afternoon services was particularly difficult in the winter months when the weather was colder and the days were shorter. In addition, inclement weather could make traveling to services difficult, especially for elderly church members. However, the consistory was not particularly understanding. The consistory noted with frustration that during the winter months attendance at the catechism services fell and sins rose.[62] In another instance the consistory complained of the poor attendance during the winter and resolved to meet with the magistrates to seek a resolution.[63] But, the consistory tried to be reasonable. The consistory recognized the attendance at the catechism services in the winter was lower, so they decided that instead of holding afternoon

---

56 Sinnema, "The Second Sunday Service," 307–311.
57 GAK, AHGK, May 14, 1623.
58 GAK, AHGK, August 22, 1623.
59 GAK, AHGK, December 28, 1638.
60 GAK, AHGK, October 16, 1640.
61 GAK, AHGK, February 25, 1641.
62 GAK, AHGK, November 20, 1645.
63 GAK, AHGK, February 28, 1646.

services at both of the Reformed churches in Kampen they would hold only services in the main church, the Bovenkerk.[64]

These afternoon services were so important because it was here the church members were educated in the Reformed faith. The Kampen consistory was extremely concerned with educating its congregants, particularly children. As other scholars have noted, Reformed churches throughout Europe were deeply concerned with educating their church members in the Reformed faith.[65] The situation in Kampen was no different. The consistory spent much of its time dealing with the Reformed schools it had established and discussed the schoolmasters frequently. In fact, the consistory complained frequently about the drunkenness of the schoolmasters.[66] More directly, the consistory was also concerned about the books the schoolmasters were buying to use for educating the children. The concern for educating children did not end at school, however. For the Kampen consistory, this concern for education connected closely with Sunday observation, particularly in the afternoon services where the catechism was preached.

Sunday church attendance was important to the consistory because it ensured the people would hear God's Word and become educated in the Reformed faith, but the consistory also stressed the importance of participating in the Lord's Supper. On numerous occasions the consistory complained of the desecration of the Lord's Supper, sometimes in conjunction with Sabbath complaints and sometimes as a stand-alone complaint.

The consistory records usually do not explicitly mention how the Lord's Supper was being desecrated. Part of the problem was simply people's absence. In September of 1639 the consistory complained that too many people were not coming to the Lord's Supper.[67] Other times, the offense dealt with drunkenness. Evidently, people preferred drinking rather than participating in the Lord's Supper. Such were the complaints, for example, on March 31, 1643 and again on July 5, 1644.[68] But, regardless of the particular transgression, what is clear is that a vital part of Sunday observance, from the consistory's perspective, was properly and piously participating in the Lord's Supper when it was celebrated. As in other Reformed traditions, pastors and elders kept lists of those who were not eligible to participate in the Lord's Supper. Those who were seeking readmission to the

---

64 GAK, AHGK, October 27, 1639.
65 Kingdon, "Reforming Religious Education," in *Reforming Geneva*, 47–69; William Lewis Spitz, *The Reformation: Education and History*, Aldershot, Great Britain: Variorum, 1997, II.58–62, V.300–302; Karin Maag, "Education and Literacy," in *The Reformation World*, ed. Andrew Pettegree, London: Routledge, 2000, 535–544.
66 GAK, AHGK, January 16, 1642; March 2, 1642; January 18, 1643; September 15, 1644.
67 GAK, AHGK, September 3, 1639.
68 GAK, AHGK, March 31, 1643; July 5, 1644.

Supper had to bring their requests to the consistory, and the consistory investigated such requests carefully. A major criterion for readmission was church
attendance.[69] The Lord's Supper was undoubtedly a major part of Dutch Reformed piety and, more specifically, participating in the Supper was part of
observing the Sabbath.

So, church attendance for the Kampen consistory included afternoon catechism services and participating piously in the Lord's Supper when celebrated.
Yet, the most important part of church attendance was listening to the preaching.
The consistory was very concerned that people attend the preaching and pay
close attention to the sermons. Furthermore, the consistory repeatedly complained of desecration that was occurring *onder [de] predicaten*, "during the
preaching."

The complaints regarding the preaching are usually not about attendance,
though they do occur. Attendance concerns were, as mentioned above, frequent
in regard to the afternoon catechism services. In comparison, the concerns about
attendance at the morning services were much less frequent. The natural conclusion is that church members in Kampen were generally quite willing to attend
the morning services. That is not to say, however, that the consistory was not
concerned with those who were absent from the morning services. For example,
in 1642 the consistory complained that young people were raucous and ranting
during the preaching.[70] Other times, the consistory complained that people did
not come to hear "God's Word," meaning they were absent from the morning
church services.[71] Yet, overall, attendance at the morning church services appears
to have been much better than at the afternoon catechism services.

When the consistory sought to remedy the profanation and desecration of the
Sabbath they frequently mentioned the preaching. Clearly, in their view, a proper
observation of the Sabbath meant attending and honoring the preaching held
during the church services. In 1640, after complaining of the profanation of the
Sabbaths the consistory resolved that the preaching needed to be emphasized.[72]
The consistory had resolved the same thing a few years earlier, noting that people
had been made aware of such a resolution.[73]

Immoral behaviors on Sundays were also a concern the consistory held but to
much less of an extent than in either the provincial synods or the regional classes.
As has been noted in the provincial synod records and the classes' records,
drinking was a continual problem. Other immoral behaviors are mentioned
occasionally, though not frequently. The general complaint about these behav-

---

69 Van Der Pol, "Diversity and Ethics in Kampen," 23–25.
70 GAK, AHGK, November 11, 1642.
71 GAK, AHGK, July 5, 1644; November 20, 1645.
72 GAK, AHGK, February 12, 1640.
73 GAK, AHGK, December 10, 1637.

iors was the "insolence" that took place on the Sabbath and, particularly, during the church services.[74] The insolence extended to the young people; the consistory complained about their "insolence" in the main Reformed church in Kampen, the Bovenkerk.[75]

The most frequent complaint in terms of immoral behavior was, of course, drinking alcohol on the Sabbath. Drinking was a nearly incessant complaint the consistory had more generally. Its occurrence on Sundays was a serious offense in the eyes of the consistory, but alcohol offenses were certainly not limited to only Sundays. Already in 1621 the consistory noted the drinking of "brandy-wine," an alcoholic drink similar to English vodka or brandy, on Sundays.[76] Again in 1624 the consistory complained of the "beer and wine" that were openly consumed, thereby desecrating the Sabbath.[77] In 1629 the drink of choice was again "brandywine," as the consistory complained yet again of the drinking on Sundays.[78]

Drinking alcohol on Sundays was desecration enough of the Sabbath, but much to the consistory's dismay, the drinking also took place during the church services. The consistory laments repeatedly the drinking that took place *onder [de] predicaten*. For instance, in 1631 the consistory complained of the people drinking, literally "tapping [the beer]," during the preaching.[79] Drunkenness was, of course, always a sin, but its occurrence during the preaching services was even more upsetting to the consistory since it meant the sinner was not only engaged in drunkenness but also not participating in hearing God's Word.

Although rarely, the consistory does mention other particular immoral offenses that occurred on Sundays. Several of the specifics mention sexual sins. In 1623 the consistory complained about young people's failure to attend catechism services and noted the "copulation" they were engaged in instead.[80] Years later, on November 3, 1641, the consistory complained of the "ugly flaunting and parading, lewdness, and other such great sins."[81] Fighting, an issue seen in previous chapters, was included in the consistory's complaint in 1639.[82]

As in the records of the provincial synods and regional classes, the issue of engaging in commercial activities, what the records called "buying and selling," came up occasionally. At the June 2, 1636 consistory meeting the consistory

---

74 GAK, AHGK, November 3, 1641; September 14, 1643; May 22, 1645.
75 GAK, AHGK, January 26, 1642; December 28, 1642.
76 GAK, AHGK, November 1, 1621. My thanks to Dr. Arnold Huijgen for confirming that I
    understood and identified this alcoholic drink correctly.
77 GAK, AHGK, February 25, 1624.
78 GAK, AHGK, December 2, 1629.
79 GAK, AHGK, May 22, 1631.
80 GAK, AHGK, May 14, 1623.
81 GAK, AHGK, November 3, 1641.
82 GAK, AHGK, May 31, 1639.

addressed the "profanation of the Sabbaths," and first on the list of offenses was the "buying and selling."[83] The same complaint of "buying and selling" was noted a few years later in 1639 when the consistory again raised the issue of the "profanation of the Sabbaths."[84] Later in the same year the consistory sought the magistrates' help in addressing the "desecration of Sabbath day" which included the "increasing buying and selling."[85] The complaint was again repeated in 1643 when buying and selling were included in a long list of "disorder" on the Sabbath.[86]

The buying and selling of goods on Sunday involved the holding of the weekly market, as mentioned in previous chapters. In 1643 the consistory complained of the "markets on Sundays" and the profanation of the Sabbaths it caused.[87] The same complaint about the markets being held on Sundays was lodged in March of 1644 and again in May of the same year.[88]

Recreation does not appear to have been the consistory's major concern, though it did come up a handful of times. In May of 1645 the consistory did press the city officials to do something about the clay-pigeon shooting taking place on Sundays.[89] That same entry also complained of the game "*ringsteken*," a traditional game where riders on horseback attempt to stab rings with their lances. The consistory sought to forbid all such "insolence" in its jurisdiction.

Work was the least mentioned complaint in terms of Sabbath observance. In 1618 the consistory complained briefly about working on Sundays, and in 1621 the issue of working on Sundays was again raised.[90] The only other time the complaint about work on Sundays came up was in 1639.[91] Mentions of working on Sundays were rare, and the few times it was mentioned the complaints were brief. Evidently, working on the Sabbath was not a problem in Kampen; the consistory was simply not concerned with work being done on the Sabbath; or the consistory resigned itself to work being done on the Sabbath. Given the concern with working on Sundays at the provincial and regional ecclesiastical levels, it seems unlikely working on the Sabbath was not an issue in Kampen. If indeed work was being done on Sundays, it is improbable the consistory would not have found such activities objectionable and worthy of attention. Most likely, then, is that the consistory had to resign itself to work being done on the Sabbath, an

---

83 GAK, AHGK, June 2, 1636.
84 GAK, AHGK, May 8, 1639.
85 GAK, AHGK, October 7, 1639.
86 GAK, AHGK, November 8, 1643.
87 GAK, AHGK, April 13, 1643.
88 GAK, AHGK, March 13, 1644; May 15, 1644.
89 GAK, AHGK, May 22, 1645.
90 GAK, AHGK, September 13, 1618; November 23, 1621.
91 GAK, AHGK, October 7, 1639.

unpleasant realization for the consistory of the reality of the situation. Unfortunately, hypothesis is all the records permit on why working on the Sabbath is not a more frequent concern for the Kampen consistory.

Remedying Sabbath Desecration

The Kampen consistory sought to remedy concerns regarding Sunday observance in several different ways. As with consistories throughout early modern Europe, the Kampen consistory barred people from the Lord's Supper as a means of punishment and an incentive to repentance. The Kampen consistory did use suspension from the Lord's Supper as a punishment for improper Sabbath observance; however, such a punishment was extremely rare. For the most part, this method was not used because discipline for Sabbath offenses was rarely aimed at one particular person. When one particular person was being addressed for Sabbath desecration that person could be suspended from the Lord's Supper. As in the May 1639 instance mentioned above, the man brought before the consistory for disrupting Sundays was in fact given a suspension from the Lord's Supper at the consistory's next meeting.[92]

Much more frequent than excommunication, the consistory sought the help of the political authorities. Given the local nature of the consistory, naturally, the appeals were almost always to the local city magistrates. The pleas were typically in the form of written letters sent to the city magistrates. The letters were generally the assignment of the presiding officer (*praeses*) of the consistory, typically a pastor, and the consistory's scribe (*scriba*). However, appeals to the magistrates could also be made in person. For example, in 1640 Jacobus Plancius and Derrick Hendrixen were sent to speak with the magistrates about the profanation of the Sabbath days.[93] In 1644 the duty to speak in person with the city mayor, the *E.E. Burgemester*, regarding the Sabbath days fell to the consistory's presiding officer and scribe.[94] Similarly, in 1645 the consistory's presiding officer and scribe sought an audience with the magistrates regarding the profanation of the Sabbaths and were promised a meeting.[95] The face to face meetings demonstrate how seriously the consistory took the problem of Sabbath desecration.

For the most part the consistory records portray the city magistrates in a positive light. Likely, the consistory realized it needed to work closely with the magistrates and considered it best to remain on friendly terms with them.[96] The

---

92 GAK, AHGK, June 23, 1639.
93 GAK, AHGK, February 5, 1640.
94 GAK, AHGK, August 30, 1644.
95 GAK, AHGK, March 30, 1645.
96 Van der Pol, "Diversity and Ethics in Kampen," 51–60.

consistory's intentional appointing of city magistrates to the consistory, as mentioned above, further demonstrates the consistory's desire to work jointly with the civic authorities. Of course, the consistory did not have much of a choice in the matter. The town council mandated that ordinarily the consistory would have two members who were also burgomasters.[97] Nonetheless, the consistory was quite willing to work closely with the town council, even if out of necessity. The consistory records note with approval that the city officials were committed to enforcing a stricter Sabbath observance. For instance, when the presiding officer and scribe spoke with the mayor in 1644 they reported that the mayor would seek that desecration of the Sabbath days would be forbidden.[98] In the same way, in 1643, when the presiding officer and scribe met with the magistrate they received a "good resolution" that an end to the "disorder" on the Sabbaths, including buying, selling, and drinking, would be executed.[99]

Yet, the records provide hints of frustration with the unwillingness of the magistrates to take greater steps to ensure a devotion to Sabbath observance.[100] The need for the consistory to send delegates to meet in person with the city magistrates regarding Sabbath desecration underscores how hesitant the civic authorities were to take action; simply sending a letter would not do. As mentioned in previous chapters, political authorities were often hesitant to take action regarding Sunday observance, and the same appears to be true in Kampen.

Sabbath and Establishing a Reformed Identity

The situation in Kampen was one of religious plurality, at least in the eyes of the Reformed authorities. The Reformed congregation was forced to deal with the lingering presence of Catholics, Mennonites/Anabaptists, Remonstrants/Arminians, and Lutherans.[101] It should be duly noted that when the consistory records

---

97 Van der Pol, "Diversity and Ethics in Kampen," 28.

98 GAK, AHGK, August 30, 1644.

99 GAK, AHGK, November 8, 1643.

100 Van der Pol, "Diversity and Ethics in Kampen, 61–62. In my view, Dr. van der Pol overstates the willingness of the civic government to enforce the piety the consistory so desired. Such is the case, for example, when he writes, "Throughout the seventeenth century the civic authorities accepted the responsibility for maintaining a Christian society. The town council and Reformed consistory agreed on the ways in which the Christian religion prescribed such social practices as those affecting public morality and Sunday observance." However, only a few paragraphs later, Dr. van der Pol does recognize that the town council "felt that it was being pulled in two different directions...Officially the town council made few concessions to religious pluralism. In practice, however, the government accommodated divergent religious interests."

101 Van der Pol, "Diversity and Ethics in Kampen," 48–51. Dr. van der Pol briefly addresses each of these groups, though he adds another category of diversity he labels "The World of

speak of Remonstrants, Catholics, or Mennonites there is no guarantee the people in question actually aligned themselves with the particular confessional group of which they were accused. For example, the complaints of Remonstrant preaching do not necessarily mean self-described Remonstrant preachers were holding forth from the pulpit; it could simply mean the consistory was concerned the preacher was advocating for Remonstrant positions or doctrines. Nonetheless, the mere fact that the consistory took the perceived presence of Remonstrants, Mennonites, Catholics, and Lutherans seriously can provide an extremely helpful lens for interpreting how the consistory conceived of its role, the role of the Reformed church, and the way proper Sabbath observance factored into the Reformed identity.

Kampen's consistory and city council were determined to squash any confessional diversity in the city. This is true for all the confessional groups–Catholics, Mennonites, Arminians, and Lutherans. But, such a strident attitude towards these groups was not the norm in the Dutch Republic. Much recent research has demonstrated that Dutch society was much less separated according to confession than other places in Europe, with several scholars even questioning the helpfulness of speaking about "confessionalization" in the Dutch Republic.[102] However, the Kampen consistory portrays none of the willingness to tolerate various confessions found in other Dutch provinces and cities.

As in the rest of the Dutch Republic, the Reformed Church was the official state-supported church, but citizens were not required to be members. Instead, as guaranteed already in the Union of Utrecht in 1579, people were given freedom of conscience. This freedom of conscience did not mean, however, that people of different religious persuasions were free to publicly practice their religions. Such public religious expressions were only permitted for Reformed Christians. In fact, as mentioned above, in order to serve in public office in Kampen it was a requirement to be a full member of the Reformed Church.

Kampen's consistory records frequently mention the Remonstrants, also called Arminians in the records. The Remonstrants were, of course, the group who lodged five main complaints with the established Reformed church in the Dutch Republic which resulted in the Synod of Dort in 1618–1619. The Re-

---

Magic." I have not included this final group because, in my opinion, a Reformed understanding of magic places it in a separate religious category than the Christians groups, albeit heretical from the Reformed point of view, addressed here. Nonetheless, Dr. van der Pol's point regarding the presence of quite diverse religious perspectives in Kampen is important and well taken.

102 Kaplan, *Calvinists and Libertines*, 5–12. Kaplan accepts that confessionalization sheds "light on developments in the Netherlands" but "also that the case of the Netherlands casts a reflective and not uncritical light back on the paradigm." In addition, see Benjamin Kaplan and Judith Pollmann, "Conclusion: Catholic minorities in Protestant states, Britain and the Netherlands, c.1570–1720," in *Catholic communities in Protestant states*, 249–250.

monstrants were condemned at the Synod and forced out of the orthodox, Reformed church. The transition in Kampen, as in many places, was not as smooth as the Reformed authorities would have liked. Not surprising given the historical context, the Kampen consistory records demonstrated a continued concern with the presence of Remonstrant adherents in the city. The consistory frequently mentioned the Remonstrants, also often referred to as Arminians.While completely cataloguing complaints about Remonstrants would require an entirely separate study, I counted nineteen complaints about Remonstrants from 1635–1645.

Several of the complaints the Kampen consistory registered regarding Remonstrants did relate to Sabbath observance. One problem was that the Remonstrants were absenting themselves from the catechism services.[103] Their absence is not all that surprising, given that several theological issues regarding the Heidelberg Catechism were among the topics the Remonstrants wanted addressed at the Synod of Dort.[104] In addition, there was the persistent presence of Remonstrant preaching in the city. Van der Pol has noted a significant presence of Remonstrant preaching prior to the Synod of Dort of 1618–1619 that had a good deal of public and political support in Kampen. Remonstrant preaching persisted after the Synod of Dort, though by then such preaching was much less popular and the consistory quickly sought to put an end to any Remonstrant presence.[105]

The consistory was also concerned with the Catholic presence in Kampen.[106] The complaints about Catholics were quite frequent. Again, formulating total calculations for complaints regarding Catholics is beyond this study, but I found fifteen complaints about Catholics from the years 1635–1645. For example, in October of 1639 the consistory complained that the "fathers" at the previously Catholic orphanage were not encouraging the children to attend the Reformed church services.[107] Undoubtedly, the consistory believed these former Catholic priests who had run the orphanage had not really given up their Catholicism at all.

The third religious group the Reformed consistory had to deal with was the Anabaptists, usually described as "Mennonites" (*Mennonisten*) in the consistory records.[108] As is now well-established, Anabaptists had a long history in the Low Countries. After the disastrous affair of 1534–35 in Munster where Anabaptist

---

103 GAK, AHGK, January 24, 1640; January 29, 1640.
104 Donald Sinnema, "The Heidelberg Catechism at the Synod of Dordt," lecture, H. Henry Meeter Center for Calvin Studies, Grand Rapids, MI, December 5, 2013.
105 Van der Pol, "Diversity and Ethics in Kampen," 33–35.
106 GAK, AHGK, January 12, 1635; August 17, 1636; June 22, 1642; March 19, 1643; June 27, 1645.
107 GAK, AHGK, October 7, 1639.
108 GAK, AHGK, May 26, 1641.

leaders captured the city and attempted to set up their New Jerusalem ended with the execution of several Anabaptist leaders, the Anabaptist movement in the Low Countries coalesced around Menno Simons.[109] As with both the Remonstrants and the Catholics, the Kampen consistory complained frequently about the presence of Mennonites in their midst, not surprising given that an Anabaptist community was found in Kampen early in the seventeenth century.[110] To give only a sense of the frequency of complaints, I counted at least twenty-three complaints about Mennonites from 1640–1646. The consistory was quite clear; Mennonites were not to be tolerated in Kampen. The complaints from the consistory varied regarding Mennonites. In January of 1642 the consistory complained about the "great annoyance" of the Mennonite presence in a local church on Christmas day.[111] In 1644 several mentions of the Mennonites appeared in the consistory records, including the indictment that the Mennonites were desecrating the Lord's Supper and failing to come and hear God's word preached at the church services.[112] Earlier, in 1641, the consistory noted that the Mennonites needed to attend the church services to "hear God's word."[113] The Mennonite presence in Kampen was persistent throughout the seventeenth century, but the consistory was resolute in its attempts to eradicate it.[114]

The final group the consistory was concerned with was the Lutherans. A Lutheran presence was found early on in Kampen, and they even attempted to establish a church in Kampen in 1619. The town council quickly squashed such an idea, but the Lutheran presence continued to be problematic in Kampen. In 1635 the consistory again struggled against Lutheran services being held in the city. The problem was temporarily resolved with the help of the city council when a Lutheran minister was expelled from the city.[115] However, such actions did not put an end to the Lutheran presence. In 1645 the consistory complained about the Lutherans and their great unwillingness to come to church services to hear God's Word.[116] But, the consistory devoted much less attention to the Lutherans than the other confessional groups found in Kampen. Other mentions in the consistory records of Lutherans were quite rare, and Van der Pol argues that by the 1640s the Lutheran presence in Kampen was increasingly tolerated.[117]

---

109 R. Po-chia Hsia, ed., *A Companion to the Reformation World*, Malden, MA: Blackwell Publishing, 2004, 121.
110 Van der Pol, "Diversity and Ethics in Kampen," 41.
111 GAK, AHGK, January 5, 1642.
112 GAK, AHGK, July 12, 1644.
113 GAK, AHGK, May 26, 1641.
114 Van der Pol, "Diversity and Ethics in Kampen," 43–45. Dr. van der Pol notes the continued issues with Mennonites in the second half of the seventeenth century.
115 Van der Pol, "Diversity and Ethics in Kampen," 45.
116 GAK, AHGK, June 27, 1645.
117 Van der Pol, "Diversity and Ethics in Kampen," 46.

The consistory's concern with the Sabbath observance should be understood within this multi-confessional space.[118] The presence of religious pluralism in Kampen helps interpret the consistory's emphasis on Sunday observance in at least two ways. First, for those Christians who were suspicious of or ambivalent towards the Reformed Church, such as *liefhebbers* or those with Anabaptist sympathies, but who were devoted to their religious piety, Sabbath observance was a clear way for them to gauge the moral rigor of the Reformed Church. One of the appeals of the Anabaptist movement in the Dutch Republic was the seriousness with which followers took their faith, in particular a pious devotion to morality. By emphasizing proper Sabbath observance, Reformed authorities were demonstrating their own seriousness regarding Christian morality in an effort to prove the reality of their devotion to the Christian faith and thereby win converts looking for a morally demanding Christian community or, at least, sustain those members desiring a strictly moral Christianity.

Second, an emphasis on proper Sabbath observance aided the Reformed Church in its efforts to portray itself as the true Christian faith. Among the multiple confessions, morality was a barometer for the validity of one's confession. The Heidelberg Catechism is explicit in this regard. Doing good works is one of the ways Christians can "be assured of our faith" since faith is known "by its fruits."[119] A frequent accusation against those accused of being heretics was their immorality. Desecrating the Sabbath only fanned the flames of those denouncing the Reformed faith. Reformed authorities, well aware of the accusations, encouraged devotion to the Sabbath in order to bolster the validity of the Reformed faith amid the claims of multiple confessions all declaring to be the one, true Christian faith.

Sunday Observance, Order, and Scandal

As argued in the previous chapters, proper Sunday observance was important for the religious authorities because it ensured a proper order in society and in the church. The Kampen consistory records support exactly such an argument. While not as frequently as in the classes' records, the consistory records did mention the "disorder" the desecration of the Sabbath caused. The consistory, in January 1627, raised the issue of the Sabbath and noted the "great disorder and desecration of Sabbath days."[120] The same complaint was raised a decade later when the consistory complained of the "disorder" that plagued Sundays and

---

118 It is on this point that Dr. van der Pol and I are in complete agreement.
119 Heidelberg Catechism, Q&A 86.
120 GAK, AHGK, January 5, 1627.

church services. Such disorder was particularly troubling when ill-advised activities were involved. In 1643 the consistory noted the "buying, selling, [brouten?], milling, drinking, clinking [of glasses], and other disorder" on the Sabbath.[121]

However, more prevalent in the Kampen consistory records than in the provincial synod records or the classes' records is the idea of scandalous behavior on Sundays. The consistory records often spoke of the "schandelijk" (spelled in a variety of ways) observance of the Sabbath. For instance, the January 18, 1643 consistory meeting mentioned that attention needed to be given to the "desecration and scandalous profanation of the Lord's Sabbaths."[122]

Scandal by its very definition connotes a public offense. The desecration of the Sabbath was, in the eyes of the consistory, so serious precisely because it was a public sin. The Reformed Church was no doubt under the watchful eye of any number of groups, including competing confessions, its own particularly dedicated members, and the general public. These groups each had their own reasons for taking an interest in the Reformed Church. Competing confessions pounced on any scandal as an opportunity to disparage the authenticity of the Reformed faith in general. Members of the Reformed Church who wanted greater strictness enforced in their church saw scandal as further proof that greater dedication to strict morality was needed in the Dutch Reformed Church. The general public's interest could have served any number of purposes, ranging from questioning the privileged position of the Reformed Church in Dutch society to calling for a loosening of the moral standards that even the pious members of the Dutch Reformed Church could not meet.

In addition to describing the Sabbath offenses as scandalous, the consistory records also complain repeatedly about the "open" or "public" (*openbaar*) desecration of the Sabbath. The consistory noted in 1629 the secular way Sundays were "openly" observed in the churches.[123] In 1640 the consistory complained about the "public" sins that were profaning and desecrating the Sabbath days.[124] The consistory was obviously concerned not only that the Sabbath was being desecrated but that it was being desecrated in such a public, open manner.

Describing the *openbaar* desecration of the Sabbath is typically used in association with drunkenness and drinking on Sundays. For instance, in May 1639 and April 1641, the consistory's complaints of the public desecration of the Sabbath included public drunkenness on Sundays.[125] Similarly, the consistory had complained years earlier about the desecration of the Sabbath days with the

---

121 GAK, AHGK, November 8, 1643.
122 GAK, AHGK, January 18, 1643.
123 GAK, AHGK, December 9, 1629.
124 GAK, AHGK, January 15, 1640.
125 GAK, AHGK, May 31, 1639; April 3, 1641.

drinking "publically of beer and wine on such days."[126] Public drunkenness was an offense everyone could see, and witnessing it on Sundays, when people were supposed to be in church, was particularly troubling for the consistory and, at the same time, damning to the piety of the Reformed Church and her members.

This *public* scandal was particularly important given the position of the Dutch Reformed Church. As mentioned earlier, Kampen citizens were not required to join the Reformed Church, an option many citizens elected to exercise. In order to maintain its reputation and attract church members, the consistory in Kampen needed the Reformed congregations to be above reproach. Public sin cast the entire Reformed faith in a bad light, and it was even more reason for suspicious, nominal Christians to forego membership. Public Sabbath desecration demonstrated to citizens in Kampen of other confessions or of no confession at all that Reformed Christians led no better lives than they did. Moreover, public Sabbath desecration reminded everyone that the Reformed Church was not the beacon of faithful Christian piety that they so desired to be.

Additionally, the public nature of Sabbath desecration served as a painful reminder that the Reformed Church was unable to completely reform Dutch society. Christine Kooi has argued that the persistence of the Catholics' Holland Mission in the Dutch Republic served as a reminder "that the reformation of soul and society was at best an uncompleted and at worst an endangered process." In the same way, open desecration of the Sabbath served as unwelcome evidence to the Kampen consistory that its desires for a holy, Reformed city were far from complete. In fact, its members were unable even to maintain complete proper Sunday observance among their own faithful. The public nature of this desecration served as an obvious marker for all to see that the Reformed faith was in danger, to again borrow Kooi's language, "of becoming one more confession in a multiconfessional society."[127]

Conclusions

Having investigated Sabbath practices and discipline via the local consistory, the Kampen consistory records have shown the Sabbath was a serious concern in the eyes of the local religious authorities. While it would be wrong to extrapolate conclusions from one local consistory to all consistories throughout the Dutch Republic, the consistory records studied in this chapter provide at least a framework for how the Sabbath was understood at the local level in the Dutch Reformation.

---

126 GAK, AHGK, February 25, 1624.
127 Kooi, "Reformed Reaction to the Holland Mission," 175.

What the consistory records have demonstrated to a greater extent than either the provincial synods or the regional classes is that the Sabbath concerns were fundamentally related to issues of confessionalization. At least in Kampen, the issues of Sabbath profanation and desecration were closely linked with attempts to establish a unique Reformed identity. The Reformed Church in Kampen faced other religious confessions, ranging from the closely related Remonstrants to the more radical Anabaptists to the hated Catholics, and enforcing a strict observance of the Sabbath was an essential way of establishing their own confession. Reformed church sermon services and education in the Reformed faith at the afternoon catechism services were important ways for Dutch Reformed church members to be inculcated in the Reformed faith and the Dutch Reformed Church.

In addition, the consistory records affirm the argument that the Sabbath was important in the Dutch Reformation because it allowed the Reformed church to establish a sense of order. Proper observance of the Sabbath ensured proper order within the Reformed Church but also within the larger society as a whole. If the Sabbath were to devolve into immoral behaviors and a lack of respect for the church services, then disorder, which the Reformed frequently equated with evil, within the Reformed community threatened to take over. If that disorder were permitted to spread to the whole of society, then society itself might unravel into immorality, violence, and general chaos.

Turning the attention back to the theological understanding of the Sabbath, the Kampen consistory's theological regulation of the Sabbath most closely aligns with the theological concerns that Johannes a Lasco and, especially, Zacharius Ursinus expressed. The primacy of the ministry of the church regarding Sabbath observance is quite clear in the Kampen consistory records. On the other hand, the concerns of a "spiritual rest" so dominant in Calvin find little expression in the consistory records. Even the complaints about immoral behavior are related not to spiritual rest from sin but, rather, to how they affect one's attendance at the preaching. The same principle holds true for the sabbatarian concerns of à Brakel and the Nadere Reformatie. The records do display some concern with recreation and work on Sundays, but the records indicate a primary concern not with rest, as à Brakel stressed, but with the way these activities interfere with attendance at the church services.

Thus, the Kampen consistory records in the first half of the seventeenth century confirm what has been seen in earlier chapters. Namely, the Sabbath was an important aspect of Reformed piety, and Reformed church authorities were insistent on proper Sunday observance. In Kampen, the particular emphasis was on the Sunday morning preaching services and the afternoon catechism services. Of course, other concerns about immorality, recreation, work, and the like also arise. In seeking to understand the consistory's concern with Sabbath desecration, the consistory records support the conclusion that the consistory deemed the Sabbath so important, consciously or unconsciously, because it was a public way in which the Reformed churches could exhibit their pious and ordered nature in the face of multiple competing confessions, such as Remonstrants, Anabaptists, Catholics, and Lutherans.

Conclusion

The most obvious and general conclusion of the previous chapters is that the Sabbath was an important aspect of the Dutch Reformation. Theologians in the Dutch Reformed tradition gave a significant amount of attention to the Sabbath. Moreover, how the Sabbath was to be understood theologically was a more complicated, controversial issue than one might suppose. The primary argument occurred over whether or not the fourth commandment was a ceremonial or moral commandment or some mix of the two. In addition, theologians needed to determine whether the Sabbath was primarily about rest or worship. If the focus was meant to be on rest, then the issue became what sort of rest the fourth commandment required.

Similarly, the church records attest to the importance of Sunday observance in Dutch Reformed churches. The church authorities at all levels were concerned that Sundays were observed properly. Most notably, Sunday observance meant attending worship services. But, Sunday observance also meant abstaining from sinful behaviors, frivolous recreational, and work. For the ordinary Dutch Reformed church member, Sunday observance was a central aspect of one's lived Christian piety. At the very least, religious authorities demanded proper Sabbath devotion even if Dutch congregants more frequently preferred desecration.

Dutch Reformed Theological Understanding of the Sabbath

As the first three chapters established, the Dutch Reformed theological tradition had surprisingly different ways of understanding the Sabbath. At times these differences were quite drastic, such as Wilhelmus à Brakel's complete rejection of the spiritual, ceremonial interpretation of the Sabbath commandment. In other instances, these differences were subtler. This is often the case when looking at John Calvin, Johannes a Lasco, and Zacharias Ursinus. For instance, Calvin denotes "spiritual rest" as the primary purpose of the Sabbath commandment, which a Lasco and Ursinus also mention albeit with somewhat less emphasis and slightly different terminology.

As demonstrated in chapter one, Calvin believed the Sabbath to be primarily about a "spiritual rest." This spiritual rest means, essentially, resting from one's own spiritual works so that God can work in him or her. In Calvin's view, the fourth commandment is not about any one day of the week; spiritual rest may begin on Sunday but should be carried out to every day of the week. The commandment does also recommend gathering for worship, something extremely important to Calvin, but it is a secondary aspect of the Sabbath itself. Even more surprisingly, the issue of work on the Sabbath is not something on which Calvin spends a great deal of time.

A Lasco's conclusions, examined in chapter two, regarding the Sabbath are much the same as Calvin's. Though he uses the phrase "interior Sabbath," he focuses on the need to spend time resting from sin and one's own spiritual works in order to allow God to work, all things found in Calvin. However, in Ursinus a greater emphasis is placed on participating in the "ministries of the church" on Sundays. While Ursinus is clear that the Sabbath includes a spiritual rest from sin and a physical rest from work, Ursinus pays much greater attention to the importance of participating in the ministries of the church. For Ursinus, much more than either Calvin or a Lasco, the importance of the Sabbath is worship, not rest, which represents a significant shift both practically and theologically from the emphasis on spiritual rest.

The Nadere Reformatie within the Dutch Reformed tradition took a radically different theological approach to the Sabbath. In the Nadere Reformatie, roughly akin to English Puritanism or German Pietism, one sees a strict Sabbatarianism. As Wilhelmus à Brakel makes clear, the Sabbath commandment is completely moral, not ceremonial and, as such, must be followed as described in the Old Testament. So, for à Brakel, the Sabbath must be observed on the seventh day of every week and requires absolute rest from all activity, though à Brakel rejects completely the notion of a spiritual rest. Worship is also required on the Sabbath, but the Sabbath requires cessation from all sorts of activities, activities about which à Brakel is pointedly specific.

In looking at the various understandings of the Sabbath in Dutch Reformed theology, it becomes quite clear that a sabbatarian understanding was not present in the early Dutch Reformed theological tradition. As argued in the first chapter, Calvin himself did not hold to a sabbatarian position, and, as discussed in the second chapter, early theologians in the Dutch Reformed tradition such as a Lasco and Ursinus were certainly not Sabbatarians. Thus, sabbatarian theology did not become a mainstay of Dutch Reformed theology in the sixteenth century.[1] It was not until the Reformed presence was more established in the

---

1 Balke, "Calvijn en de Zondagsheiliging," 185–186. Balke, correctly, briefly makes the point that Calvin's understanding was not Puritan.

Dutch Republic that Sabbatarianism became a widely acceptable theological position. As the third chapter argued, the emphasis on a strict, sabbatarian understanding of the fourth commandment originated with the Nadere Reformatie under the influence of English Puritanism. Such a view of the Sabbath would last throughout the seventeenth century and was clearly articulated in the popular work of Wilhelmus à Brakel. Therefore, it is safe to conclude that sabbatarian theology was not present early in the Dutch Reformed theological tradition but was a later theological development found primarily in the Nadere Reformatie.

Obviously, Dutch Reformed theology did not have one uniform attitude towards the Sabbath. It is impossible, then, to speak of the "Dutch Reformed" understanding of the Sabbath as some identifiable, unified entity. As a result, the obvious question to ask is which of the theological understandings of the Sabbath found clearest expression in the lived experience of Dutch Reformed Christians. The question can be asked of Dutch Reformed clergy, casual church goers, full church members, and everyone in between. To answer that question the final three chapters turned to church records to seek answers.

Sabbath Practices in Dutch Reformed Church Records

The Sabbath in the Dutch Reformation was far from being simply a theological discussion point. As the Dutch provincial synod records, regional classes' records, and Kampen consistory records demonstrate, the Sabbath was a frequent point of discussion. Dutch church authorities considered Sabbath observance an important point of order and policed it as such. The various church governing bodies lamented the desecration of the Sabbath and consistently sought to encourage and enforce better Sunday observance. While their efforts seem to have had little positive results, their efforts were persistent from the early years of the Dutch Reformed presence in the second half of the sixteenth century and into the first half of the seventeenth century.

While the theological understanding of the Sabbath was quite varied, the actual disciplining and practicing of the Sabbath appears to have been much more uniform. As the final three chapters showed, from the expansive provincial synods to the local consistory the ecclesiastical governing bodies were concerned, albeit to varying degrees, about Sabbath observance. The concerns focused on two overarching categories. First, concerns regarding unacceptable behaviors on the Sabbath were a frequent source of contention. These included a number of blatantly immoral behaviors such as sexual promiscuity, fighting, and drunkenness. But, undesirable behaviors could also include less insidious activities. Recreational activities, such as sailing, shooting clay pigeons, and playing games, were all activities the authorities sought to curb. Similarly, the issue of buying and selling on Sundays, typically at the Sunday markets, is found throughout the records. While generally not objectionable activities, these were not acceptable behaviors for the Sabbath.

Second, the governing bodies were concerned with church services on the Sabbath. This was particularly true in Kampen but can be found at the provincial synods and regional classes as well. Complaints about disruptions during the preaching services are frequent, though the specifics of such disruptions are not always clear. Attendance at these services was also a point of contention. This is particularly true regarding the afternoon catechism services. Church members were quite unwilling to attend these services, much to the distress of the authorities. The complaints did include morning preaching, though Dutch congregants were more willing to attend these church services. The issue of the Lord's Supper was not raised frequently at the provincial or regional levels, but the concern did come up often in Kampen. Tending to the ministry of the church on Sundays included attendance and attention at morning sermon services, afternoon catechism services, and, at least in Kampen, proper participation in the Lord's Supper.

Other Sabbath issues were occasionally raised but were not the focus of the authorities' concerns. Most surprising, the discussion of work on the Sabbath comes up relatively infrequently. Likely the infrequent complaints about work are the result of people not typically working on the Sabbath, though such a conclusion is not definite. Similarly, people's activities at their homes rarely are addressed. Discussions of whether or not people spent their Sabbaths at home engaged in pious Bible reading or prayer are generally not found in the records.

What the church records at all levels in the Dutch Reformed polity demonstrate is that Sabbath concerns were found early on in Dutch Reformed congregations and classes. Church authorities complained about Sabbath desecration in the latter decades of the sixteenth century just as the Reformed presence in the Low Countries was gaining significant traction. Thus, while Dutch Reformed theologians did not make sabbatarian arguments until the seventeeth century, how church authorities sought to enforce the Sabbath was quite sabbatarian in nature early in the life of the Dutch Reformed churches. The early presence casts serious doubt on the conclusions of previous scholars, several of whom were noted in the above Introduction, who have credited English Puritanism with the sole origination of an emphasis on strict Sabbath observance. Certainly my work demonstrates that in practice the Dutch Reformed churches sought a strict observance of the Sabbath before Puritan influences had effectively reached the Dutch Republic. In other words, the theology of the Sabbath in the Dutch Reformed tradition did not match how church authorities attempted to enforce Sabbath practices. In the Dutch Reformed churches in the final third of the sixteenth century Sabbath practices were quite strict and tended towards Sabbatarianism even though such theological positions were not widely held until decades later. Such an incongruity between theology and practice raises further issues regarding how a theology of the Sabbath and Sabbath practices were related in the Dutch Reformed tradition.

Sabbath Theology and Practice

Throughout this project the attempt has been to analyze the interplay between the Dutch Reformed theology of the Sabbath and actual Sabbath observance within the Dutch Reformed churches. The relationship between theology and religious practice is notoriously complicated.[2] In this study I have largely given attention to the way theology has impacted actual practice. That is to say, the study began with theology and then examined practices. Those practices were subsequently interpreted in light of the theology of the Sabbath as Calvin, a Lasco, Ursinus, and à Brakel articulated it.

What this study has demonstrated is that the transition from a theology of the Sabbath to actual Sabbath practices was not seamless. Religious authorities, often themselves theologians, did seem to appropriate the theological traditions of the Sabbath within the Dutch Reformed sphere. The church records pick up the emphasis on participation in the ministries of the church, present in Calvin, a Lasco, and à Brakel but stressed most by Ursinus. Similarly, the church governing bodies recognized the importance of abstaining from immoral behaviors, a sort of spiritual rest Calvin and a Lasco emphasized.

However, if the church records are to be believed, the average church member was much less willing to incorporate the theological ideas of the Sabbath into her or his religious piety. Dutch Reformed church members appear to have been quite willing to attend morning sermon services. However, the same cannot be said for the afternoon catechism services. The poor attendance at these services was a battle the church authorities continually waged. The same can be said for church members' behaviors regarding Sabbath observance. While it cannot be said with certainty how widespread such scandalous behavior actually was, it was widespread enough for church authorities to repeatedly complain about such activities. A good number of Dutch church members were not content attending church and resting at home on Sunday, often their only day off work for the week.

---

2 Christine Helmer, "Theology and the study of religion: a relationship," in *The Cambridge Companion to Religious Studies*, ed. Robert A. Orsi, Cambridge: Cambridge University Press, 2012, 230–254. Helmer briefly addresses the tension and provides what she believes to be a helpful way forward.

Instead, they were drawn to a wide variety of activities ranging from drinking at the tavern to shopping at the market to playing any number of games. These Dutch Reformed Christians were, at best, ignorant of the theological under-standing of the Sabbath which the Dutch theological tradition advocated. At worst, they simply rejected such theological viewpoints and the subsequent implications. The Dutch Reformed theology of the Sabbath, in all its various strands, was certainly not completely welcome in the lived religious experience of many Dutch Reformed congregants.

But, as religious studies scholars have noted, religious practice can influence theology in a variety of important ways.[3] Admittedly, those influences have not received as much attention in this project but should not be discounted. It can be difficult to decipher exactly how religious practice might influence theology; proving causation is even more difficult. For instance, did people's proclivity to recreational activities on Sunday influence à Brakel's insistence on a complete cessation of activity on the Sabbath? Or, did people's lack of attendance at cat-echism services cause Ursinus to place a greater emphasis on the ministry of the church as essential to proper Sabbath observance? Such influences are certainly possible, if not likely, but also extremely difficult to delineate completely.

Order, Pluralism, and Confessionalization

As I have argued throughout, the role of the Sabbath in the Dutch Reformation should be interpreted in two major ways. First, as described in the Introduction, the Sabbath was an important way for the Dutch Reformed church authorities to establish order within their churches and, additionally, in the larger society. The sense of order the Sabbath provided comes through in several ways. Theologi-cally, Calvin, a Lasco, Ursinus, and à Brakel all at least mention the topic of order in their discussion of the Sabbath. For some, such as à Brakel, Sabbath worship was required to take place on Sunday, in part because it established order within the church. For others, such as Calvin, a Lasco, and Ursinus, Sabbath observance on Sunday was simply a way of maintaining order within Christ's church. In addition, the church records frequently use the language of "disorder" when addressing complaints about the Sabbath. When Sabbath desecration is dis-cussed it is often designated as *ongeregeldheid*, meaning "disordered" or "un-regulated." *Onordentlickheden*, another term meaning "unorderly" is also used

---

3 Two of the clearest examples of this, in my opinion, are the following: Robert A. Orsi, *Thank You, St. Jude: Women's Devotion to the Patron Saint of Hopeless Causes*, New Haven, CT: Yale University Press, 1996; Leigh Eric Schmidt, *Holy Fairs: Scotland and the Making of American Revivalism*, Grand Rapids, MI: William B. Eerdmans Publishing Co., 2001.

to describe the desecration of the Sabbath. Thus, in terms of both theology and practical discipline, the topic of the Sabbath was deeply connected with order in the church and in society more broadly.

Second, the Sabbath contributed to the confessionalization goals of the Reformed ecclesiastical authorities. In other words, Sabbath practices were a way church authorities sought to establish a Reformed identity in a multiconfessional space. As has been well established, the Dutch Republic contained a number of Christian confessions within its borders, not to mention a Jewish and Muslim presence.[4] As the sixth chapter demonstrated, this was certainly the case in the city of Kampen. More broadly, the provincial synods and regional classes also frequently connected Sunday observance with issues of other confessional groups. Sometimes this meant that Catholics were holding their own worship services or Reformed members were attending Catholic worship services. Even Anabaptists, typically known for their strict morality, could occasionally be the subject of a complaint about Sabbath observance.

Related to this second point is my third argument that the Sabbath was important because it was vital to the reputation of the Reformed churches. Sunday observance was an easy visible, public way in which to evaluate the piety of Reformed Christians. Maintaining the appearance of piety was particularly important in the polemical battles with Remonstrants, Catholics, and Anabaptists. Impious behavior was a certain way to undermine the veracity of one's confessional group; the true church would, naturally, also be the most pious one. The church records contain ample evidence that the church authorities were acutely aware of the public nature of Sunday observance. Most notably, the church records frequently describe the *openbaar*, meaning "public," desecration of the Sabbath. The records also speak of the *schandelijk* observance of the Sabbath, denoting the public scandal such poor observance of the Sabbath caused. Clearly, church authorities recognized the public nature of Sunday observance and the damage desecration of the Sabbath caused to the reputation of the Reformed confessional identity.

Implications for Understanding the Reformation

Assuming the above conclusions are valid, my research alters or, at least, nuances how both the Protestant Reformation, more generally, and the Dutch Reformation, more specifically, are understood. In addition to the issues of order, pluralism, and confessionalization addressed above, this is true in at least four ways. It is worth mentioning briefly these ways in which a more complete un-

---

4 Hsia, "Introduction," in *Calvinism and Religious Toleration*, 1–7.

derstanding of the Sabbath in the Dutch Reformation adds to the fullness of understanding the Dutch Reformed tradition and the Protestant Reformation more broadly.

First, tracing the theological understanding of the Sabbath in the Dutch Reformed tradition demonstrates that in several important ways the Dutch Reformed Church was far from simply replicating Calvin's theological thought. As several scholars, most notably Richard Muller, have convincingly argued, to call the Dutch Reformed theological "Calvinist" does serious injustice to the development of the unique theological tradition within the Dutch Reformed tradition.[5] Clearly, a theologian such as Wilhelmus à Brakel has a much different theology of the Sabbath than Calvin ever did. Even Zacharius Ursinus, while much closer to Calvin's understanding of the Sabbath, develops his theology of the Sabbath in ways that at least nuance how Calvin understood the Sabbath. Examining theological notions of the Sabbath establishes yet another way in which the Dutch Reformed Church developed its own unique tradition and was far from simply being "Calvinist" if that term means adopting all of Calvin's theological ideas.

Second, my research further adds to discussions about the interplay between religious authorities and lay church members. While even the distinction between lay believers and church elites is somewhat faulty given the amount of overlap, such interactions did exist. As other scholars have noted, interactions between church members and church governing bodies, be they synods, classis meetings, or consistories, were often conflicted. On the other hand, other scholars have found that such interactions could also be quite amicable and cooperative. My research adds further depth to the picture of interactions between church authorities and lay people. The church records primarily tend towards the former depiction of tension between religious authorities and common citizens. However, at least in regard to Sunday observance, the church bodies showed considerable restraint and refrained from drastic, draconian punishments. In this way, perhaps the religious authorities sought a more amicable, cooperative relationship with their congregants even if it meant moderating their demands for piety.

Regarding Sunday observance, Dutch citizens were frequently unwilling to give in to the wishes of the church officials. While church authorities continually pushed for better Sunday observance, they also realized the limits of their authority and seemed to resign themselves to a certain amount of inevitable Sabbath desecration. Such a situation verifies that lay church members certainly were

---

5 Richard A. Muller, "Calvin and the 'Calvinists': Assessing Continuities and Discontinuities between the Reformation and Orthodoxy, Part One" *Calvin Theological Journal* 30, no. 2 (November 1995): 345–375; Muller, "Calvin and the 'Calvinists': Part Two," 125–160.

not powerless but, rather, had significant agency in their lived religious experience.

Third, the notion that the Sabbath was only a particular point of emphasis for Puritan or pietistic strands within the Protestant Reformation needs to be revisited. As has been made clear, Sunday observance was important to Dutch religious authorities early on in the existence of the Dutch Reformed Church, both theologically and practically. While English Puritanism certainly influenced a theological tendency towards Sabbatarianism in the Dutch tradition, a strict, sabbatarian Sunday observance was the goal of Dutch church authorities and the demand for such Sunday observance was quite inherent within the Dutch Reformed Church.

Finally, my research demonstrates again the complexity of the relationship between ecclesiastical and political authorities. This was undoubtedly true throughout the Protestant Reformation, but the Dutch situation was also quite unique. At all levels of church polity, Dutch ecclesiastical governing bodies often appealed to their political counterpoints to better regulate Sunday observance. Yet, the political authorities responded with varying degrees of willingness. These exchanges indicate that for a variety of reasons political authorities were unwilling to completely support the Dutch Reformed Church, and this wavering support included demanding strict Sunday observance. Given the lukewarm response, religious authorities needed to turn to other avenues for regulating behavior, but their alternatives were limited to their own church members. This limitation significantly hampered the impact they could have on Sunday observance within the overall society. Surely the relationships between religious and political powers in Dutch communities was a continual struggle for power and control yet a struggle that was mitigated since both parties also recognized the need for cooperation.

Opportunities for Further Research

The role of Sunday observance in the Dutch Reformation and the theological understanding of the Sabbath still require further study. In terms of theology, the opportunities for further research are quite varied. Perhaps most importantly, given its importance for the Dutch Reformed tradition, the Synod of Dort's decisions and discussions regarding Sabbath observance need more attention. Also, theological strands on the edge of Dutch orthodoxy need more attention. Most notably, this includes Jacobus Arminius and later the Remonstrants. It might also include other theologians important in the Nadere Reformatie such as Willem Teellinck, Herman Witsius, and Jodocus van Lodenstein, among others.

This need for further research is particularly true for actual Sunday observance in Dutch Reformed congregations, especially at the local level. What might studies of other Dutch consistories reveal about how the local church authorities attempted to regulate Sabbath observance? Additionally, studies of other local communities may possibly uncover even further how ordinary church members responded to or, equally as likely, did not respond to demands of Sunday observance.

Finally, the focus of Sabbath observance here has been mostly on the second half of the sixteenth century and the first half of the seventeenth century. To more fully understand Sunday observance in the Dutch Reformation more research is needed into the practices of the Dutch congregants in the second half of the seventeenth century. Did Sabbath concerns persist in the church records throughout the latter portion of the seventeenth centuries? Were the complaints more or less frequent, and did they include the same sorts of concerns or were they quite different? Answers to all of these questions will only add more color to our understanding of life in the Dutch Reformed Church and, particularly, how the Sabbath was policed and practiced.

While the opportunities for further research abound, what this study has shown is that proper Sabbath observance was a vital part of the Dutch Reformed identity. The Dutch theological tradition moved over time from viewing the Sabbath as a spiritual rest to participation in the ministries of the church to a sabbatarian demand for complete cessation of activity on the first day of every week. The Dutch ecclesiastical authorities adopted each theological view to a certain extent, though the overall emphasis was on participating in the ministry of the church. The sabbatarian propensity towards complete rest was present at all ecclesiastical levels in the Dutch church records from the early years of the Dutch Reformation, though the focus was always towards participation in the church services. The Dutch Reformed church members did not always comply, finding it difficult to abstain from recreational and sometimes even immoral behaviors and to attend the afternoon catechism services. However, in an effort to establish a Reformed confessional identity and maintain a pious order within the church, the Dutch Reformed church authorities continued to emphasize a greater devotion to the Sabbath even as church members were so frequently prone to Sabbath desecration

Bibliography

Primary Sources

Manuscript Sources

Archief van Gemeente Kampen (AGK). "Acta der vergaderingen van de Classis Kampen (1618–1651)." X.I.A.18.

–. "Acta der vergaderingen van de Classis Vollenhove (1597–1636)." X.I.C.157.

–. "Register van handelingen van de Algemene Kerkeraad van Kampen (1618–1900)." In the "Archief Hervormde Gemeente Kampen (AHGK)." II.A.9–20.

Printed Sources

Abels, P.H.A.M. /A. Ph. F. Wouters, eds. *Provinciale Synode Zuid-Holland: Classis Delft en Delfland 1572–1620.* Vol. 7 of *Classicale acta, 1573–1620.* Den Haag: Instituut voor Nederlandse Geschiedenis, 2001.

Aquinas, Thomas. *Summa Theologica.* Translated by Fathers of the English Dominican Province. Benziger Brothers, 1947.

Augustine. *City of God.* Vol. 2, Series I of *Nicene and Post-Nicene Fathers.* Edited by Philip Schaff. Buffalo: The Christian Literature Company, 1887.

–. *Reply to Faustus the Manichæan.* Vol. 4, Series I of *Nicene and Post-Nicene Fathers.* Edited by Philip Schaff. Buffalo: The Christian Literature Company, 1887.

Bouterse, J., ed. *Particuliere Synode Zuid-Holland: Classis Rotterdam en Schieland 1580–1620,* Vol. 3 of *Classicale acta, 1573–1620.* Den Haag: Instituut voor Nederlandse Geschiedenis, 1991.

–. ed. *Provinciale Synode Zeeland: Classis Walcheren 1601–1620, Classis Zuid-Beveland 1579–1591.* Vol. 4 of *Classicale acta, 1573–1620.* Den Haag: Instituut voor Nederlandse Geschiedenis, 1995.

Brakel, Wilhelmus à. *De Redelijke Godsdienst: In welke de Goddelijke waarheden van het genadeverbond worden verklaard, tegen partijen beschermd en tot beoefening aangedrongen, alsmede de bedeling des verbonds in het Oude en Nieuwe Testament en de ontmoeting der kerk in het Nieuwe Testament, vertoond in een verklaring van de Openbaring van Johannes.* Leiden: D. Donner, 1893.

–. *The Christian's Reasonable Service in Which Divine Truths Concerning the Covenant of Grace are Expounded, Defended Against Opposing Parties, and Their Practice Advocated, as well as The Administration of this covenant in the Old and New Testaments.* Edited by Joel R. Beeke. Translated by Bartel Elshout. 3 Vols. Grand Rapids, MI: Reformation Heritage Books, 1992.

–. *The Christian's Reasonable Service.* Translated by Bartel Elshout. 4 Vols. Grand Rapids, MI: Reformation Heritage Books, 2012.

Calvin, Jean. *Institutes of the Christian Religion.* Edited by John T. McNeill. Translated by Ford Lewis Battles. Philadelphia: Westminster Press, 1960. Reprint, Louisville, KY: Westminster John Knox Press, 2006.

–. *Institutes of the Christian Religion.* Translated by Henry Beveridge. Grand Rapids, MI: Eerdmans, 1989.

Calvin, John, *Calvin's First Catechism: A Commentary.* Edited by I. John Hesselink. Louisville, KY: Westminster John Knox Press, 1997.

–. *Calvin: Theological Treatises.* Translated and edited by J.K.S. Reid. Louisville, KY: Westminster John Knox Press, 1954.

–. *Commentaries on the Epistles of Paul the Apostle to the Philippians, Colossians, and Thessalonians.* Translated by John Pringle. Edinbourgh: Calvin Translation Society, 1851.

–. *Commentaries on the Four Last Books of Moses Arranged in the Form of a Harmony.* Translated by Charles William Bingham. 4 Vols. Edinburgh: Calvin Translation Society, 1852–55.

–. *Commentary on a Harmony of the Evangelists Matthew, Mark, and Luke.* Translated by William Pringle. 3 Vols. Edinbourgh: Calvin Translation Society, 1845–1846.

–. *Commentary on the Epistle of Paul the Apostle to the Hebrews.* Translated by John Owen. Edinbourgh: Calvin Translation Society, 1853.

–. *Commentary on the First Book of Moses Called Genesis.* Translated by John King. 2 Vols. Edinbourgh: Calvin Translation Society, 1847–1850.

–. *Instruction in the Faith (1537).* Translated by Paul Fuhrmann. Philadelphia: John Knox Westminster Press, 1949.

–. *Ioannis Calvini Scripta Ecclesiastica. Volumen II: Instruction et Confession de Foy Dont on Use en L'Eglise de Geneve; Catechismus seu Christianae Religionis Institutio Ecclesiae Genevensis.* Edited by Anette Zillenbiller and Marc Vial. Gene`ve : Librairie Droz, 2002.

Calvini, Ioannis. *Opera quae supersunt Omnia.* Edited by Guilielmus Baum, Eduardus Cunitz, and Eduardus Reuss. 59 Vols. Corpus Reformatorum. Braunschweig: C.A. Schwetschke, 1863–1900.

Calvin, John. *The Sermons of M. Iohn Calvin upon the fifth booke of Moses called Deuteronomie…,* Translated by Arthur Golding. London: Henry Middleton, 1583.

Cox, Robert, ed. *The Whole Doctrine of Calvin About the Sabbath and the Lord's Day: Extracted from His Commentaries, Catechism, and Institutes of the Christian Religion.* Edinburgh: Maclachlan and Stewart, 1860.

Dennison, James T. *Reformed Confessions of the 16th and 17th Centuries in English Translation.* 4 Vols. Grand Rapids, MI: Reformation Heritage Books, 2008–2014.

Dooren, J.P. van, ed. *Particuliere Synode Zuid-Holland: Classis Dordrecht 1573–1600.* Vol. 1 of *Classicale acta, 1573–1620.* Den Haag: Nijhoff, 1980.

Ecumenical Creeds and Reformed Confessions. Grand Rapids, MI: CRC Publications, 1987.

Gelderen, J. van and C. Ravensbergen, eds. *Provinciale Synode Overijssel: Classis Deventer 1601–1620, Classis Kampen 1596–1601 en 1618–1620, Classis Steenwijk/Vollenhove 1601–1620*. Vol. 6 of *Classicale acta, 1573–1620*. Den Haag: Instituut voor Nederlandse Geschiedenis, 2000.

Jensma, Theunis W. *Uw Rijk Kome: Acta van de Kerkeraad van de Nederduits Gereformeerde Gemeente te Dordrecht, 1573–1579*. Dordrecht: Uitgeverij J. P. van den Tol, 1981.

Kingdon, Robert M., Thomas A. Lambert, Isabella M. Watt, Jeffrey R. Watt, and M. Wallace McDonald, eds. *Registers of the Consistory of Geneva in the Time of Calvin*. Grand Rapids, MI: Eerdmans, 2000.

Knuttel, W. P. C. *Acta der particuliere synoden van Zuid-Holland, 1621–1700*. 6 Vols. 's-Gravenhage: Nijhoff, 1908–1916.

Koffeman, Leo, ed. "Hoe Calvijns is het Nederlands Calvinisme?". Special Issue, *Kosmos en oecumene: maandblad gewijd aan het samen-leven in kerk en wereld* 24, no. 9 (1990).

Kok, M., ed. *Provinciale Synode Zuid-Holland: Classis Leiden 1585–1620, Classis Woerden 1617–1620*. Vol. 5 of *Classicale acta, 1573–1620*. Den Haag: Instituut voor Nederlandse Geschiedenis, 1996.

Kuyper, Herman H. *De Post-Acta of Nahandelingen van de Nationale Synode van Dordrecht in 1618 en 1619 Gehouden, Naar den Authentieken Tekst in het Latijn en Nederlandsch Uitgegeven en met Toelichtingen Voorzien, Voorafgegaan door de Geschiedenis van de Acta, de Autographa en de Post-acta dier Synode en Gevolgd door de Geschiedenis van de Revisie der Belijdenisschriften en der Liturgie, Benevens de Volledige Lijst der Gravamina op de Dortsche Synode Ingediend. Een historische Studie*. Amsterdam: Höveker & Wormser, 1899.

Lasco, Johannes a. *Joannis a Lasco Opera tam edita quam inedita*. 2 Vols. Edited by Abraham Kuyper. Amstelodam: Müller, 1866.

–. *Forma ac ratio tot Ecclessiastici Ministerij, in pereginorum, potissimum vero Germanorum Ecclesia: instituta Londini in Anglica, per Pientissimum Principem Anglicae etc. Regem Eduardum, eius nominis Sextum: Anno post Christum natum 1550. Addito ad calcem libelli Privilegio suae majestatis. Autore Joanne a Lasco Polinae Barone*, Frankfurt, 1555.

–. *Toute la forma & maniere du Minstere Ecclesiastique....*In *Marian Protestantism: Six Studies*, Edited by Andrew Pettegree. Brookfield, VT: Ashgate, 1996.

Micron, Marten. *De Christlicke Ordinancien der Nederlantscher Ghemeinten te Londen (1554)*. Edited by Willem Frederik Dankbaar. 's-Gravenhage: M. Nijhoff, 1956.

Müller, E.F. Karl. *Die Bekenntnisschriften der reformierten Kirche*. Waltrop: Hartmut Spenner, 1903. Reprinted in 1999.

Niemeyer, H.A. *Collectio confessionum in ecclesiis reformatis publicatarum*. Lipsiae, 1840.

Olevianus, Caspar. *A Firm Foundation: An Aid to Interpreting the Heidelberg Catechism*. Translated and edited by Lyle Bierma. Grand Rapids, MI: Baker Books, 1995.

Ravensbergen, C., ed. *Provinciale synode Gelderland: Bd. 1. Classis Nijmegen 1598–1620. Classis Tiel/Bommel 1606–1613. Classis Tiel 1613–1620. Classis Bommel 1614–1620. Bd. 2. Classis Zutphen 1593–1620. Classis Over-Veluwe (Arnhem) 1598–1620. Classis Neder-Veluwe (Harderwijk) 1592–1620*. Vol. 9 of *Classicale acta, 1573–1620*. Den Haag: Huygens ING, 2012.

Reitsma, Johannes and S. D. Van Veen. *Acta der provinciale en particuliere synoden gehouden in de noordelijke Nederlanden gedurende de jaren 1572–1620.* 8 Vol. Groningen: J.B. Wolters, 1892–1899.

Reuter, Quirinus, ed. *Zacharias Ursini Opera Theologica.* 3 Vols. Heidelberg, 1612.

Roelevink, J., ed. *Particuliere Synode Zuid-Holland: Classis Dordrecht 1601–1620, Classis Breda 1616–1620,* Vol. 2 of *Classicale acta, 1573–1620.* Den Haag: Instituut voor Nederlandse Geschiedenis, 1991.

Rutgers, Frederik L. *Acta van de Nederlandsche Synoden der zestiende eeuw.* Dordrecht: Van den Tol, 1980.

Schilling, Heinz, / Klaus-Dieter Schreiber. *Die Kirchenratsprotokolle der Reformierten Gemeinde Emden, 1557–1620: Teil I: 1557–1574.* Köln: Böhlau, 1989.

–. *Die Kirchenratsprotokolle der Reformierten Gemeinde Emden, 1557–1620: Teil II: 1575–1620.* Köln: Böhlau, 1992.

Teellinck, Willem. *Noodtwendigh Vertoogh, aengaende den tegenwoordighen bedroefden staet van Gods volck.* Middelburg, 1627.

Tertullian. "*An Answer to the Jews.*" In *Latin Christianity: Its Founder,* Tertullian, edited by Alexander Roberts, James Donaldson, and A. Cleveland Coxe, 283–324. Vol. 3. The Ante-Nicene Fathers. Buffalo, NY: Christian Literature Company, 1885.

Ursinus, Zacharias. *A Verie Profitable and Necessarie Discourse Concerning the Observation and Keeping of the Sabbath Day....* Translated by John Stockwood. London: Harrison, 1584.

–. "Catechesis minor, perspicua brevitate christianum fidem complectens." In *Zacharias Ursini Opera Theologica,* edited by Quirinus Reuter. 3 Vols. Heidelberg, 1612.

–. *The Commentary of Dr. Zacharius Ursinus on the Heidelberg Catechism.* Translated by G.W. Williard. Grand Rapids, MI: Eerdmans, 1956.

–. *The Commentary of Dr. Zacharius Ursinus on the Heidelberg Catechism.* Edited by Eric D. Bristley. Translated by G.W. Williard. The Synod of the Reformed Church in the U.S., 2004. http://www.rcus.org/wp-content/uploads/2013/09/UrsinusZ_HC-Commentary-17-NEW-HC.pdf.

Verschoor, A.J., ed. *Classis Gorinchem 1579–1620.* Vol. 8 of *Classicale acta, 1573–1620.* Den Haag: Instituut voor Nederlandse Geschiedenis, 2008.

Voetius, Gisbertus. *De sabbatho et festis.* In *Selectae Disputationas Theologicae Volume III.* Ultrajecti, 1651.

Secondary Sources

Amos, Norton Scott / Andrew Pettegree / Henk F. K. van Nierop, eds. *The Education of a Christian Society: Humanism and the Reformation in Britain and the Netherlands: Papers Delivered to the Thirteenth Anglo-Dutch Historical Conference, 1997.* Aldershot: Ashgate, 1999.

Apperloo-Boersma, Karla / Herman J. Selderhuis, eds. *Power of Faith: 450 Years of the Heidelberg Catechism.* Göttingen: Vandenhoeck & Ruprecht, 2013.

Asselt, Willem J. van. *Johannes Coccejus: Portret van een zeventiende-eeuws theoloog op oude en nieuwe wege.* Heerenveen: Groen, 1997.

Balke, Willem. "Calvijn en de Zondagsheiliging." *Theologica Reforma* 37, No. 3 (September 1994): 176–186.

Bates, Gordon. "Typology of Adam and Christ in John Calvin." *Hartford Quarterly* 5, no. 2 (1965): 42–57.

Bauckham, Richard J. "Sabbath and Sunday in the Medieval Church in the West." In Carson, *From Sabbath to Lord's Day: A Biblical, Historical, and Theological Investigation*, 300–309.

–. "Sabbath and Sunday in the Post-Apostolic Church." In Carson, *From Sabbath to Lord's Day: A Biblical, Historical, and Theological Investigation*, 252–298.

–. "Sabbath and Sunday in the Protestant Tradition." In Carson, *From Sabbath to Lord's Day: A Biblical, Historical, and Theological Investigation*, 311–342.

Bayes, Jonathan F. *The Threefold Division of the Law.* Newcastle upon Tyne: The Christian Institute, 2012.

Beeke, Joel R. "The Dutch Secnd Reformation (Nadere Reformatie)." *Calvin Theological Journal* 28, no. 2 (1993): 298–327.

–. *Assurance of Faith: Calvin, English Puritanism, and the Dutch Second Reformation.* New York: Peter Lang, 1991.

Benedetto, Robert / Darrell L. Guder / Donald K. McKim. *Historical Dictionary of Reformed Churches.* Lanham, MD: Scarecrow Press, 1999.

Benedict, Philip. *Christ's Churches Purely Reformed: A Social History of Calvinism.* New Haven and London: Yale University Press, 2002.

Bergsma, Wiebe. "The Intellectual and Cultural Context of the Reformation in the Northern Netherlands." In Amos, Pettegree, and Van Nierop, *The Education of a Christian Society*, 243–261.

–. *Tussen Gideonsbende en publieke kerk: een studie over het gereformeerd protestantisme in Friesland, 1580-1650.* Hilversum: Verloren, 1999.

Berkhof, Hendrikus. "The Catechism in Historical Context." In *Essays on the Heidelberg Catechism*, edited by Bard Thompson, Hendrikus Berkhof, Eduard Schweizer, and Howard Hageman, 76–92. Eugene, OR: Wipf and Stock Publishers, 2016.

Berkvens-Stevelinck, Christiane / Jonathan I. Israel / G. H. M. Posthumus Meyjes, eds. *The Emergence of Tolerance in the Dutch Republic.* Leiden: E.J. Brill, 1997.

Bierma, Lyle / Charles D. Gunnoe / Karin Maag / Paul W. Fields. *An Introduction to the Heidelberg Catechism: Sources, History, and Theology: with a Translation of the Smaller and Larger Catechisms of Zacharias Ursinus.* Grand Rapids, MI: Baker Academic, 2005.

Bierma, Lyle. "Olevianus and the Authorship of the HC: Another Look." *The Sixteenth Century Journal* 13, no. 4 (1982): 17–27.

–. "Remembering the Sabbath Day: Ursinus's Exposition of Exodus 20:8–11." In *Biblical Interpretation in the Era of the Reformation: Essays Presented to David C. Steinmetz in Honor of His Sixtieth Birthday*, edited by Richard A. Muller and John Lee Thompson, 272–291. Grand Rapids, MI: W.B. Eerdmans, 1996.

–. "The Purpose and Authorship of the Heidelberg Catechism." In Bierma et al., *An Introduction to the Heidelberg Catechism*, 49–74.

–. "Ursinus and the Theological Landscape of the Heidelberg Catechism." In *The Spirituality of the Heidelberg Catechism: Papers of the International Conference on the Heidelberg Catechism Held in Apeldoorn 2013*, edited by Arnold Huijgen, 9–24. Göttingen: Vandenhoeck & Ruprecht, 2015.

–. *The Theology of the Heidelberg Catechism: A Reformation Synthesis.* Louisville: Westminster John Knox Press, 2013.

Blacketer, Raymond A. *The School of God Pedagogy and Rhetoric in Calvin's Interpretation of Deuteronomy.* Dordrecht: Springer, 2006.

Blei, Karel. *The Netherlands Reformed Church, 1571–2005.* Translated by Allan J. Janssen. Grand Rapids, MI: William B. Eerdmans Publishing Company, 2006.

Boer, Erik A. de. *The Genevan School of the Prophets: The Congregations of the Company of Pastors and Their Influence in 16th Century Europe.* Genève: Librairie Droz, 2012.

Briels, J.G.C. *Zuid-Nederlanders in de Republiek 1572–1630: een demografische en cultuurhistorische studie.* Sint-Niklaas: Danthe, 1985.

Brienen, T., et al., *De Nadere Reformatie: Beschrijving van haar voornaamste vertegenwoordigers.* 's-Gravenhage: Boekencentrum, 1986.

Broeke, Cornelis van den. *Een geschiedenis van de classis: classicale typen tussen idee en werkelijkheid (1571–2004).* Kampen: Kok, 2005.

Broeyer, F. G. M. "Gisbertus Voetius, God's Gardener. The Pattern of Godliness in the *Selectae Disputationes*," In Wisse et al., *Scholasticism Reformed*, 127–154.

Brown, Harold Ogden Joseph. *John Laski: A Theological Biography, A Polish Contribution to the Protestant Reformation.* Ph. D. Dissertation: Harvard University, 1967.

Carson, D.A., ed. *From Sabbath to Lord's Day: A Biblical, Historical, and Theological Investigation.* Grand Rapids, MI: Zondervan, 1982.

Cheung, Kwok Ting. "The Sabbath in Calvin's Theology." Ph.D. Dissertation: University of Aberdeen, 1990.

Clemens, Deborah Rahn. "Foundations of German Reformed Worship in the Sixteenth Century Palatinate." Ph. D. Dissertation: Drew University, 1995.

Coldwell, Christopher. "Calvin in the Hands of the Philistines, Or, Did Calvin Bowl on the Sabbath." *Confessional Presbyterian* 6, (January 1, 2010): 31–49.

Crew, Phyllis Mack. *Calvinist Preaching and Iconoclasm in the Netherlands, 1544–1569.* Cambridge: Cambridge University Press, 1978.

Dalton, Hermann. *Johannes a Lasco. Beitrag zur Reformationsgeschichte Polens, Deutschlands und Englands.* Nieuwkoop: De Graaf, 1970.

Deursen, Arie Th. van. *Bavianen en slijkgeuzen: kerk en kerkvolk ten tijde van Maurits en Oldebarnevelt.* 4th Ed., Assen: Van Gorcum, 1974, 1991, Franeker: Uitgeverij Van Wijnen, 2010.

–. *Het kopergeld van de Gouden Eeuw.* Assen: Van Gorcum, 1978–1981.

–. *Plain lives in a golden age: popular culture, religion, and society in seventeenth-century Holland.* Translated by Maarten Ultee. Cambridge, New York: Cambridge University Press, 1991.

Dixon, C. Scott/Dagmar Freist/Mark Greengrass, eds. *Living with Religious Diversity in Early-Modern Europe.* Farnham, England: Ashgate, 2009.

Dixon, C. Scott. *Contesting the Reformation.* West Sussex, UK: Wiley-Blackwell, 2012.

Duke, Alastair C. *Dissident Identities in the Early Modern Low Countries.* Edited by Judith Pollmnn and Andrew Spicer. Burlington, VT: Ashgate, 2009.

–. *Reformation and Revolt in the Low Countries.* London: The Hambledon Press, 1990.

–, Gillian Lewis, and Andrew Pettegree, eds. *Calvinism in Europe, 1540–1610: A Selection of Documents.* Manchester: Manchester University Press, 1992.

–, Judith Pollmann, and Andrew Spicer, eds. *Public Opinion and Changing Identities in the Early Modern Netherlands: Essays in Honour of Alastair Duke*. Leiden: Brill, 2007.

Durkheim, Emile. *The Elementary Forms of the Religious Life*. New York: The Free Press, 1915.

Elliott, John Paul. "Protestantization in the Northern Netherlands, A Case Study: the Classis of Dordrecht, 1572–1640." Ph. D. Dissertation: Columbia University, 1990.

Elliott, Mark W. "Calvin and the Ceremonial Law of Moses." *Reformation & Renaissance Review* 11, no. 3 (December 2009): 275–293.

Elshout, Bartel. "The Theology of Wilhelmus à Brakel (1)." Lecture at Puritan Reformed Seminary, Grand Rapids, MI, August 29, 2014. https://www.youtube.com/watch?v=wnOkwCiPxGY&list=PLHKxt9HSA8B72xMBzMHU8kIUT9aUu5rUw&index=1.

Engelberts, W.J.M. *Willem Teellinck*. Translated by Annemie Godbehere. Amsterdam: Scheffer & Company, 1898.

Engelke, Matthew. "Material Religion." In Orsi, *The Cambridge Companion to Religious Studies*, 209–229.

Engle, Randall D. "A Devil's Siren or an Angel's Throat: The Pipe Organ Controversy among the Calvinists." In *John Calvin, Myth and Reality: Images and Impact of Geneva's Reformer; Papers of the 2009 Calvin Studies Colloquium*, edited by Amy Nelson Burnett, 107–125. Eugene, OR: Wipf and Stock, 2011.

Farley, Benjamin Wirt. *John Calvin's Sermons on the Ten Commandments*. Pelham, AL: Solid Ground Christian Books, 2011.

Finney, Paul Corby, ed. *Seeing Beyond the Word: Visual Arts and the Calvinist Tradition*. Grand Rapids, MI: Eerdmans, 1999.

Fitzsimmons, Richard. "Building a Reformed ministry in Holland, 1572–1585." In *The Reformation of the Parishes: The ministry and the Reformation in town and country*, edited by Andrew Pettegree, 175–194. Manchester: Manchester University Press,

Ford, James Thomas. "Preaching in the Reformed Tradition." In *Preachers and People in the Reformations and Early Modern Period*, edited by Larissa Taylor, 65–88. Leiden: Brill, 2001.

Frijhoff, Willem/Marijke Spies. *Dutch Culture in a European Perspective, 1650: Hard-Won Unity*. Translated by Myra Heerspink Scholz. New York: Palgrave Macmillan, 2004.

Frijhoff, Willem. "How Plural were the Religious Worlds in Early-Modern Europe? Critical Reflections from the Netherlandic Experience." In Scott, Freist, and Greengrass, *Living with Religious Diversity*, 21–51.

–. "Shifting Identities in Hostile Settings." In Kaplan et al., *Catholic communities in Protestant states*, 1–17.

–. *Embodied Belief: Ten Essays on Religious Culture in Dutch History*. Hilversum: Uitgeverij Verloren, 2002.

Gaffin, Richard B. *Calvin and the Sabbath*. Fearn, Ross-shire: Mentor, 1998.

Geertz, Clifford. *The Interpretation of Cultures*. New York: Basic Books, 1973.

Gelderblom, Arie-Jan/Jan L. de Jong/Marc van Vaeck, eds. *The Low Countries as a Crossroads of Religious Beliefs*. Leiden: Brill, 2004.

Gelderen, Martin van. *The Political Thought of the Dutch Revolt, 1555–1590*. Cambridge: Cambridge University Press, 1992.

Gilpin, Lawrence A. "An Analysis of Calvin's Sermons on the Fourth Commandment." *Presbyterian* 30, no. 2 (September 1, 2004): 90–105.

Goeters, J.F.G. "Entstehung und Fruhgeschichte des Katechismus." In *Handbuch zum Heidelberger Katechismus,* edited by Lothar Coenen, 3–23. Neukirchen: Neukirchener Verlag, 1963.

Gootjes, Nicolaas H. *The Belgic Confession: Its History and Sources.* Grand Rapids, MI: Baker Academic, 2007.

Goudriaan, Aza/Fred van Lieburg. "Introduction," in *Revisiting the Synd of Dordt (1618–1619),* IX–XIV.

–, eds. *Revisiting the Synod of Dordt (1618–1619),* Leiden: Brill, 2011.

Grochowina, Nicole. "Confessional Indifference in East Frisia." *Reformation & Renaissance Review* 7, no. 1 (April 2005): 111–124.

Groenendijk, L.F. "De Oorsprong van de Uitdrukking 'Nadere Reformatie.'" *Documentatieblad Nadere Reformatie* 9, no. 4 (1985): 128–134.

Groenhuis, Gerrit. *De predikanten: de sociale positie van de gereformeerde predikanten in de Republiek der Verenigde Nederlanden voor 1700.* Groningen: Wolters-Noordhoff, 1977.

Hall, David D. *Worlds of Wonder, Days of Judgment Popular Religious Belief in Early New England.* New York: Knopf, 2013.

–. ed. *Lived Religion in America: Toward a History of Practice.* Princeton, N.J.: Princeton University Press, 1997.

Hansen, Maurice G. *The Reformed Church in the Netherlands Traced from A.D. 1340 to A.D. 1840, in Short Historical Sketches.* New York: Board of Publication of the Reformed Church in America, 1884.

Harkness, Georgia. *John Calvin: The Man and His Ethics.* New York: Henry Holt and Company, 1931.

Helmer, Christine. "Theology and the study of religion: a relationship." In Orsi, *The Cambridge Companion to Religious Studies,* 230–254.

Heron, Alasdair I.C. "Calvin and the Confessions of the Reformation: Original Research." *Hervormde Teologiese Studies/ Theological Studies* 70, no. 1 (2014): 1–5.

Hof, W. J. op 't. "Studie der Nadere Reformatie: Verleden en Toekomst." *Documentatieblad Nadere Reformatie* 18, no. 1 (1994): 1–50.

–. *Bibliografische lijst van de geschriften van Willem Teellinck.* Rotterdam: Lindenberg, 1993.

–. *Engelse piëtistische geschriften in het Nederlands, 1598–1622.* Rotterdam: Lindenberg, 1987.

–. *Willem Teellinck (1579–1629): Leven, Geschriften en Invloed.* Kampen: De Groot Goudriaan, 2008.

Hollweg, Walter. *Neue Untersuchungen zur Geschichte des Heidelberger Katechismus.* Neukirchen: Neukirchener Verlag, 1961.

Hsia, R. Po-chia/Henk F. K. van Nierop, eds. *Calvinism and Religious Toleration in the Dutch Golden Age.* Cambridge: Cambridge University Press, 2002.

Hsia, R. Po-chia. "Introduction." In Hsia and Van Nierop, *Calvinism and Religious Toleration,* 1–7.

Huijgen, Arnold, ed. *The Spirituality of the Heidelberg Catechism: Papers of the International Conference on the Heidelberg Catechism Held in Apeldoorn 2013.* Göttingen: Vandenhoeck & Ruprecht, 2015.

Hyde, Daniel R. "Regulae de Observatione Sabbathi: The Synod of Dort's (1618–1619) Deliverance on the Sabbath." *Puritan Reformed Journal* 4 (2012): 161–184.

Israel, Jonathan I. *The Dutch Republic: Its Rise, Greatness and Fall, 1477–1806.* Oxford: Clarendon Press, 1995.

Janse, Wim. "A Lasco und Albert Hardenberg. Einigkeit im Dissens." In Strohm, *Johannes a Lasco, 1499–1560,* 261–282.

–. *Albert Hardenberg als Theologe: Profil eines Bucer-Schülers.* Leiden: E. J. Brill, 1994.

Jewett, Paul King. *The Lord's Day: A Theological Guide to the Christian Day of Worship.* Grand Rapids, MI: W.B. Eerdmans Publishing Company, 1971.

Jones, Rosemary L. "Reformed Church and Civil Authorities in the United Provinces in the Late 16th and Early 17th Centuries, As Reflected in Dutch State and Municipal Archives." *Journal of the Society of Archivists* 4, no. 2 (1970): 109–123.

Jong, Peter de, ed. *Crisis in the Reformed Churches: Essays in commemoration of the great Synod of Dordt, 1618–1619.* Grand Rapids, MI: Reformed Fellowship, Inc., 1968.

–. "The Conflict Between Calvinism and Anabaptism in the Netherlands." Master's Thesis: University of Washington, 1963.

Joy, Christopher. *The Dutch Language in Britain (1550–1702): A Social History of the Use of Dutch in Early Modern Britain.* Leiden: Brill, 2015.

Jürgens, Henning P. *Johannes a Lasco in Ostfriesland: der Werdegang eines europäischen Reformators.* Tübingen: Mohr Siebeck, 2002.

–. *Johannes a Lasco, 1499–1560: ein Europäer des Reformationszeitalters.* Wuppertal: Foedus-Verl, 1999.

–. *Johannes a Lasco: Ein Leben in Buchern Und Briefen.* Wuppertal: Foedus, 1999.

Kaplan, Benjamin/Judith Pollmann. "Conclusion: Catholic minorities in Protestant states, Britain and the Netherlands, c.1570–1620." In Kaplan et al., *Catholic communities in Protestant states,* 249–264.

Kaplan, Benjamin/Bob Moore/Henk van Nierop/Judith Pollmann, eds. *Catholic communities in Protestant states: Britain and the Netherlands c.1570–1720.* Manchester, UK: Manchester University Press, 2009.

Kaplan, Benjamin. *Calvinists and Libertines: Confession and Community in Utrecht, 1578–1620.* Oxford: Clarendon Press, 1995.

Kingdon, Robert M. *Reforming Geneva: Discipline, Faith and Anger in Calvin's Geneva.* Genève: Librairie Droz S.A. 2012.

Klooster, Fred. "Calvin's Attitude to the Heidelberg Catechism." In *Later Calvinism: International Perspectives,* edited by W. Fred Graham, 409–430. Kirksville, MO: Sixteenth Century Journal Publishers, 1994.

–. "The Priority of Ursinus in the Composition of the Heidelberg Catechism." In *Controversy and Conciliation: The Reformation and the Palatinate, 1559–1583,* edited by Dikran Hadidian, 73–100. Allison Park, PA: Pickwick Publications, 1986.

–. *The Heidelberg Catechism: Origin and History.* Grand Rapids, MI: Calvin Theological Seminary, 1987–1988.

Knappen, M. M. *Tudor Puritanism: A Chapter in the History of Idealism.* Chicago: University of Chicago Press, 1970.

Knippenburg, Hans. *De religieuze kaart van Nederland: omvang en geografische spreading van de godsdienstige gezindten vanaf de Reformatie tot heden.* Assen: Van Gorcum, 1992.

Kooi, Christine. "'A Serpent in the Bosom of our Dear Fatherland': Reformed Reaction to the Holland Mission in the Seventeenth Century." In Gelderblom, De Jong, and Van Vaeck, *The Low Countries as a Crossroads of Religious Beliefs*, 165–176.

–. "Paying off the sheriff: strategies of Catholic toleration in Golden Age Holland." In Hsia and Van Nierop, eds., *Calvinism and Religious Toleration*, 87–101.

–. "Popish Impudence: The Perseverance of the Roman Catholic Faithful in Calvinist Holland, 1572–1620." *The Sixteenth Century Journal* 26, no. 1 (1995): 75–85.

–. *Calvinists and Catholics during Holland's Golden Age: Heretics and Idolaters*. Cambridge: Cambridge University Press, 2012.

–. *Liberty and Religion: Church and State in Leiden's Reformation, 1572–1620*. Leiden: Brill, 2000.

–. Review of *Nieuw en ongezien: kerk en samenleving in de classis Delft en Delfland 1572–1621*, by A. Ph. F. Wouters and P. H. A. M. Abels. *The Sixteenth Century Journal* 27, no. 2 (1996): 532–533.

Koopmans, Joop W. *Historical Dictionaries of Europe: Historical Dictionary of the Netherlands*. New York: Rowman & Littlefield, 2016.

Kromminga, Diedrich H. "How Did John Calvin Regard the First Day of the Week?." *The Banner* (May 8, 1936): 437.

–. "John A Lasco: Polish Calvinist and Reformer." *The Calvin Forum* 5, no. 5 (December 1939): 88–89

–. "The Heidelberg View of the Fourth Commandment: Does It Conflict with Calvin's?." *The Calvin Forum* 6, no. 8 (March 1941): 161–164.

–. "The Heidelberg View of the Fourth Commandment: Is it Scriptural?." *The Calvin Forum* 6, no. 9 (April 1941): 187–190.

Kuyper, H.H. *De Post-Acta of Nahandelingen van de nationale Synode van Dordrecht in 1618 en 1619 gehouden een Historische Studie*. Amsterdam, 1899.

Lambert, Thomas A. "Preaching, Praying and Policing the Reform in Sixteenth Century Geneva." Ph.D. Dissertation: The University of Wisconsin-Madison, 1998.

Lang, August. *Der Heidelberger Katechismus und vier verwandte Katechismen*. Leipzig: Deichert, 1907.

Lauer, Stewart E. "John Calvin, the Nascent Sabbatarian: A Reconsideration of Calvin's View of Two Key Sabbath-Issues." *Confessional Presbyterian* 3, (January 1, 2007): 3–14.

Lindeboom, Johannes. *De confessioneele ontwikkeling der reformatie in de Nederlanden*. 's-Gravenhage: Martinus Nijhoff, 1946.

Maag, Karin / John D. Witvliet, eds. *Worship in Medieval and Early Modern Europe: Change and Continuity in Religious Practice*. Notre Dame: University of Notre Dame Press, 2004.

Maag, Karin, ed. *Lifting Hearts to the Lord: Worship with John Calvin in Sixteenth-Century Geneva*. Grand Rapids, MI: William B. Eerdmans Publishing Company, 2016.

–. "Early Editions and Translations of the Heidelberg Catechism." In Bierma et al., *An Introduction to the Heidelberg Catechism*, 103–117.

–. "Education and Literacy." In *The Reformation World*, edited by Andrew Pettegree, 535–544. London: Routledge, 2000.

–. *Seminary or University?: The Genevan Academy and Reformed Higher Education, 1560–1620*. Aldershot, England: Scolar Press, 1995.

Marnef, Guido. *Antwerp in the Age of Reformation: Underground Protestantism in a Commercial Metropolis, 1550-1577.* Baltimore: Johns Hopkins University Press, 1996.

McDannell, Colleen. *Material Christianity: Religion and Popular Culture in America.* New York and London: Yale University Press, 1995.

McGuire, Meredith B. *Lived Religion: Faith and Practice in Everyday Life.* New York: Oxford University Press, 2008.

McKee, Elsie Anne. *The Pastoral Ministry and Worship in Calvin's Geneva.* Genève: Librairie Droz S.A., 2016.

-. *Diakonia in the Classical Reformed Tradition and Today.* Grand Rapids, MI: W.B. Eerdmans, 1989.

Meertens, P.J. *Letterkundig leven in Zeeland in de zestiende en de eerste helft der zeventiende eeuw.* Amsterdam: Noord-hollandsche Uitgevers Maatschappij, 1943.

Mentzer, Raymond A. "The Synod in the Reformed Tradition." In *Synod and Synodality: Theology, History, Canon Law and Ecumenism in New Contact: International Colloquium Bruges 2003,* edited by Alberto Melloni and Silvia Scatena, 173-186. Münster: Lit Verlag, 2005.

Miller, Stephen. *The Peculiar Life of Sundays.* Cambridge: Harvard University Press, 2008.

Mochizuki, Mia M. *The Netherlandish Image After Iconoclasm, 1566-1672: Material Religion in the Dutch Golden Age.* Aldershot, England: Ashgate, 2008.

Mout, Nicollete. "Erasmianischer Humanismus und reformierter Protestantismus zur Zeit a Lascos." In Strohm, *Johannes a Lasco, 1499-1560,* 21-34.

Müller, Johannes M. *Exile Memories and the Dutch Revolt: The Narrated Diaspora, 1550-1750.* Leiden: Brill, 2016.

Muller, Richard A. "Calvin and the 'Calvinists': Assessing Continuities and Discontinuities between the Reformation and Orthodoxy, Part One." *Calvin Theological Journal* 30, no. 2 (November 1995): 345-375.

-. "Calvin and the 'Calvinists': Assessing Continuities and Discontinuities between the Reformation and Orthodoxy, Part Two." *Calvin Theological Journal* 31, no. 1 (April 1996): 125-160.

-. "Was Calvin a Calvnist?." Lecture at Westminster Seminary California, Escondido, CA, February 28, 2012.

-. *After Calvin: Studies in the Development of a Theological Tradition.* Oxford: Oxford University Press, 2003.

-. *The Unaccommmodated Calvin: Studies in the Foundation of a Theological Tradition,* Oxford: Oxford University Press, 2001.

Neuser, Wilhelm. "Die Erählungslehre im Heidelberger Katechismus." *Zeitschrift für Kirchengeschichte* 75 (1964): 309-326.

Ney, Theodor Julius. "Zacharius Ursinus," In *Allgemeine Deutsche Biographie: auf Veranlassung und mit Unterstützung seiner majestät des Königs von Bayern Maximilian II.* Vol. 39. 369-372. Leipzig: Duncker & Humblot, 1895.

Nierop, Henk van. "Introduction." In Gelderblom, De Jong, and Van Vaeck, eds., *The Low Countries as a Crossroads of Religious Belief,* 1-7.

-. "Sewing the bailiff in a blanket: Catholics and the law in Holland." In Hsia and Van Nierop, eds., *Calvinism and Religious Toleration,* 102-111.

Nijenhuis, Willem/Christiaan G.F. de Jong / Jacob van Sluis, eds. *Gericht verleden: ker-khistorische opstellen aangeboden aan prof. dr. W. Nijenhuis ter gelegenheid van zijn vijfenzeventigste verjaardag*. Leiden: J.J. Groen, 1991.

Nijenhuis, Willem. *Ecclesia Reformata: Studies on the Reformation*. 2 vols. Leiden: Brill, 1994.

Nijenhuis, Willem. *Hoe Calvinistisch Zijn Wij Nederlanders?*. Amsterdam: Historisch Documentatiecentrum voor het Nederlands Protestantisme, 2009.

Oberman, Heiko A. *Spatscholastik und Reformation, Vol. 1: Der Herbst der mittelalterlischen Theologie*. Translated by Martin Rumscheid and Henning Kampen. Zürich: EVZ Verlag, 1965.

–. *Zwei Reformationen: Luther und Calvin, Alte und Neue Welt*. Berlin: Siedler Verlag, 2003.

Old, Hughes Oliphant. *The Reading and Preaching of the Scriptures in the Worship of the Christian Church: Vol. 4, The Age of the Reformation*. Grand Rapids, MI: Eerdmans, 2002.

Opitz, Peter. *The myth of the Reformation*. Göttingen, Germany: Vandenhoeck & Ruprecht, 2013.

Orsi, Robert A. *Thank You, St. Jude: Women's Devotion to the Patron Saint of Hopeless Causes*. New Haven, CT: Yale University Press, 1996.

–. *The Madonna of 115th Street: Faith and Community in Italian Harlem, 1880–1950*. New Haven: Yale University Press, 2002.

–., ed. *The Cambridge Companion to Religious Studies*. Cambridge: Cambridge University Press, 2011.

Ozment, Steven E./Marc R. Forster/Benjamin J. Kaplan, eds. *Piety and Family in Early Modern Europe: Essays in Honour of Steven Ozment*. Aldershot, England: Ashgate, 2005.

Parker, Charles. "Cooperative confessionlisation: lay-clerical collaboration in the Dutch Catholic communities during the Golden Age." In Kaplan et al., *Catholic communities in Protestant States*, 18–32.

–. "Obedience with an Attitude. Laity and Clergy in the Dutch Catholic Church of the Seventeenth Century." In Gelderblom, De Jong, and Van Vaeck, *The Low as a Crossorads of Religious Beliefs*, 177–195.

–. "The Moral Agency and Moral Autonomy of Church Folk in the Dutch Reformed Church of Delft, 1580–1620." *Journal of Ecclesiastical History* 48, no. 1 (January 1997): 44–70.

–. *Faith on the Margins: Catholics and Catholicism in the Dutch Golden Age*. Cambridge: Cambridge University Press, 1998.

–. *The Reformation of Community: Social Welfare and Calvinist Charity in Holland, 1572–1620*. Cambridge: Cambridge University Press, 1998.

Parker, Geoffrey. *The Dutch Revolt*. London: Penguin Books, 1977, Reprinted 2002.

–. *Spain and the Netherlands, 1559–1659: Ten Studies*. Short Hills, N.J.: Enslow Publishers, 1979.

Parker, Kenneth. *The English Reformation: A Study of Doctrine and Discipline From the Reformation to the Civil War*. Cambridge: Cambridge University Press, 1988.

Parker, T. H. L. *Calvin's Preaching*. Louisville, KY: Westminster/John Knox Press, 1992.

Pater, Calvin A. "Calvin, the Jews, and the Judaic Legacy." In *In Honour of John Calvin: Papers from the 1986 International Calvin Symposium*, edited by E.J. Furcha, 256–296. Montreal: McGill University Press, 1987.

Pestalozzi, Carl. *Heinrich Bullinger. Leben und ausgewählte Schriften*. Elberfeld: K.K. Friderichs, 1858.

Pettegree, Andrew, A. C. Duke, and Gillian Lewis. *Calvinism in Europe, 1540–1620*. Cambridge: Cambridge University Press, 1994.

–, *The Reformation of the Parishes: The Ministry and the Reformation in Town and Country*. Manchester: Manchester University Press, 1993.

–, *The Reformation World*. London: Routledge, 2000.

–. "The Spread of Calvin's Thought." In *The Cambridge Companion to John Calvin*, edited by Donald K. McKim, 207–224. Cambridge: Cambridge University Press, 2004.

–. *Emden and the Dutch Revolt: Exile and the Development of Reformed Protestantism*. Oxford: Clarendon Press, 1992.

–. *Marian Protestantism: Six Studies*. Aldershot, England: Scolar Press, 1996.

Pieters, Albertus. "Calvin's View of the Fourth Commandment." *The Calvin Forum* 6, no. 7 (February, 1941): 134–137.

–. "Three Views of the Fourth Commandment." *The Calvin Forum* 6, no. 6 (January 1941): 119–121.

Pol, Frank van der. "Religious Diversity and Everyday Ethics in the Seventeenth-Century Dutch City Kampen." *Church History* 71, no. 1 (March 2002): 16–62.

–. *De Reformatie te Kampen in de Zestiende Eeuw*. Kampen: Uitgeversmaatschappij J.H. Kok, 1990.

Pollmann, Judith. "Off the Record: Problems in the Quantification of Calvinist Church Discipline." *The Sixteenth Century Journal* 33, no. 2 (2002): 423–438.

–. *Catholic Identity and the Revolt of the Netherlands, 1520–1635*. Oxford: Oxford University Press. 2011.

–. *Religious Choice in the Dutch Republic: The Reformation of Arnoldus Buchelius, 1565–1641*. Manchester: Manchester University Press, 1999.

Polman, Bert. "A History of Music in the Christian Reformed Church." In *Proceedings, a Conference on Liturgy and Music in Reformed Worship, July 18–20, 1979, Grand Rapids, Michigan*, edited by A. James Heynen, 18–33. Grand Rapids, MI: Board of Publications, Christian Reformed Church, 1979.

–. "A History of Worship in the Christian Reformed Church." In *Psalter Hymnal Handbook*, edited by Emily R. Brink and Bert Polman, 109–119. Grand Rapids, MI: CRC Publications, 1998.

Pont, J.W. *Geschiedenis van het lutheranisme in de Nederlanden tot 1618*. Haarlem: E.F. Bohn, 1911.

Primus, John H. "Calvin and the Puritan Sabbath: A Comparative Study." In *Exploring the Heritage of John Calvin*, edited by David E. Holwerda, 40–75. Grand Rapids: Baker Book House, 1976.

–. *Holy Time: Moderate Puritanism and the Sabbath*. Macon, GA: Mercer University Press, 1989.

Ravenswaay, J. Marius J. Lange van/Herman J. Selderhuis, eds. *Reformed majorities in early modern Europe*. Göttingen: Vandenhoeck & Ruprecht, 2015.

Reitsma, Rients. *Centrifugal and Centripetal Forces in the Early Dutch Republic: The States of Overijssel, 1566-1600.* Amsterdam: Rodopi, 1982.

Reuver, Arie de. "Wat is het Eigene van de Nadere Reformatie." *Documentatieblad Nadere Reformatie* 18, no. 2 (1994): 145-154.

–. *Sweet Communion: Trajectories of Spirituality from the Middle Ages Through the Further Reformation.* Translated by James de Jong. Grand Rapids, MI: Baker Academic, 2007.

Roodenburg, Herman. "Smelling Rank and Status." In *Class Distinctions: Dutch Painting in the Age of Rembrandt and Vermeer,* edited by Ronni Baer, 41-53. Boston: Museum of Fine Arts Publications, 2015.

–. "Social Control Viewed from Below." In *Social Control in Europe Volume 1, 1500-1800,* edited by Herman Roodenburg and Pieter Spierenburg, 145-158. Columbus, OH: The Ohio State University Press, 2004.

–. *Onder censuur: de kerkelijke tucht in de gereformeerde gemeente van Amsterdam, 1578-1700.* Hilversum: Verloren, 1990.

Schilling, Heinz. *Civic Calvinism in Northwestern Germany and the Netherlands: Sixteenth to Nineteenth Centuries.* Kirksville, MO: Sixteenth Century Journal Publishers, 1991.

–. *Religion, Political Culture, and the Emergence of Early Modern Society: Essays in German and Dutch History.* Leiden, New York: Brill, 1992.

Schmidt, Leigh Eric. *Holy Fairs: Scotland and the Making of American Revivalism.* Grand Rapids, MI: William B. Eerdmans Publishing Company, 2001.

Schotel, Gilles Dionysius Jacob. *De openbare eeredienst der Nederl. Hervormde Kerk in de zestiende, zeventiende en achttiende eeuw.* Haarlem: Kruseman, 1870.

Schuringa, Gregory D. "Orthodoxy and Piety in the *Nadere Reformatie:* The Theology of Simon Oomius." *Mid-America Journal of Theology* 20 (2009): 95-103.

Selderhuis, Herman, ed. *Handbok of Dutch Church History.* Göttingen: Vandenhoeck & Ruprecht, 2015.

Sinnema, Donald. "The Drafting of the Canons of Dordt: A Preliminary Survey of Early Drafts and Related Research." In *Revisiting the Synod of Dordt (1618-1619),* 291-311.

–. "The Heidelberg Catechism at the Synod of Dordt." Lecture at the H. Henry Meeter Center for Calvin Studies, Grand Rapids, MI, December 5, 2013.

–. "The Second Sunday Service in the Early Dutch Reformed Tradition." *Calvin Theological Journal* 32, no. 2 (November 1, 1997): 298-333.

Smid, T.D. "Bibliographische Opmerkingen over de Explicationes Catecheticae van Zacharias Ursinus." *Gereformeerde Theologisch Tijdschrift* 41 (1940): 228-243.

Smith, James Frantz. "John A'Lasco and the Strangers' Churches." Ph.D. Dissertation: Vanderbilt University, 1964.

Solberg, Winton U. *Redeem the Time: The Puritan Sabbath in Early America.* Cambridge: Harvard University Press, 1977.

Spaans, Joke. "Orphans and students: recruiting boys and girls for the Holland Mission." In Kaplan et al., *Catholic communities in Protestant states,* 183-199.

–. "Public opinion or ritual celebration of concord?: politics, religion and society in the competition between the Chambers of rhetoric at Vlaardingen, 1616." In Duke, Pollmann, Spicer, eds., *Public Opinion and Changing Identities,* 189-209.

–. "Reform in the Low Countries." In *A Companion to the Reformation World,* edited by R. Po-chia Hsia, 118-134. Malden, MA: Blackwell Pub, 2004.

–. "Religious policies in the seventeenth-century Dutch Republic." In Hsia and van Nierop, *Calvinism and Religious Toleration*, 72–86.

–. *Haarlem na de Reformatie: stedelijke cultuur en kerkelijk leven, 1577–1620.* 's-Gravenhage: Stichting Hollandse Historische Reeks, 1989.

Spicer, Andrew. *Calvinist Churches in Early Modern Europe.* Manchester: Manchester University Press, 2007.

Spierling, Karen. *Infant Baptism in Reformation Geneva: The Shaping of a Community, 1536–1564.* Burlington, VT: Ashgate, 2005.

Spijker, Willem van 't. "Broonen van de Nadere Reformatie." In *De Nadere Reformatie en het Gereformeerd Piëtisme*, edited by T. Brienen, K. Exalto, J. van Genderen, C. Graafland, W. van 't Spijker, 5–51. 's-Gravenhage: Boekencentrum, 1989.

–. "De Nadere Reformatie." In *De Nadere Reformatie. Beschrijving van haar voornaamste vertegenwoordigers*, edited by T. Brienen, K. Exalto, J. van Genderen, C. Graafland, W. van 't Spijer, 5–16. 's-Gravenhage: Boekencentrum, 1986.

Spitz, Lewis William. *The Reformation: Education and History.* Aldershot, Great Britain: Variorum, 1997.

Springer, Michael Stephen. *Restoring Christ's Church John a Lasco and the Forma Ac Ratio.* Aldershot, England: Ashgate, 2007.

Sprunger, Keith L. "English and Dutch Sabbatarianism and the Development of Puritan Social Theology (1600–1660)." *Church History* 51, no. 1 (1982): 24–38.

Sprunger, Keith L. *The Learned Doctor William Ames: Dutch Backgrounds of English and American Puritanism.* Chicago: University of Illinois Press, 1972.

Steen, Jasper van der. *Memory Wars in the Low Countries, 1566–1700.* Leiden: Brill, 2015.

Stek, John. "The Fourth Commandment: A New Look." *Reformed Journal* 22, no. 6 (July 1, 1972): 26–29.

Strand, Kenneth Albert, "Sabbath and Sunday in the Reformation era." In *Sabbath in Scripture and History*, edited by Kenneth A. Strand and Daniel Augsburger, 215–228. Washington, D.C.: Review and Herald Publishing Association, 1982.

Strauss, Gerald. *Enacting the Reformation in Germany.* Aldershot: Variorum, 1993.

Strietman, Elsa and Peter Happé, eds. *Urban Theatre in the Low Countries, 1400–1625.* Turnhout: Brepols, 2006.

Strohm, Christoph, ed. *Johannes a Lasco, 1499–1560: Polnischer Baron, Humanist, und europäischer Reformator: Beiträge zum internationalen Symposium vom 14.–17. Oktober 1999 in der Johannes a Lasco Bibliothek Emden.* Tübingen: Mohr Siebeck, 2000.

Sturm, Erdmann Karl. *Der junge Zacharias Ursinus: Sein Weg vom Philippismus zum Calvinismus (1534–1562).* Neukirchen: Neukirchener Verlag, 1972.

Swigchem, C.A. van. *Een blik in de Nederlandse kerkgebouwen na de ingebruikneming voor de protestantse eredienst.* The Hague: Voorhoeve, 1979.

Te Brake, Wayne. "Emblems of Coexistence in a Confessional World." In Scott, Freist, and Greengrass, *Living with Religious Diversity*, 53–79.

Tracy, James. *The Founding of the Dutch Republic: War, Finance, and Politics in Holland, 1572–1588.* New York: Oxford University Press, 2008.

Trueman, Carl R. "Reformed Orthodoxy in Britain." In *A Companion to Reformed Orthodoxy*, edited by Herman J. Selderhuis, 261–291. Leiden: Brill, 2013.

–/ R. Scott Clark, eds. *Protestant Scholasticism: Essays in Reassessment.* Carlisle: Paternoster, 1999.

Vanhaelen, Angela. *The Wake of Iconoclasm: Painting the Church in the Dutch Republic.* University Park, PA: The Pennsylvania State University Press, 2012.

Visser, Derk. *Zacharias Ursinus, The Reluctant Reformer: His Life and Times.* New York: United Church Press, 1983.

Visser, Hans. *De geschiedenis van den sabbatsstrijd onder de gereformeerden in de zeventiende eeuw.* Utrecht: Kemink en Zoon, N.V., 1939.

Visser, Piet, / A.A. den Hollander / Michael D. Driedger / Gary Waite, eds. *Religious Minorities and Cultural Diversity in the Dutch Republic: Studies Presented to Piet Visser on the Occasion of His 65th Birthday.* Leiden: Brill, 2014.

Vliet, Jan van. *The Rise of the Reformed System: The Intellectual Heritage of William Ames.* Eugene, OR: Wipf & Stock, 2013.

Waite, Gary. *Reformers On Stage: Popular Drama and Proganda in the Low Countries of Charles V, 1515–1556.* Toronto: University of Toronto Press, 2000.

Westerbeek van Eerten, J. J., *Anabaptisme en Calvinisme. Tafereelen uit de vaderlandsche kerkgeschiedenis der 16e eeuw, 1531–1568.* Kampen: Kok, 1905.

Whitford, David M., ed. *Reformation and Early Modern Europe: A Guide to Research.* Kirksville, MO: Truman State University Press, 2008.

Wisse, Maarten/ Marcel Sarot/Willemien Otten/W. J. van Asselt, eds. *Scholasticism Reformed: Essays in Honour of Willem J. Van Asselt.* Leiden: Brill, 2010.

Woltjer, J. J. *Friesland in hervormingstijd.* Leiden: Universitaire Pers, 1962.

Wouters, A. Ph. F./P.H.A.M. Abels. *Nieuw en ongezien: kerk en samenleving in de classis Delft en Delfland 1572–1621.* 2 vols. Delft: Eburen, 1994.

Zachman, Randall C. *John Calvin As Teacher, Pastor, and Theologian: The Shape of His Writings and Thought.* Grand Rapids, MI: Baker Academic, 2006.

Zijlstra, Samme. "Anabaptists, Spiritualists and the Reformed Church in East Frisia." *The Mennonite Quarterly Review* 75, no. 1 (2001): 57–73.

–. *Over de ware gemeente en de oude gronden: Geschiedenis van de dopersen in de Nederlanden 1531–1675.* Hilversum: Verloren, 2000.

Zwierlein, Cornel. "Der reformierte Erasmianer a Lasco und die Herausbildung seiner Abendmahlslehre 1544–1552." In Strohm, *Johannes a Lasco, 1499–1560*, 35–100.

Index of Names

Abels, P. H. A. M.   20, 138, 157, 170–173, 177, 180 f., 184, 186 f., 200
Ames, William   23, 108 f.
Aquinas, Thomas   21, 45
Asselt, Willem van   109–111
Augustine, of Hippo   21, 55, 58, 123

Bauckham, Richard   17, 58
Beeke, Joel   24, 107–109
Benedict, Philip   23, 25, 188
Bierma, Lyle   12, 17 f., 38, 45, 58, 70, 89, 91, 93–95
Brakel, Wilhelmus á   18, 20, 25, 33, 35, 107, 109, 112–130, 132, 158 f., 194 f., 221, 223–225, 227 f., 230
Burman, Franciscus   110

Calvin, John   11, 17 f., 20 f., 23–25, 33, 35, 37–73, 76–79, 82, 84 f., 87 f., 90–93, 95, 102, 104–107, 109, 112 f., 115, 123, 126, 128–130, 132, 151, 158 f., 194 f., 204 f., 216, 221, 223 f., 227 f., 230
Cocceius, Johannes   21, 110 f.

Deursen, Arie Th. Van   18, 135, 148 f., 154, 160, 172
Duke, Alastair   26 f., 77, 135, 137, 154, 197, 199

Elliot, John Paul   20, 143, 170
Elshout, Bartel   85, 113–127
Essenius, Andreas   112

Frederick III, Elector of the Palatinate   89 f.
Frijhoff, Willem   27, 30, 141, 151

Gaffin, Richard   17, 37 f., 41–43, 62
Gelderen, J. van   92, 170, 180, 185
Gootjes, Nicolaas   76, 157

Hardenburg, Albert   11
Heidanus, Abraham   110
Hof, W. J. op 't   107–110
Hoffman, Melchior   78

Israel, Jonathan   44, 52, 60, 107, 111, 114, 126, 135 f., 141–143, 197–199, 201, 204

Janse, Wim   78
Joris, David   78–79
Jürgens, Henning   77 f.,

Kaplan, Benjamin   26, 29, 200, 215
Kingdon, Robert   37, 65–69, 192, 209
Klooster, Fred   90 f.
Knuttel, W. P. C.   19, 139, 149, 153
Kooi, Christine   12, 19, 26–29, 152 f., 170, 187, 200, 220

Lasco, Johannes a   11, 18, 20, 25, 35, 75, 77–89, 93, 105 f., 112, 115, 123, 128–130, 132, 158, 195, 221, 223 f., 227 f.
Lauer, Stewart   18, 38, 42

Maag, Karin   12, 40, 76, 90, 98, 209
McKee, Elsie   17, 44, 64, 66 f.

Mentzer, Raymond   12, 135
Micron, Marten   80
Muller, Richard   17, 35, 41, 109, 112 f., 230

Nierop, Henk van   27, 157

Olevianus, Caspar   90 f.

Parker, Charles   12, 16, 19, 23, 26, 29, 31, 37,
    41, 142, 153 f., 200
Perkins, William   108
Pettegree, Andrew   76, 78 f., 81, 135, 137,
    157, 209
Pol, Frank van der   198–200, 202, 204, 210,
    213–218
Pollmann, Judith   19, 26, 29, 31, 133 f., 154,
    205, 215
Primus, John   18, 38, 41 f., 44, 56 f., 70

Ravensbergen, C.   170, 177, 179–185, 187,
    191 f.
Reitsma, Johannes   19, 131, 138–141, 144–
    156, 197–199, 201
Reitsma, Rients   131, 138–141, 144–156,
    197–199, 201
Roodenburg, Herman   19, 31, 149, 164, 200
Rutgers, Frederik   92, 135–138, 171

Schilling, Heinz   19, 80, 107, 205

Selderhuis, Herman   24, 39 f., 75 f., 90, 98,
    171, 199
Sibilla, Gijsbert Janszoon   13, 166–168
Simons, Menno   78–79, 217
Sinnema, Donald   20, 105, 151, 208, 216
Solberg, Winton   23, 159
Spaans, Joke   19, 27, 153, 157, 182, 200
Spijker, Willem van 't   107
Springer, Michael   18, 38, 79–81
Sprunger, Keith   23 f., 109, 159

Teellinck, Willem   108–110, 113, 158, 231

Ursinus, Zacharias   17 f., 20, 25, 33, 35, 45,
    75, 77, 89–91, 93–106, 112, 115, 123, 126,
    128–130, 132, 158, 195, 221, 223 f., 227 f.,
    230

Veen, S. D. van   19, 131, 138–141, 144–156
Visser, Derk   89, 91, 111, 193
Visser, Hans   18, 21, 27, 89, 111, 193
Voetius, Gisbertus   21, 109–113

Witte, Emmanuel de   13, 164 f., 168
Wouters, A. Ph. F.   20, 138, 157, 170–173,
    177, 180 f., 184, 186 f., 200

Zijlstra, Samme   26

Index of Subjects

Afternoon, Worship Services 20, 66, 68, 80, 86, 151, 154, 159–160, 172, 180, 189, 192, 194, 203, 207–210, 221, 226

Amsterdam 13, 18 f., 35, 105, 109, 143, 164 f., 197, 200 f.

Anabaptists 25–28, 75, 79, 101, 110, 120, 151 f., 154 f., 191, 199, 214, 216, 221 f., 229

Attendance, Church 25, 66–69, 92, 135, 151, 160, 164 f., 178, 180, 189, 194, 206–210, 221, 226–228

Authorities 15 f., 24 f., 28 f., 31, 73, 77, 81, 109, 129, 132–134, 137, 139, 143, 145–147, 151, 153–157, 177, 184, 186–188, 190 f., 198–200, 214, 216, 218, 221, 223, 225–232

– Political Authorities 19, 28–30, 33, 65, 108, 131, 133, 154–157, 184, 187 f., 190, 213 f., 231

– Religious Authorities 24, 27–31, 65, 67, 134, 145, 147, 156 f., 160 f., 163 f., 168 f., 171, 174, 178, 190, 192 f., 195, 218, 220, 223, 227, 230 f.

Baptism 20, 37, 65, 80, 86, 121, 156

Bars 30, 86, 116, 147 f., 179–181, 183

Belgic Confession 76, 92, 99, 156 f., 200

Calvinists 17, 26, 28 f., 35, 108, 112 f., 152, 200, 204, 215, 230

Catechism 17, 20, 30, 39, 44, 48–50, 66, 69, 71, 80–82, 84–87, 89–98, 150, 180, 208 f.

– Catechism Services 15, 37, 66, 86, 132, 151, 159 f., 173, 192, 207 f., 210 f., 216, 221, 226–228, 232

– Emden Catechism 81 f., 82, 84–89, 105

– Genevan Catechism 40, 43, 48–50, 59, 61 f., 65 f., 71, 85, 92

– Larger Emden Catechism, London 81–82, 84

Catholics 25–29, 75, 110, 137, 143, 151–153, 155, 190–192, 198, 214–217, 220–222, 229

Ceremonial 21, 45–47, 49 f., 53, 55, 58–61, 73, 82, 98–101, 103–105, 111, 118, 120–124, 126–128, 130, 223 f.

– Fourth Commandment As 58, 122

Children 48, 66, 81, 85 f., 91, 94, 100, 103, 117, 137, 151, 155 f., 165, 168, 191, 208 f., 216

City 19, 58, 78, 118, 131, 141, 143, 155, 157, 186, 197–201, 204 f., 208, 212–217, 220

Classis 20, 31, 35, 131, 135–138, 143, 145 f., 153, 168–178, 180, 182–193, 204, 230

– Classis Bommel 170, 175 f., 192

– Classis Breda 138, 170, 175, 193

– Classis Delft 20, 138, 170, 172, 174–176, 180 f., 184, 186, 192 f.

– Classis Deventer 170, 174–176, 180, 185, 192

– Classis Dordrecht 20, 138, 163, 170, 173–176, 179–181, 184, 186–188, 192 f.

– Classis Gorinchem 170, 175 f., 179, 181, 183 f., 191 f.

– Classis Kampen 170, 175 f., 189, 192

– Classis Leiden 170, 175 f., 192 f.

- Classis Neder-Veluwe 170, 176, 181 f.
- Classis Nijmegen 170, 174–176, 179–181, 183–185, 192
- Classis Rotterdam and Schieland 138, 172, 174–176, 178, 186, 192–193
- Classis Steenwijk/Vollenhove 170, 176
- Classis Tiel 170, 174–176, 179, 185, 187, 192
- Classis Tiel/Bommel 170
- Classis Walcheren 170, 172, 175 f., 179, 181, 186, 188, 192
- Classis Woerden 170
- Classis Zuid-Beveland 170, 175 f., 188, 192
- Classis Zutphen 170, 175 f., 180, 191 f.
Commandment 15, 22, 37, 41, 44–53, 55 f., 58–64, 67, 71–73, 82–88, 92–96, 98 f., 101, 104, 107, 111, 114–117, 119–122, 124–130, 149, 223 f.
Complaints 28 f., 34, 68, 131 f., 138–149, 151–154, 156, 160, 163, 169, 173–178, 181–183, 185–195, 205–207, 209 f., 212, 215–217, 219, 221, 226, 228, 232
Confessional 16–18, 38 f., 76, 78, 89, 91, 151 f., 200, 215, 218, 229
- Confessional Groups 19, 28, 215, 217, 229
- Confessional Identity 35, 191, 229, 232
Confessionalization 19, 26, 215, 221, 228 f.
Consistory 19, 35, 66–69, 79, 81, 136 f., 146, 169, 171–173, 195, 201, 203–222, 225
- Consistory Records 18 f., 31, 65 f., 68 f., 133, 195, 200–202, 204–207, 209, 213–222
Count Enno III, of Ostfriesland 78–79
Countess Anna (Maria of Holstein-Gottorp), of Ostfriesland 79

Dancing 32, 131, 144, 147–149, 160, 163, 179, 181, 184, 194
Deacons 102, 135 f., 159, 171, 203 f.
Delft 13, 20, 143, 157, 164 f., 170, 201
Desecration 25, 28 f., 86, 120, 131, 133, 137–140, 142, 144–146, 150, 152–157, 161, 172, 176–178, 183–190, 192 f., 205–207, 209–214, 218–223, 225 f., 228–230, 232
Deuteronomy, Book of 37 f., 40, 55–62, 64, 70 f.
Deventer 201
Discipline 15 f., 18–21, 25, 30 f., 35, 37, 79 f., 136 f., 171, 188, 190, 195, 200, 213, 220, 229
Disorder 29, 72, 131, 150, 155, 179, 184, 186, 188, 191, 212, 214, 218 f., 221, 228
Disruptions 150, 159 f., 164 f., 168 f., 179, 226
Dogs 164, 168
Dordrecht 20, 33, 38, 92, 105, 137 f., 143, 154, 171, 187 f., 200 f., 204 f.
- Canons of Dort 200
- 1578 Synod of Dordrecht 137
- 1618–1619 Synod of Dordrecht 137
Drenthe 134, 136, 140, 142, 198
Drinking 32, 116, 144, 147–149, 160, 172, 179–181, 183–185, 189, 194, 206, 209–211, 214, 219 f., 228
- Drunkenness 84, 86, 88, 131, 163, 207, 209, 211, 219 f., 225

Education 40, 66, 68, 92, 94, 110, 112, 136, 157, 191 f., 209, 221
Elders 79, 102, 135 f., 159, 171, 203 f., 209
Emden 11 f., 19, 76–82, 85, 89, 92, 135, 205
- Synod of Emden 92, 135–138, 171, 203
Excommunication 136, 213
Exodus, Book of 17, 45, 52 f., 58–60, 62–64, 70, 101, 126

Fighting 141, 148 f., 181 f., 188, 194, 207, 211, 225
Fourth Commandment 15, 18, 37, 39–42, 44–46, 48–53, 55, 57–63, 67–73, 82, 84, 86 f., 92, 94–98, 101 f., 104, 113–115, 119–122, 125–129, 195, 223–225
Friesland 75, 77–79, 81, 85, 131, 134, 136, 140–142, 149 f., 156 f., 170, 198

Gelderland 134, 136, 140–142, 147, 150, 170, 183, 193
Genesis, Book of 51 f., 62, 64, 122

Geneva 17, 20, 37, 40, 48–50, 65–69, 71, 76, 80, 89, 92, 102, 192, 204 f., 209
Geography 141 f.
Groningen 19, 21, 131, 134, 136, 138, 140–142, 149, 154, 170, 198, 201

Haarlem 19, 23, 26, 143, 157, 200 f.
Heeren Staten 29, 131, 155 f., 186 f.
Heidelberg 18, 39, 76, 89–94, 97, 150
– Heidelberg Catechism 18, 25, 39, 84, 89–98, 104 f., 200, 207 f., 216, 218
Holland 19, 26–28, 76, 111, 136, 138 f., 143, 148, 152 f., 156, 163, 170, 193, 198, 200 f., 204, 220

Immorality 86, 88, 148 f., 155, 159, 181, 194, 218, 221
Insolence 153, 182, 188, 206, 211 f.

Jesuits 153 f., 191 f.
Jews 21, 27 f., 38, 40, 43, 45–48, 51 f., 54–56, 58–61, 98 f., 105, 110, 120, 124, 127
Joris, David 75, 78 f.

Kaatsen 131, 148, 156, 179, 182 f.
Kampen 12, 19, 109 f., 135, 139, 189, 197–205, 207, 209–218, 220 f., 226
– City of Kampen 35, 197, 229
– Kampen Consistory 197, 201–207, 209 f., 213, 215–221, 225

Leiden 19, 21, 24, 27, 34, 67, 75 f., 78, 85, 105, 107, 109–111, 113, 142 f., 201
Liefhebbers 35, 200, 218
Lived Religion 30, 113, 130
London Strangers' Church 78
Lord's Supper 35, 37, 66, 78, 80, 85, 121, 136, 172, 200, 202, 204, 206, 209 f., 213, 217, 226
Lutherans 26–28, 110, 214 f., 217, 222

Magistrates 147, 157, 186–188, 199, 204, 208, 212–214
Markets 146 f., 150, 159, 178, 182 f., 189, 212, 226

– Buying 117, 147, 182 f., 209, 211 f., 214, 219, 226
– Selling 117 f., 147, 182 f., 211 f., 214, 219, 226
Marriage 80, 131, 154
Mennonites' 216
Middelburg, 1581 Synod of 110, 201
Moral 21 f., 29, 45 f., 50, 58–60, 79, 82, 98, 100 f., 103, 105, 111, 114, 120–126, 128, 154 f., 191, 218 f., 223 f.
– Fourth Commandment As 58, 122

Nadere Reformatie 18, 24, 35, 106–113, 130, 132, 144, 158 f., 221, 224 f., 231
– North Holland 134, 136, 138, 140, 142–144, 147 f., 150, 152 f.
Nehemiah, Book of 118, 147

Observance 15–20, 23–26, 28, 31 f., 38, 42, 46 f., 50, 54, 60, 62, 77, 82 f., 85 f., 94, 104 f., 108–111, 114–116, 119 f., 122–125, 128, 131–133, 138, 145 f., 151 f., 154, 159, 173 f., 176 f., 184, 186 f., 189–191, 193 f., 197, 201, 205–207, 212–216, 218 f., 221, 225–229, 231 f.
Order 16, 21, 24–26, 28 f., 32, 35, 39 f., 42 f., 45–48, 52–56, 63, 66, 70–72, 79 f., 85 f., 97, 99–103, 108, 111 f., 114, 118, 128, 132, 135, 139, 145, 150, 154 f., 159–161, 168, 172, 176, 187 f., 190, 195, 202, 215, 218, 220 f., 224 f., 228 f., 232
Orthodoxy 24, 35, 109, 112, 230 f.
Overijssel 134, 136, 139–142, 170, 197–199, 201, 204

Pacification of Ghent 198
Piety 15, 24–26, 35, 37, 60, 63, 77, 101, 108–110, 113, 133, 177, 191, 210, 214, 218, 220 f., 223, 227, 229 f.
Placards 143, 156, 187 f.
Pluralism 26 f., 214, 218, 228 f.
Preaching 20, 37, 66 f., 76, 91, 101 f., 104, 121, 131, 149–151, 155 f., 165, 172, 178–182, 191 f., 198, 202, 208, 210 f., 215 f., 221, 226

- Preaching Services   180, 204, 206, 211, 221, 226
Profanation   131, 138, 153, 173, 179 f., 182, 184, 186, 188–191, 210, 212 f., 219, 221
Prohibitions   42, 88 f., 93, 116, 118, 129, 158
Protestant   15–17, 20, 23, 26–29, 31, 35, 67, 75 f., 78 f., 82, 91, 102, 109, 113, 141, 151, 153, 159, 198 f., 215, 229–231
Provincial Synod
- of Drenthe   134, 136, 140
- of Friesland   131, 134, 136. 140
- of Gelderland   134, 136, 140, 149
- of Groningen   134, 140
- of North Holland   111, 134, 136, 140, 143, 186
- of Overijssel   134, 136, 140, 156
- of South Holland   111, 135–136, 140, 143–145
- of Utrecht   135–136, 140, 148
- of Zeeland   135–136, 140, 152
Public   25–27, 39, 45, 48 f., 59 f., 72, 79 f., 88, 94, 96, 98 f., 101 f., 104, 106, 111, 119– 121, 123, 128 f., 132, 136 f., 147 f., 153, 180, 182, 186 f., 198, 200, 204, 207, 214– 216, 219 f., 222, 229
Puritans   38, 108
- English Puritanism   23 f., 107 f., 224– 226, 231
- Puritanism   23, 38, 109

Recreation   87, 105, 111, 146, 148 f., 159– 161, 178 f., 194, 212, 221
Remonstrants   26, 28, 108, 110, 187, 200, 202, 214–217, 221 f., 229, 231
Rest   15 f., 22, 33 f., 44, 46–48, 50–54, 56 f., 59–65, 72, 82, 87–89, 92–97, 99–101, 103–105, 113–117, 119–122, 124–126, 129, 142, 183, 194, 215, 221, 223 f., 232
- Physical Rest   22, 64, 72 f., 88, 95, 128, 194, 224
- Rest from Work   44, 46, 48 f., 62, 64, 73, 96, 104, 106, 117
- Spiritual Rest   22, 44, 48–51, 59 f., 62, 64 f., 72, 82, 88, 93, 95, 104, 106, 125 f., 129 f., 132, 145, 194 f., 221, 223 f., 227, 232

Rhetoric Games   182
Rotterdam   108 f., 112, 138, 143, 170, 172, 174–176, 178, 186, 192 f., 200
Rural Lands   150, 183 f.

Sabbatarian   16, 18, 22–24, 37–39, 41 f., 50, 70, 72, 94, 104 f., 128, 130, 158 f., 194 f., 221, 224–227, 231 f.
Sabbath   11, 15–26, 28 f., 31–35, 37–65, 67– 73, 75, 77, 82–89, 91–134, 137–161, 163 f., 169 f., 172–195, 197, 201 f., 205– 207, 209–216, 218–232
Sacraments   37, 45, 48 f., 56, 83 f., 92, 94, 96, 101 f., 104, 200
Scandalous   152, 206, 219, 227
Scholasticism   109 f., 112 f.
Sermon   13, 15, 18, 37, 39 f., 42–44, 55–64, 66–71, 80, 86 f., 132, 136, 160, 164 f., 168, 171, 206, 210, 221, 226 f.
Services   15, 25, 35, 37, 48, 56, 63 f., 66–69, 72, 79–81, 86, 88, 92, 100, 104, 111, 129, 132, 136, 148–151, 153–155, 159 f., 163– 167, 169, 178–181, 185, 189 f., 192, 194 f., 200, 203–211, 216 f., 219, 221, 223, 226 f., 229, 232
Sheriff   27, 173, 186–188
Shooting   131, 148, 156, 160, 179, 182–184, 190, 212, 225
- Clay-Pigeon Shooting   179, 183, 190, 212, 225
South Holland   19, 21, 111, 135 f., 139 f., 143–145, 148–150, 153 f., 156, 186
Sunday Observance   15, 25 f., 28–31, 42, 77, 108, 111, 130, 132 f., 138, 141, 150, 154 f., 157, 163 f., 169, 186, 205–207, 209, 213 f., 218, 220 f., 223, 225, 229–232

Ten Commandments   15, 33, 43, 49, 53, 55, 58, 66, 68, 70, 80, 82, 85–87, 96, 101, 113 f., 121 f., 124
The Hague, 1586 Synod of   33, 163, 201
Toleration   27, 151, 198, 229

University   11 f., 16 f., 19 f., 23, 26 f., 29–32, 37 f., 40 f., 76, 78, 81, 92, 95, 97, 109, 133, 135, 148 f., 163, 182, 198, 227 f.

- University of Franeker   110
- University of Heidelberg   95
- University of Leiden   110
- University of Utrecht   110
- University of Wittenberg   75
Utrecht   18, 21, 29, 110, 112, 135 f., 139–
   142, 147 f., 155, 170, 201
- Union of Utrecht   215

Walcheren   21, 172
Westminster   35, 37, 39, 44, 49
- Westminster Longer Catechism   39
- *Wonderjaar*   77, 81
Work   11 f., 15–22, 24–28, 31, 33, 35, 38 f.,
   42–45, 48–57, 59–65, 68–73, 79–85, 87–
89, 91–106, 109, 111–113, 115–119, 122,
   125, 127 f., 131–133, 136, 138 f., 143–145,
   147–150, 153, 156, 158–161, 163, 170,
   183–185, 194, 200, 202, 205, 212–214,
   218, 221, 223–227
Worship   15–17, 22, 25, 30, 34, 37, 39, 44–
   48, 51–54, 56, 58–60, 63–69, 71–73, 77,
   79–81, 88, 92 f., 97–105, 115, 120 f., 123,
   125–130, 132, 144 f., 148–150, 152–155,
   157, 159 f., 163 f., 167, 178–180, 185, 187,
   191 f., 194 f., 200, 203 f., 223 f., 228 f.

Zeeland   109, 135 f., 140–144, 149, 154, 156,
   170, 193, 201